Palgrave Studies in Minority Languages and Communities
Series edited by Gabrielle Hogan-Brun, University of Basel, Switzerland

Titles include:

Glyn Williams
SUSTAINING LANGUAGE DIVERSITY IN EUROPE

Máiréad Nic Craith
EUROPE AND THE POLITICS OF LANGUAGE

Anne Judge
LINGUISTIC POLICIES AND THE SURVIVAL OF REGIONAL LANGUAGES IN
FRANCE AND BRITAIN

Anne Pauwels, Joanne Winter and Joseph Lo Bianco (*editors*)
MAINTAINING MINORITY LANGUAGES IN TRANSNATIONAL CONTEXTS
Australian and European Perspectives

Máiréad Nic Craith
LANGUAGE, POWER AND IDENTITY POLITICS

Yasuko Kanno
LANGUAGE AND EDUCATION IN JAPAN

Nancy Hornberger (*editor*)
CAN SCHOOLS SAVE INDIGENOUS LANGUAGES?

Susanna Pertot, Tom M. S. Priestly and Colin H. Williams
RIGHTS, PROMOTION AND INTEGRATION ISSUES FOR MINORITY
LANGUAGES IN EUROPE

Jean-Bernard Adrey
DISCOURSE AND STRUGGLE IN MINORITY LANGUAGE POLICY FORMATION

Linda Tsung
MINORITY LANGUAGES, EDUCATION AND COMMUNITIES IN CHINA

Janet Muller
LANGUAGE AND CONFLICT IN NORTHERN IRELAND AND CANADA

Bernadette O'Rourke
GALICIAN AND IRISH IN THE EUROPEAN CONTEXT

Miquel Strubell and Emili Boix-Fuster
DEMOCRATIC POLICIES FOR LANGUAGE REVITALISATION: THE CASE OF
CATALAN

Durk Gorter, Heiko F. Marten, Luk Van Mense and Gabrielle Hogan-Brun
MINORITY LANGUAGES IN THE LINGUISTIC LANDSCAPE

Vanessa Pupavac (*editor*)
LANGUAGE RIGHTS IN CONFLICT
Serbo-Croatian Language Politics

Diarmait Mac Giolla Chríost
WELSH WRITING, POLITICAL ACTION AND INCARCERATION

Peter Sercombe and Ruanni Tupas (*editors*)
LANGUAGE, IDENTITIES AND EDUCATION IN ASIA

Keith Langston and Anita Peti-Stantić
LANGUAGE PLANNING AND NATIONAL IDENTITY IN CROATIA

Dovid Katz
YIDDISH AND POWER

Forthcoming titles:

Graham Hodson Turner
A SOCIOLINGUISTIC HISTORY OF BRITISH SIGN LANGUAGE

Nkonko M. Kamwangamalu
LANGUAGE POLICY AND ECONOMICS IN AFRICA

Rhys Jones and Huw Lewis
NEW GEOGRAPHIES OF LANGUAGE

Palgrave Studies in Minority Languages and Communities
Series Standing Order ISBN 978–1–403–93732–2
(*outside North America only*)

You can receive future titles in this series as they are published by placing a standing order. Please contact your bookseller or, in case of difficulty, write to us at the address below with your name and address, the title of the series and the ISBN quoted above.

Customer Services Department, Macmillan Distribution Ltd, Houndmills, Basingstoke, Hampshire RG21 6XS, England

Yiddish and Power

Dovid Katz

First published 2015 by
PALGRAVE MACMILLAN

Palgrave Macmillan in the UK is an imprint of Macmillan Publishers Limited,
registered in England, company number 785998, of Houndmills, Basingstoke,
Hampshire RG21 6XS.

Palgrave Macmillan in the US is a division of St Martin's Press LLC,
175 Fifth Avenue, New York, NY 10010.

Palgrave Macmillan is the global academic imprint of the above companies
and has companies and representatives throughout the world.

Palgrave® and Macmillan® are registered trademarks in the United States,
the United Kingdom, Europe and other countries.

ISBN 978–0–230–51760–8

This book is printed on paper suitable for recycling and made from fully
managed and sustained forest sources. Logging, pulping and manufacturing
processes are expected to conform to the environmental regulations of the
country of origin.

A catalogue record for this book is available from the British Library.

A catalog record for this book is available from the Library of Congress.

Typeset by MPS Limited, Chennai, India.

Contents

List of Maps, Charts, Boxes and Images

Maps

Charts

Boxes

Images

Acknowledgements

Dr Giedrė Beconytė (Vilnius University, Lithuania) has graciously designed and produced all the maps, charts and graphics in this book as well as the front cover.

Sincere thanks are due for various forms of assistance to the Albert Einstein Archives, Hebrew University of Jerusalem; Professor Diana K. Buchwald (editor and director of the Einstein Papers Project, California Institute of Technology); Roza Bieliauskienė (Vilnius); Dr Julian Breeze (Bangor, UK); Chaim Chernikov (New York); Professor David Crystal (Holyhead, North Wales); Irina Izhogina (Brest, Belarus); Julia Rets (St Petersburg); Geoff Vasil (Vilnius); and above all, to Palgrave Macmillan's series editor Dr Gabrielle Hogan-Brun whose persistence, patience and wise counsel over the years have in fact enabled the book to become a reality. Sincerest thanks to Palgrave Macmillan's Elizabeth (Libby) Forrest for helping to see the project through to completion, and to my outstanding editors Francesca White and Jane Hammett for their many corrections, improvements and suggestions, and for their generosity of spirit at each stage of proofing.

Images are credited on site. Special thanks for providing images and kindly permitting their use in this volume are due to Dr Moshe Rosenfeld, Rose Chemicals, London; Rahel Fronda of the Bodleian Libraries, University of Oxford; and Dr Hermann Suess of Fürstenfeldbruck, Germany.

Translations of texts from Aramaic, German, Hebrew, and Yiddish are by the author. In many instances, punctuation and division into paragraphs, absent in the original, have been added in the translations to enhance clarity.

As ever, none of the colleagues who have so generously assisted bears any responsibility for the views or shortcomings herein.

Preface

In this discourse, power (generally with a lower-case 'p') will be taken in the general sense beloved of philosophers, as part or whole of an entity's ability to impact its environment, including the status and behaviour of other entities. There is for any empirical linguistic study, presumably, a verifiable modification resulting from the impact of the influencing force.

That stands in sharp contrast to the political, societal force of language authority that is part of a government or state authority; these are enforced or defended by some threatening state institutions such as police, army, navy or other forces bearing weapons that are in the first instance meant to deter, in the medium term to subjugate and in the final instance to damage or destroy (even in such social senses as depriving people of degrees or documents necessary to acquire employment or other benefits).

With the exception — and quite a tragic exception it ended up being — of some parts of the Soviet Union in its earlier interwar history in the twentieth century, the power that concerns Yiddish is strictly non-state power. But for the participants in various language-related projects and debates, it can be every bit as important as state power issues.

There is no special aim here to follow the paradigms set by books in the various sub-disciplines of language and power, among many others — Bain 1993; Butler and Keith 1999; Fairclough 1989; or the earlier language and liberty literature, for example, Hayakawa 1939/1952; Sampson 1979. In a deeper sense, they are all sub-chapters of Benjamin Lee Whorf's brilliantly enduring isolation of cultural determinism, where such exists that is inherent in, and specific to, individual languages. From the uniqueness of individual languages and their world view, it is only a leap to postulate 'acquired ideas and paradigms' that result from conscious innovations to the language that 'come with a purpose' (Whorf 1964). These ideas have been somewhat revived in twenty-first-century parlance by Daniel Everett (2012), as an issue somewhat apart from the more abstract (and sometimes obtuse) pro- and anti-Chomsky debates over innateness. While the Chomskyan debate is more about absolute truths, the Worfian debate is more about what is more interesting for you or another individual to decide to study. What a boring world it would be if there were not folks drawn to one vs the other of these choices as a matter of personal preference.

The chapters on Yiddish and power here may, it is hoped, shed light on the power of individuals and groups to shape language for 'wider things', precisely because of the political powerlessness of Yiddish and other minority languages whose adherents have by and large never aspired to a state of their own. This is not to be confused with languages of people who believe their homelands to be occupied and aspire to a nation-state with a national language in the future. The real stateless languages are inherently stateless, and Yiddish is one of the stateless languages par excellence.

If the book betrays excessive personification (anthropomorphization, agentivization) of Yiddish, in the attempt to argue from innovators to language per se, that is part of the methodology invoked, and should not be taken overly literally — nor, needless to say, personally.

A preface even to a book in English about Yiddish should cite at least one Yiddish word. One of the Yiddish words whose etymology continues to lead to verbally violent confrontations between passionate supporters of one or another theory is *khóyzək* (Lithuanian Yiddish *khéyzək*). It translates 'the act of making fun (of something or someone)', 'mocking' or 'ridicule', but is written using classical Hebrew spelling that would, if an accurate representation of the word's origin, derive from an etymon like ḥṓzɛq, from the Semitic triconsonantal stem √ḥzq which refers to strength and not humour, and is itself a noun translated through the ages as 'power', 'strength', 'force' or 'fortress'. An ample philological literature has grown up around the origin of Yiddish *khóyzək* (see Rivkind 1955; Reiman 1962; Weinreich 2008: A292–A293).

Leaving aside which etymology might be accurate (we just don't know), there is the socio-synchronic reality in Yiddish-speaking civilization, over time and space, that a word spelled as if it is the ancient Hebrew for 'strength' means 'making fun' and that dissonance itself has been the source of much ongoing Yiddish folklore. The beloved Yiddish poet of Whitechapel, London, A. N. Stencl (1897–1983) used to often cite one old saying: 'The *khóyzək* [strength] of the weak [powerless] is to poke some fun at the strong [powerful]'. That is just about a metaphor for this book.

Maps

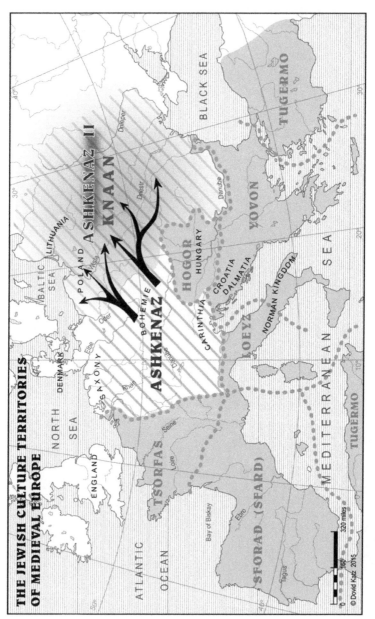

Map 1   The Jewish culture territories of medieval Europe

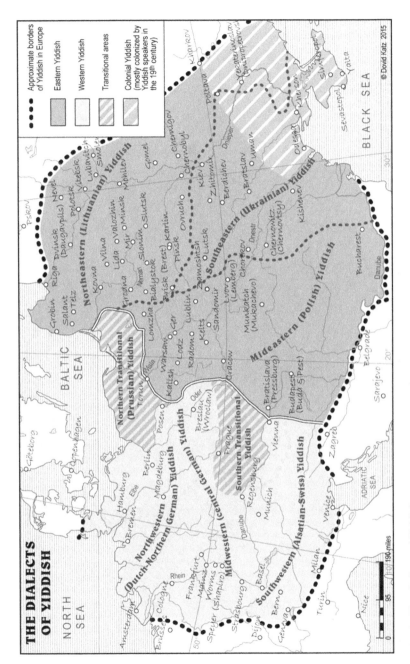

Map 2 The dialects of Yiddish

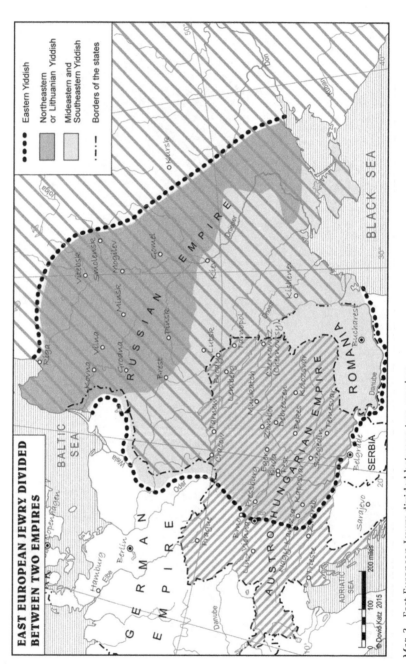

Map 3   East European Jewry divided between two empires

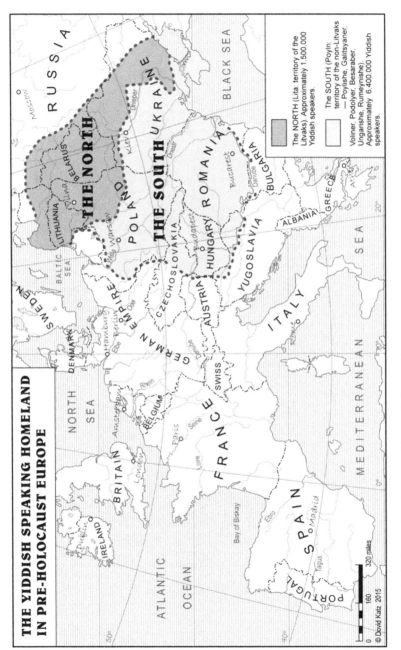

Map 4 The Yiddish-speaking homeland in pre-Holocaust Europe

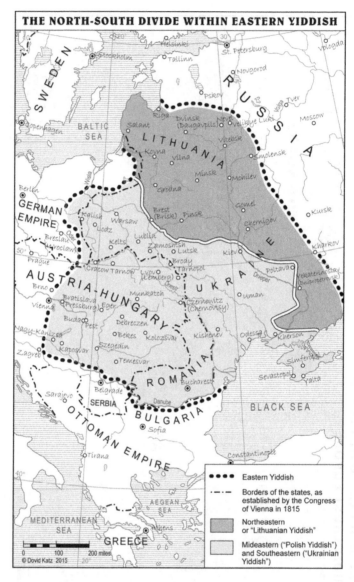

Map 5   The north–south divide within Eastern Yiddish

1

A Yiddish Romance with Powerlessness

And the Jewish people to whom I gladly belong and with whose mentality I have a deep affinity have no different quality for me than all other people. As far as my experience goes, they are also no better than other human groups, although they are protected from the worst cancers by a lack of power. Otherwise I cannot see anything 'chosen' about them.

— Albert Einstein
(from a 3 January 1954 letter to Eric Gutkind)

Jewish Powerlessness was proclaimed as an explicit heritage by the nascent liberal-secularist Yiddishist movement in Eastern Europe when it came into its own in the last decade of the nineteenth century. Y. L. Peretz (1852–1915), a native of Zámoshtsh (Zamość), Poland, was both a pioneering master of the Yiddish short story and a theoretician of the evolving Yiddishist (pro-Yiddish language) movement. He launched his *Yídishe biblyoték* ('Yiddish Library') in Warsaw in 1891, the first of a series of literary anthologies in the tradition of smaller East European peoples seeking to raise their vernaculars to European literary status. He prefaced the volume with a programmatic plan for the still-novel movement that transcended by far the scope of 'just literature'.

Two volumes of a comparable literary anthology (but without a political 'programme for change' agenda), the *Yídishe fólks-biblyoték* ('Yiddish People's Library') had been published a short time earlier by his competitor, the humorist Sholem Aleichem (Sholem Rabinowitz, 1859–1916), in Kiev, Ukraine, in 1888 and 1889.

The appearance of such serious Yiddish literary miscellanies was itself more than a remarkable accomplishment in its time. It was a

7

sensationalist statement, the more so in the case of Peretz's explicit proclamation, so to speak, of the Yiddishist movement. It was a kind of double marvel. An untended vernacular rising almost overnight, as it were, to be the language of a serious modern literature in the tradition of 'Europe', and, the rise itself lying somewhere near the core of a new understanding of Jewishness as a modern secular culture imbued with liberal (socialist/leftist/humanist/universalist/pacifist) values. Millennia of religious texts did not even have to be jettisoned along with strict religious observance to rabbinic dictum. They could readily be reinterpreted and well fit the bill of modern notions of literature, culture, folklore, history and a broad-based national heritage that can see the beauty, vitality and usefulness of many kinds of inherited culture without subscribing to a religious, nationalist or 'fact-based' claim to truth or superiority. That is a little analogous to modern Egyptians and Iranians who take pride in their countries' glorious ancient heritage, no matter how rejected those ancient cultures are as 'representing higher truth' by their own or their nations' majority Muslim faith.

For all its masses (millions, in fact) of speakers in Eastern Europe, such a rapid social and societal rise of Yiddish on the European model was not expected. Accrediting Peretz in this history is not to diminish the achievements of many and diverse pro-Yiddish forerunners in preceeding decades and centuries (see Katz 2007: 72–4, 174–6, 188–192, 200–4, 246–56). But unlike his antecedents, Peretz was consciously founding the new Yiddishist movement per se, in a framework of secular(ist) cultural diasporism with generous elements of contemporary socialist liberalism. His founding editorial includes telling passages:

> Our enemies say that Jews in general are leeches and blood suckers, criminals and scoundrels. And those who make fun of us say that the Jewish brain is like a rotted-out Hosanah branch, the heart — like a pebble, the skin — neglected, its limbs all crooked and lame.
>
> Our own chauvinists say however that Mr Israel is God's beloved only child — belief in God is there at the cradle, the pillow at his head is trust in higher powers, his swaddling clothes — curtains from the Temple, his saliva apron — the curtain over the Torah ark, his bandage — the holy belt of Moses, his heart — the liver of angels, his brain — the holy ark with the cherubs, and his financial musings — holy grass of the Lebanon.
>
> So we will put it simply: We Jews are people like all people. We have our strong and our weak points. We're no gods but neither are we devils. Just people. And, people have to educate themselves, study

continually, becoming more intelligent, better and finer people with each passing day.

By nature we are the same as all people. Nevertheless our nation is not like other nations, because our life is different and our history is different. Our teacher has been — the Diaspora.

Actually, we have a lot to thank the Diaspora for. A lot of strong points, but a lot of weak points too. In the millennial struggles of life in eras gone by, when all the nations stored up power and used it for murder, burning-stakes and subjugation, we stored up our powers to be used for tolerance, being able to bear our burdens and wait things out in order to make it through the bad times. The usual kind of power grows only to the point at which it meets a greater force; then it bursts like a soap bubble. *Our* power will not be encountering any superior forces. That is why a lot of those nations went under, while we live, and will live, forever...

For as long as we have been in the Diaspora, we have on our conscience, on our Jewish conscience, not a single drop of foreign blood. The fanaticism of nations splashed mud all over our flag, and we went and washed it off with our own blood.

And because we are in the Diaspora, because we always eat at a table of strangers, always hapless guests in this world, our hopes are for humankind, and humanity is our most sacred ideal. That is why our egoism (self-love) is the purest kind of love of people! Because we perceive that as long as love of people does not triumph, as long as there is petty envy and enmity, competition and wars, things will be bad for us. That is why we always pray for peace, that's why our hearts are like a sponge for all the newest ideas, that's why we have a heart, feelings and empathy for all people who are suffering, the exiled and the pursued. That is why we are called 'merciful and children-of-the-merciful'.

(Peretz 1891: 5–6 [from the Yiddish])

Peretz saw socialism as a potent force of modernity that could from a literary and folkloristic point of view readily and constructively absorb the ancient heritage. He was one of the builders of a Yiddishist tradition that was started some decades earlier by those who saw love of the language of the people as a cardinal element of a new kind of nineteenth-century East European Jewish culture that was in its way itself part of the multifaceted phenomenon subsumed under one of the incarnations of nationalism.

The energetic architects of the Yiddishist movement succeeded, after a fashion. Collectively, and with remarkable speed, they raised the vernacular

Box 1.1   An 'Address' for a stateless language

Menke Katz Collection

By the 1890s, this picture postcard image of Y. L. Peretz sitting at his famous desk at Tzigliana Street no. 1 in Warsaw became a symbol of literary sophistication and authority for Yiddish. Young writers from all over Eastern Europe made the pilgrimage to Warsaw to show Peretz their work and hear his opinion about whether they have a future. Among them were the future masters as I. J. Singer, Dovid Bergelson and Lamed Shapiro.

Few people knew that in an earlier incarnation, Peretz had been a fireman in his hometown Zamoshtsh (Zamosc, Poland).

Courtesy of the Menke Katz Collection.

to the status of a European language that could impress open-minded outsiders as well as already-convinced insiders with the quality and quantity of literary output and successful use in education, and in political and cultural movements (see Goldsmith 1976, 1987; Fishman 2005).

Influenced deeply by the surrounding non-Jewish language nationalisms, particularly of the smaller and long oppressed peoples of Eastern Europe who fell between the vast German area to the west and the Russian area to the east, Yiddishism aimed to 'match the neighbours' in the sophistication and range of uses that could be attained by the folk-language-turned-national-language, but without a state. In most cases, it was also without wanting a state, for that is the true definition of stateless cultures par excellence: their champions want a lot for them, but the desiderata do not include an army, a navy or a police force.

This went hand in hand with a firm belief in a potentially rosy future of inter-ethnic harmony in the framework of humanistic multicultural states that would happily make way for cultural autonomy of minorities, including the weak and the dispersed minorities. Confidence came from belief that it would all come to pass as the Russian Empire would in one's lifetime evolve, be reformed or in some versions be replaced, and the region would somehow become a place for cultivation of all the area's peoples and their cultural aspirations. And language aspirations were — and generally are — at the heart of such aspirations in a culture marked by its own distinct language. Yiddishists like Peretz, and several generations of his followers, saw in Jewish powerlessness a virtue that could in fact underpin the new and bold movement in the new and better world that they were certain would succeed the Russian Empire, and perhaps more so in the already more progressive Austro-Hungarian Empire (though, there, liberal tendencies had led some Yiddish speakers and numerous Jewish leaders to aspire to German culture and get rid of Yiddish altogether).

Yiddishism was thus allied with various movements of the day aiming for what we might today call multicultural environments under the benevolent and generous roof of the majority culture of the Good State that would soon become a tent of refuge for all her ethnic constituents (usually called 'nationalities' in the Eastern European lexicon).

Secular reincarnations of traditional messianic yearnings were not seldom at work. Who of us does not recycle internally that with which we grew up, even as we aim to remix and reconfigure it into our later decisions about higher truths? The emotional and usually unconscious transference of erstwhile unquestioning religious belief into unquestioning political belief in this or that movement or faction came into play. The deeply religious mindset and culture-set could thus continue, particularly in the soul of many a later nineteenth- and twentieth-century young East European Jew, with the content having changed from a classic religious Ashkenazic Jewish society to one of humanistic optimism. The movers and followers alike were believers in inherent goodness, generosity of spirit and tolerance as fundamental human qualities that would in due course come to the fore of public life, overpowering evil inclinations. Here, too, ancient religious notions were readily recast into a modern mould rather than just being abandoned, even when practitioners rejected rituals and observances that had been a sine qua non of Jewish life for millennia, and whose rejection would label the rejecters as potential apostates, evil-doers and misleaders-of-others in the eyes of the long-standing rabbinic and communal elite (and, in most times and places, the eyes of the traditionally religious 'silent majority').

It is fair to say that the adoration of powerlessness (in some political sense of intuitive preference for the underdog), characteristic of classic modern Yiddishism, was, and has continued to this day, though in a very different form, associated with political and social leftism and liberalism of various stripes. But make no mistake, there is a direct line of ideas from that early Yiddishism to today's left-of-centre (and occasionally further left) liberal, minority-espousing and generally anti-conservative pro-Yiddish twenty-first-century sentiment, which is often intertwined with equal rights for all, feminism, gay rights or environmentalism — though as we shall see in due course right and far-right causes have in recent years for the first time in the history of the language sometimes instrumentalized the 'cause of Yiddish' and even some academic Yiddish studies.

Yiddishism stood in contrast to Hebraism, which arose in the midst of the same East European Jewish population in the selfsame nineteenth century, in the same families. But the Hebraist language ideology was based on resurrecting the language of the Hebrew Bible, and ultimately, for those who followed the trend to its conclusion, forsaking one's home and environment and migrating to the ancestral homeland. At the time that homeland was Arab-populated, and much of it largely sizzling desert or malaria-infested swampland within the Turkish Empire. To take all that on, in other words, consituted life-plans born of extraordinary personal fearlessness in line with mainline nationalism. That genre of nationalism normally entails the notions of a nation-state in a presumed historic homeland, and the readiness to achieve it by undaunted combat with much loss of life as in any war, against the perceived wrongful 'current occupier'. The idea, common enough in European nation-states, sounded eerily unreal, sometimes to the point of hilarity among a European Jewry that had been a wholly unarmed pacifist minority in others' lands for some two millennia.

In that sense, the classic Hebrew–Yiddish conflict is but one chapter, a chapter of linguistic surrogates — or sublimations — of the power vs powerlessness debate. The broader issues were splendidly summed up in David Biale's classic *Power and Powerlessness in Jewish History* (Biale 1986). More recently, however, the subject has returned with renewed force, usually in the form of a latter-day incarnation of old Hebraism, featuring attempts to discredit powerlessness as a purportedly shameful feature of weakness in Jewish history. On occasion these arguments make use of studies that demonstrate how the image of an inherently weak and 'effeminate' Jew was a feature of modern anti-Semitism (see Robertson 1999: 151–232; see also Aschheim 1982; Biberman 2004). Uncomfortably for some, this is one of the cases where Jewish nationalism borrowed selectively from anti-Semitism, in a well-intentioned effort to construct a new and 'normal' Jew who would not suffer from alleged weaknesses, which anti-Semites and Jewish nationalists alike often saw as 'part of a problem' that needed to be rectified (rather than as, say, part of other non-problematic sets of features of wholly peaceful groups).

The most prominent recent work in this mould from the 'pro-power' camp, successor to the earlier 'Hebraist-Zionist' side of the debate, is Ruth Wisse's *Jews and Power* (Wisse 2007), an important book that merits a rejoinder (surely each debate should have at least two sides). However, that is decidedly not the task of the volume at hand (for some discussion, see Nextbook 2008). All sides agree that there is an empirical evidence trail for a long tradition of powerlessness as a virtue, and that that tradition was challenged in modernity by Zionism and occasionally by other forms of Jewish nationalism. This can be studied in its own context rather than as an evaluation of merits and faults in a twenty-first-century context of debates that are ultimately themselves incarnations of an older intra-group quip: 'But what is good for the Jews?'

A sizable swathe of the debate is menacingly anachronistic, not only in the temporal but more importantly in the cultural sense, because the characteristic of powerlessness was never called such or considered such in traditional Yiddish. On the contrary, the sum total of traits inherent in eschewing actual statelike or physical-prowess grade authority would all be expressed in an array of positive ways that do not sport a *-less* type negational suffix. They would be among the most admirable human traits, expressed by affectionate Yiddish terms such as (where the *-r* forms are masculine): *eydele(r)*, 'genteel/courteous person'; *táyerinke(r)*, 'dear [with diminutive adjective/adverb suffix here agentivized] person'; *záydene(r)*, 'gentle [lit. silk-like, soft-charactered] person' and *neímesdiker*, 'pleasant'. By contrast, Yiddish insults often include the nuance of physical adeptness (for threatening or harming others) along with a primarily character-related epithet, most famously *gróber yung* ('boor' or 'uncouth individual', lit. 'heavy-set young man'), where the social quality of coarseness is the same word as the physical quality of serious weight (in premodern East European Jewish society a figurative feature of prime health and strength rather than obesity).

The religious preincarnation

Peretz's elucidation of the merits of Jewish powerlessness was framed in the context of a modern humanistic brand of Jewish culture, whose language for future cultural achievements was to be Yiddish, then the vernacular language of virtually all of East European Jewry. Elsewhere in the same essay, he explicitly disowns the 'chauvinism' of traditional Jewish religious ideas about chosenness, or, as he puts it, the notion that 'Mr. Israel is God's beloved only child'.

Nevertheless, it would be naive to think that Peretz pulled out of thin air the notion of powerlessness being a real or potential national virtue, or, as is sometimes heard, that he rather mechanically adapted the language-based nationalisms of the nineteenth century to the specific situation of East European Jewry. In some measure, he was recycling ideas from traditional religious literature, itself in Hebrew and in Aramaic, to a reincarnated existence in the here and now, in a secular European reconceptualization, expressed in his own rich and vibrant Yiddish. His ideas had in part come vertically down the line from the ancient Jewish sources he and his socialist contemporaries had come to utterly reject as religious truth. Nevertheless, the huge moral authority of the ancient texts would inevitably lead to the question of whether powerlessness as a purported Jewish value is present or not in those ancient texts. The Hebrew Bible is not a strong candidate, given its devoted emphasis on the people fighting endless wars in order to be in the land they believe God gave them, and the prophets rebuking them to follow God's will in the land He had given to them.

The sources for powerlessness as a kind of doctrine come later. There is evidence that from the fall of Jerusalem to the Romans in 70 AD, powerlessness was verily in the mainstream Jewish tradition, even if that mainstream idea is in the twenty-first century relegated to the marginality called 'ultra-Orthodox' within the Jewish totality. Putting aside value judgements, it would be the ultra-Orthodox who are the lin-ear continuers of the two-millennium mindset, and the rest of modern Jewry that deviates in one or another direction. Most famously, the Babylonian Talmud and the homiletic literature from its period records the Three Oaths. The narrower context of the central passage concerns a discussion of attempts by one Rabbi Zeira to leave his exilic home in Babylonia and relocate to the Land of Israel. Another rabbinic sage, Yossi ben Chanina, holds forth on the problems triggered by that outwardly simple proposition by explaining the Three Oaths.

> What are these three oaths? One, that the people of Israel may not storm the wall. Two, that the Holy One, Blessed be He, made the people of Israel take an oath not to rebel against the nations of the world. And three, the Holy One, Blessed be He, made the nations of the world take an oath not to oppress the people of Israel too much.
>
> (Babylonian Talmud, Kesubos/Kethuboth [Marital Contracts] 111a [from the Hebrew, within Aramaic text])

If ever there was an explicit national recipe for powerlessness and paci-fism, there it is. Not *necessarily*, of course, because this short text could have been taken as an opinion or as a tradition with an expiry date, and that is exactly how it *is* taken — as just one non-binding opinion — by modern Orthodoxy and religious Zionism. But for today's Haredi ('ultra-Orthodox') camp, it is a cardinal principle of post-exilic, pre-messianic Jewish life and law (see Ravitzky 1996).

Around the start of the second millennium AD, the Jewish cultures of Europe were in the process of formation. Among them were Ashkenaz, in the Germanic-speaking area of central Europe, Sepharad on the Iberian Peninsula and Knaan on Slavonic-speaking territory (see Map 1; Katz 2007: 19–24).

Yiddish is the historic language of the Ashkenazim (*Ashkenázi* = 'Ashkenazic Jew', pluralized hebraically via suffixation of -*im*). Motivated most frequently by massacres, expulsions and the intolerance emanat-ing from medieval Christian central Europe, Ashkenazim migrated in various directions, principally eastward. Over centuries, Eastern Europe became the centre of Ashkenazic civilization. In the famed terminology of Max Weinreich, Ashkenaz II (in the East) arose, as 'geography was transformed into history' (Weinreich 1973: I, 5, 2008: I, 3).

It could be argued that Ashkenazic civilization took powerlessness further than most by seeing in it a deep and essential national religious characteristic, closely linked with preparedness for martyrdom, should the need arise. The elevation of martyrdom over, say, baptism, including insincere baptism to save one's life (with the intention of returning one day to the fold), is one of the single most potent examples of empirically demonstrable powerlessness that one could ask for. If any one event played a primeval role in the rise of Ashkenazic martyrdom (ergo powerlessness) it was the First Crusade (see Chazan 1987, 1996). There was a firm Ashkenazic dedication to at least the strong possibility of graciously accepting death to 'sanctify the name of God' over any form of attempted physical resistance, least of all trying to kill the attacker. To this day, there is enormous emotive power in the Yiddish phrase *af kídesh hashém* (lit. 'for Sanctification of the Name', Ashkenazic Hebrew *kidush hashéym*), that can follow any of a number of verbs for 'die', to indicate that the supreme sacrifice is being made for the highest ideal of sanctifying the holy name of God. The term invokes a permanent aura of hallowed memory. Incidentally, this little-discussed feature of Ashkenazic civilization was much in evidence during the Holocaust, with no diminution of acknowledgement to the minority that put up staunch and inspirationally brave resistance, and equally no disrespect to the silent majority for whom armed resistance was not even a conceptual option. (A survey spanning the history of Ashkenazic martyrdom is provided in Shepkaru 2006: 161–278.)

It goes without saying that, in traditional Ashkenazic society, the practice of passivity vis-à-vis violence from the majority was inextricably linked with a belief in *ganéydn* (paradise, lit. 'Garden of Eden') in the afterlife that was every bit as psychologically real, and vivid and immediate, as the empirical realities of everyday life. It is by no means only a culture of 'death by one's own violent hand' that can go hand in hand with certitude about life after death, as westerners sometimes imagine, in response to contemporary suicide bombers or pilots.

But the reaction to violence, the readiness for martyrdom and the concomitant certainty about the rewards of the afterlife are only one of the complex components of a political-temporal powerlessness. In the sense of a divine prohibition on taking up arms for political reconquest of the Land of Israel, this 'specially Jewish form of legalized powerlessness' was not only enshrined in rabbinic law and lore, it was also closely linked with belief in the Messiah who was alone authorized to enable the people of Israel to reclaim their ancient homeland in that End of Days. Nowadays, this issue is best known from the various Jewish anti-Zionist ultra-orthodox groups that reject the State of Israel (Ravitzky 1996). In recent years, their best-known exploit was

Box 1.2   From the days of early Ashkenaz

The gravestone in Mainz of Rabeynu Gershom (960–1028), "the Light of the Exile" who is considered to be the symbolic founder of Ashkenazic Jewish civilization in Europe.

The studyhouse of Raṣhi (1040–1105), the greatest Bible and Talmud commentator of all time, adjoined the   in Worms. He left there in 1065.

This pillar from the old synagogue in Worms contains a Jewish letter "chronogram" for the year corresponding to 1174–1175. The 1272 prayerbook containing the first dated Yiddish sentence (see pp. 21, 22, 84, 97) was kept at the synagogue for centuries.

probably their participation in an event hosted by a president of Iran (Santos 2007).

Communal power

But in both the modern incarnation of secular (and leftist) Yiddishism, and in the thousand-year-old traditional profoundly religious civilization of Ashkenaz, there was never any prohibition on power in an array of non-violent and non-state senses. For the good of the community (that which has been satirized as 'good for the Jews'), political skills in forging alliances with those in power to promote good relations, commerce, prosperity and tranquillity were highly valued. There was even a name for the professional post of a power-broker or 'interceder' with the authorities of the state, the *shtádlen* (Israeli *shtadlán*), and for his craft — *shtadlónes* *(shtadlanút)*. With the rise of modern liberal movements, the goals shifted somewhat to the forging of more contemporary kinds of alliances, for example, with non-Jewish radical groups committed to equality of all peoples in a given country and beyond. In either case, powerlessness in the sense of not desiring an army, a navy and a police force or an exclusive sovereign territory does not translate into a lifetime of submissiveness in other realms.

Within the thousand-year civilization of Ashkenaz, there were elaborate power structures between organized Jewish communities, differing in time and place, with every bit as much in the way of power struggles, ambitions and prizes of various sorts, as among anyone. That was, and is, at any rate, the norm. Still, there were mystical movements that encouraged even daily-life submissiveness, such as a medieval Ashkenazic work in Hebrew that encourages losing disputes here in this world to make way for a better time in the world to come, as distinguished from the posthumous fate of those who use cunning and subterfuge to gain the upper hand in this life.

Such advice notwithstanding, Ashkenazic Jewry, while one of the most non-violent societies in human history, and never coveting sovereign power (before the rise of the modern Zionist movement in the late nineteenth century among a minority within it), or participation in local power (before the rise of the socialist and diaspora autonomy movements at the same time), was not a society of Jewish monks and nuns. There have been many studies of Ashkenazic society in different periods, and particularly of the *kohol* (*kahal*) or formal internal Jewish community structure.

Ashkenazic Jewish trilingualism

In addition to being conversant with at least one co-territorial non-Jewish vernacular, Ashkenazic civilization comprised three distinct Jewish languages (see Spolsky 2014). Only one of them, Yiddish, was spoken by all Ashkenazic Jews. The other two, inherited from the ancient Near East and imported, as it were, deep into Central Europe, were not vernacular but they were very far from being 'dead languages'. Not only were the ancient, pre-Ashkenazic texts read, studied, recited and cited, but — and this is crucial — various kinds of scholars and writers continued without interruption to write *new* works in both.

First there was Hebrew, language of most of the Hebrew Bible (the Old Testament in Christian culture), the Mishnah and a large number of classical and post-classical texts. It was used in Ashkenaz for an array of genres that included letters between learned men, community records, commentaries on Bible and Jewish law, and historical works. While everybody could perhaps read some basic Hebrew and recite prayers and blessings, only some, mostly male, could truly understand an unseen text and even fewer could write the language. Those who could were among the elite of society, the equivalent of today's 'intellectuals' or 'chattering classes'. An even smaller number of elites was able to fluently study the two genres of traditional literature that were the highest in the eyes of the society: Talmud and Kabbalah. The most central texts of both are in Aramaic.

Internal Ashkenazic Jewish trilingualism can be interpreted as a progression of sociolinguistic prestige that starts from Yiddish and progresses upward through Hebrew and then to Aramaic (see Chart 1.1). That is certainly true, but it is only part of the story. Because Yiddish was the only spoken language of all Ashkenazim until modern times, it was obviously also the spoken language and usually the sole thinking language of the most erudite master of Talmud or Kabbalah — though his variety of Yiddish would have been (and in traditional societies, still is) very different; laced, for example, with a much higher concentration and frequency of lexical items deriving from the Semitic (Hebrew and Aramaic) component within Yiddish, and a concomitantly lower percentage of Germanically derived words (see Katz 2004: 37–44; 2007: 45–9).

There were myriad ways in which proficiency in reading and writing Hebrew and Aramaic were interrelated with the structure of authority, prestige and status in various Ashkenazic communities (see, for example, studies in Glinert 1993).

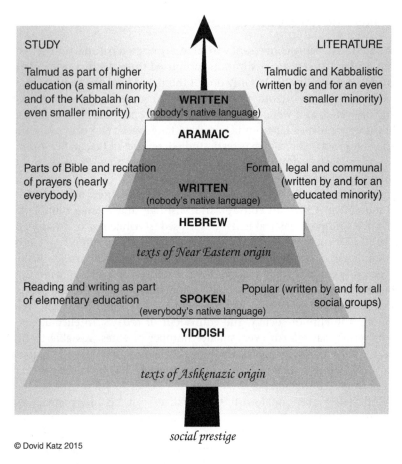

STUDY

Talmud as part of higher
education (a small minority)
and of the Kabbalah (an
even smaller minority)

LITERATURE

Talmudic and Kabbalistic
(written by and for an even
smaller minority)

WRITTEN
(nobody's native language)

ARAMAIC

Parts of Bible and recitation
of prayers (nearly
everybody)

Formal, legal and communal
(written by and for an
educated minority)

WRITTEN
(nobody's native language)

HEBREW

texts of Near Eastern origin

Reading and writing as part
of elementary education

Popular (written by and for all
social groups)

SPOKEN
(everybody's native language)

YIDDISH

texts of Ashkenazic origin

social prestige

© Dovid Katz 2015

Chart 1.1   Three Jewish languages in Ashkenaz

Naturally, this left out nearly all the women in Ashkenaz and, for that matter, a majority of men too. For them, expression in writing could only come in the vernacular, Yiddish, and for a long time it lacked any single firm literary tradition or stylistic norm. Moreover, it *had* to lack such a tradition. It was spoken and written for centuries over a large and expanding geographic territory that at its apex stretched from Italy in the southwest and the Netherlands in the northwest to deep into Slavic territory in the east. It had no formal or sacred status even *within* the society of its speakers, let alone the possibility of recognition or stand-ardization with the help of any nation-state, even during and following the Renaissance and the rise of the vernaculars of Europe (though, to be sure, these events directly and indirectly inspired Yiddish advances too).

The late master scholar of Yiddish literature, Khone Shmeruk (1921–97), used the earliest known single dated sentence in Yiddish to make a much larger point. The sentence, which translates, roughly, as 'May a good day shine upon him who carries this *mákhzer* [prayerbook for festivals] into the synagogue', is penned into the hollows of the large first word of one of the canonical Hebrew prayers in the famed Worms manuscript of 1272 (now housed in Jerusalem). Shmeruk saw in the graphic relationship of the 'opportunistic' Yiddish line within the hollows of the large Hebrew calligraphed word a symbol of 'filling the gaps'.

> And so, the graphic position of the first dated Yiddish literary document reflects in great measure, and for a long period of time, the status and the possibilities of Yiddish and of Yiddish literature within the larger and multifarious culture of the bilingual [Yiddish and Hebrew] Jewish society of Ashkenaz. The space that is dedicated for the blessing in Yiddish reflects the limited possibilities that were open to Yiddish literature from its very beginnings in the empty 'gaps' that remained for it in the framework of Jewish cultural life.
>
> (Shmeruk 1988: 13 [from the Yiddish])

Clearly, the development of different kinds of Yiddish, in different times and places, by different groups and for different purposes, would entail the quest for success that is closely tied to a wish for some kind of power in the internal, nongovernmental sense of a stateless culture's internal structures. In a society that is highly literate, with a rich tradition of attention to detail and love of text and nuance, it is perhaps scarcely a surprise that the different kinds of power sought over the centuries that would follow would be linked to individualistic styles of Yiddish, entailing the kind of corpus planning often thought of by modern sociolinguists as being a function of the state and its language academies in modern societies, or at least of high-authority institutions like churches or royal chanceries.

However, 'some kind of' is not really good enough. This book will try to pinpoint and understand some of the highly specific kinds of power envisaged by various movements and trends that used Yiddish-specific means toward their ends, or had some specific kind of Yiddish in mind as a presumed actual end.

At the same time, we will try to trace some of the 'new kinds of Yiddish' that came into being as the primary cultural symbol,

Box 1.3   Oldest known Yiddish documents with a date

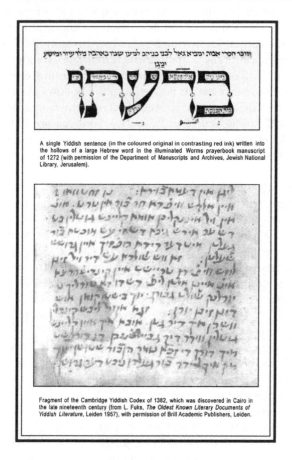

A single Yiddish sentence (in the coloured original in contrasting red ink) written into the hollows of a large Hebrew word in the illuminated Worms prayerbook manuscript of 1272 (with permission of the Department of Manuscripts and Archives, Jewish National Library, Jerusalem).

Fragment of the Cambridge Yiddish Codex of 1382, which was discovered in Cairo in the late nineteenth century (from L. Fuks, *The Oldest Known Literary Documents of Yiddish Literature*, Leiden 1957), with permission of Brill Academic Publishers, Leiden.

product and vehicle for one or another new Jewish tendency, and its empowerment.

Prior to the modern period, there will not have been a lot of explicit thought or pronouncement on a topic called 'Yiddish', not to mention that the language did not have a stable name (see Weinreich 1973: I, 321–33, III, 332–43, 2008: 315–27, A302–A312). The conscious and self-conscious notion of 'language' in the modern western sense was not a part of traditional Ashkenazic culture. Hence the historiography and sociology of Yiddish has unanimously regarded any and all forms of the 'Yiddish movement' as a product of westernization in the nineteenth century and beyond in Eastern Europe and, more specifically, as one of the direct or indirect offspring of the Haskalah (German-Jewish Enlightenment) movement. Founded earlier in 'the west', in Berlin, in the late eighteenth century by Moses Mendelssohn (1729–86), the original German-Jewish incarnation of the movement sought to obliterate Yiddish, which it regarded as an ugly, corrupt and morally damaging Jargon (*Zhargón*). The idea was to give rise to 'good Germans of the mosaic faith'. When these modernizing, westernizing ideas were carried eastward, however, to the Slavonic and Baltic lands where Yiddish was the primary vernacular of millions of speakers, ideas would evolve, sometimes in unexpected ways. Yiddish and Hebrew were both moulded into modern literary vehicles on western models, instead of being discarded in favour of the majority national language. This eventually gave rise to the Yiddishist and Hebraist movements and their (usually) related political and societal counterparts. Typically a leftist, egalitarian local cultural autonomy model was the dominant ideology for Yiddishism, while nationalist territorial aspiration, in the form of return to the ancient homeland, was the Zionist concomitant to modern Hebraism. On the way, both underwent impressively rapid qualitative and quantitative development as European-scale literary languages (see Katz 2007: 228–46).

Yiddish and Power will seek to demonstrate that from its very beginnings in medieval Europe — and centuries before any conscious structuring of language movements, and their corpus-planning components, and their conscious emulation of the 'rising new national language movements' — there was a potent societal force at work entailing wilful and even individualistic reform of written conventions that could come, if successful, to be emblematic of the new cultural force and the new power over the imagination, the mind, public interest and, by extension, the potential for economic developments.

In other words, various details of written usage, from the 'kind of Yiddish' in the largest sense down to details of usage, orthography and typography, were repeatedly combined and recombinated by founders of new kinds of power *within* the stateless society of Ashkenaz.

The unusual internal, societal social power commanded by writing in Jewish society certainly plays a key role here. It is possible to construct an upward curve of prestige from 'Yiddish speaker' (everyone) to ever smaller subsets on a continuum encompassing: 'reader of a limited set of sacred Hebrew texts' → 'reader with comprehension of the same' → 'reader/comprehender of unseen Hebrew texts' → 'reader of Aramaic texts' → 'writer of Hebrew texts' → 'writer of Aramaic (as well as Hebrew) texts' and so forth. Naturally, this list could be expanded into a monograph with ample exemplification and nonlinear progressions, and such a study, say, on 'The Notion of Linguistic Prestige in Traditional Ashkenaz' is a desideratum.

The purpose of the present exploration however is to pinpoint a number of conscious digressions from the societal norm, a norm itself a product of cultural inheritance and reinterpretation of pre-existing configurations into new realities: for example, the reincarnation of erstwhile Hebrew-Aramaic bilingualism into Hebrew-Aramaic-Yiddish trilingualism, where the final member of the hyphenated set is the one universal vernacular, and the other or others are highly used sacred, academic and liturgical languages.

The vernacular starts out with its natural power only: the fact that it is the sole and unique mode of verbal communication in Ashkenazic society. In a society with a near-universal rate of literacy, the potential is there for any new empowering movement to try to make some special new use of it. It's for us to look and see what happened.

The result can be explosive: suddenly giving the power of alternative knowledge to everyday people, thereby, in one fell swoop, upsetting the balance of societal power of Old Ashkenaz.

I
Old Yiddish in Western Ashkenaz

2
Gentile Culture Empowers Simple Jews

Early Ashkenaz presents two contrasts. First, it was one of the most 'totally self-immersed' and self-contained Jewish societies in European history, where only the tiny percentage who were (necessarily male) scholars had real prestige in town. Yet it yielded as its first popular counterculture the adoption and adaptation of absolutely — and, from the viewpoint of the conservative Jewish society, sensationally — non-Jewish medieval knightly epics and romances, taken with little hesitation from deeply Christian civilization, as reading and listening material, spiritual escape and entertainment that every simple woman (and man!) could enjoy.

Second, one of the most peaceful and nonviolent groups in the continent's history, that of Ashkenazic Jewry, had as its first counterculture love for these medieval knightly romances featuring as their regular fare duels, wounds, intrigues, murders, plots, love affairs and the dashing allure of physicality. That people love the faraway in literature is no surprise, but that this could develop in such a successfully normative, legalistic and highly regulated set of communities is nevertheless noteworthy, given the near-absolute authority of Jewish law and lore as interpreted by the rabbinic elite, and the near-total absence of anything approaching rebelliousness.

On closer inspection, the contrasts can be somewhat toned down. Reading and listening to tales, and even enjoying them, is not a contradiction to being altogether different in one's own life, no more so then than now. Moreover, in a society where the 'seriously regarded' reading (and writing) was all in Hebrew and Aramaic, the two Northwest Semitic languages imported by European Jewry from their erstwhile Near Eastern home, there needed to be some kind of personal and social release valve for the vast majority of the population — virtually all women and an overwhelming preponderance of men (nobody will ever know the statistics) — who were 'simple' and unable to partake of those Hebrew and Aramaic pleasures, therefore needing stories in the vernacular that anyone can enjoy. And who doesn't enjoy tales from a distant unknown that take one out of one's everyday routine?

But first, some background is in order regarding the norms against which this powerful counter-cultural movement emerged.

Ashkenaz within nascent Jewish Europe

Somewhere around a thousand years ago, the various Jewish culture areas were taking shape in Europe, each with diverse kinds of internal and communal power but no state-like power. But power they did covet, not least in the prestige of self-identification, whereby, with the magnificent tool of language, one can have a nation-construct of sorts without armies, navies, wars or other such 'irksome realities'. Relying on the humour, and frankly the deep Jewish pleasure, of recycling biblical names for their new homes, they often just picked obscure biblical place names that bore some kind of phonetic similarity to their new homes. The map of primeval Jewish Europe (Map 1) shows: the French-speaking area became *Tsorfas* (or *Tsarefat*), invoking a number of the consonants of forms of *Francia*; the Iberian Peninsula became *Seforad* (*Sfard, Sefarad*), after a kind of Spania (*p* and *f* are positional variants of the same phoneme in Northwest Semitic). Both names occur in the same passage in the book of Obadiah, one of the 'twelve minor prophets' (1: 20). With even more intrepid wit, Hungary became *Hogor* (or *Hagar*) after the similar-sounding name of Abraham's concubine (Genesis 16) — not even a place name. As it happens, the specific origins of relating the German-speaking central European area to *Ashkenaz* are more obscure (see Katz 1998 for explanations to date). But even here there is general clarity, in so far as the biblical chronology of nations, in Genesis 10, places the original fellow called Ashkenaz right in the category of Indo-European or Japhetic peoples, after Japheth, one of the sons of Noah in the biblical account, the others being Shem (begator of the Semitic peoples) and Ham (of the African peoples). Well, we learn early on that 'The sons of Jafeth [were]: Gomer, and Magog, and Madai, and Javan, and Tubal, and Meshech, and Tiras. And the sons of Gomer: Ashkenaz, and Riphath, and Togarmah' (Genesis 10: 2–3). That last-named son, again, via playful phonetic similarity, became the name for the Jewish culture area corresponding with Turkey. The Slavonic lands, then known for the slave trade (cf. slave, Slav in many European languages) were called *Knaan* after an ancient link of Noah's curse upon Canaan, son of Ham, as per Genesis 9: 25 (see Katz 2014).

The Jewish civilization called Ashkenaz, its people *Ashkenazim* (singular: *Ashkenazi*), was characterized from the start by Yiddish as its universal and only spoken Jewish language right through the modern period when western-civilization-inspired diversifications took root (see Katz 2007: 173–92). The language itself came about as an intricate and delicate fusing of local Germanic city dialects with the Semitic remnants preserved by the first settlers. The relative stability of the fusion formulas (for example, infixing of a Semitic verb stem in a Germanic verbal paradigm) spread over time and space by the spread of the Ashkenazim. But for many centuries, Yiddish just *was*; it was not tended to with anything like the philological expertise or conceptual sanctity of Hebrew and Aramaic.

The elites of early Ashkenazic society were the class of 'rabbinic scholars' or, in a more generic sense, the learned in the Holy Jewish Books: 'the Ashkenazic Library' comprising a vast corpus from the Hebrew Bible (and especially the 'Ashenazic canon' within it), to the latest written-in-Ashkenaz treatise. The class of ordained masters of the required learning were called *rabónim*, which is generally translated as 'rabbis', but it is one of those translative equivalents that does damage to the meaning by virtue of built-in anachronization. The term was often in a kind of competition with the more emotive *talmídey khakhómim* (lit. 'students of the wise men' or by derivation 'wise pupils', 'wise men' because 'student' is a lifelong accolade in a milieu where learning is supposed to continue for life).

On the one hand, it is important to appreciate that 'rabbi' should not be taken in the sense of a modern congregational pastor type. And on the other, this elite class made up, so to speak, of the 'intellectuals'. They were literate and learned in a certain corpus of texts that was based on the Torah-centric interpretation of the universe, but they were not strictly limited to its subject matter — the Jewish law, practice and philosophy that occupied most of their time. The genres of Ashkenazic rabbinic literature may have featured such regulars as the treatise (Biblical, Talmudic and Kabbalistic commentaries were three cardinal genres); the commentary, the commentary-on-commentary (supracommentary), responsa (questions and answers on law, real or invented as a literary device), the legal ruling and, much less frequently, liturgical poetry, which tended to blossom after massacres and expulsions as elegies for the perished.

But the vast majority of the Jewish population — and virtually all the women — were excluded not only from the societal possibilities of learning and accomplishment in the arena of Hebrew and Aramaic texts, but from the simple pleasure of reading too. The 'pleasure of reading' is a potentially powerful tool in any society, empowering the reader to broaden his or her horizons and be entertained or diverted by exposure to ideas, narratives, presumed wisdom and all sorts of material that inter alia enhances the conversation and the aura of worldliness in the intercultural sphere perchance above and beyond that of the hallowed rabbinic class itself. In other words, empowerment via knowledge for simple people, albeit not the Jewish kind sensu strictu, could be effected via a literature in the vernacular, without necessarily violating any Jewish law.

One of the simplest ideas in fathoming the origins of Yiddish literature is therefore that of empowerment of the majority, in an implicit — or not so implicit — challenge to the exclusivity of 'access to the written word' by an elite that was regarded by the population as possessing the supreme knowledge and authority in the eyes of the society in question, that of the Torah and the cumulative body of interpretation that came to be regarded as inherently correct, all in the absence of state authority. It cannot be stressed too strongly that there was no substantive challenge to rabbinic authority in the earliest Yiddish literature. On the contrary, there is every reason to believe that its readers, writers and enablers were by and large no more or less observant and pious than anyone else.

Empowerment need not entail direct challenge in the sense of opposition to extant norms in some anachronized modern sense of rebellious resistance. It can entail the raising up of a 'low' segment of the population to a higher level, which reduces the societal differential between levels by enabling those ostensibly unempowerable in some way (for example, being female) to achieve influence and prestige in a novel way not forbidden by law. One way, a priori rather curious, is knowledge of Jewish versions of works of literature that are enjoyed by the non-Jewish majority population.

In the case of Ashkenaz, the added complexity of empowerment-via-the-written-word being altogether different, and by-and-large unrelated languages, makes the scenario more intriguing, especially when it is one and the same Semitic right-to-left alphabet used for all the Jewish languages. The rabbinic elite's *actual* power, in the sense of determining law and judging disputes and generally running the internal life of the community, was derived from a literature they read, and that some of them continued to write, in two ancient Semitic languages, Hebrew and Aramaic, though philologists have of course been able to isolate obvious Yiddish influences (particularly calques) in their writings (Noble 1958). The new Yiddish counterculture was in the vernacular, upping the ante of its psychological competitiveness in a remarkable way: 'it', the sole vernacular language of the people, was being used *only* by a nascent popular counterculture, and was in fact not used *at all* by the elites for the writing of *their* rabbinic, legalistic, religious and communal literature, all produced in the two ancient Near Eastern languages of Ashkenaz.

When similar-looking manuscripts are wholly different

A prerequisite for fathoming this first reach for 'Yiddish power' is the need to comprehend the very special notion of literacy in Ashkenaz and other traditional Jewish societies. One often reads and hears that literacy was close to 100 per cent. That is quite accurate but it needs to be defined and, when it is, it is not quite *that* rosy. Nearly all boys and most girls learned the Jewish alphabet at a very early age, and could read elementary Hebrew of the Five Books of Moses (the *khúmesh*), men more so because they studied for longer and more intensively. Men could read the entire daily prayerbook, and women could read or recite those prayers that were part of their much more limited canon (for example, the blessing for Friday evening eve-of-Sabbath candles).

But this kind of literacy does not imply the ability to understand unseen texts in Hebrew, much less in Aramaic. Nor does it imply the ability to understand all (or much, or any) that is being prayed or recited, though certainly comprehension is higher for texts studied. Such calculuses are all subject to a cardinal linguistic fact of Ashkenazic society. If a word in the text happens to be close or identical to a Hebrew or Aramaic word in the Semitic Component of Yiddish, in other words, synchronically a part of Yiddish, then it will be readily understood. For example, the everyday person might not understand everything in the Grace after Meals, but he (and equally she!) will catch the blessings for *hatslókho* ('success') and *parnóso* ('making an adequate living') from the Yiddish cognates *hatslókhə* and *parnósə*, even more so when the Yiddishized pronunciation comes to dominate in prayers (unlike the formal Sabbath reading of the Torah where such Germanic-inspired phonological developments as post-tonic reduction may not be used and the classical stress-marks, usually on the final syllable, need to be followed (cf. Katz 1993b).

In the case of the actual Pentateuch, the *tóyre* (Torah), each passage was particularly deeply ensconced within the culture, as a result of the entire text being read in annual cycles in the synagogue. This was accompanied by a strong tradition of studying the weekly portion extensively before its Sabbath reading in the synagogue. But a lot of the comprehension came from the traditional translations, first oral and then written, into Yiddish. Much was memorized by a system of phrase-by-phrase translation that continues to be used today in traditional Haredi communities (on its origins and development, see Katz 1990b). No matter how it is dressed up, perhaps as 'specialized literacy', it is also in many cases, plain and simple — limited literacy. It is the relationship of the non-scholarly reader to sacred and hallowed passages, whether to be studied in the Torah, or recited as prayer, or known from other traditional usages. It is decidedly not the ability to transfer the native knowledge of a language to the written medium. That could only happen in the one spoken Jewish language of Ashkenaz — Yiddish.

And here we come to one of the most remarkable contrasts in written language. Difficult as Hebrew was, and immensely difficult as Aramaic was, for the majority of simple folk, the use of the same Jewish alphabet that everyone had studied for sacred purposes was splendidly easy and automatic fun for use with the vernacular. Yiddish itself arose in a kind of 'Big Bang' confrontation between the Semitic the first settlers, who were to become the Ashkenazim, brought with them and the German dialects that they found and which contributed the majority of the lexicon and grammatical machinery (see Katz 2007: 23–7).

A classical philologist might harp on about a thousand-and-one incompatibilities between the Northwest Semitic writing system and the new Yiddish language. The Semitic system is purely consonantal at its core, with diacritic systems added much later for sacred texts where pronunciation needed to be codified. In the case of Tiberian ('classical') Hebrew and Aramaic vowels, stress and the cantillation system (known together as the 'accents', or in Yiddish as the *trop*) were added to the Old Testament late in the first millennium AD. The new Yiddish language was mostly Germanic, and even with the 'mobilization' of letters that had lost their consonantal value as vowels (most famously the letter áyin for *e* vowels; see Steinschneider 1863; also alef for *a* and *o* vowels, double yud and other combinations for diphthongs), it was far from a perfect match initially, from the point of view of a 'professional language teacher'. The application of a primarily consonantal Northwest Semitic alphabet to a medieval largely Indo-European language in the heart of Europe leaves issues that have been studied extensively (see, for example, Timm 1987).

Yet for the people of Ashkenaz it was not only a good match; it evolved into a perfect one. The familiar letters plus the familiar language made for a written language immediately, one conceptually concurrent with the (also conceptual) birth date of Yiddish. This is quite analogous to other Jewish languages and varieties that were over time and space written in the Jewish alphabet (see Weinreich 2008: 45–174). It didn't matter that the spelling system was fluid, sometimes representationally imperfect or not based on a fixed older writing tradition. The basic phonetic formula of 'letters freed up because they had lost their old Semitic consonantal pronunciation being used as the basic vowels' was in part a straightforward continuation of a process well under way in the Aramaic period preceding the Yiddish-European epoch of Jewish history (see Birnbaum 1953).

For, say, a late fourteenth-century Christian European looking *in*, or for someone nowadays looking *back*, the manuscripts of Hebrew and Aramaic rabbinic writings and those of the earliest known works of what we now call 'Old Yiddish literature' would appear rather similar, exhibiting 'the same' exotic 'Hebrew' alphabet and the same regional 'hands', as palaeographers dub individual handwritings. Two rather similar-looking European Jewish manuscripts might even be dated to the same period. For example, a certain manuscript dated 1382, apparently from Italy, contains an enlightened compendium of works on Jewish ethics and philosophy in Hebrew, and hence was written for one or an ultimately small number of learned Jewish males who would be inclined to study it. It contains Hebrew translations from Arabic, such as a rendition of the Arabic treatise on improvement of personal ethics by the Sephardic Jewish scholar (and neoplatonist) Solomon Ibn Gabirol (±1021–±1058), and a number of works by Aristotle. The Hebrew renditions are generally translations of Arabic versions rather than the Greek originals. Parts of the manuscript, including an ethical treatise in verse, were apparently Hebrew originals (for a detailed description of the manuscript see Margoliouth 1909–15: III, no. 867: 158–60).

The same British Library that faithfully preserves that manuscript also holds another, dated around the same time, at 'shortly before AD 1384'. This one comes from Ashkenaz, the Jewish culture-area on German-speaking soil, and is written in a 'fine' hand. Like many manuscripts, it is a compilation of various works, including prayers for both days of the Jewish new year holiday according to the Ashkenazic rite, with poetic pieces traditionally recited produced in full, and a dual-column presentation of the Torah (Pentateuch) readings for these days. One column provides the biblical text 'as she is' without the vowel and accent diacritics (a reader in synagogue must read from the scroll which contains this ancient 'minimalist' version) alongside a parallel column with the diacritics (excellent for someone preparing to do the formal reading by looking back and forth during practice). The manuscript is likewise described by the British Museum's famed Hebrew manuscript master, G. Margoliouth (for a detailed description of the manuscript see Margoliouth 1905: II, no. 672: 312).

However, to Yiddish specialists from the second half of the twentieth century onward, a contemporaneous date, the year 1382, has been a kind of magic number. It is the year triumphantly trumpeted as the year of the 'first dated Yiddish literary manuscript'. The manuscript was to be found in the treasure trove of Judaica that the famed Moldavian-born scholar Solomon Schechter (1847–1915) discovered in the 'Cairo Genizah' in the 1890s. A genizah is a place for the proper ritual 'burial' of no longer usable Jewish sacred writings, which may not, by Jewish law, be burned or thrown out as rubbish. Schechter took many treasures to Cambridge, England, where they remain faithfully guarded to this day. In the autumn of 1953, it was (re)discovered in Cambridge by Leo Fuks (1908–90), a Jewish scholar who hailed from Kalish, Poland and settled in the Netherlands in 1934. In 1957, Fuks published the manuscript in a two-volume set handsomely produced by Brill of Leiden (Fuks 1957). That in itself was part of the prestige-winning path for a Yiddish studies that was barely recognized in the circles of the relevant academic disciplines of the time. There are debates on whether Fuks should be crowned the discoverer or the rediscoverer of the 1382 manuscript (see Gininger 1954; Marchand 1960), but these are immaterial to the present discussion, because he is *the* discoverer as far as anybody's knowledge of the manuscript is concerned, a category that obviously subsumes the small group of scholars and others interested in such things.

However, a much more explosive debate centred upon what *name* should be given to the language of these 1382 'oldest known literary documents of Yiddish literature', as Fuks put it proudly in the title of his two-volume Brill edition of 1957. He thereby launched a scholarly debate instead of shirking it. That itself was an accomplishment that Fuks was not given much credit for in his day, when the 'friends' and 'foes' lined up instead according to 'academic-ideological' camps. These are the camps in Yiddish studies known as 'Germanists' (who look at Yiddish from the viewpoint of Germanic studies) and 'Yiddishists' (looking at Yiddish from within, structurally and synchronically, on its own terms). The 'academic Yiddishist' spirit was itself derived from the cultural, societal and political East European Yiddishist movement which, thanks to Ber Borokhov (1913a, 1913b), developed its viable academic 'wing' on the eve of World War I (see Katz 2007: 274–8). Borokhov's academic (and generally likewise ideologically Yiddishist) followers in 1960s academia and beyond rushed to the 'defence' of the language of the 1382 'Cambridge Codex', insisting it was Yiddish. After Fuks himself, then librarian at the Rosenthaliana Library in Amsterdam, in his preface to his edition (Fuks 1957: I, xxvi–xxix), came the top guns in the field: Max Weinreich (1894–1969) in New York, the leading historian of the Yiddish language (in Weinreich 1960), and Solomon A. Birnbaum (1891–1989), another towering figure, then resident in London (see Birnbaum 1961). They were basically responding to the 'Germanists' who had pounced on Fuks for this or that fault of his edition, or, in fact, the sum total of its faults. The spirit of that whole era in Yiddish studies is expressed by Florence Diana Donsky's 1971 MA thesis about the major Germanic work contained in the Cambridge Codex: *Dukus Horant: Middle High German or Yiddish?* (Donsky 1971).

Yet the 'Germanists' in that 1960s debate were in no way 'anti-Yiddish', much less anti-Jewish. Still, looking back, it is obvious that the sociology of Yiddish studies at the time was such that the 'academic Yiddishists', for whom it was personally important that the language of this manuscript be called 'Yiddish', were not only Jewish themselves, but in their own way activists in the modern Yiddish language movement, itself rather embattled vis-à-vis the Jewish mainstream. However those who said, 'Hey, but this is just German with the odd Yiddish word or two, albeit in the Jewish alphabet and partly on Jewish themes' were non-Jews who were equally building the post-war field of Yiddish studies in the west (arguably 'more than equally' because they were helping Yiddish gain acceptance in an academic marketplace which had almost always excluded Yiddish, mostly because of the snobbism and anti-Yiddishism of the *Jewish* academics who established modern 'Judaic Studies' in the first place). The major proponent of the idea that this manuscript was written in 'German with Hebrew letters' was James W. Marchand (1959: 385–91).

In recent decades, however, the field of Yiddish has matured beyond the stage where a scholar's ethnicity could be inferred from his or her opinion on a question of whether a certain manuscript is written in 'language X' or 'language Y' (or more bluntly here: 'in a kind of German in Jewish letters' vs 'in a kind of Yiddish'). Jerold Frakes was among those who broke the mould. He came to Yiddish studies from Germanics, but found something wrong in the Germanists' approach.

In his *Politics of Interpretation: Alterity and Ideology in Old Yiddish Studies* (Frakes 1989) he took a staunchly Yiddishist line. Like anyone breaking a cast-iron mould, he had to sometimes go too far (cf. Katz 1990a).

I have long held, along with the Germanists, that the particular manuscript is some kind of 'Jewish German' (that is, German with minor Yiddish-usage influence and with major Judaic cultural influence, not least in part of its content and its use of the Jewish alphabet and Yiddish spelling conventions); and, at the same time, that this opinion says next to nothing about the spoken language of the time, which I am certain was, among Ashkenazim, Yiddish. Alongside other evidence, I have cited the centuries-old sociolinguistic phenomenon of Yiddish-speaking writers trying hard to 'write some kind of standard German' (whether they really knew standard German or not), albeit in Jewish letters, as well as the written record of 'indisputable Yiddish' among the oldest *non*-literary documents known; for example, personal letters (see Katz 1990b: 25–30).

Empowerment: gentile ('Christian') culture — minus Christianity

For linguistics and sociolinguistics the nature of language is vital and the differences between Yiddish and German, even at the earliest time, are a key point of debate. A range of other, non-literary documents from 'before, during and after' the time of that particular manuscript, now in Cambridge and dated 1382, are in fact 'Yiddish' according to all (see, for example, Frakes 1–14, all from the twelfth, thirteenth or fourteenth centuries). In the work at hand, 'Frakes' plus a number refers to Frakes 2004. But (retrospectively interpreted) Yiddishness, at stake in the history of the language, is, strange as it may sound, somewhat less relevant to the study of the writing system and internal societal power.

What is at stake for this 'other' set of questions is in part a continuum of writing systems. The Jewish alphabet documents of early Ashkenaz constitute a structural continuum that is related to prestige in a society where the written word has utmost sanctity and honour, and temporal powers of governments and armies are resolutely frowned upon. In this discussion about the power issues associated with some of the different Yiddish writing traditions down the centuries, the 'Yiddishist vs Germanist' disputes about what to call the actual language retrospectively, of any single document that may have disproportionately attracted the passions of modern scholars (though for excellent reasons, like 'being "literary" plus having a date'), are likewise of limited relevance.

On the other hand, notions of 'literariness' are not irrelevant, because they go to the heart of prestige, influence and power, in contrast with, say, a personal letter where interpersonal communication or exchange of information is the object, and there is no thought of acquiring societal prestige or engaging in some sort of creativity. That kind of basic literacy, being able to write a letter in a vernacular, when the vernacular had no firm standardized tradition yet but did have a general formula, was indeed close to universal and therefore not particularly a source of any specific person's status.

The arena of language-and-power studies can draw upon the various philological and linguistic debates without worrying the researcher about 'who is right'. The very circumstance that some modern specialists have thrown considerable ink at trying to 'prove' that the 1382 Cambridge Codex is 'German', and others have in turn done the same to 'prove' that it is 'Yiddish' *does* reflect on a major substantive issue of the period in question. There is a relationship between the twentieth-century debate and a question that did not concern most of the debaters.

Let us take the 'Yiddishist' premise that Yiddish was the language of the Ashkenazim from the outset, in other words that the specific fusion process entailing Germanic and Semitic via fixed formulas, with some Romance too, applied to the speech of the first generation of settlers who were by definition the pioneer Ashkenazim (after Mieses 1915: 30; Shiper 1924, 1933; Birnbaum 1929: 270, 1939: esp. 43, 1979: 44–57; Weinreich 1939b: 49, 1954: esp. 78–9, 1959: esp. 565; Katz 1987b, 1993a, 2007: 24–9).

Or, conversely, we could take the premise of the opposing 'Germanist' school. They took the position that Ashkenazim first spoke (some kind of) German which eventually evolved into (some kind of) Yiddish. In fact, a number of German-Jewish scholars of the nineteenth century 'Wissenschaft des Judentums' school developed this view, starting with the movement's founder, Leopold Zunz (1832: 438). For Zunz and his followers, it was a matter of 'honour' that Jews were proper Germans who originally spoke the true German language before it was 'corrupted'. But in the twentieth century, the view that Yiddish followed German as the language of early Ashkenazim was generally supported by Jewish scholars who were (a) trained in Germanic linguistics, and (b) less identifiably ideological Yiddishists. Among them were Jechiel Fischer (later, in Israel, Bin-Nun) and Nathan Ziskind. Ziskind nevertheless felt the need to conclude his paper with a post-Holocaust tribute to the sanctity of Yiddish in Jewish life, as if the need to demonstrate that his linguistic opinion in favour of a later dating of the origin of Yiddish should not be misconstrued as implying a non-Yiddishist ideological position in mid-twentieth century Jewish life in New York City (see Fischer 1936/Bin-Nun 1973: 24–46, 61, 73–7; Ziskind 1953: 104–6).

In *either* scenario — irrespective of modern suppositions and reconstructions of the actual Jewish spoken language — a form of written literary Jewish language that aimed to approximate 'Germans' German' would have had a cachet that might have posed a direct cultural challenge to Ashkenazic society, wherein the only prestige of writing usually came from the (to most people) obscure Hebrew and Aramaic rabbinic writings, mostly commentaries on ancient texts, legalistic treatises and responsa, among others.

Turning to the content of the Cambridge Codex, both its 'secular' and 'Jewish' sections are written in very German genres and styles of the day, modelled on contemporary German epic poetry. It can be construed as a simple case of the content reconfirming the form: a Germanizing or gentilizing tendency that would have been seen to undermine rabbinic 'sole cultural prestige in society' by providing an alternative model of the prestige of reading, writing, manuscripts, and an alternative usable literature for pleasure, edification, entertainment and, consciously or otherwise, social prestige too.

It is tantalizing that this was a 'modernesque' movement of utilizing gentile (or 'secular') culture without it being a Christianizing (or 'missionizing') threat posed to the Jewish religion. There was no such inkling. The most curious detail in the scholarly debate over whether the Cambridge Codex is 'Yiddish' or 'German' was probably sparked by one of the various 'Yiddish Tests' proposed by Marchand: 'If Yiddish, the document should contain at least .01 per cent Hebrew words' (Marchand 1959: 386–7). I had the pleasure of meeting Marchand at the first annual Oxford Winter Symposium in Yiddish Language and Literature (December 1985). Much of our private talks at the Eagle and Child Pub on St Giles focused on that one line of his. I think I got him to agree to drop his percentage requirement, and he got me to agree that a text of a 'certain length' always has Semitic-derived words, by the very nature of Yiddish (the terminological difference here occasioned by my introduction of the term 'Semitic Component' instead of 'Hebrew' or 'Hebrew-Aramaic' as part of my own insistence that Hebrew and Aramaic are separate languages that were *not* merged into a hodgepodge, plus my long-standing belief in the importance of Aramaic in the history of Yiddish; see, for example, D. Katz 1991).

As fate would have it, the one and only Semitic-derived word in the Cambridge Codex is a 'deeply Yiddish word' with a long history that does not speak lovingly of Jewish–Christian relations in earlier centuries, but at least it is one that rings out with humour more than bitter denigration (or at least we like to think so). It is the word *tíflə*, a frankly disrespectful (but not vulgar) word for 'church' or 'Christian house of worship'. The Yiddish humour derives in part from its 'metathetic' association with *tfílə* ('prayer', 'holy prayer', in older Western Yiddish also 'prayerbook'). Paradoxically adding to the mystique, in recent centuries, *tfílə* is a Yiddish word for prayer that can be used interdenominationally and with respect for other cultures or universal culture. While təfīlṓ 'prayer', the classical Hebrew etymon of *tfílə*, is well attested in the Old Testament, *tíflə*'s etymon, tiflṓ , occurs but three times: at Jeremiah 23: 13, where King James has 'folly'; at Job 1: 22, where the good king's scholars use 'charge with wrong[doing]' (where 'wrong[doing]' translates the Hebrew 'gave tiflṓ'); and finally at Job 24: 12, where it is again 'folly'. Modern translations generally opt for the more general and less specificity-satisfying gloss 'unseemliness'.

It seems from the attestations known to date that only in Ashkenazic times, in other words in the linguistic hands of Yiddish speakers, did *tíflə* acquire the connotation of a Christian church. Max Weinreich's (2008: 193–5) discussion of the topic is thorough, even if he might have been mistaken when he tried to somehow make the Cambridge Codex more politically correct for later twentieth-century Jewish–Christian relations by claiming that in this manuscript the word is neutral (but conceding, in a sort of giveaway, that, 'If for example, we were told that there was anti-Jewish agitation in the church, the word *tíflə* would have a definitely negative emotional charge'; Weinreich 2008: 195).

The word *tíflə*, for some philologists the only indisputably and exclusively Yiddish word in the entire manuscript, was however not at all meant to be neutral. It is both humorous and resplendent with undaunted mockery of the majority religion, right in the middle of a Germanic knightly romance, *Dukus Horant*, that is taken for pleasure (and at pleasure) entirely from that very majority milieu.

This also takes us to the heart of 'Yiddish and power' in the Cambridge manuscript of 1382. While a very small proportion of males was truly reading and writing the rabbinic literature of their time in Hebrew and Aramaic, the advent of a good story taken from the non-Jewish majority environment and put into Jewish lettering with some tinkerage empowered Jewish men and women of all educational, social and economic classes to enjoy a work of literature, to be led into thinking of a scene wholly different from everyday surroundings. And what is more, it enabled them to enjoy it *without* coming anywhere near the forbidden territory of apostasy, blasphemy or even some (anachronistically imposed) 'equality of religious traditions'. The first power that Yiddish writing conferred on men and women was the ability to enjoy a work of literature of whatever quality, and to have some frankly disrespectful, though ultimately hilarious, fun with originally Christian elements. By changing at some points the word, let us posit, *kirkhn* to *tíflə* on some but not all occasions, there is a would-be literary hand at work, not a mechanical 'koshering process', because *kirkhn* would do as a neutral designation for 'church'. It just would not have the reader or listener roaring with laughter as *tíflə* would, in consequence of the contextual humour of the somewhat pejorative Yiddish colloquialism transplanted into the heart of a very gentile tale of medieval chivalry. Christian culture without Christianity in older Yiddish literature was a feat of sorts.

While *kirkhn* → *tíflə* adds elements of self-confident humour to the milieu of this non-rabbinic imported-from-the-gentiles literature, other cases of 'de-Christianization' in the Codex and throughout Old Yiddish literature are intended simply to make the work acceptable to Jewish audiences. Another Cambridge Codex substitution avoids mention of the 12 apostles. In Codex scholarly debates, it is characteristic that Marchand saw this (using common sense) as a replacement for an unacceptable Christian reference (for example, Marchand 1961: 62), while Eli Katz (much like Max Weinreich in the case of *tíflə*) preferred to think it was 'because the concept of the twelve disciples was alien to the Jewish audience for whom this version was intended', while going on to accurately characterize it as 'an instance of de-Christianization of the Germanic material, a characteristic occurrence in Germano-Judaic and Old Yiddish literature' (Katz 1963: 16–17; more of the debates on the use of this word in the Codex are summarized in Donsky 1971: 66–8).

Such instances of de-Christianization are a hallmark of Old Yiddish literature. Whether they simply enable a Jewish readership or audience to enjoy a story or performance without being disturbed by (for them) offensive material (and there is no need to present it otherwise), or whether the substitution is done cleverly enough to provide a certain humour as an added bonus, the fact of de-Christianization is there.

As Yiddish literature developed, a reverse kind of literary playfulness involving Christian–Jewish tension came into play. For example, in Yiddish versions of the tale of *Ditrikh of Bern* (=Verona) and *Hildebrand*, about two friends who are exiled, there is a scene where the wounded knight Hildebrand is offered 'chicken and fish', a traditional Ashkenazic dish, instead of the various references to refreshment in the German text from which such Yiddish works were adapted.

To be sure, the genre that Frakes (xviii) aptly calls 'secular epic' is the central literary genre in the early centuries of Yiddish writing. Early on, it came, via a classic and recurring patterning of Ashkenazic civilization, one that may be seen to mirror the synthetic structure that is the Yiddish language to start with, to encompass a fusion of inherited Near Eastern (Jewish) content with European (Germanic) form. A most notably recurring instance involved the application of the epic genre to Jewish narratives, not least those of the Old Testament in their Jewish incarnation as interpreted and expanded upon by generations of midrash (classic legends, Yiddish *médresh*). Some of these are to be found in the selfsame Cambridge Codex, including *Abraham our Father* (Frakes 5) and *Joseph the Good Man* (Frakes 6). While most scholars do find 'Jewish midrashic' and other post-biblical references here, sometimes successfully, there were enough parallels in Middle High German for Marchand (1959: 387) to define these too as more Germanic than Jewish, given the popularity of some of these same biblical accounts in Christian society.

Yet early Yiddish literature was also developing a more sophisticated model: that of the original Yiddish work, on a Jewish topic, in a language that is clearly Yiddish. The earliest, sadly undated, versions may be from the same general period as the vaunted Cambridge document that had the 'fortune' of having the oldest date on a literary manuscript, and of having a post-history so notable (as a codex appearing to hail from Egypt; waiting for centuries in the Cairo Genizah, found there by Schechter and brought to Cambridge; being discovered anew for the world of Yiddish by the Polish-born emigré to the Netherlands Leo Fuks; having the benefit of so much scholarly disputation, right down to the word *tíflə*).

The most famous of these works reveals a synthesis of European form (knightly epic) and Near Eastern content (biblical narrative as developed further by the Jewish post-biblical story-spinning tradition). Not surprisingly, the books of Samuel and Kings, what with kings, loves, feuds, intrigues and wars, fit the synthesis rather well. The *Shmuel bukh* ('Samuel Book'), dated by Frakes to the late fifteenth century (and earlier by Weinreich to the period 1300–1480), is a sophisticated retelling of the tales of the Books of Samuel. The material is Jewish. The humour is achieved by juxtaposing Jewish life of then and there (medieval Europe) with the biblical heroes (of the ancient Land of Israel) who obviously had a very different lifestyle. The young Max Weinreich assembled a list during his pre-war Vilna period. There is a reference to High Priest Eli as *der rébe* ('the *rebbe*' or 'local rabbi or teacher of children') and Samuel as *der yúngər rébə* ('the young *rebbe*'). The passage (1 Samuel 7: 13), 'So the Philistines were subdued, and they came no more within the border of Israel' is rendered, 'So the Philistines were no longer allowed into the country of the Jews'. When the prophet Samuel offers hospitality to Saul and his servant, it is of course the mandatory 'chicken and fish' (see Weinreich 1928a: 93–4).

The *Shmúel bukh*, or Samuel Book (Frakes 47), first appeared in print in Augsburg in 1544, a year after its sequel in the Bible, the *Mlókhim bukh*, or Kings Book, in Augsburg (Frakes 45; see Fuks 1965). It too contains that unique synthesis of ancient narrative with European form enlivened via humorous anachronism and other devices.

But all the while, the 'properly secular' works, derived from obviously *non*-Jewish sources, were being written and distributed, right alongside the 'Jewish-theme works'. There was the Yiddish epic work *Vidvilt*, derived from the *Wigalois* of the thirteenth century, and featuring the Arthurian romance of Gawain and his son Vidvilt (Frakes 80). There was the Yiddish *Kinig Artis houf* (*King Arthur's Court*) in itself, which has a complex manuscript history (see Frakes 111 and 112). Until not very long ago, a Yiddish saying that translates roughly as, 'That fellow thinks his little place is *King Arthur's* court' was still current in East European Yiddish.

Historians of Yiddish literature are generally agreed that the one indisputable masterpiece of Old Yiddish literature is *Bovo d'Antouno* ('*Bovo of Antona*'). It too is a secular romance, based on the Italian *Buovo d'Antona* (Levita 1541a). The 'renderer into Yiddish' was Elye Bokher, known in the Christian world as Elijah Levita (1469–1549), a phenomenally gifted linguist and author who escaped Germany for Italy, where he taught Hebrew to Christian scholars. His books on Hebrew and Aramaic philology are philologically dazzling and intellectually daring. Given his output on that front, the achievements of his 'sideline' in matters Yiddish are exponentially more phenomenal. His philological output includes a Hebrew lexicon with some remarkable Yiddish etymologies (Levita 1541b), a Yiddish-Hebrew-Latin-German dictionary with 'Yiddish first' (Levita 1542), a translation of the Psalms (Levita 1545), and *Bovo D'Antono*, written around 1507 and published in 1541 (Frakes 33). The love story of Bovo and Druziana could not have found favour in the eyes of the rabbinic elite. It features unmaskedly risqué scenes. At one point, Druziana removes her blouse to seduce Bovo. It doesn't have the intended effect. He fails to even glance at her chest, at which point 'author's humour' comes into it, when the narrator turns to the reader to say, 'Not likely that would be the outcome if this had happened to Elye Bokher' (see Frakes 120–2; also Katz 2007: 66–7, 69–70, 83–5, 93, 94, 278).

This work, *Bovo of Antona*, was adopted from the Italian, where *Buovo d'Antona* was itself adopted, through a chain of translations and adaptations, from the Anglo-Norman romance of Bueve de Hantone (*Sir Bevis of Hampton* in English), based on a semi-mythical founder of Southampton. The Yiddish version contains the first known use in a Germanic language of *ottava rima*, an Italian stanza form comprising eight 11-syllable lines with an AB-AB-AB-CC rhyme scheme. Such structural templates make for a splendid backdrop for the level of cultural give and take between Yiddish and the national European literatures. Ancient Jewish imagery is invoked to strengthen the cross-cultural ambience. When the medieval knightly Guidon, Duke of Antona, suffers from an ailment in his old age, his advisors suggest bringing in a wife, in a scene deliciously reminiscent of King David's last days, when his counsellors sought him out the fair Shunamite (I Kings 1). Much further on in the tale, their son Bovo, at one point a poor stable hand in a faraway land, has to fight a duel with a much mightier opponent. Not being able to find a sword, he picks up an old wooden beam and uses it to devastating effect, not unlike David slaying Goliath with his catapult. (1 Samuel 17: 40). There is interreligious humour as well. When Druziana fears that Bovo will leave her for good, he reassures her with the line: 'May I get baptised if I don't come back to you!' Even greater is the hilarity when the sultan in a distant Islamic land, who orders that Bovo convert to Islam or be hanged, pursues the parallel 'gently gently' approach at the same time, asking his underlings to somehow persuade him to join the Muslim *kóel*. This linguistic, interfaith and intercultural humour, using an emotive 'inside Jewish' word for 'community' (Ashkenazic Hebrew *kóhol*, Israeli and gentile *kahál*), assumes an audience (a) of certain worldliness and sophistication and (b) happy to be entertained with materials that would not please the elites of their own society — the Hebrew and Aramaic reading and writing rabbinic classes.

It is of no small importance to the story of Yiddish and power that the first great work of Old Yiddish literature is explicitly dedicated to a female readership. The rhymed Yiddish of the first lines reads:

I, Elye the Levite, the writer serving all pious women, with respect and graciousness, realize full well that many women hold a grudge against me for not printing some of my books for them, in Yiddish, so that they might enjoy them and read them on Sabbaths and holidays. So I want to tell the truth. It seems to me the right thing to do, as I have written some eight or nine books in our sacred languages, and I have begun to put them through the press, as I reach the end of my days, and today or tomorrow might find myself on my back, and all my books and my poems will be forgotten. So if nobody deflects me from my purpose, I will print them all, one after the other [...].

(Elye Bokher 1541: [1] [from the Yiddish])

Later in the preface he explains that he had adapted it from an Italian book 34 years earlier. Hence we know it was written around 1507.

From medieval times onward, there were protests from rabbis and ethicists against the 'corrupting' gentile influence of secular romances, it being self-evident that the books referred to are in the vernacular. One of the most famous symbolic prohibitions is in the twelfth- or thirteenth-century *Séyfər khasídim* ('Book for the Pious'), which famously issued an edict that reads:

A person must not cover a sacred book with pieces of parchment upon which something of romance works is written [...] There was a case of a person who covered his *Khúməsh* [copy of the Five Books of Moses] with leather on which alien things were written, nonsense about the quarrels of kings and nations. A righteous man came and cut it right out!

(Séyfer khasidim §141 = Margaliot 1957: 148; no. 88 in Finkel 1997: 55 [from the Hebrew])

Scholars have argued about the Europeanism *romants* that occurs here. Some would refer it to genre, other to language (and for a certain generation of scholars, the obvious question of which language this refers to had to be skewed; Margoliot has 'Laaz [Italian] or Greek', Finkel reads 'Latin'). But the clarifying sentence about the 'quarrels of kings' makes clear the subject matter that is being derided, irrespective of the language in which it is written, and if this was something being widely read, then we know it is a work in the vernacular.

But the 'quarrels of kings' studied in the biblical books of Samuel and Kings could not be challenged. It is, after all, the Holy Jewish Bible. When the Yiddishized European genre of the knightly epic poem came to render even *those* books into a European, albeit Yiddish, format, the scope for protest was stymied, as ever more Yiddish speakers were being in one way or another empowered.

3
Power of the Printing Press

There have been many opinions about the readership declarations in the forewords (including title pages, prefaces, introductions) or afterwords (often short colophons) to older Yiddish printed books. These 'declarations', most strikingly, would appear on the title page of books, announcing that the book is for women, and occasionally that it is for women and men who are like women in being Yiddish (rather than proper Hebrew or Aramaic) readers, a somewhat comic way of actually saying something vernacular like: 'Buy this book, it is for regular people like you and me who like a good fun read, not for those great rabbis busy with their legal works in those inscrutable languages.'

The readership declarations have been argued about and interpreted variously, often in reference to gender issues. Many twentieth-century observers were quick to latch on to a dichotomy of male versus female readership but, as many of these comments state explicitly, the real meaning is something akin to 'all women and the vast majority of men', in other words the entire population minus the minority of rabbinic elites and other Jewishly learned males.

Some Yiddish words are included in a manual to help Christians learn Yiddish in 1514. Some Yiddish quotations from witnesses in rabbinic court cases are cited from 1519 and 1523. A single Yiddish Passover song, *Almekhtiker got* ('Almighty God'), was included in the Passover Haggadah of Gershom Cohen in Prague in 1526. But the appearance of actual Yiddish printed books is generally thought to have started with *Mirkéves ha-míshne* (the biblical Hebrew meaning being 'the second chariot' but in the popular Ashkenazic mind easily interpretable as *Mirkéves ha-Míshne* ('chariot for the Mishnah' or something that would help one read texts like the Mishnah, the Hebrew compendium of Jewish law completed in Palestine around 200 AD). It appeared in

Krakow in or around 1534 (see Shlosberg 1938). It is a biblical concordance, and the afterword, in a 'biblically recombinated' Hebrew,
contains an explosive allusion to the book being an aid in preparing
for debates with Christians about the Old Testament (in other words,
knowing what the Hebrew for this and that really means thanks to
this concordance, so as to be able to refute Christian interpretations
(cf. Weinreich 1923a: 123).

> Because his [the opponent's] words are as a hammer that shatters a
> rock, and as fire; [so it will be] as a consolation and a restoring of
> the spirit for blinded eyes, showing the highway for him who is lost,
> so that one should not have to go up against snakes and scorpions
> in a desert, so strengthen yourself and buy my book, and not silver,
> because its merchandise is better than all merchandise!
>
> (*Mirkéves ha-míshne* 1534: epilogue [from the Hebrew])

In other words, this first (known) printed Yiddish book has a kind of
higher mission, to empower non-elites of the majority to learn enough
biblical Hebrew to go out there and not get floored by learned Christian
polemicists, in an age of polemics centred in no small measure upon the
meaning of certain theologically explosive words in the Old Testament.
In a concordance, these words need to be 'buried far and deep' among
masses of everyday words. But one would assume that the difference
between the 'young woman' who would give birth in Isaiah 7: 14 and
the usual biblical word for 'virgin' would be in there.

Incidentally, this concordance brings as separate entries the same
biblical word with different endings (for person, number, tense, etc.),
making it a lot easier for someone without proper knowledge of the
language to look up 'words' in the usual European sense, rather than
'roots', as is the norm for Semitic languages, whose lexicography generally has a single entry for each tri-consonantal root. That would be
much harder for someone not too familiar with the structure of the language and its usual pattern of roots with various prefixes and suffixes.
Whoever knows the language in some degree can quickly pick out those
affixes and head for the root.

The incendiary, semi-camouflaged afterword to the first known
Yiddish book in history, the Krakow ±1534 *Mirkéves ha-míshne*, was
composed in difficult Hebrew. Perhaps that was a message to the elite —
the limited circles of learned males who could make head or tail of
this kind of Hebrew — that this book is kosher, actually, and they
need not be too alarmed. This highly coded colophon is signed by

Image 3.1 Frontispiece of *Mirkéves ha-míshne* (Krakow 1534). At the top is the Lithuanian coat of arms (the horse-riding warrior); left centre the Polish eagle; to the right (the snake with human prey) the Italian House of Sforca (added in honour of Queen Bona of the Sforcas, wife of King Zygmunt the elder, who was the reigning monarch when *Mirkéves ha-míshne* appeared). The interspersed Hebrew words make up the line, 'May the King of Kings raise and lift up the star of their hosts', which can just as easily mean, with delightful Hebrew ambiguity, 'their lucky star' in the sense of zodiacal constellations
Source: Image courtesy of the Bodleian Libraries, University of Oxford.

the printer-publishers, the three Helitz (or Halicz) brothers, Shmúel (Samuel), Ósher (Asher) and Elyókim (Elyakim), though the concordance itself is attributed to one Reb Anshil. No doubt scholarly and pious perusers of the work would have felt vindicated for their doubts or opposition about bringing such 'power to the people', when, around 1537, those same 'anti-Christianizing' Helitz brothers themselves converted to Christianity. Years later, one recanted before his death and relocated to Constantinople (see Baumgarten (trans. Frakes) 2005: 42). Needless to say, publication of the book involved rather more intrigue than we shall ever know.

The difficult Hebrew of the afterword was meant to assuage the fears of the elite that this first-ever Yiddish printed book would spread *too much* power among everyday people, and a sacred cause is alluded to as a kind of defence of the project: the need to defend against missionarism.

The opening salvo of the three-page (six-column) foreword in Yiddish, for the general reader, is one of the most memorable in the history of Yiddish and power:

> Since it has become an everyday thing, for all secret things and books to be published [or: come to light] in Taytsh [i.e. 'in transation' or 'in the translated language' = 'in the vernacular'] in order that every simple person should have knowledge [...].
>
> (*Mirkéves ha-míshne* [1534: 1] [from the Yiddish])

Later on the same page there is an appreciation of the degree to which the new application of the technology of the Jewish letter book brings a certain self-sufficiency of educational capacity to the simple family among the far-flung and isolated:

> If someone lives in isolation [could also be translated: 'far from a Jewish community'] and has a son, and there is nobody with whom the boy can study, and his father is not very educated but nevertheless has this little book, he can study the entire Bible with his son, translate every word and understand its meaning. If the father cannot read anything but *Taytsh* [i.e. Yiddish], it [the Yiddish translation] is here written after every word [of the original Hebrew] Or, if the father does not have time, but he has a wife or daughter who can only read *Taytsh*, then she can also succeed to teach the boy to translate the entire Bible.
>
> (*Mirkéves ha-míshne* [1534: 1] [from the Yiddish])

Paradoxically, empowerment issues result in various paradoxes that bear an oblique relationship to the question of whether they are 'new' or 'original' in any modern western sense. Let us engage in a simple thought experiment. A work — whether an adaptation from a German

or Italian epic, or something 'created for the first time *in* Yiddish' —
reaches Ashkenazic readers for the first time. That work, let us say
a medieval-style epic with knights and fights, blood and love and
'naughtiness', may upset a certain elite rabbinical scholar on various
grounds of inappropriateness, lowliness of spiritual level, un-Jewish
tone and feel and so forth. However, that work cannot begin to offend
the same way a translation into the vernacular of a hallowed Hebrew
or Aramaic text can offend. After all, its mastery had always been the
privileged proprietary domain of the scholar, and one that is not meant
in orthodox thinking to be 'watered down' for unmediated direct
popular consumption.

Until the rise of Yiddish printing, that entire Jewish civilization,
semiotically encapsulated in two classical Jewish languages imported
into Europe from the ancient Near East, was by definition available to
the small minority of males who could truly navigate the more difficult
texts within that literature (in other words, far beyond the simple reciting of prayers and Pentateuch portions and blessings). Suddenly, with
the advent of Yiddish printing, it was open to a translator or publisher
wishing to do something heroic for his people, or simply to make
money by producing a desirable product for the wider market.

The translator and publisher enabled simple people to 'know things'
that only elites knew before. But what kind of things? It is strangely
appropriate that the first known book that is substantially Yiddish,
the 1534 *Mirkéves-ha-míshne*, is neither 'new' in the sense just out-
lined nor a 'translation'. It is a lexicographic work to help one read
and understand biblical Hebrew. It 'could have been' just an innocent
Bible concordance cum dictionary to help Jewish people study biblical
Hebrew, but the explosive, if difficult to read, short afterword reveals
that it was a conscious effort at empowerment of a maximum number
of defenders of the faith, in the wider Jewish interest: defence of the
realm of an embattled faith against a Christian majority's insistence on
disputations and debates about Old Testament meanings. Strange as it
may sound today, that particular dispute and its many ramifications
(particularly the question of whether Jesus Christ per se is 'predicted' in
Isaiah, Daniel and elsewhere) were at the 'high end' of Jewish–Christian
theological troubles. The 'low end' was made up of the likes of blood
libels, accusations of desecration of the wafer, usury issues and the
frequently unhappy results of expulsions, punishments and — time and
again — massacres.

The first 'roughly straight Yiddish translations' of sacred texts were
printed in the early 1540s. Some believe the oldest to be the bilingual

Isny edition of *Shir ha-yíkhud* ('Song of Unity'), dated at '1540 to 1542' (Cowley 1929: 360). It is an early Ashkenazic Hebrew liturgical poem, with seven parts corresponding to the days of the week. Some believe it to contain an esoteric mystical layer of meaning. The whole business of empowerment, when looked at more closely, reveals a range of levels, and, as with all human power scenarios, there is game-playing and teasing, directed at one's listener or reader. The foreword to this early 1540s edition of the *Shir ha-yíkhud* contains this tease:

> What is easy in here, everyone can understand by himself, and what is difficult he must let go of [...] It is no good to entrust to anyone, least of all to the ladies. The mind of simple people cannot comprehend so much, so he [the translator] made short shrift of a lot [of those things].
>
> (Shir ha-yíkhud, ±1540–1542 [from the Yiddish])

What is rather colloquially expressed here was to become part of a tradition of centuries of printed 'edited translations' that *partly* empower the majority while making it clear that they must not know higher or esoteric things that are not for them. Of course, all the foreword (or afterword) statements of intent need to be taken with a pinch of salt. They are part of a marketing effort, which included a drip-drop strategy of imparting knowledge of things previously available only to educated elites while simultaneously covering their backs vis-à-vis the unchallengeble rabbinic authorities.

A much larger book that appeared in 1542 in Isny was the *Séyfer mídes* [séjfər mídəs] ('Book of Good Traits'), also an adapted translation of an earlier Hebrew work. The book mentions the expulsion of the Jews from France in 1395 and may have originated in the early fifteenth century.

Ethics are for everyone, and rabbis, one could surmise, should only have been happy that works to improve moral and ethical standards appeared in the vernacular. There is no challenge here to anyone. Still, the declarations are informative. On the title page, right underneath the name of the book, there are six half-lines in big type, in the classic style of recombinating biblical and Talmudic phrases. It starts off with *Noshim shaanonoys*, 'Women who are at ease' (Isaiah 32: 9). The recombinated lines translate approximately as:

> Women of leisure, secure and fresh, whose honour is all in the princess within: time-wasting brings about whoredom. Let her read this

book with trepidation, and she will add to herself wisdom and multiply her Godfearingness.

(*Séyfer mídes* 1542 [from the Hebrew])

Words are not minced. The tone of the title page implies in some measure that the 'special race of women' requires a book like this to keep its house in order. This Hebrew mini-poem on the title page would *not* have been understood by the average reader of the book; it is part of a publishing tradition that has elegant Hebrew (unintelligible to the actual reader of the book) material that makes the book look and feel more prestigious, a kind of 'title page hebrewgram'. That title page text was perhaps more a message to the *men*, and perhaps in some cases, the fathers or husbands of the intended readers, assuring them that this is *not* about empowerment or gender competition — unlike the case of secular romances bringing about the circumstance of Ashkenazic women — and men too, of course — who could not read a line of Talmud but could have read a Yiddish version of a famous European work. What we have here is a counter-blow struck by the power-for-men and leave-women-in-their-place attitude. But that is only on the title page, in Hebrew, written for the sake of soothing the male fear over women having such access to a work of Jewish ethical literature rich in that old male bastion of Judaic lore, law and custom.

The frontispiece has an elegant Hebrew paraphrase from Isaiah making it clear in big letters that this is a book for the ladies. It is apparent that 'literature for women' is the *excuse* here for publishing in Yiddish, and the makers of the book proceed from 'women' (on the motto page) to 'whosoever' (in the preface) to 'everyman' (in the afterword), taking care to give prominence to the pleasure and edification of women and girls at each juncture. The progression 'women' → 'whosoever' → 'everyman' is rather explicit.

In the foreword, some logic, after a fashion, is provided: people feel lusts and the burning of the Evil (often meaning 'sexual') Inclination (the *yèytser hóre*), and 'that is why we have written this *Séyfer mídes* in *Taytsh*, so that everybody would be able to understand it', going on to explain that the unnamed producer of this volume is being enabled by God to write this book 'that is called in Hebrew *Séyfer mídes*'.

A major gender-based differentiation may be found in the realm of proportionalities. For women, Yiddish literature was close to 100 per cent of the literature they could enjoy and study (yes, study; many works like *Séyfer mídes* are books meant to be studied, not just 'read' in the sense of a story or poem), while that proportionality was the case for many (or even most) but not all men. There was, to be sure, an unknown proportion of men who could and did enjoy various writings in Hebrew, whether ancient or more recent, who could *also* enjoy Yiddish. From the point of view of truly enjoying something that is read, it was one of three languages (for most people), two of three (for few), or three of three (for very few) in the case of men. For women, and indeed for most men, it was one of one, full stop.

The *Séyfer mídes* also has a few pages with the first ever published rules of Yiddish spelling for *Jewish* readers (a Christian Hebraist had written out a version of Yiddish spelling rules in his Hebrew grammar back in 1514). This is important because Yiddish publishing was seeking a Europe-wide market (well, at least one comprising most of Central and Eastern Europe). The spelling and indeed lexical decisions which these early publishers made often involved choosing between various manuscript traditions and between dialect areas. The result was a kind of 'lowest common denominator printed Yiddish' with a relatively standard spelling.

The commercial rise of Yiddish printing in the 1540s is therefore a watershed. The title page of the *Séyfer mídes* is in square Hebrew characters with full vowel pointing, characteristic of Bibles and prayerbooks, but its six lines of Hebrew verse are an original recombination of phrases and terms to say something very clear to the reader who is highly educated enough to fully understand these lines; in gender terms, the title page can even be taken as an assurance to elite males that this book can only improve the morals of their womenfolk, in other words: 'Not to worry!' At the same time, for the reader-buyer her- or himself, the prestige of owning a book with such a learned title page is a statement of something to be proud of.

However, this early Yiddish-printing 'luxury item' bequeaths to us not only the Hebrew title page, and the Yiddish introduction, but a supplement at the end that is far more than a 'colophon' or 'afterword'. It is almost self-consciously a launching pad for the new enterprise of European Yiddish publishing. 'European' because the language being symbolically codified in these spelling rules, hapless as their formulation may be, is one that would in large measure serve the interests of Yiddish publishing for centuries.

Here we come to the interface of language standardization and the empowerment of the non-elite overwhelming majority of the population for a stateless language whose publishing sector took off in the 1540s (with no implied diminution of respect for the singular Yiddish 'appearances in print' prior to that date). This new empowerment needed the rudiments of standardization, not in any modern sense of 'the one correct spelling/usage/form' as opposed to all the 'nonstandard ones' but nevertheless, for the time and place, an overall standard based on broadly consistent 'main points' that would, for all its internal variation and variability, allow for the widespread dissemination of a variety of works to the majority.

Moreover, the standard was a standard in at least one important sense. Variation was regulated vis-à-vis where it could and where it could not occur. It was clear that the stressed *é*, for example, must always be represented by áyin (ע), while stressed *á* could be represented by álef (א), or by nothing (zero). It *is* therefore part of a rule-governed system that *zakh* ('thing') could be spelled either זך or זאך while *bet* ('bed') has to be בעט. No big deal for the readers, writers or typesetters. Only a big deal to us moderns, for whom complete uniqueness of representation has become some kind of principle of legitimacy or correctness. Fully standardized orthography is not a cultural universal.

There had of course *been* a Yiddish writing tradition for centuries before these '1540s rules', as Max Weinreich so eloquently pointed out in his first book *Shtáplen* (Weinreich 1923a: 107). From the meagre scraps of written Yiddish words preserved from the eleventh century onward (see Frakes 1–4), and from preserved proper names (Shiper 1924), it is evident that a Yiddish writing tradition developed *without* the power of either state or 'church' (remember that the elites of Ashkenaz were only interested in the 'accuracy' of a Hebrew or Aramaic written form, and even here there was leeway in most things post-biblical with respect to vowels, letters that functioned as vowels, and more).

Yiddish provides a powerful example of the centripetal force of language standardization in the absence of academies or governments. Yiddish nevertheless developed a small but vital base set of writing conventions. The most famous of these set in, as noted earlier, at the genesis of the language per se. They included recycling of the ancient letter áyin ('ayin), originally presumed to have been the grapheme for the [+low] or pharyngeal consonant [ʕ] in ancient Hebrew and Jewish Aramaic. Its recycling for the (usually stressed) vowel /e/ (/e/ [ɛ] as well as /e:/ [ē] and eventually various diphthongizations in Yiddish dialects, for example, [ej], [ɛj]), is one of the instances of Ashkenazim recycling phonetically lost consonantal graphemes into useful new (usually vocalic or diphthongal) graphemes in the European spirit of consonants and vowels being equally marked. This major adjustment is crucial, because Yiddish managed 'on its own', centuries before the sixteenth-century rise of Yiddish printing, to effectively and collectively 'reform' an almost purely consonantal Semitic alphabet into a European alphabet. In some cases, Semitic pharyngeal/laryngeal consonants 'lasted for a while' before disappearing, succumbing to the overwhelming force of the European phonetic environment (see Katz 1993b: 68–71). That feat was accomplished by various European Jewish languages, but not in the same way. In the case of Yiddish the bold reassignment of áyin from the Semitic consonantal repertoire to the European vowel inventory became an early characteristic feature of the Ashkenazic writing system (this term being wide enough to include place names, transcriptions of foreign languages and other material not necessarily 'Yiddish' in everybody's opinion). Its importance in Ashkenazic history was first recognized by the remarkable Friedrich Christian Benedict Avé-Lallemant (1809–92) of Lübeck, a German police chief, crime novelist and expert on Rotwelsch, the German underworld language, who ultimately became one of the great scholars of Yiddish too (see Avé-Lallemant 1862: 296–8). Correctives as well as polemics were added by nineteenth-century German-Jewish 'Wissenschaft des Judentums' scholar Moritz Steinschneider (1816–1907), the master bibliographer of Europe's Judaica, in an 1863 paper called, with classic Steinschneiderian brevity, 'Der Vocalbuchstabe ע' (Steinschneider 1863). In the twentieth century, the great Yiddish philologist and Jewish alphabet palaeographer Solomon A. Birnbaum (1891–1989) added much more on two other 'phoneticizing features' that actually got under way in the ancient Near East in Jewish writing, and were transplanted to Europe and to Yiddish: double vov for /v/ (which, after consistent application, eventually freed up beyz/beth <ב> for univalent plosive /b/), and double yud <יי> for various /ej/ and /aj/ diphthongs (see Birnbaum 1979: 112–6).

But to return to the 1542 *Séyfer mídes* and its complex implications: we had noted the Hebrew title page that reassured learned menfolk about the importance of keeping their womenfolk informed about morals and ethics, and the very different Yiddish preface which talks about the need to make these things known to everyone. The afterword contains the first known attempt at published rules for Yiddish spelling for popular Jewish usage. They contain nothing original, which is useful, implying that they are descriptive; they correlate the usage of vowel letters with the Hebrew system of sub- and supralinear vowel points. This correlation is itself instructive of the internal complexities of Ashkenazic culture. While Yiddish was the only vernacular, and nobody actually 'spoke' any Hebrew, much less Aramaic, a vast majority of the Jewish population was well familiar with the names of the Hebrew vowel points, because they are traditionally taught with the elements of reading at a young age, to nearly all boys and (many) girls (separately). So we have the situation of the Hebrew vowel points, from a language nobody spoke, invoked to help define the sound equivalent of the spelling of a language everybody spoke but that did not have a stable writing tradition. As convoluted as this may all sound to moderns, these notions, expressed with the traditional vocabulary for each feature, would have been the singularly straightforward method of discussing such topics in traditional Ashkenaz. It is equally accurate today in traditionalist Ashkenazic Haredi, mostly Hasidic communities, worldwide, where boys' and girls' education alike begins with basic literary in the Hebrew letters and names of the vowel points as rendered by Ashkenazim, and which remain to this day among the earliest childhood memories of any traditionally brought-up Ashkenazi, be it in Antwerp, the Stamford Hill district of London, the Boro Park area of Brooklyn, the Haredi community in Jerusalem or many more.

Besides an obscure polemic with some who allegedly use vowel points poorly, the author provides seven relatively clear rules, linking Yiddish letters with Hebrew vowel points. They are the correlations between the following:

Yiddish letter	Hebrew vowel-point name (and Ashkenazic reflex)
yud	khírik (/i/) and tséyrə (/ei/ and /ai/ diphthongs)
alef	kóməts (/o/) and pásekh (/a/)
vov	mlópm (/u/ or /ü/) and khóuləm (/ou/ and /au/ diphthongs)
ayin	segl (/e/ vowels, ranging from [ɛ] to [ē] etc.)
double yud	/ei/ and /ai/ diphthongs
final alef	a silent letter that the author calls a 'decoration'
vov yud	/au/, /oe/ etc. diphthongs

It may not sound like much to moderns: a stateless, powerless language had over centuries developed conventions that were widely used, and that were, at the dawn of the age of Yiddish publishing, put into an afterword of a book. But for that language it is a watershed: the rise of a publishing tradition in the spoken language, producing books readable by all, men and women alike. Taken symbologically, the spelling rules in the afterword, the first published linguistically self-conscious document intended for a Jewish audience, represent the launch of a certain kind of pan-Ashkenazic 'Yiddish power' that acquires a retrospective conceptual significance when we bear in mind the broad European expanse of Yiddish-speaking territory.

The afterword including the spelling rules is signed by 'Plóyni Almóyni', a popular expression for 'Anonymous' or, more literally, 'Such and such a person' (after Ruth 4: 1; classical Hebrew: *pəlōní ʔalmōní*; older Western Yiddish approx. *plóuni almóuni*). Incidentally, the afterword with the spelling rules starts off with a curious dedication to an apparent lady patron who bankrolled the work:

> To God Almighty an exclusive oath! We send our sincere greetings to all women and girls. And in the first place to the honourable and pure lady, Morada, doctor of the free art of healing, resident of Guenzburg, a generous woman. After I understood that you have craving and desire for the *Book of Good Traits* [Séyfer mídes], so I have taken it on myself with the help of God, blessed be He, the Almighty, and have on this day done it, and although I should not take upon myself such a thing, it is after all written in the Sayings of the Fathers [in the Mishnah]: 'Where there is no man, try to be a man.' I therefore want everybody, and ask women and girls and whosoever will read from this *Book of Traits*, and might find something wrong in it should not think the worst of me.
>
> (*Séyfer mídes* 1542, afterword [from the Yiddish])

Like the other editions produced by the Christian Paul Fagius 'for' Jewish readers, the *Séyfer mídes* contains his trademark logo of three leaves. This logo of the Christian publisher is therefore a potent symbol of the empowerment of Yiddish in the 1540s. Not only were Fagius's books of the early 1540s, in Isny, produced to a much higher standard than the Helicz brothers' prints in Krakow from a typographical and production point of view. The 'proper Christian' Fagius and the 'proper Jew' Elijah Levita, both German-born, were a proud pair of interfaith colleagues, a far cry from the Polish-born Jewish brothers who produced a concordance as a polemic against missionaries, only to convert themselves and subsequently be banished from the Jewish community.

Paul Fagius did very well from publishing and selling Yiddish books. He published the first four chapters of Genesis in Yiddish and Hebrew in 1543, and a selection of favourite books from the Old Testament in 1544. It is telling for interfaith publishing history that Fagius issued two prints of this Jewish Bible anthology, one for Jews and another, with a German title page and introduction, for Christians. This is an outgrowth of the gentile-culture aspect of early Yiddish power: Yiddish was the bridge between Judaic and Christian culture in Central Europe, many theologians of both faiths would have been made most uncomfortable at the time by any such characterization.

Nevertheless, it is important that the two founding 'firms' of Yiddish printing came from the two sixteenth-century 'halves' of Ashkenaz: the Helicz brothers from the east, destined to become the dominant centre of Yiddish in the centuries following, and the team of a great Jewish philologist and a Christian humanist in the west, still a potent centre of Yiddish. It has been proven that Western Yiddish and Eastern Yiddish were already two distinct dialect blocs within the Yiddish language in the sixteenth century. But there is 'not much in it' when one compares the prints of Krakow in Eastern Yiddish territory with Isny (Yiddish *Áyzne*, deep in Western Yiddish; now Isny im Allgäu in southeastern Baden-Württemberg, Germany, part of the district of Ravensburg).

The overall similarity in the Yiddish used by publishers from both east and west, say in Krakow and Isny, while suppressing the vibrancy of the living language and its local forms, served to enhance the power of Yiddish publishing. By being supra-dialectal, it became a pan-Yiddish, pan-Ashkenazic enterprise. It was appearing in a relatively uniform style for pan-Ashkenazic consumption, making it a viable product both economically and culturally. Books were intended for as large a distribution as possible throughout the Ashkenazic diaspora, which by then included a large swathe of Central and Eastern Europe. Forms associated with any one dialect area were decidedly not good for a book's pan-Ashkenazic distribution. Max Weinreich has called this language 'Written Language 1' (to distinguish it from the new East European based modern literary language of the nineteenth century). He accurately dubbed that older Literary Language I a 'minimum common denominator' language. By avoiding what is regional, emotive and colourful, it served well for forging out of Yiddish a powerful medium for the conveying of 'information in print' to a population that had an extraordinarily high degree of literacy. But it was therefore, perhaps inevitably, a Yiddish lacking in plasticity, vitality and regional dynamism. That was all being developed in the course of natural spoken language development throughout Yiddish-speaking Europe, and *that* is a kind of power that would not burst onto the stage of Ashkenazic history until the early nineteenth century.

For modern linguists, of course, those works that defy the sterile standardization of early printed Yiddish are the ones with the linguistic magic. For example, the Amsterdam 1658 edition of a Hebrew–Yiddish dictionary for pupils, *Khínukh kóton* (Yiddishized: *Khínəkh kótn*, lit. the 'Little Education' or 'Little Educator'), lists Eastern Yiddish *zéydə* along with Western Yiddish *hárlə* for 'grandfather'; Eastern *bóbə* with Western *fráiə* for 'grandmother'; Eastern *múmə* with Western *mémələ* for 'aunt'; and so forth. Other editions opt instead for the neutral pan-Yiddish literary forms which are closer to German and lacking in local colour. For example, the Amsterdam 1761 edition of the same work gives *éltər fótər* for 'grandfather' and *éltər mútər* for 'grandmother' (see Katz 1990b: 198–201).

A symbological coup: the *máshkit* font — just for Yiddish

Nearly all Yiddish works published in the sixteenth century (and for centuries after that too) used a special type font just for Yiddish. To be able to easily read the letters, a modern reader has to spend a lot of time studying them, such are the differences. In a civilization centred on words, texts and quotations from ancient works, typefaces take on a major symbolic importance after the invention and spread of printing. Both Christian and Jewish printers produced pre-1500 books (incunabula) in Hebrew and Aramaic, in both Italy and the Iberian Peninsula (Spain and Portugal). Hebrew printing got under way in Italy in 1475, about a quarter of a century after Johannes Gutenberg's fabled invention in Europe of the printing press at Mainz.

The founders of Jewish typography, Christian and Jewish alike, were irresistibly attracted to the creative process of fashioning a modern Jewish-letter typeface *in addition* to the classic 'square' Jewish letters. These square characters are called *merúbe* (Israeli *merubá*), which means 'square' (they are also known as *ksav Ashúri*, literally 'Assyrian script' because the Jews adopted it after the 586 BC Babylonian exile, and eventually abandoned the ancient 'paleo-Hebrew script', which looks completely different and can be read today only by specialists). The new fonts were modelled on actual Ashkenazic and Sephardic writing of the period (sometimes called 'Hebrew cursive'). The printers, inspired by the aesthetic and functional variation in the new Latin and Gothic fonts (and the different styles being developed for each), used square letters for the text of the Bible and Talmud and other classic works. In the case of the Bible, they usually included the intricate system of vowel points and accents. They used their more creative adaptations of the contemporary popular written forms of the day for the commentaries on these texts and other later writings. The Christian Daniel Bomberg's printing enterprise pioneered editions of the Bible and both Talmuds that remain standard to this day. But it was the Jewish (originally Ashkenazic but Sephardicized) Soncino family that set the mould for the genre of the commentary, which was usually printed *around* the main text. The differences between the newly created contemporary fonts were considerable. Not only is there a great deal of variation in handwriting, but it is natural that Sephardic-oriented printers, whether Christian or Jewish, would use Sephardic script as a model, while those oriented toward the Ashkenazic lands would look to their constituency's typical handwriting. The result was a wide array of styles for commentaries. The specific style of Sephardic cursive that the Soncino family printers used for commentaries became known as Rashi script after the most popular commentator, Rashi (Solomon ben Isaac, 1040–1105), to both the Bible and Talmud. (Rashi, an Ashkenazic Jew who lived centuries before, did not use that script. But names have a way of sticking; to this day the font is known as just 'Rashi' or 'Rashi letters'.)

After many years of scholarly speculation, the late master Judaica bibliographer Herbert Zafren of Cincinnati cracked the mystery of how the third major kind of early Jewish type, the unique separate font for Yiddish, came about, starting with the prints of the Helitz brothers in Krakow in the 1530s (if not earlier). What came to be the Yiddish type font in the 1530s had previously been one of the competing (and now abandoned) typefaces for rabbinic commentaries based on the Ashkenazic handwriting of the time (see Zafren 1982, 1986–7). When the Soncino Rashi script won the battle of the commentaries, the font based on Ashkenazic handwriting was left without a function. From the 1530s for over 300 years thereafter Ashkenazic publishing used (a) the *máshkit* font for Yiddish, (b) square Jewish (or 'Assyrian' — *ashúri*) for the classic Hebrew and Aramaic texts, and (c) Soncino's Rashi font for Hebrew and Aramaic commentaries. A typical Ashkenazic page often has all three fonts: a three-script culture to go with a three-language culture, although not in one-to-one correspondence. Instead, the three fonts roughly correspond to three strata in Jewish history. Square Jewish type was for the classical texts from the Near Eastern period in Jewish history, principally the Bible and the Talmud. The so-called Rashi font was principally for works of rabbinic scholars in Hebrew or Aramaic hailing from the European period in Jewish history and equally in use for Ashkenazic- and Sephardic-origin works.

Herbert Zafren thus discovered the origin of the special Yiddish font, often called *máshkit* (formerly also *méshit*, *máshet*, *máshket*, etc.),which came to be used for Yiddish alone. But Zafren's masterful unravelling of the mystery of origin is a question separate from the structural and symbolic status the typeface quickly came to acquire. In 1540s Ashkenaz it had become the special, unique typeface of Yiddish, giving Yiddish books a style and panache of their own; one which might be looked down upon by scholars but was looked up to by the silent majority of Ashkenazim, who were thereby empowered with a printed literature of their own by this remarkable development in a stateless society with no centralized governmental or quasi-governmental forces at work. Incidentally, the origin of the name *máshkit* is unknown and the word continues to inspire etymological speculations, the earliest of which were offered by Elijah Levita in his *Tishbi*, where he reports investigating and rejecting an Arabic origin (Levita 1541b: 109–10).

The three-font visual 'look' of certain kinds of Ashkenazic sacred-book pages was a huge step in Yiddish empowerment in a society like Ashkenaz: it brought the universal vernacular right 'up onto the page' of some truly sacred books, both such as were in wide use (for example, prayerbooks), and such as were more for reference or possession. Moreover, it brought typographical stability for a three-alphabet/font and three-language Jewish Ashkenaz.

The right-to-left Jewish letter typography arose in emulation of the productions of left-to-right European gentile typography. There was a desire to replicate the structural variety of typestyles, in a case of noteworthy cultural mirroring. The same Ashkenazic culture that was so adamant about separating things out was enthralled by the prospect of mirroring its own complexities using the invention for distinct internal cultural and semiotic differentiation. The development of the European Latin-based alphabet custom of using *bâtarde* (*bastarda*) typefaces for the vernacular to distinguish vernacular text from the classic languages provided the model. But it is an explanation that only goes so far. After the first few years (or, more likely, the first few books), the Jewish mirror practice could have gone out of fashion. What happened was that the letters became popular precisely because they were similar to the Ashkenazic handwriting on which they were based; the font had a homely, heart-warming quality, setting it prominently apart from the formality of the difficult-to-understand mainly-for-scholars classical texts. And on that count, the symbolism of the typography had another level too. The mindset of Ashkenazic civilization is not one of universalism or levelling out in the interests of efficiency or standardization. It is a culture of seemingly infinite differentiation, a culture that takes pleasure in the minutest of splitting hairs. The result was: square letters for the basic texts, Rashi letters for the scholars, and Yiddish letters for the language spoken by the people. Nuanced Jewish reproduction of a Christian custom could fit right into the Ashkenazic way of thinking.

Image 3.2 Title page of the Freiburg 1584 edition of the Yiddish translation of the Five Scrolls from the Old Testament. The book's title is in square Hebrew characters. The description is in Rashi (rabbinic cursive) letters. The third large paragraph is in Yiddish in *máshkit* letters. This page illustrates two languages, three styles and three alphabets. Typographical Yiddish power was by then well established in consequence of the strikingly unique and different *máshkit* font
Source: Moshe Rosenfeld Collection, courtesy of Rose Chemicals, London.

Christian influences

The Christian 'hand' in the rise of Yiddish publishing — the first major manifestation of Yiddish and power — was not limited to a Jewish mirroring of classical vs vernacular language typeface. There was prominent actual Christian participation in the rise of Yiddish printing, which

Image 3.3 The Ashkenazic 'Yiddish-incorporating sacred page', featuring in this case all three Jewish languages (Hebrew, Aramaic and Yiddish), and all three classic fonts ('square Hebrew' for classic text, 'Rashi' for rabbinic commentary and '*máshkit*' for Yiddish) survived in many shapes and forms between the 1540s in Western Ashkenaz and (with regional variation) the 1840s deep in modern East European Yiddish. This page is from the end of the three-font era, as *máshkit* would soon be discarded. It is the beginning of the book of Job (Vilna 1842). The top left (conceptually 'main') box launches the biblical text in Hebrew. The box to its right initiates the classic Aramaic translation (the Targum). Both these texts are in classic square Hebrew with full vowel pointing. Then comes Rashi's commentary and some others in Rashi font. At the bottom of the page, the homely, unmediated, understood-by-all Yiddish, in its own vaunted font, serves to both translate the biblical text and selectively incorporate elements of commentary

Source: Courtesy of the Menke Katz Collection.

was the first major Ashkenaz-wide episode of Yiddish and power in European history. This might surprise moderns. After all, Ashkenazic civilization was in some ways extraordinarily insulated from Christian culture, and 'episodes' like the Crusades (from 1096 onward), the Rindfleisch massacres (1298), violence in the wake of the Black Death (1348–9) and numerous discriminatory and humiliating laws, expulsions and murders did not help interfaith relations, to use the anachronism. Nevertheless, the spirit of the Renaissance, Humanism and the Reformation all led to certain cracks in that particular wall of total separation, cracks that were filled mostly by eager open-minded scholars on both sides (the Christian side in the age of Reformation included Catholics as well as Protestants). One of the cross-cultural heroes on the Jewish side was Elijah Levita who taught Hebrew to, and copied Kabbalistic manuscripts for, Petras Giddies of Vitter (1471–1532), a clergyman who rose to the rank of a Roman Catholic cardinal (from 1517).

However, the story becomes murkier in so far as three 'kinds of Christians' were involved in the rise of Yiddish publishing in the 1530s and 1540s: (a) Jews about to convert to Christianity, like the three Helicz (or Halicz) brothers who produced *Mirkéves ha-míshne* in 1534; (b) born Christians who had commercial or theological interests (ranging from the study of Hebrew and Aramaic in the spirit of European humanism to missionary activity or various and subtle combinations of both); and, finally, the murkiest group, (3) Jews who had previously converted and did not want their Jewish origins known, leaving researchers even today surmising about 'accusations' (from either side!) that they had once been Jewish or even that they had Jewish origins. After *Mirkéves ha-míshne*, the Helitz brothers followed up in 1535 with *Azhóres Nóshim* ('Admonitions for Women'), which, they explain on the title page, was adapted from the works of the great Ashkenazic rabbis Judah Mints (c. 1408–1506) and the twelfth-century Samuel of Worms. In the late 1530s, they released *Múser un hanhóge* ('Ethics and Behaviour'), a Yiddish version of a famous ethical work by the great Ashkenazic scholar, Asher ben Jechiel (c. 1250–1327), known as 'the Rosh' from his acronym. And in 1537 the Helitz brothers were baptized. The Jews of Krakow (and elsewhere) organized a bitter boycott of their books and refused to pay the debts that had piled up. Although lacking a single Christian or missionary allusion, anything and everything they produced was retroactively tainted by this most painful act of community betrayal in the eyes of Ashkenazic civilization. Launched in this 'baptism by fire' in every sense of the term, Yiddish publishing was a highly suspect proposition from the outset. The Helitz brothers and their many new Christian friends petitioned the king of Poland, Sigismund I ('The Old', 1467–1548). The king was a devout Catholic who protected the rights of Jews, Greek Orthodox Christians and nascent Lutherans. He issued a decree on 28 March 1537, ordering the Jews to buy up the remaining stock of the Helitz brothers' books. But the dispute flared up further. By the end of 1539, the brothers had to obtain another royal decree ordering the Jewish community to buy up their stock of (mostly) Yiddish books — almost 3,500 volumes. The Jewish community of Poland handled things in a Jewish diasporic way. They obeyed the king, paid for all the books and according to an old (but unproven) tradition, set them on fire. One of the three brothers (historians dispute which) changed his name to Paul and went on to publish the first New Testament in Jewish letters in 1540 (essentially a transcription of the Lutheran German translation) as well as a handbook in 1543 to enable Christians to learn Yiddish for business purposes. He became a missionary among Jews. The brother originally named Shmuel eventually renounced his baptism, returned to the Jewish faith, moved to Constantinople (Istanbul) and in 1552 printed a Bible with a colophon containing his contrite statement of repentance.

The 'western part of the story' remained at least somewhat less murky. As far as we know, brief rules for Yiddish spelling began to appear in 1514 in Latin works on Hebrew grammar (Boeshenstein 1514). But the first real Christian Hebraic pioneer of Yiddish published was Paul Fagius (1504–49). Like many Humanists, he had 'classicized' his original name, Bucklin, by translating it to Latin (*Bucklin = Fagius* = 'beech tree'). He was a German (*apparently* a born Christian — his enemies would challenge that), who became professor of Hebrew at Strasbourg and eventually at Cambridge University in England, where he died. Fagius translated Hebrew books into Latin, edited a famous Aramaic translation of the Bible and wrote several tracts trying to prove the truth of Christianity. The lines of cross-cultural communication can actually become delightfully elaborate. Elijah Levita, when he was around 70 years old, became *his* teacher of Hebrew, Aramaic and Yiddish, in other words all *three* Ashkenazic Jewish languages.

Diversity and 'target readership declarations'

By the 1540s, when Yiddish publishing began to flourish, the language had its relatively codified spelling and usage rules and its own special type font, which had the warmth and immediacy of lettering based on contemporary local (Ashkenazic) handwritings. There was also a healthy variety of genre already in the first decade of Yiddish printing. The 'onward march' of this 'people's education' movement can be gauged by growing diversity of genre and the declarations of 'target readership', much as these need to be taken with caution. The following examples are offered in the spirit of giving a feel for 'kinds' of books and for their 'declared' intended readerships.

The 1544 Pentateuch published in Konstanz, by Fagius (and with his three-leaf logo proudly on the title) features a quotation from the prophets in the original Hebrew:

> And they shall teach no more every man his neighbour, and every man his brother, saying: 'Know the Lord'; for they shall all know Me, from the least of them unto the greatest of them, sayeth the Lord [...].
> (Jeremiah 31: 33 [in Christian Bibles often 31: 34])

The Yiddish introduction that follows, titled with the traditional Hebrew-derived word *hakdómə* ('preface'), popular to this day, contains an important argument for the shift, so to speak, from education-by-specialist-teachers to self-education (itself possible only in Yiddish, of course), one that is poignantly justified by a frequent tragedy of Ashkenazic history:

> We see, that for all our sins [traditional psycho-ostensive expression preceding the recounting of bad news] that [...] the organized communities have constantly been disrupted by frequent expulsions [of Jewish people], that where there were once ten communities one barely finds one now, for our many sins, heads-of-households find themselves forced to reside in villages, but it is not within everyone's means to employ a teacher to teach his children, and because of all this, great ignoramuses are growing up. Therefore we have been moved to print in *Taytsh* [Yiddish] the *Khúməsh* [Five Books of Moses, Torah] and the *Megíləs* [the Five Scrolls, i.e. Song of Songs, Ruth, Lamentations, Ecclesiastes and Esther] and the *haftóurəs* [modern standard Yiddish *haftóyrəs*, the readings from the prophets that follow the weekly Torah portions at Sabbath morning services], according to the way various learned Jews and rabbis have translated the Hebrew into *Taytsh*, and we have compared the various translations and versions with each other and given each passage in the form we found best [...] So then, any head-of-household who can read *Taytsh* will be able to teach his children, and enable them to understand

the *Khúmǝsh*, and we have therefore chosen renderings that follow
in *Taytsh* word-for-word.

(Khamisho khumshey Touro 1544: [1] [from the Yiddish])

This revealing book from the dawn of Yiddish printing provides a core
version of the 'Ashkenazic canon' which can be more loosely called the
'Ashkenazic Bible', in other words the portions of the Old Testament
that were genuinely studied intensively and needed for everyday: the
Five Books of Moses (*Khúmǝsh* [= 'the five' being Genesis, Exodus,
Leviticus, Numbers, Deuteronomy], modern English usage *chumash*,
Torah, Pentateuch); the portions from the Prophets (haftaroth) read
after the Torah portion each Sabbath; and the Five Scrolls (being the
Song of Songs, Ruth, Lamentations, Ecclesiastes, Esther). Other perhaps more 'specialized' parts of the Ashkenazic canon include Psalms,
though on occasion for 'reciting as prayer' than for study of the text.
Big chunks of the Old Testament were simply not regularly studied and
were considered the purview of specialists (and at certain times and
places regarded as more of interest for Christians).

This was a project, alongside 'selling the book', of empowering
householders who read Yiddish (nearly everybody) themselves to teach
their children, without having to pay a professional teacher who was
learned and therefore proficient in the original Hebrew. It was a bit of
an economic and social revolution, and the apologetics about it applying principally in the case of 'expulsions' ring somewhat concocted.
This is after all one of the two 'core curriculum' books of universal
Ashkenazic elementary education — the biblical canon (the other
being the prayerbook) and it was being offered to the public in a handy
edition in Yiddish *only* (not the more dutiful bilingual style that would
eventually become so widespread — Hebrew 'on top' and Yiddish
'below'), with just one-word Hebrew headings and catchwords, often
familiar as the name of the section or book. The book was rendered
more attractive still by marginal notes, which the introduction tells
us relate important explanations and interpretations by the popular
Rashi (Ashkenaz 1040–1105), the rather more-for-the-learned Abraham
Ibn Ezra (Sepharad ±1092–1167) and the Radák (Provencal grammarian and commentator David Kimhi or Qimḥi 1160–235). The upshot
was that this edition wanted to compete at the 'higher market' level of
offering rabbinic interpretations that the traditional teacher would be
expounding from the original Hebrew, in the Rashi typeface. And all
this was being offered in Yiddish, in the (for that time and place) easy
and enjoyable *máshkit* typeface that was based on popular Ashkenazic
handwritings of the day.

Image 3.4 Start of Genesis 1 from the 1544 Konstanz *Khúməsh* (Pentateuch). The large letters in square scribal style for the first word *Bréyshis* ('In the beginning') suggest a classical Hebrew style text, except perhaps for the small final *sof* character (far left), which could have resulted from the scribe's miscalculating the space needed (in the original, the anomaly is curiously the reverse: a large first letter, beyz [b]). Conversely, an off-size letter evokes the original whether smaller *or* larger.

The larger-type first word in Square Hebrew is Yiddish *ey* (first component of term for 'before', in modern Yiddish *éydər*), itself then a daring use of square characters for Yiddish-language material. But the primary power play here is the attempted imitation of the learned man's biblical text, which would have the original Hebrew text in Square Hebrew and marginal notes in smaller type, also in Hebrew, in the so-called Rashi font used for rabbinic commentaries. Here, the square Hebrew letters and Hebrew language are duly replaced by *máshkit* and Yiddish language as the central text, and the marginal notes are in Yiddish but, very audaciously, in Rashi font, which would normally be reserved for the original rabbinic commentary on a sacred text. One 'justification' would be that these marginal notes do indeed quote from various classical commentaries; the very first one at the top is from 'the Redák' (David Kimhi or Qimḥi)

Source: Image courtesy of Dr Moshe Rosenfeld of Rose Chemicals, London.

The ratio of Ashkenazic power relations is in a sense represented by choices in typography. The means are visual and graphic but the larger psychological quest is to replicate the look and feel of the original with the vernacular newly ruling this very special space of the most sacred of books. The individual formulas that comprise the attempt can be schematized as follows:

Usual biblical edition	The Konstanz *Khúməsh* of 1544
Larger main text vs smaller marginal notes/commentary	Maintained
Use of distinct fonts for main text vs marginal notes/commentary	Maintained
Use of Square Hebrew main text vs Rashi font commentary	Square Hebrew changes to *máshkit*; Rashi font maintained
Use of Hebrew (or Aramaic) in both main text and commentary	Both changed to Yiddish

Of all these features, the boldest would have been the use of the Rashi font for commentary text in Yiddish, and this did not, in fact, result in a viable tradition. But it was an audacious power play and a symbolic marker for an epoch in which Yiddish power, thanks to the advent of Yiddish printing, was coming out in multiple parts of Ashkenazic Europe in the 1540s.

The preface's audacity keeps pace. There is discussion of how the volume will help folks to spell contemporary Hebrew-derived names correctly, and how to cope with the various names for God in the Hebrew Bible when studying and pronouncing. And, if ever this age of Yiddish empowerment took on a unisex character, this book said it out loud:

> And also the women who are in the synagogue will hear the cantor reading out the weekly portion of the Torah, and they will be following in this *Taytsh Khúməsh* the same portion and its Haftorah, reading it, and have **the same holy intent** with their heart for the sake of heaven. [bold type added]
>
> (Khamisho khumshey Touro 1544: preface [from the Yiddish])

Still, after the brave new world where simple people teach their children without the need for a teacher, and where women can follow along properly in the synagogue and equal men in the all-important realm of *kavónə* 'sacred intent during prayer', all thanks to this switch-to-Yiddish, is there a final measure of humility and admitted fallibility:

> But there is no person who is such a saint and perfect being, that he will do only good and no bad, and so we ask everyone that will read in this book and find mistakes, to please judge us in a lenient spirit.
> (Khamisho khumshey Touro 1544: preface [from the Yiddish])

Before turning to essential Hebrew grammar, the preface ends with the promise that if this book will be 'accepted among many readers' then, 'We will soon with the help of Blessed God, also bring to press the other books of the entire Twenty-Four, including the Former Prophets, the Latter Prophets, and the Hagiographa'. *Ésrim-v(ə)árbə* ('the twenty-four'), probably by then pronounced *Svárbə*, is an older Yiddish name for the entire Hebrew Bible (in other words, the 24 books of the Old Testament according to the traditional Jewish divisions of books).

It is telling that this ambition did not materialize, not for this press in the 1540s, and not for any other, in the sense intended by this statement of intent, for hundreds of years. In the late 1670s, when *two* competing complete Jewish Bibles did appear in Amsterdam, they were not overly successful. Both were 'straight translations' with none of the explanatory traditional material that Yiddish readers so loved. Both were far from the living tradition of Bible study. Much later in the time and space of Yiddish, in nineteenth-century Eastern Europe, there were multi-volume sets of the entire Jewish Bible with Yiddish translation and warm, traditional commentary. But this very topic can be more a diversion than an enlightening path of enquiry for the point at hand, precisely because Ashkenazic society was focused on the 'Ashkenazic canon' within the Old Testament and not on the entirety of the text of the 'Hebrew Bible'. In fact, dabbling too much in those 'other books' (for example, Later Prophets) was considered suspicious other than in the hands of the most trusted, pious, established rabbinic scholars. A future study will determine the degree to which Christianity's 'use' of books such as Isaiah and Daniel, among others, played a role in an unspoken policy of Ashkenazic society to keep a diplomatic distance.

As a final flourish, instead of a usual colophon with information about the printer, the last page has a quotation from the great scholar Elijah Levita, who we know had helped the Christian(!) publisher of this book, Paul Fagius get his Jewish publishing act together, irrespective of whether Levita had a hand in a version of this particular book or not. This afterword contains an explanation of a historical question that has occurred to many a Jewish child over the generations while studying (especially a boy for a bar-mitzvah celebration) the haftorah (*haftóyrə*), or portion from the Prophets. It is the question 'Why do we have haftorahs at all?' The final page starts with a heading that itself begins with a biblically cadenced 'Thus sayeth' (Ashkenazic Hebrew: *koy omar*, older Western Ashkenazic *kou ōmar*). It is a quote from the publisher's famous Jewish friend. In modern standard Ashkenazic: 'Koy omar Eylióhu ha-Léyvi Ashkenázi ha-mədákdek bəsífroy shel Tíshbi' ('Thus sayeth Elijah the Levite Ashkenazi the grammarian in his book of *Tishbi'* [= Levita 1541b]). And it continues with a quote from the *Tishbi* explaining that during the period of the evil king Antiochus (a Hellenistic Seleucid monarch, ±215–164 BC, famous in Jewish history from the story of the rebellion memorialized in the holiday Chanukah), it was forbidden to read the Torah out loud, and so Jews under his evil dominion found parts of the Prophets that had some connection with the Torah portion of the week that could itself not be read out. Levita cites the occasionally obvious link of a certain Torah portion and its corresponding haftorah. For example, Noah (starting at Genesis 6: 9) is 'supplemented' by a haftorah from Isaiah, which contains the passage 'For this is as the waters of Noah unto me' (Isaiah 54: 9). While there is nothing remotely *anti*-traditional in Elijah's explanation of the haftorahs that his friend Fagius has chosen as the book's finale, it is unusually 'fact-oriented', in other words modern, vis-à-vis the more traditionally Ashkenazic homiletic explanations that prefer legend and especially legend-with-a-moral over proposed 'straight' historical explanations.

Still, there is a 'problem' with this first convoluted chapter of the 'new Yiddish power' scenario of the 1540s. The apparent publisher, the Protestant Paul Fagius, who had been such close friends with Elijah Levita, and was quite prepared (if indeed it was his press, as assumed) to release such an intensely 'Jewish-Jewish' book with not a trace of 'Christian intent', almost simultaneously released another edition with his own introduction which is replete with anti-Semitic and missionary motives, going so far as to condemn the Jews for distorting the true faith, as do the Catholic papists! The true explanation of an interplay of commercial and theological motives, and of a possible change in Fagius's stance during those years, is not yet known, and may never be known. There is a lot of intrigue, including the question of whether Paul Fagius and Michael Adam, who issued some Yiddish works, are one and the same person. The story's twists and turns have occupied

Yiddish literary historians since the rise of modern Yiddish literary studies nearly a century ago (see, for example, Borokhov 1913b: nos 3–4; Weinreich 1923a: 94–103; Shtif 1928). It is not unexpected in cultural history that such factors play their part in the precise way a major new revolution in communications technology (in this case, printing) makes its first major public splash. As Ecclesiastes once put it, there is nothing new under the sun.

4
Women of Western Ashkenaz

The extensive introduction to the Konstanz 1544 Yiddish edition of the 'Ashkenazic core Bible' (Pentateuch, Prophets readings, Five Scrolls) speaks not only of heads-of-household (in other words: men) who would now be able to teach their children themselves, in Yiddish, without needing a professional teacher, especially in such times when, as we are told, expulsions have decimated proper communities. It also has something for women:

> This book is also for the benefit of women and girls. Typically, they can all read *Taytsh* well but squander their time on books of nonsense like *Ditrikh of Bern*, *Hildebrand* and the likes of them, which are nothing but lies and concoctions. These same women and girls can now find their entertainment in this edition of the *Khúmash* [Five Books of Moses], which is all pure and clear truth.
>
> (Khamisho khumshey Touro 1544: preface [from the Yiddish])

The age of printing brought new dynamism and substance to a Yiddish revolution that flew in the face of centuries of women being the widely perceived (and duly accepted) primary readers of secular knightly romances in their Yiddish renditions (previously in copied manuscripts). But in terms of Yiddish and power it is in fact counter-revolutionary, rather than revolutionary, for a rather simple reason: with the likes of *King Arthur* or *Hildebrand*, women, like 'the men who were [in this sense] like women', were knowledgeable about another cultural tradition, albeit an inferior one in the eyes of the civilization; knowledgeable nevertheless. That was the 'revolution'. The 'counter-revolution' was the effort that would extend over large swathes of time and space to dislodge the likes of *King Arthur* and replace him with select portions of the internal Jewish tradition that was previously not available to them in any comprehensible, hence meaningful, form.

It is scant surprise that a sales-minded preface-writer would appeal to both the male and female potential buyers of a book being marketed. The spiel for men about the expulsions and so forth may actually ring less than convincing vis-à-vis the largest part of the potential book market that was never at a single point in time 'expelled', no matter how a martyrological minority community narrative is written. In any case there would be no overnight social revolution of ridding the society of teachers who were expert in Hebrew so that parents would sit with their children using this particular Yiddish Bible; advertising has remained advertising through the ages. Still, it would sell some books, and slowly but surely would move Yiddish power forward in Ashkenaz.

The mention of the 'women's issue' here, by contrast, rings 'true', not necessarily in the sense of any higher 'truth' but in the sense of invoking something that is genuinely 'in the air' in the society in question and has something to say to the cultural historian looking at all this retrospectively around half a millennium later.

Beyond basic literacy and the few blessings women traditionally articulate, virtually the entire 'Hebrew and Aramaic library' that was at least *open* to all males was with rare exceptions closed to women. There were over the centuries many different precise constructions in various Ashkenazic communities as to how much it was 'proper' for a girl or woman to excel in the knowledge traditionally acquirable only by males. Modern Yiddish literature now and again features an extreme exceptional case which is enabled by its very exceptionality and the length to which the woman would have to go, most famously in Isaac Bashevis Singer's short story *Yentl der yeshíve-bòkhər*, 'Yentl the Yeshiva student', rendered into the Barbra Streisand film *Yentl* (1983). While the hyperbole of such situations is an obvious literary device, it does illustrate the underlying inability of females to access what this culture considers 'the serious books' in any internal Ashkenazic sense.

Carrying the argument a stage further — and this could even be tested empirically today in Hasidic and other Ashkenazic Haredi communities — no amount of Bible translation or explication in the vernacular can truly satisfy the intellectual needs of part of the female population, in a society where men so inclined have ready access to a desired degree of study of the original text and the vast corpus of cherished commentaries, in the two ancient languages, Hebrew and Aramaic. Learned Ashkenazic men had maintained the ancient linguistic heritage to such a high degree that late in the nineteenth century one determined

Hebraist-Zionist Lithuanian Jew, Eliezer (local Yiddish: Léyzer) Perelman (later Eliezer Ben-Yehuda) was able to revive Hebrew as the basis of the new and successful vernacular Israeli language. A Yiddish translation of the primarily studied books of the Bible could never be for women what the enormously sophisticated Hebrew and Aramaic literature provided for men. The Yiddish Bible translations were inherently incapable of satisfying the intellectual needs of Ashkenazic women, period. And that is why it is common sense that Ashkenazic women were in fact the 'first and foremost readers' of *Dukus Horant, Hildebrant, Ditrikh of Bern, Kinig Artus hoyf* ('*King Arthur's Court'*) and others. At some distant unknown point in the past, a specific characteristic of Ashkenaz developed that has yet to be studied: while men are the scholars of Jewish literature in Hebrew and Aramaic, women are better-read and more knowledgeable in other kinds of literature in the vernacular. Indeed, they are often more proficient in both reading and writing Yiddish in traditional communities, as well as the co-territorial non-Jewish language. An echo can be empirically observed today. Hasidic girls' schools in English-speaking countries have consistently higher levels of knowledge of both written Yiddish *and* English than the boys' schools. This was duly observed in London by a feature writer for the *Telegraph* in 2011 (Brown 2011: 29). There are two parts to the explanation for this fact, which continues to stymie some outsiders. The first explanation is that it has become accepted that girls and women have those realms to excel in as a kind of de-facto compensation for the intellectual *Jewish* pleasures denied them. There is no law, after all, that says, 'Thou shalt not enjoy a good story that comes from the peoples of all the earth.' The second factor is one that can boast a degree of demonstrable explanatory adequacy, but is rather more mundane. When 'higher Jewish studies' (Talmud, higher levels of Codes of Law and even more sophisticated biblical commentary) are off-limits, a swathe of classroom time is ipso facto freed up. In olden days this may have been in less formal settings sometimes and with smaller groups or at home, and today it is in Hasidic girls' schools in places like Stamford Hill in London or Boro Park in Brooklyn, New York. Today, it may mean more Yiddish language, more Hebrew language — and much more study of the national, non-Jewish language and other allowed subjects — and more books intended for edification and practice in those languages. It is no more and no less than a continuation of a primeval Ashkenazic tradition that once upon a time expressed itself in the Yiddish adaptations of *Hildebrand, Ditrikh of Bern* and *King Arthur* being thought of as primarily for Jewish women. It is an Ashkenazic constant that has changed markedly in form.

Occasionally the name of a 'commissioning lady' is found in older Yiddish manuscripts and printed books. Her name was sometimes embedded in a rhymed preface or colophon. A 1532 manuscript containing Yiddish versions of Psalms and Proverbs was written by Eliezer, son of Israel of Prague, for 'my patroness Peslin' (the more modern Yiddish forms of this female forename: *Pesl, Pés(h)ke*). A Yiddish version translation of the Hebrew *Sayings of the Fathers*, a tractate of the Mishnah with many famous dictums for everyday life, was compiled in Italy around 1580 by Anshel Levy. It contains a long rhymed colophon dedicated to his patroness Perlin (modern Yiddish: *Perl, Pérlke*). But such instances are few and far between, and the degree to which some norm can be extrapolated from them is disputed.

Although questioned by scholars (and rightly so), the targeted readership declarations in the extensive corpus of Yiddish published works over decades and centuries simply constitute too voluminous a corpus to mean 'nothing' or to be the result of some presumed conspiracy to lead some future scholars of the twenty-first century 'off the trail'. When a certain comment about readership is repeated over decades and centuries, over big swathes of Europe, by a variety of publishers and authors, there is every reason to feel confident of at least a direct relationship between that comment and *some* aspect of reality, even if the relationship is oblique, complex and never to be fully known. But that does not mean that men did not read these books. It does not even mean that some very learned Ashkenazic scholars did not quietly find some pleasure in them either (and human pleasure can include 'keeping tabs on what the other half are up to'). It just means that the invention of printing empowered the women of Ashkenaz to have a literature which they enjoyed reading, discussing and passing on, and that they became much more sophisticated and 'European' for being regular readers of a literature written in the language that they spoke. And yes, it also meant that in some ways they were, from that 'European' point of view, rather more sophisticated in terms of familiarity with chatter of the wider gentile world than some of their most learned menfolk. For a society like Ashkenaz, that is power.

One of the major trendsetter here was the literary giant of sixteenth-century Yiddish letters, Elijah Levita. In the preface to his *Bovo d'Antona* (Isny 1541), he writes:

> I, Elye the Levite, the writer, serving all pious women, with respect and graciousness, realize full well that many women hold a grudge against me for not printing some of my books for them, in *Taytsh*,

so that they might enjoy them and read them on Sabbaths and holidays. So I want to tell the truth. It seems to me the right thing to do, as I have written some eight or nine books in our sacred languages, and I have begun to put them through the press, as I reach the end of my days, and today or tomorrow might find myself on my back, and all my books and my poems will be forgotten. So if nobody deflects me from my purpose, I will print them all one after the other.

(Elijah Levita/Eylióhu Bókher 1541: preface [from the Yiddish])

One of Levita's less talked-about works is his Psalms translation, published in Venice in 1545. The title page proudly announces the translation to be 'by the learned man Élye Bókher Ashkenázi ha-Léyvi' ('the Levite', hence Levita). The publishers are also named on the title page as 'Cornelius Adelkind and Meir bar Yakov a man of Frentz, in partnership'. The rhymed preface on the following page (in a rather more homely and authentic colloquial Yiddish than the book itself) begins: 'You pious women who have in mind the wish to praise the Almighty' and quite a way down, as a kind of advertising afterthought, the page mentions also the possibility of *melámdim* (elementary-level teachers) using this particular *Tílim* (the popular Yiddishized pronunciation for standard *Təhílim* 'Psalms' in a rare instance of violating Hebrew root-norms in the orthography of a word to reflect the everyday pronunciation of its Yiddish reflex). Levita certainly sees no contradiction in commending the here-and-there naughty, and delightfully pleasurable, *Bovo d'Antona*, and the ultra-upright book of Psalms, traditionally from the pen of King David himself, as two Yiddish works for women he is 'serving' in his capacity as an author. That is a telling symbolic aspect of the intended diversity for the intellectual benefit of the declared female audience.

Co-publisher Cornelius Adelkind (Jewish despite the name, which he claimed to have taken in honour of his employer) included the following afterword to the 1545 Psalms edition:

In my younger days I published many precious and large sacred books, and put all my energy into it, as one can see from all of [Daniel] Bomberg's prints where I am inscribed [mentioned] at the beginning or the end. Now that I have grown old, I have thought things over, that I have done nothing for the pious women and for those men who had no time to study in their younger years or even later, and who would nevertheless spend their time on Sabbath or a holiday with reading Godly tidings and not about *Ditrikh of Bern* or

'*The Good Luck of the Beautiful Girl.*' And so for their sake, those who would gladly read God's word, one finds very few books that are written in Yiddish and well translated, so I went to Mr Elye Bokher to translate some books for me, and first of all, the book of Psalms.

(Cornelius Adelkind's Yiddish Psalms edition, 1545, afterword [from the Yiddish])

The upshot seems to be, that whether one is publishing a literary 'secular' work, or a translation of a Jewish sacred text, and whether one is discrediting the former when marketing the latter on allegedly 'Godly' grounds (and who does not stress X's virtues when marketing X?), the prime audience of women is time and again explicitly delineated. What we may never be able to recover now is sociolinguistic data about how it was for a hypothetical male who occasionally read one of these books, or indeed for one who read them all the time. It is for the moment fodder for nothing more than sociolinguistic thought experiments with not much in the way of empirical data. On this point any attempt at sociolinguistic reconstruction using modern Haredi communities, in the internet age, would be hopelessly anachronistic.

The growing enterprise of Yiddish and empowerment of women was being trumpeted in sundry new works. That first publishing 'generation' of religiously ambiguous (and, for moderns, confusing) founders of Yiddish publishing (Judaizing Christians, Christianized Jews, Jews who would later be baptized, humanistically oriented Christians and more) gave way to further generations of 'Yiddish publishing by simply Jewish publishers' in the most clear and conventional sense of 'Jewish' and with none of the complications of the founding generation of Yiddish publishing in sixteenth-century Europe.

While the Hebrew and Aramaic literature continued to reign supreme in society and its internal power structures, it is inescapable that Yiddish-in-print was a new and potent Ashkenazic counterculture. Countercultures and cultural reformations (and ensuing counter-reformations) can start with tentative steps and incrementally acquire their audacious and 'overtly revolutionary' proclamations as a second step. The unambiguously Jewish publisher-printer Chaim ben Dovid Shokher turned to Yiddish after moving from Augsburg to Ichenhausen, where in 1544 he printed a Yiddish prayerbook. It was compiled from various earlier manuscripts by his son-in-law, Yosef bar Yokor, who says in his preface:

I have not translated this prayerbook from my own head but have taken what seems to me the best from those I have read through. The prayers were constructed in very difficult language, and for all our sins, you barely find one in a thousand who knows what they mean. I therefore consider the people who pray in Hebrew and don't understand one word to be utter fools. I for one would just like to know what kind of devout intention [*kavóne*, Israeli *kavaná*] they could possibly have. We therefore came to the conclusion that we would publish this prayerbook in Yiddish and many more books later on.

(Yosef bar Yokor 1544 [from the Yiddish])

As ever, 'counterculture leader' types may also be audacious on other points. Yosef bar Yokor's afterword referencing 'an old hag and a young girl' would be regarded by the powers-that-be in Ashkenazic culture as an outrageous appendage to the holy canonical prayerbook, all the more so when being touted as a Yiddish replacement for the universal Hebrew (and Aramaic) original.

I allowed it to go on sale for one crown, but I swear by my head, it is well worth ten, as you will very well see for yourself. When you take a look at other prayerbooks, you will verily conclude that the difference is as great as that between an old hag and a young girl.

(Yosef bar Yokor 1544 [from the Yiddish])

It is moreover significant that the argument about needing to understand prayer would make this more a book for men than women, because it is men alone who are commanded to recite the thrice-day prayers. This is a stark contrast vis-à-vis many works of the period that are explicitly for women and the special and limited commandments which obligate them in such realms as prayer.

In 1552, Cornelius Adelkind's son, Daniel Adelkind, published in Venice his *Mítsvous ha-Nóshim* ('Commandments for Women'), which is charmingly rendered on the title page as *Frouen bikhlan* (modern Yiddish: *Fróyen-bikhl*): 'Little Book for Women'. It is noteworthy that the selection of Yiddish book names of the period was conscious of the need for the intimately attractive in the vernacular to trump any perceived requirement for literal translation. This too is a symbolical feature of the inherent internal separateness of Yiddish publishing in the overall Ashkenazic culture, where 'matching' Hebrew per se was not an issue.

Commandments for Women is an elaborate Yiddish guide to those religious and ritual precepts which women were specifically required to know and keep. The book is divided into three sections dealing with major areas of Jewish women's law: the complex laws of menstrual purity (which include the laws of the *míkvə* or ritual bath); of challah (ritual Sabbath bread); and of Candle Lighting. The three are known by the acronymic *khánə* (Ashkenazic Hebrew *kháno* = khálo (challah bread) + nído (lit. 'ritually unclean woman, during her period and until the ritual cleansing in the *míkvə*', but by extension: 'the laws of the *nído*') + *hadlóko* (lighting [of the Sabbath candles]). The acronymic is delightfully homophonous with the Yiddish pronunciation of the ever popular name *Khánə* (Hanna/Chana).

The table of contents is written in a much more authentic Yiddish (that is, closer to the vernacular) than many of the more literary works, especially those adapted from German books, and includes some charming prayers, thoughts and feelings. The afterword is signed by the publisher's (retired?) father Cornelius Adelkind:

> Dear women! Please accept this book in a good way, from my son Daniel, who has printed it for your sake. It has been reviewed by a pious rabbi and a dear *rébitisn* [honorific term for a rabbi's wife, often learned in her own right] in the expectation that every woman can well find this little book to be of use, as if she had learned these laws from the Talmud, and we thereby ask God to grant us eternal life, so asks and desires Cornelio Adelkind [Adil Kind].
>
> (Adelkind 1552, afterword [from the Yiddish])

Yiddish empowerment continued to expand through less esoteric and limited parts of the Ashkenazic sacred library. In 1560 Leyb Bresh's Pentateuch appeared. It was titled *Khamísho khúmshey Tóuro* ('The Five Books of the Torah') *im ktsas péyrush Ráshi vəím* (with some of the Rashi Commentary and with) *ha-haftóurəs ákher kol sédro vəsédro* (the haftorahs following each and every Torah section). By providing rather more than usual of the famed commentary of Rashi in Yiddish, this Ashkenazic-canon Bible was elevating what could be accessed by virtually the entire population to a level previously attained only by Hebraically literate men; note that many men of modest learning, not Talmudic scholars by any means, would have been able to follow *just* the biblical text and but a little of Rashi's commentary, especially his most famous exegetical explanations, some of which even entered spoken Yiddish. In one fell swoop, Bresh's *Khúməsh* put this higher-than-just-the-text Ashkenazic Bible capability into the hands of the entire population, enhancing the burgeoning Yiddish counterculture. As ever, the visual typographical component played its part. By providing the Rashi commentary excerpts in a separate column in smaller type, this book provides a further stage in the psychological mirror-imaging of a 'real' original-language Bible, with the main text in square Hebrew characters and the Rashi text in smaller Rashi type font. Here, both columns are in *máshkit* but the smaller size of the Rashi column, along with Hebrew-in-Hebrew catchwords in square Hebrew type to help relate each comment to the appropriate passage in the original Hebrew, offers a book that gives something of the look, feel and panache of the original. But it is all in Yiddish. This importance of the volume in Yiddish cultural and social history is not diminished, allowing for its time and place, by what would be our modern-day complaints about the translation itself — not least that it is considered to be based on Paulus Aemilius's earlier Augsburg 1544 Pentateuch (see Joffe 1954: 111).

Bresh's 'Yiddish duplicate' of the prestigious standard-issue Hebrew Pentateuch-with-Rashi, laid out with columns and contrastive typography to mirror the original, would obviously have been of use to many men too, for whom reading and understanding Rashi did not come especially easy, particularly through adulthood, ever further from the years of childhood education in a *khéydər* (traditional school) with a *məláməd* (traditional teacher). But for *women* to be proudly walking around with a *Khúməsh mit Ráshə*, that has separate columns and typography for the two, would be an important day in Ashkenazic history, a day that came at different times and places, when works like the Cremona 1560 Yiddish Pentateuch with Rashi edition, and its successors down the line, arrived in a given place and started to be bought and used. It is hard to exaggerate the prestige of multi-columned sacred books in the vernacular that mirrored the size and typographical dualism of the Hebrew and Aramaic 'real ones'.

There is a single line in the preface that is socially telling, even though it is astutely phrased in the negative — a lament about men who do not study, and about women who, sadly, imitate them:

> We haven't studied much, and the wives, young women and girls see the men not studying, and then they also don't study [...].
>
> (Bresh 1560, preface [from the Yiddish])

All in all, this is a sophisticated piece of mid sixteenth-century Yiddish marketing in Cremona, and one that reveals rather more about the society in question than the scholarly works of the time and place.

The classic Western Yiddish vocabulary for the three kinds of women (classified by position in the life cycle) is also a memorable feature of

Leyb Bresh's preface: *di váybər un bókhərəs* [or: *bakhúrəs*] *un piltsls*. The word for 'wives' or 'women' (*váybər*, cf. German *weiber*) is Germanic; for young women of marriageable age it is from Hebrew (*bókhərəs/bakhúrəs*, cf. post-biblical Hebrew *baḥūróθ*), and for little girls it is from Romance (sg. *piltsl*, cf., for example, French *pucelle*, Italian *pulcella*; see Weinreich 2008: 405–6).

As in many a new enterprise, things settle down after a first tortuous and 'intense' start-up. For much of the rest of the sixteenth century, Yiddish publishing focused on women's books but was by no means limited to women in real life. It continued in both Eastern Europe (principally in its place of origin, Krakow) and in a variety of places in Western Ashkenaz, including Basel, Freiburg and Venice, and in the 'great border city straddling west and east Ashkenaz' — Prague. Amsterdam would become a paramount Yiddish publishing centre rather later.

So much of the scholarly literature's guesses about the precise nature of the readership of Yiddish books has to be just that — whether or not it is couched in academic terminology. Still, two conclusions are in order. The first, the primacy of women, is where common sense and explicit delineation on title pages and in introductions coincide fully. In Jewish, and certainly in Ashkenazic history, there is nothing particularly 'feminine' in the inherent attractive capacity of, say, the biblical book of Daniel, not one of those studied in the Ashkenazic canon, and hence culturally risqué in any case. But when the Yiddish *Donĭəl bukh* appeared in Krakow in 1588, published by the very kosher and admired publishing family Prostitz (sometimes Prosnitz), the title page announces the Yiddish version to be 'beautiful, clear and entertaining to read for women and girls' (*váybər un méydləkh*). This whole new ('western'!) style of ascetic lightness, literary desirability and capacity to entertain was far from the core values of the ultra-pious, male-dominated Ashkenazic society. It was one of the clearest manifestations of a new kind of 'woman power' in Ashkenaz, one with a solid commercial backbone (production, selling and purchase of books), that at the same time extended the prestige of the book from the learned to all. Finally, with the spread of the implicit notion of 'literature' which can include religious and secular alike, there arose the curious situation in which some serious sinning can take place in a story without shaking the fundamentals of the community in 'real life'. It is a point where social prestige, ergo power, is rising to challenge the internally binding legal power of the rabbinic status quo that continues in force every bit as much as before the first Yiddish book came off the press. Whether it was the respective religious duties of men and women, or

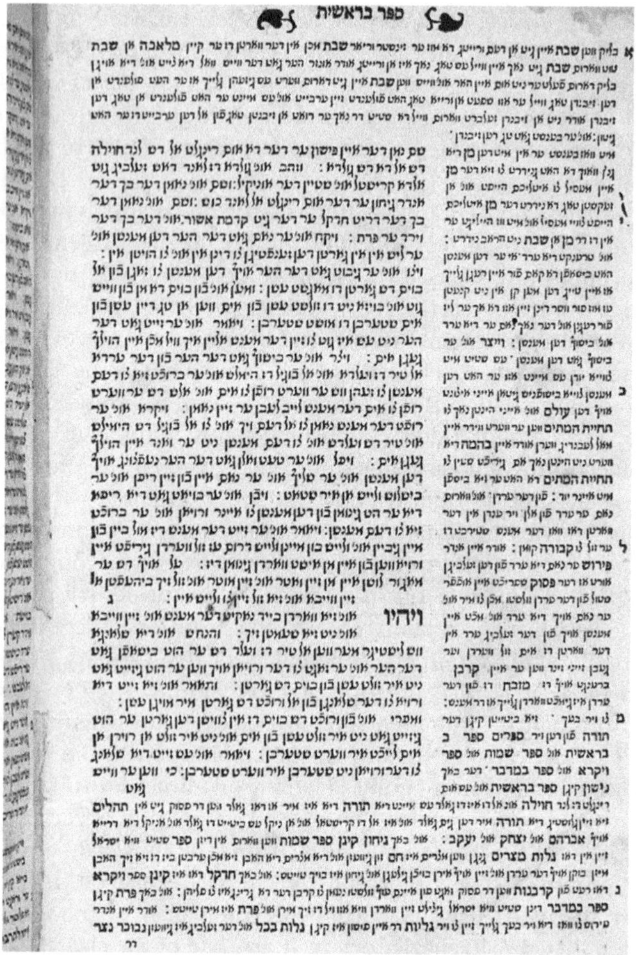

Image 4.1   Page from Leyb Bresh's Cremona *Khúməsh* of 1560, where the rise of the sixteenth-century Yiddish movement evidences two further steps: first, the providing of a continuous (though abridged) Yiddish text translation of Rashi, rather than just odd marginal notes; second, the visual statement of the wrap-around commentary, usual for Hebrew commentaries on Hebrew texts. There is however a definite retreat in the use of different sizes of Yiddish *máshkit*: the attempt to use rabbinic commentary 'Rashi font' for Yiddish text had by now been abandoned, possibly because of complaints, as Yiddish publishing continued to test what the cultural market of Ashkenaz could bear in the new age of printing

Source: Image courtesy of the Bodleian Libraries, University of Oxford.

belief in the divinity of the entire Torah and the virtually infallible 'Oral Law' of generations of rabbinic authorities who interpreted it for contemporary life, the literature in Yiddish, both secular and translative or interpretative of the internal culture, did not challenge any of those basic tenets of Ashkenazic civilization. A woman who was the first on her street to own and enjoy a good epic romance or a Bible translation and had books of her own of various kinds was a woman with much more prestige and social status than her perhaps bookless grandmother, but she did not in the least challenge the practices around, say, birth, marriage and the daily laws. For all Ashkenazim, Yiddish reading and non-Yiddish reading, the God-given Torah was the only law of the land for those 'fortunate' enough to be born into its 'chosen' people, and it was just a bit of good luck that the new invention of printing, and the new field of Yiddish publishing, finally combined to produce new delights for the non-Hebrew, non-Aramaic reading of Ashkenaz, which were not in the least bit forbidden.

But that is not to say that there was no opposition. There was opposition. As is the case with many culture-expanding movements in history, the results of that opposition are not always entirely predictable. Yes, the secular stories were somewhat suppressed, but a new revival in the Yiddish writing and publishing sphere arose where least expected: in the realm of the depths of religion itself. This is the phenomenon earlier referred to as 'counter-reformation'.

Second, it was only a matter of time before female Yiddish writers would emerge in Ashkenaz, breaking one of the major taboos of many centuries of Ashkenazic mores. It is something that would happen only when the Ashkenazim moved eastward and their literature became part of a religious awakening. It is hard to exaggerate the cultural significance of typefaces, columns, relative sizes and shapes and so forth in a society as book-centred as Ashkenaz. It might even be true to say that, relatively and proportionately considered, these 'Christian inventions' had even greater import for the small, weak and stateless Ashkenazic minority that mirrored them with such fervour.

5
The Neo-Religious and the Jewish-Secular

The year when a pivotal book appears can be a handy (albeit arbitrary) way to mark out a general timeframe, all the more appropriately in a culture where books are at the core. The disproportionality of 'book culture' in Ashkenaz is also, in some measure, a function of statelessness as synthesized with a highly authoritative internal text-based culture. The period from 1534, when *Mirkéves ha-míshne* appeared, and through the late sixteenth century, was the period of the rise of Yiddish publishing, itself a power-shifting phenomenon that added social prestige, commercial possibilities and a much more widespread knowledge of things both religious and secular to the majority of a previously literarily unfranchised population — and, most emphatically, to the women of Ashkenaz. This new rise in cultural social power did not challenge the extant religiously determined power relations in society. It may have created certain tensions and potential conflicts, some of which will be the focus of this chapter, but it did not reject the divinity of the Torah or the absolute authority of the cumulative rabbinic interpretation of its law over the generations. That was in itself quite a balancing act.

As noted earlier (p. 21), the late master historian of Yiddish literature, Khone Shmeruk, boldly 'metaphorized' the visual aspects of the oldest known dated Yiddish sentence (1272), where the Yiddish words fill in the gaps inside the calligrapher's letters of a single word, as symbolic of the early development of Yiddish literature: the filling in of the odd gap left by the Hebraic literature of Ashkenaz (Shmeruk 1988: 13). The same can be said, hundreds of years later, when the invention of printing eventually reached Yiddish. It is just that printing made way for a new empirical situation with vast — instead of tiny — gaps.

84

Neo-religious Yiddish literature

The concept 'neo-religious' can be pressed into service, in the context at hand, to refer to novel, previously unheard-of practices that profess the same devotion to accepted religious beliefs as the accepted canonical prayers, laws, rituals and customs but which by their very novel conveyance in Yiddish fly in the face of traditions and practices. The previous chapter surveyed a variety of works of note. These included a Bible concordance to help Yiddish speakers come to grips with biblical Hebrew, at least in part so that they could cope with polemics with Christians; Yiddish-only Bible editions; Bible translations with rabbinic commentaries in Yiddish translations; books of women's laws in Yiddish that would help women accurately follow the complex precepts for spheres of life in which they are commanded by Torah law to do certain things (and could now follow from a printed book themselves); books of Jewish customs.

Neo-religious use of Yiddish attempts to convey, celebrate, educate, proclaim and explain aspects of the Jewish religion and heritage, while in fact rebelling against standard practice of conveyance in one of the sacred languages. If such 'expansion of the realm' were to be taken as 'neutral' by great rabbinic authorities, it would hardly be an issue of 'power'. It was not, however, taken as neutral. It had caused major controversy well before the age of Yiddish printing.

The book that contains the first known lines about a 'Yiddish power dispute' is a collection, in Hebrew, compiled from the statements and episodes in the life of the Maharíl. Maharíl is an acronym for one of the great formative rabbis of Ashkenaz, Rabbi Jacob Mollin (±1360–1427), who established *Mínheg Ashkenaz* (the Custom of Ashkenaz as a formal set of practices, traditions and laws). His faithful pupil Zalmen of St Goar produced the *Séyfer Maharíl* ('Book of Maharíl') to preserve his master's wisdom and comments. It circulated widely for centuries in manuscript form. Since the first printed editions in the mid sixteenth century, it has been reprinted frequently and in traditional communities to this day.

In the *Séyfer Maharíl* we are told, in a casual Hebrew style:

He [the Maharíl] said: 'Those rhymed songs that they come up with in *loshn Ashkenaz* ['Language of Ashkenaz' = Yiddish] on the Unity and on the Thirteen Principles, if only they wouldn't do it! The reason is that most simple people think that all the commandments depend on that alone, and they give up on a number of Thou-shalts and Thou-shalt-nots, such as wearing *tsítsis* [the fringed vest], *tfíln* [putting on phylacteries], studying Torah and the like. They think they fulfil their obligations by reciting those rhymes with *kavónə* ['devout intent in Jewish prayer and fulfilment of commandments']. But those rhymes are only an allusion to the main tenets of the Jewish religion and not even one of the six hundred and thirteen commandments which Jews are commanded to perform!

(Zalmen of St Goar 1556: 103a [from the Hebrew])

We may never know whether the two Yiddish rhymed songs that the Maharíl mentions were in fact Yiddish translations of Maimonides' 'Thirteen Articles' (of the Jewish faith) and the Kalonymus family's 'Song of Unity of old Ashkenaz', one of the oldest faith poems of Ashkenaz, or just possibly, Yiddish paraphrases or semi-original compositions based on the original Hebrew. (In the case of the latter, a poem by one of the founding families of Ashkenaz, Kalonymus, could conceivably have been created in Yiddish as well as in Hebrew.)

Not only was there a neo-religious Yiddish movement by the fourteenth and fifteenth centuries, as in the singing of Yiddish versions of hallowed Hebrew texts, rather than the original Hebrew, but there was also a direct comment about a rebelliousness moderns would rather tend to associate with late nineteenth-century and subsequent Jewish culture: a 'secular revolution' whereby Jews stop fulfilling their inherited religious commandments, but continue to 'sing' about them in the vernacular as a kind of 'cultural heritage'. Anachronistic as the idea may sound, applied backward in time many centuries to medieval Ashkenaz, this is a comment about Jews who *did* rebel against the civilization and, in the modern sense of 'secularize', did indeed secularize Judaism into songs in the vernacular in place of fulfilling various commandments. Still, the parallel should not be stretched: it is far from obvious whether these 'strayers' would have, say, worked on the Sabbath or eaten food that was not as strictly kosher as rabbinic law would demand. Nevertheless, Zalmen of St Goar's sentence is one of these one-liners that testify to the existence of a phenomenon that would otherwise have remained quite unknown.

Clearly then, there were some Jews in the fourteenth century in the ultra-believing society of Ashkenaz who did not obey all the normative commandments and expressed their religiosity by singing songs on the basic principles of the Jewish faith in their native language, Yiddish, rather than in the society's sacred languages. There is no hint that the Maharíl has anything against (or for) Yiddish per se, and it would be indefensibly anachronistic to deduce 'language policy' here. But from its very beginning, Yiddish empowered non-scholars, simple people, to express their Jewish faith and enjoy singing in their native language. It is the empowerment of the vernacular and the vernacular is Yiddish. It is predictable that the native language of the population should represent the masses, who are not masters of exalted classical languages. What is surprising in the case of Yiddish is that modern scholarship and popular Jewish culture alike have forgotten that a 'Yiddish rebellion' of sorts has been under way in Jewish life for many centuries and is not *only* a product of the nineteenth- and twentieth-century Yiddish movement (Yiddishism). And few realize that some creative forms (for example, verse based on basic Jewish tenets) Yiddish has taken on within Jewish society have (a) existed and (b) been controversial, for many centuries.

In addition to rhymed couplets inserted into illuminated prayerbook manuscripts (known from the 1272 Worms machzor, or festival prayerbook) and songs about God and the Jewish faith (known from the Maharíl's complaints), Yiddish came into use for certain types of Jewish vocational training, especially for community positions requiring deep Jewish knowledge but not as deep as that required of a fully ordained rabbi. One such occupation was that of the ritual slaughterer, who must have mastery of a complicated legal literature about the insides of the animal and many intricacies of Jewish law about various details. Not every community could afford to have a rabbi do its slaughtering. The long and short of it is reported by the Maharíl in his own collections of responses to legal questions that came his way:

> There was a learned man who composed a work on the laws of slaughtering in a charming rhymed poem in *loshn Ashkenaz* ['language of Ashkenaz' = Yiddish], with a comprehensive commentary. And he did it with good intention, for he had seen that there were some simple people in the provinces, not to mention ignoramuses who cannot grasp or understand on their own even just the laws of slaughtering from a work in *loshn kóydesh* ['language of the sacred' = Hebrew]. It is even constantly necessary to explain everything to them [...]. And those in [the language of] Ashkenaz are explained very well. Nevertheless it is not the practice to give licence to slaughter on the basis of these, even though everything forbidden in the [actual actions under the] laws of slaughtering counts as a sin of the

actual Torah. [...] Every householder who can read the commentary of Rashi in the Torah, or the holiday prayerbook [...] and there are some who never served a genuine scholar! All these are reckoned unto the Valley of Fools [wordplay on Genesis 14: 3]. They look things up in the works of our rabbis, the compilers of Codes [...] but according to the reasoning in a given case, the application of a law can change! [...] There is no deciding on questions of law other than by the Talmud!

Maharíl (after Satz 1977: 92–3 [from the Hebrew])

The irreplaceable knowledge required in this culture is not ultimately 'knowledge of the law', but rather the ability to understand a page of Talmudic debate, which is mostly in Aramaic, rather than just a page of Hebrew summary of laws of one of the codifiers. Mastery of Yiddish legal manuals would not remotely qualify one to adjudicate legal issues. The power and human authority related to relationships of the three Jewish languages of Ashkenaz are exquisitely exemplified — and, for moderns, explained — through these few lines from the Maharíl's responsa. Without being intimately familiar with the debates and opinions (the history of debate and case law, as it were), one could go wrong in a specific case, and verdicts would in any event inherently lack the requisite authority. All three of the languages of Ashkenaz eerily come into play in the Maharíl's critique. Moreover, we learn of the practice of producing in the Yiddish language manuscripts of works on the laws of slaughtering that rhyme (not exactly the most typical use of rhyme in any culture, but a further example of exotic east–west amalgamation in Ashkenaz). In other words, a cultural form popular from *outside* the culture, in the related vernacular, was being applied in manuscripts dedicated to teaching the laws of slaughtering to ritual slaughterers who did not have the requisite rabbinic education to understand the argumentation in Hebrew and Aramaic original sources about cases that might require a difficult judgement. The judge has to be educated beyond having recourse to a list of laws. On early Yiddish slaughtering law manuscripts, see Shmeruk (1988: 17–24). Shmeruk, a master Yiddish literary scholar who followed the evidence rather than what is 'attractive and popular' for moderns, actually demonstrated that early writings on slaughtering law played a rather larger role in the earlier history of Yiddish literature than (we) literary or Yiddishist romantics might like.

However, it was not only ritual slaughtering that bothered the Maharíl in connection with Yiddish (and where, perhaps, the pleasurable feature of rhyme added to his disquiet). He was likely most concerned about the Jewish religious laws of women. The Maharíl's comments about ritual slaughtering manuals in rhymed Yiddish were made in a by-the-way tone, in the course of a legal reply to a rather different question. That itself is significant in the discourse analysis for this period, and perhaps it is a universal of legalistic writing that answering a question provides opportunity for some considered digression on a secondary topic upon which the writer wishes to comment. But the question on women was direct. It came from a man with the popular Jewish name Chaim, who had written to the great rabbi, in the late fourteenth or early fifteenth century, asking approval for a project to produce a work in Yiddish about the laws of 'family purity'. In its original and in English it is a euphemism for the laws of sex between a married couple as they relate to the wife's menstrual cycle, and we encounter a discussion of a book for women containing a major section on these matters under the traditional name of 'the [by Jewish law] menstrually impure woman', that is, the *nídə* (Ashkenazic Hebrew *nidɔ*, Israeli *nidá*). In outline, sex is prohibited from the day a woman expects her period until after seven full days following the end of the period (after Leviticus 15: 19–33), and she must be legally 'clean' before being able to resume relations with her husband. The legal and practical questions that come up are the subject of an entire tractate of the Talmud and countless rabbinic tomes. Traditional Orthodox Jews take these laws every bit as seriously today as thousands of years ago. The one major change in post-biblical times concerns the ceremony of purification following the end of the ritually unclean period. The Bible dictates that the woman take two turtle doves or pigeons to the priest on the eighth post-period day, and 'the priest shall offer the one for a sin offering and the other for a burnt offering' (Leviticus 15: 29–30). In post-temple Judaism the ritual bath (*míkve*) replaces those animal sacrifices. For the Bible and traditional communities, these are laws given by God and of paramount importance. Jewish humour over the centuries has repeatedly drawn material from people who might just succumb to the temptation of illicit sexual relations, but would never in their life transgress one of the technical laws of purity, such as the requisite ritual bath; they would engage in the greater sin (the illicit union) but not the smaller one (failing to observe the laws of ritual purity). So, if the purity couldn't be observed, they would forego the larger sin too.

There has for a long time been a question as to how much the couple themselves, and particularly the wife, can determine vis-à-vis her status without private detail being recounted before the rabbi. For the people in question, for whom obeying the law is far more important than any modernesque 'privacy' concept, the situation can be vexing in places where a doubt arises and there is no qualified rabbi. To return to the mysterious Chaim, who penned the question on these matters concerning his plan to produce a manual in Yiddish for couples to be able to ascertain the law in a given situation, the Maharíl got 'rather upset' at the idea:

> It is a matter of urgency for me to reply to my cherished and dear learned friend, Reb Chaim, may you live and be well. I was totally astounded by you, to learn that you are thinking about writing in Yiddish that which you know [...]. But our rabbis the codifiers did not intend [for their compilations of laws to serve the ignorant] but rather for pupils to go on to higher learning, and for *them* to inform women of the laws relevant to them [...]. And on top of everything [the proliferation of 'experts' who cannot read the Talmud itself and just look up the law in one of the compilations in Hebrew], you go ahead and try to foist on us even newer products that scatter the Torah among the scatterbrained, the simple people and frivolous women, and to give them 'a monument and a memorial' [*yod vo-sheym/yad va-shem*, lit. 'a hand and a name,' Isaiah 56: 5, here in the sense of 'enduring authority'], to study and to teach from your Yiddish book the issues relating to menstruation and blood spots, which our earlier and later masters dwelt upon in great detail, even as waters that have no end. God forbid, God forbid that such a thing would have been found among your fathers and forefathers, notwithstanding that we see [in Yiddish] many books on the laws of what is forbidden and what is permitted, and menstruation, and the *challah* bread, and the laws of Passover and holidays and various other topics.
>
> Maharíl (after Assaf 1942–3: 41–2 [from the Hebrew])

We learn, first, of the existence of a popular legal literature in Yiddish during the fourteenth and fifteenth centuries (and obviously earlier — a literature does not come into being overnight, and the Maharíl knows of it as a widespread 'problem'). Second, we are apprised of the power structure that defined the trilingualism of Old Ashkenaz. It is a given that Aramaic is necessary for a scholar who can adjudicate legal questions. He or she needs to be able to read all about it in the original Talmud, most of which is in Aramaic; the modern notion of a linguonym like 'Aramaic' is not a term that is even mentioned in the medieval Hebrew text here. Hebrew is of course necessary for studying the Bible as well as the codes and compilations of laws (for example, Maimonides and the Tur) which occupy the rungs of medium learnedness.

With the possible lapse of the alleged case of those who sing the songs of the principles of Judaism and the unity of God in Yiddish but don't bother to adhere to other commandments (one of 'the Maharíl's complaints'), these are instances of neo-religious Yiddish: taking universally accepted matters of Jewish law and faith, and rendering them in a pleasurable songful way in the vernacular. Far from being happy with this spread of knowledge (and presumably the devout belief that accompanies it), and the potentially entertaining (hence joyous) celebration of both through rhyme or song, the generation's leading rabbi is in fact furious over the concomitant loss of rabbinic *power*: ability to judge questions of everyday life might pass from those learned in the intricate Aramaic debates of the legalistic Talmud to simple folks who can read some rhymed book in their own language and think they 'know'. The feature of rhymedness seems to be adding insult to injury. But we must not be too hasty to read the heart of the Maharíl, or others, and to think that his only interest was in protecting the 'class interests' of the rabbinate — though that would be an understandable factor, too; after all, in many cases their one livelihood, after many years of intensive higher education, came precisely from serving as a community judge, arbiter, ritual slaughterer and so forth. There was also the professionalism required of any judge or lawyer who must have spent years studying law to achieve his position of authority. How many of us would be happy with a 'Joe the Plumber' judge who can 'look up the law' in a rhyming law book in his own language if he is illiterate in the language in which the legal debates resulting in the law history are (exclusively) recorded? All the more would the requirement of formal qualification be vital in a society where the law is believed with a full heart, not half a heart, to have been given directly by God to Moses for His chosen people of Israel.

In Ashkenaz, the language aspect is an inherent and inseparable part of the narrative of internal power. The most learned need Aramaic: that is where the legalistic debates are. The middle (and upper middle) learned have Hebrew. And the vast majority of folks, and all of the women, have only Yiddish. And early on in Ashkenazic cultural history, Yiddish and power was a potent issue as the inventive side of human nature exerted itself, managing not only to 'fill gaps' in the Shmerukian sense (which Shmeruk intended primarily to account for the growth in the number of genres of nascent Yiddish literature, from zero onward, in a society dominated by the learned written languages), but to expand the power of 'the Yiddish reading population' (potentially near-universal among Ashkenazic Jewry) into realms previously occupied exclusively by 'the Aramaic reading' and in some cases the intermediate-grade 'Hebrew reading'. The Shmerukian sense of 'filling gaps' is complementary with, rather than contradictory to, a the-glass-is-half-full analysis of a rising Yiddish written corpus.

The tradition of neo-religious Yiddish, a kind of low-level feature in the very traditionalist, conservative, obedient society of Ashkenaz, was naturally able to enjoy a rush of good fortune with the commercial launch of Yiddish publishing from the 1530s and 1540s onward. The new technology brought into play not only the ability to mass-produce a book in the vernacular, but also the free-enterprise factors of supply and demand, and ultimately, of a factor that has not often been discussed in the historiography of Yiddish culture: anonymity. In those earlier centuries, only a person wealthy or lucky enough could come by a manuscript in the vernacular whose content was something that excited them, and a purchase or inheritance or commissioning of such a thing was a conspicuous expensive acquisition. Now, with the advent of printing, anybody could relatively cheaply acquire a book in the vernacular. Mass production and low prices resulted in the loss of exceptionality in the ownership of a product and a comfortable rise in the anonymity enjoyed by the purchaser. This might have enraged some elites, who wanted literature and culture kept in the realm of the learned, with perhaps some extension to the class of 'wealthy benefactors'.

A language in which the power of authority and prestige was in practical times tied up with manuscripts shifted to one where the printed book was able to give rise to an alternative basis for some kind of prestige (if not authority), by definition in the hands of a rather different and vastly larger sector of the population.

'Secular Yiddish' literature

The modernist's convenient categories of 'secular' and 'religious' are useful for discussing previous epochs of civilizations markedly different from our own, as long as they do not lead to the fallacy that they are necessarily similar to recent or present understandings. Still, a specialized definition, with detailed delimitations for the purpose at hand, seems preferable to the coining of yet more academic neologisms. Max Weinreich famously tackled the issue for Ashkenaz in his memorable essay '*Yidishkayt* and Yiddish' in the 1953 festschrift on the seventieth birthday of 'Judaism as a Civilization' proponent Mordecai M. Kaplan (1881–1983). Weinreich demonstrated something that every traditional un-westernized Ashkenazi knows 'instinctively':

> In traditional Ashkenazic Jewry, it must be firmly kept in mind, religion was no part-time job, no Saturday versus Sunday pastime, as it happens to be in some cases today. It was a way of life and, even more important, an outlook on life.
>
> (Weinreich 1953: 481–2)

Traditional Yiddish does not even have a homely, old word for 'religion' or 'religious' because these concepts did not exist in the language in their precise western sense. From the nineteenth century onward, when westernization was under way, and terms for such concepts became necessary, such nativized imports as *relígyə* ('religion') and *religyéz* ('religious') gained currency. But the rooted words that ring with the Yiddish of old all refer to superlative degrees of keeping the laws meticulously and with all one's heart, and they are words whose dictionary definitions are quite different: *frum* (lit. 'pious' and 'observant'), *érləkh* (lit. 'honest'), *mákpəd* (lit. '(be) meticulous'), *l'məhádrin* ('[to do something/ for something to be done] in the most beautiful/meticulous way [beyond the letter of the law]'). Frequently the concept is expressed via a nominal agentive phrase rather than any kind of verb or adverb. A respected, well-liked keeper of the commandments, which of course include laws about respect, courtesy, gentleness, honesty and other attributes as well as the 'religious edicts' in the stricter sense, can be called *a shéynər yid* (lit. 'a beautiful Jew') or *a záydənər yid* (lit. 'a silken Jew'). In the post-Holocaust era, secular Yiddish educators latched on to such non-secular concepts in their effort to demonstrate a realm of specificities that are in some sense untranslatable as an argument for the ongoing need for Yiddish and, in some cases, exceptionality of the language (see Landis 1964).

In traditional Ashkenaz, there was no separate word for 'religious' because there was no separate concept of 'religious'. There was the Jewish way of life, with precepts and laws governing very many parts of life that moderns would not consider to be religious-devotional activities. There were myriad prayers or blessings that had to be said upon getting up, upon going to sleep, before and after eating, after visiting the lavatory, upon seeing a rainbow, and sundry other occasions. Men had to pray a full canon of specific prayers three times a day. The laws of food and eating, extending to the separation of meat and dairy products even among permitted foods, and the belief in a single true account of the world's creation, and the divinely ordained role of the Jewish people, are all among the facets of life that added up to more than the sum of their parts, to a totality of life which was very remote from the modern idea of living a life but reserving some time on the weekend, be it Saturday or Sunday, for attendance at a house of worship.

Nevertheless, as noted, there was never a commandment along the lines of 'Thou shalt not enjoy a good read in thy spoken language' and this gap enabled the 'invasion' for hundreds of years of the likes of *Dukus Horant, Ditrikh of Bern, Hildebrand, Bovo of Antona* and *King Arthur* into the Ashkenazic imagination via Yiddish and via the recycling of books in German or Italian into Yiddish renditions, thereby providing the power of knowledge of the wider world and its literature to the very people excluded from the primary literature of Ashkenaz in its own terms: the Hebrew and Aramaic literatures that continued to be written, mostly on matters of Jewish law, but with much latitude for including discussion on external issues.

So, for Yiddish and power, secular Yiddish may be defined as material from non-Jewish culture transmitted to a Jewish community via the Yiddish language (or, in some cases, a Judaized German in Jewish letters). It includes the so-called *romants* condemned by the twelfth–thirteenth-century *Séyfer Khasídim* ('Book for the Pious') as being unworthy for even 'paperwise-posthumous' reuse in a leather binding for a sacred book. There is dispute as to whether *romants* here refers to the genre or the language type, but in either case, the nature of the challenge is fairly evident. It surely includes also the *Dukus Horant* epic in the Cambridge Codex of 1382 (Frakes 9); the medical document on bloodletting of 1396–7 (Frakes 12); a traveller's charm against knights from before 1465 (Frakes 17); and a variety of documents from various spheres of life.

However, those documents that contain versions of tales of knights and battles recycled from non-Jewish works are most explicitly secular Yiddish, because they represent conscious pleasure in literature rather than, say, the need for knowledge of a medical procedure which is rather more pragmatic and culturally neutral. A more sophisticated definition would include the notion of *replacement*, even if it is only a kind of 'replacement in the heart'. In this 'higher threshold' definition, something secular Yiddish is a phenomenon — say a story or epic poem, whether in writing or listened to as a performance — that provides aesthetic pleasure and new material that has come from outside Jewish civilization, and that provides a certain thrill that is *not* attainable from one's habitual and familiar life and practices. It is well known that Jewish law is much more focused on 'transgressions of deed' than the 'transgression of the heart' which is more associated with Christian civilization. What might a rabbi or deeply pious Jewish Ashkenazi *feel* about somebody being immersed in stories of kings and knights that have come from — to put it plainly — the Christians, even if Christian religious references are deleted? Would it be resentment, and might there be in some cases a touch of envy of the curious? This is important because, put simply, in the case of a knightly romance in Yiddish, there is *no* danger to the income, authority or stature of the rabbi who would be needed to adjudicate a question in Jewish law, whether about the 'clean' and 'unclean' days in a couple's private life, whether a slaughtered animal may be eaten, or even about a monetary dispute between two parties who have come to a rabbinic court for a solution. In other words, in the case of knightly romances, there were no practical issues of everyday life, in sharp contrast to neo-religious Yiddish, which is strictly Jewish in content, but involves an immediate shift of a certain body of knowledge (hence, internal authority and power) from the Hebrew and Aramaic reading minority to the Yiddish-only reading majority.

That is a power-related irony of older Ashkenaz and older Yiddish. The secular works were a spiritual power-grab by the 'masses'. The neo-religious works were, after a fashion, a much *more* daring power-grab by those same masses. It is verily an opposition of the heart, and one that would, in one form or another, perhaps be better rephrased as Ashkenazic receptiveness to outside culture. That is rather different from the 'physical' receptiveness to words and other raw linguistic 'matter' that Yiddish has always revelled in 'borrowing' and rapidly 'remaking' in a deeply unique Yiddish-Jewish way. *That* very separate phenomenon was famously described in Max Weinreich's 'Form vs Psychic Function in Yiddish' (Weinreich 1936).

Then there is gender. On the one hand, it is one of the most important issues; on the other, our knowledge of proportions of female and male readers of any Yiddish work is forever going to remain a point of conjecture, no matter how many title-page prefaces use and repeat formulas about the book being for women, including Elijah Levita's announcement of his cumulative output 'for the ladies' at the start of his literary masterpiece, *Bovo d'Antona* (see pp. 42–3). Any retrospective 'research of buyers and readers' will of necessity remain a thought experiment. It is most productive to abandon ideas of determining arithmetic proportions of different groups of readers, and to think instead of the human mind and its need for edification, entertainment, aesthetic pleasure and diversion from the usual. For all the belief in the world in the divinity of the Torah and the eternal applicability of the laws derived from it by the rabbinic authorities over the ages, all of that too must of necessity be part of 'the usual' in the traditional society. So yes, certainly, and by intuitive fiat, stories, epics and tales from outside, stripped of offensive-to-the-beholder Christian references, could be a magnificent guilt-free endeavour as simple as the (western) pleasure of reading literature.

There is no denying that different modern readerships and students of Old Yiddish literature, no matter how small the numbers, are inevitably influenced by the orientations of the scholars whose books they read. Frakes (2004) is perhaps the first post-tendentious historian of Old Yiddish literature, giving equal voice, with the necessary dispassionate distance of the scholar, to secular and religious, literary and non-literary texts, providing a wide, sweeping view of the range of older Yiddish writing. But that is not to say that the earlier 'more tendentious' works are 'bad'. On the contrary, they are equally invaluable, and far from deceiving ourselves about anyone's neutrality, it is wholly in order when such neutrality is not claimed, and each scholar is left to openly champion his or her cause, the more so in the case of those who produced monographs or translated editions of individual works, with full contemporary cultural and linguistic detail, that gripped their imagination.

It is moreover no secret that the 'tendencies' of Yiddish literary scholars have been closely 'alignable' with the major forms of twentieth-century Jewish politics, with emphasis on its interwar incarnations, which in the field of Yiddish lasted more or less intact in émigré environments until about the end of the twentieth century, coming to an end with the disappearance of the last fully pre-war-acculturated survivor-scholars. Those tendencies are superbly clarified in Mendelsohn's masterpiece, *On Modern Jewish Politics* (= Mendelsohn 1993; see also Gutman et al. 1989). To turn to the matter at hand, socialists, communists, anti-Zionists, anti-religionists and cultural secularists of many stripes were eager to stress 'the secular' in Old Yiddish literature to find an old and usable lineage for what they were doing, for what they believed and for what they wanted to build: a modern Yiddish culture with the pedigree of an older history. There were others whose secularism became tempered as time went on, and they might, in the course of 'moving from the left towards the centre', be inclined to also include religious works from bygone centuries. After the Holocaust, the major new centre for Old Yiddish literary studies was for many years Israel, where a Hebraist framework that inherently tended more toward religious than secular, for direct and indirect reasons, took hold. Modern Zionism, for both its fervently religious and fervently secular sectors, and the many varieties intermediate, shares a synthesis of ancient religious texts with modern nationalistic yearnings.

For the postmodernist age, it is best to view all of the above as equally valuable, and to 'allow' each to stress what is most dear to him or her with the understanding that we all end up telling one side of a story, and should consider ourselves fortunate if we succeed in accomplishing even that with any success, all the more so when we *say* that that is what we are up to.

By that criterion, the sharpest grasp of secularism as a category of inquiry for the whole of the history of Yiddish was that of Max Erik (born Zalmen Merkin, 1898–1937). He was a native of Poland and victim of Stalin's purges of 1937. Erik relocated from the free Polish Republic to the Soviet Union in 1929. Like other Yiddish writers of the time (for example, Moyshe Kulbak 1896–±1937), his most individualistically successful work was achieved in his *pre*-Soviet period, and after having the innermost depths of creative freedom stifled, he was himself purged, arrested and murdered by Stalin's regime. Luckily for posterity, a number of his major works appeared in book form before his relocation to the Soviet Union. In the field of Old Yiddish literature, his two masterpieces are *Vegn alt-yídishn román un novéle* ('About the Old Yiddish Novel and Novella', Warsaw 1926) and *Di geshíkhte fun der yídisher literatúr. Fun di éltste tsaytn biz der haskóle-tkúfe* ('The History of Yiddish Literature. From the oldest times until the Haskalah Period', Warsaw 1928). It is only natural that in some ways later discoveries of manuscripts (and even printed books) would render Erik's work 'technically' outdated here and there. Erik could not have discussed the 1272 sentence in the holiday prayerbook or the 1382 Cambridge Codex written in Egypt, and a number of other documents then unknown. But 'facts are cheap' at the end of the day, and none of these change the conceptual picture. Anyone who has studied Erik can almost supply his or her own unique cadences to 'fit in' those discoveries rather seamlessly. As for his secularist and possibly anti-religious, pro-leftist and other 'tendencies', we *know* about those, and therefore regard Erik, to start with, as a kind of advocate for the idea of a big-ticket secular Yiddish literature in the earlier centuries of Ashkenaz.

Knowing this information about a scholar's intellectual and political orientation, and factoring it in, with no prejudice to the religious literature which may have interested him less (not so much less, as it happens, because he found the universal aspects in all the literature he studied), can be useful also for judging the many 'cultural battleground' or 'cultural union' works, such as the *Shmúel bukh* ('Book of Samuel') and the

Mlókhim bukh ('Book of Kings'). It is agreed that the union of orient and occident is a happy and even 'romantic' one (biblical material, medieval European epic poetic form); but the 'secularist' will see in them a development of European literature, arguing that Old Testament narrative also played a prominent role in many works of Christian European literature. The 'Judaist' who wishes to see the internal 'true Jewish spirit' in Old Yiddish literature might make a determination that the medieval genre of epic poetry was simply a useful and pleasurable device in the larger cause of Jewish biblical education.

As often happens in academic polemics that stretch over decades and are conducted between the living and the deceased in different periods of scholarly and wider understanding of the subject in question, the precise point of debate shifts to a space that is inherently one of a number of possible focal points of disagreement, and is perhaps a 'tad to the side' of what 'should have been' the central point from, say, our vantage point (which could even be a disadvantage). Unable to 'hook' Erik for his presentation of an uninterrupted chain of secular Yiddish literature (in the sense of 'material imported from the contemporary Gentile world'), late twentieth-century scholars simply passed him over for those of his followers who were more politically correct for the postwar, post-Holocaust era, and tried to challenge his paradigms on factual grounds. Most famous of these was Khone Shmeruk, a master scholar of texts and the literary history of their authors in the widest sense, who for most of his prolific academic career concentrated on establishing the facts and building blocks of the history of Yiddish literature, place by place and subject by subject. His own works were so important, and his success in supervising younger researchers in Jerusalem so pronounced, that he established an Israeli School of Old Yiddish literary studies, one so linked to himself that it declined precipitously when in the 1990s he stunned his contemporaries by remarrying, after he was widowed, and resettled in his native Warsaw, where he died in 1997 at the age of 76.

That the long-dead Erik was able to 'answer back' was thanks to his devoted follower, the New York Yiddish scholar Elias Schulman (1907–86). Instead of trying to take on Shmeruk himself — many who tried to do that lived to regret it, so vast was Shmeruk's academic knowledge and influence in the field of Yiddish literature, so devastating his fabled dismissals of lesser scholars — Schulman had the inspired idea of republishing Erik's classic 1928 *Geshíkhte*, with his own new introduction. That introduction openly took on Shmeruk in the form of a humble introduction to the great Erik (and moderns looking even at the table of contents would see that Erik's work is that of a great scholar, not of a leftist thinker dabbling in literature for 'socialist argmentation').

With that minimal background to 'Erik vs Shmeruk' we can look more closely at their debate (on Erik see Shulman 1968, 1979; on Shmeruk see Lifschitz 1981 and Katz 2001; on Shulman see Gris 1981).

The theory of live performance in Old Yiddish times

With a lot of hard evidence from Old Yiddish texts themselves (a methodology on which no later critic could possibly fault him), Erik had proposed that many of those early rhymed, entertainingly written epic Yiddish poems were in fact on occasion performed before an audience by a reader or entertainer. For secularist Erik it was absolutely natural to surmise that this practice was parallel to the performance of gentile works for gentile audiences in medieval Europe. (Almost as natural, one could add today, as for even religious Jewish folks to attend a non-offensive non-Jewish performance, just as their non-Jewish neighbours might attend a more 'exotic' performance in the same town or even on the same street.) Erik never claimed that these works were *only* for performance and that nobody ever read them as one would read a book or manuscript.

The evidence Erik adduced is not to be scoffed at, though to be sure it is in part circumstantial. For example, the biblical account records in several passages the episode of King David at the end of his life: the old king feels cold, his aides find him the beautiful Avishag the Shunamite to warm him, but he does not 'know her', as the biblical phrase goes (1 Kings 1: 1–4). Erik notes that the portion of Elijah Levita's *Bovo d'Antona* (written c. 1507, published 1541) modelled on those passages had grown to two strophes (16 lines), and in the Yiddish Book of Kings, the *Mlókhim bukh*, to 13 strophes (104 lines). Erik delights in summarizing the romantic and sexual overtones added by the *Mlókhim bukh's* author: Avishag demands, after a certain period, that David take her for a wife. In this particular narrative, the elderly David regrets that God has forbidden him more than 18 wives (a post-biblical legend), whereupon Avishag retorts in anger that he is probably wriggling out of it because of a loss of sexual prowess. Upon hearing this, David immediately calls in his lawful wife Bath-Sheba and, as Erik puts it, 'demonstrates his manhood right on the spot, like a young man who had just got married'.

Next, Erik adduces evidence of live performance from the fact that these works were sung to tunes that became well known; the *Shmúel bukh's* author uses the verb *zíngən* ('sing'). The phrase *b'nígn Shmúəl bukh* ('[to be sung] according to the melody of the *Shmúel bukh'*) occurs in other, later works, making it evident that it was a known entity, something like a theatre song or ditty that can long outlive the show whence it derives. Erik cites this from as late as 1686, proving that the melody remained popular for centuries, because it was *sung*. Singing is inherently a manner of performing.

Then comes evidence from parts of the text that seem made for the performer to be saying out loud to his audience. For example, in a crucial Yiddish *King Arthur* manuscript, the audience is humorously warned that poor Vidvilt cannot move, being bound to the tree, and that is exactly where he will remain 'until you give me some very good wine to drink!' — in other words, the actor is inviting folks to buy him a drink during the interval. Erik even produced the German text from which this was 'borrowed'. He sees powerful influences from the world of gentile entertainment that could be rendered into Yiddish with just minor changes, which could manifest themselves by the application of European technique to internal Jewish material. For Erik this is all the growth of the partly gentile-inspired development of the novel, the epic and other genres which were internalized and which enabled the growth of an internal Yiddish literature and performance culture that would in the fullness of time also draw on native raw cultural material (see Erik 1926: 14–30).

In his full-blown history of older Yiddish literature (Erik 1928), he went beyond these and many other impressive (and occasionally conclusive) proofs for the simple, logical and in a sense obvious idea that there was 'an occasional entertainment component in all these things' (and for the sake of sticking to the point we have ignored here many important sub-categorizations Erik made; for example, between works for recital and works for singing). Erik was out to construct a structural *history* of older Yiddish literature. He boldly divided his masterpiece into Book 1 and Book 2. Book 1 is called *Di shpílman tkúfe fun der yídisher literatúr* ('The *shpílman* Period of Yiddish Literature'). Book 2 is *Di múser tkúfe fun der yídisher literatúr* ('The Musar ['Jewish Ethics'] Period of Yiddish Literature').

Looking backwards as well as at his interwar contemporaries, Erik in a sense outdid them all. Here was a history of earlier Yiddish literature with its own structure and with the eye of a master who uses small details of far-flung manuscripts to construct imposing edifices. He even outdid the century's greatest Yiddish linguist, Max Weinreich, who in the same year (1928) published in Vilna his outstanding *Bílder fun der yídisher literatúr geshíkhte* ('Scenes from Yiddish Literary History').

Weinreich's book is a beautiful guide to the works, the language, the libraries and the cultural history, an indispensable book to this day. But it was Erik who did for the study of Old Yiddish literature what Weinreich was already doing, and would do ever more magnificently, for the history of the Yiddish language, with the good fortune to live for many more years, after the war, in New York City, where he completed his monumental *History of the Yiddish* before his death in 1969 (Weinreich 1973; in English: Weinreich 1980 and 2008).

With the advantage of hindsight, however, Erik's structure was latched on to a single word that was intellectually by no means central to his thesis or to his conceptualizations of the two postulated periods, but a word that would turn out to be 'not very attractive' for Yiddish literary scholarship after World War II and the Holocaust. In other words, Erik chose a not-too-viable name for his amassed evidence that the power of Yiddish extended beyond the entertainment of reading to the entertainment of live performance. That word was *shpílman*. It was taken without apology or hesitation from the German *Spielmann*, in the sense of a wandering entertainer of the European Middle Ages who gave performances for the public at fairs, markets, castles and other venues. They, the *Spilleute*, were credited by some with keeping alive in the Germanic dialects tales and legends in a time when much of what was being properly recorded in writing was religious. Erik's rather innocuous idea that something similar existed among Jews and was instrumental in building the foundations of early Yiddish literature might have simply been one of many of his points had it not been elevated to the name of the first *period* of Yiddish literature in his work. The *shpíl-layt* (or *shpíl-mèner*) could have become just a member of the set of names of Yiddish (quasi-) professions for which modern Yiddish sometimes even 'remembers the names', for example, *badkhónim* ('wedding jesters'), *leytsónim* ('clowns' or 'jesters'), *narn, narónim* ('clown-fools'), *klezmórim* ('musicians' and by extension 'singers' or any kind of 'musical performers') and even certain types of *magídim* ('travelling preachers' who had to do some acting to keep their audience's attention). Their moralistic discourses in some cases included storytelling, legends, humour and even singing (sometimes cantorial, sometimes folksy, nearly always with a certain recital melody reminiscent of the Talmudic chant of Jewish learning; cf. Kahan-Newman 1995).

What grated after the war was what seemed to be Erik's 'mechanical adoption' of a term from German cultural history and its transposition to Yiddish, with all that that implied to a post-Holocaust and in part Israel-centred generation of scholars. So much of Erik's empirically demonstrable claims of parts of old Yiddish literature being part of entertainment as well as literature are solid and do not depend on anyone needing to accept that there was a specifically Jewish or Yiddish profession called *shpílman* that corresponded 'completely' or 'mechanically' (or even partly!) to the German *Spielmann*. That we are even arguing about (in some senses) 'one word' in different spellings (or even in different alphabets/languages) goes to the heart of Erik's, retrospectively speaking, unfortunate choice of name for his period. Had he called it, say, the 'Secular Period' or the 'Folk Entertainment Period' of Old Yiddish literature, there would perchance have been no such post-war battle. Incidentally, Yisróel Tsinberg (Israel Zinberg) also accepted the existence of a Jewish or Yiddish *shpílman* but did so regarding various individual texts, for example, *King Arthur* (see Tsinberg 1937: 74), and he did so rather more casually, remarking on the Jewish 'entertainment professions' in which he calmly lists the *shpílman* alongside the *badkhónim, leytsónim* and so forth (1937: 38). In cases like the *Shmúel bukh*, Tsinberg finds internal evidence, just like Erik, for it being written to be performed (1937: 135); he just never made a theory out of it, and never referred to the major early works of Yiddish literature as constituting a *shpílman* period.

After the war, there was for some a symbolic portent to an issue that goes beyond a German-derived word that did not survive in the original sense into any modern Yiddish dialect; such a survival would have lent the needed authenticity. Retrospectively speaking, the offence taken itself is rather ironic, as Baumgarten points out, because the word *shpílman* occurs three times in the Yiddish-glorified 'first literary work of Yiddish literature', as it is now known, the 1382 Cambridge Codex, which Erik could not have known about and which a neo-Erikean could now flaunt with some glee (see Baumgarten 2005: 142). What might have been somewhat unconsciously offensive is the entire notion of Yiddish literature developing as a pale and watered-down Jewish version of the gentile entertainment industry of the day; somehow not quite right for the sociological, Judeo-centric constructions of post-war scholars in the Jewish academic mainstream. Nobody bothered to notice the non- (or much less) ideological Tsinberg's portrayals of the entertaining professions in straight religious Hebrew for such occasions as the festive holiday of Purim, based on the biblical book of Esther (Tsinberg 1937: 38).

The first salvo came from Khone Shmeruk's pen in a 1967 review of Leo Fuks's edition of the Augsburg 1543 edition of the *Mlókhim bukh* that was based on the book of Kings. The immediate opponent was therefore his contemporary Fuks, who was by then renowned for his rediscovery of the Cambridge Codex itself (Fuks 1954) and his hand-some two-volume edition thereof (Fuks 1957).

> L. Fuks is a faithful adherent of the *shpílman* theory of Yiddish literature. We know that from his previous publications and also from his introduction to the *Mlókhim bukh*. [...] The original texts of Old Yiddish Literature have so far not confirmed the existence of a Jewish '*shpilman* class'.
>
> Indirectly, the most that could be demonstrated is that Jewish authors used in their works conventional forms — poetic, linguistic and stylistic, whose origin can perhaps be found also in the German so-called *Spielmann* literature, but not only there. These forms were also widespread in German folk poetry and in spheres of literature that had no relationship to the *shpíllayt*. To these possible *shpílman* clichés there belong in the first instance the turnings [of the narrator's speech] to a listener, which are very widespread throughout the literature of the Middle Ages. Such appeals to listeners are to be found in the *Mlókhim bukh*. Fuks cites three such instances of addressing [the hearer] in his introduction (vol. 1, p. 24), to support the *shpílman* theory. But these quotes are no more than typical conventions, which must not under any circumstances be taken literally.
>
> (Shmeruk 1967: 210 [from the Yiddish])

In the 1960s and 1970s, the study of Old Yiddish literature was in fact invigorated by the debates noted already (pp. 34–6) concerning the Cambridge Codex. Even if some of these academic skirmishes, with hindsight, seem a little quaint ('What language is it?'), they certainly energized Yiddish studies, providing excitement and diversity for a small, weak field whose chances of survival in academia are perennially in doubt. Even the somewhat pompous name 'Cambridge Codex' was giving Yiddish a new academic cachét in some circles, not only for Germanists and Yiddishists interested in Old Yiddish but for anybody interested in Yiddish, which 'in general' meant modern Yiddish and for many modern Jews meant only off-colour words and jokes that were all that was left of their ancestors' rich language heritage. Now, Yiddish had its own 'Codex'. Sometime in those years the New York Yiddish satirist Avrom Shulman (1913–99) told me: 'Nu, Dovid, now they are finally interested in Yiddish it's certainly not in Sholem Aleichem, much less anything we have written, it's all about *épɔs a kódeks-shmódeks*' ('some kind of codex-shmodex').

In the academic sphere, however, the buzz about 'the Yiddish Codex' even played a prominent role in the agenda of the first academic conference on Yiddish at Oxford, in August 1979 (Oxford, rather than Cambridge, the codex's home, because it was at Oxford that an embryonic Yiddish programme was quietly growing). It brought together Yiddish scholars from around the world, and especially from the United States, Germany and Israel, with the contingents interested in Old Yiddish coming largely from the latter two countries. The academic grand master of the entire conference, what with his unparalleled knowledge of all stages of Yiddish literature, was Professor Shmeruk. Only this time, Shmeruk's critique of Erik and his *shpílman* theory was not to be part of a book review of one of Fuks's editions of Old Yiddish literature. It would link the academics' excitement about the Codex with a sweeping denunciation not only of Erik's *shpílman* theory. In a wider sense, Shmeruk implicitly went on to critique all of the ideologically Yiddishist (that is, pro-Yiddish in modern Jewish culture, which often implies leftist, secularist, non-Zionist) school of Yiddish literary studies: Erik, Tsinberg, Weinreich — the lot. Shmeruk, an ideological Hebraist in his long Israeli period, was willing and able to criticize the academic heroes of the Yiddishists from a position of vast erudition, and without concern about his ensuing unpopularity in the dwindling culturally Yiddishist circles in the United States, Israel and elsewhere during the period. He seemed to enjoy being the target of bitter polemics as long as these came from journalists and writers rather than professional scholars. He had no match in the academic field of Yiddish literature, and scholars could only benefit from his erudition and criticism, whatever their cultural persuasions in the socially and nationally multifarious field of Yiddish.

Shmeruk concluded his presentation to the Oxford conference with this: 'It's an insult to the great Yiddish author and great Hebrew philologist Elye Bókher to say that he was some kind of *shpílman!*', drawing applause and supportive laughter. The published version appeared later the same year in Yiddish in the most prestigious Yiddish literary journal of the time, the *Góldene keyt* in Tel Aviv (Shmeruk 1979). It was entitled: 'Tsi ken der Kéymbridzher manuskrípt shtitsn di shpílman-teórye in der yídisher literatúr?' ('Can the Cambridge Manuscript underpin the *shpílman* theory of Yiddish Literature?'); even rejection of the pompous word 'codex' in favour of the neutral 'manuscript' in the title was vintage Shmeruk. He began by framing the question which led to the answer in the first place: what kind of professions did those early Yiddish writers have, and how did they earn their daily bread? The long and short of it is that Shmeruk masterfully dissected and then put into the incinerator all of the academically loose or unproven senses of *shpílman* in Erik's theory, and went way beyond Erik in the course of doing so: back to Leo Landau. Landau had used the term in a far more circumscribed sense in his work on Yiddish *King Arthur* editions. Shmeruk extended his precision demolition work outward to German literary studies, where he showed how limited in literary scope, chronological framing and breadth of usage the concept has been, even for Germanic studies.

Thus, the master historian of Yiddish literature, himself a Jewish nationalist, Zionist and 'public anti-Yiddishist' in the modern cultural senses, put his vast erudition and talent into demolishing Erik's poor choice of the term *shpílman*, and the way in which Erik extended it as a metaphor for the oldest period of Old Yiddish literature. One could (and can) mount a spirited defence of Erik. For example, in erecting a usable and durable structure for bygone periods of a literature that few scholars even thought existed in his day, Erik was able to demonstrate that a superficially diverse corpus of texts had much in common that could be extrapolated from internal textual evidence and the cultural and literary background of both form and content. Moreover, he determined the features that define that corpus to be predominant in the earlier periods under investigation, giving another empirical motivation for a term that would tie the features and the time to help distinguish them from a later time and a corpus in which those features are diminished or absent. In choosing a name for that earlier period, he picked a word that he liked, that an earlier scholar of older Yiddish literature, Leo Landau, had used, taking it from German literary studies. The initially neutral word *shpílman* could in any case be a blanket term for an array of professions that actually have names in Yiddish: *badkhn, klézmer, lets, zínger* and more. Erik, instead of devising a neologism, adopted an existing term to a clearly defined conceptual space.

For Shmeruk, though, the term was a symptom of what had been wrong with the historians of Yiddish literature in the pre-war East European Yiddishist tradition, and he was quick to elevate a symptom into a symbol. In the paper's final broadside, he turned to the underlying conflict between a post-Holocaust Jewish-nationalist, Zionist, Hebraist centre of Yiddish studies and its antecedent East European pre-war incarnation as the academic component of the Yiddishist movement, in the Borokhovian sense (Borokhov 1913a).

We have limited ourselves to issues of attribution. But there is something very closely connected to the *shpílman* theory: the aspiration to determine a dominant 'secular' [Yiddish *véltləkh*, lit. 'worldly', often implying 'somewhat non/anti-religious'] character of Yiddish

literature in the period that has been thought of as shpilmanesque.
[...] Nevertheless, this 'secular' postulate concerning Old Yiddish literature is a matter which deserves a separate study, but as an issue in
the study of modern Yiddish literary research. In doing so, it is necessary to take into consideration the socio-ideological atmosphere
from which this research arose in 1920s Eastern Europe. However,
both this quite important matter, together with research into the
appeal of the *shpílman* theory and of the *shpílman*-image among
Yiddish writers in the twenties, deserve a separate study, that does
not have overly direct connections with Old Yiddish literature.

(Shmeruk 1979: 265 [from the Yiddish])

In fact, it is hard to disentangle research into old Yiddish literature per
se from a study of the researchers' mode of thinking. This difficulty
is encountered whether the researcher concerned was a pre-war ideological Yiddishist in Eastern Europe (like Erik) or a post-war ideologoical
Hebraist in Israel (like Shmeruk). Any effort to make a total and neat
break would probably fail in both instances. A hypothetical de novo
researcher, expert in the relevant languages and cultures, who had for
the sake of argument never read Erik or Shmeruk or any other twentieth-century scholarly treatment, looking only at the original texts
would him- or herself come up against analogous issues, howsoever differently framed (or, as the Yiddish expression would have it, *di zélbikə
kálə, ándersh gəshléyərt* — 'the same bride but differently veiled'). In
the context of the task at hand, a researcher rapidly encounters power-
related issues, both in the texts studied and in the scholarly tradition.

In the surrounding majority-culture gentile society, there was Latin
and there was the vernacular of the majority, which was increasingly
being used for various purposes, representing slowly growing power-
of the majority — of what the majority of people in the country speak.
Then there was the Jewish minority, within which the people who
wielded the most power over the others (who mostly happily and voluntarily accepted their leadership as part of a God-given constellation),
read and wrote Hebrew and, if they were very learned, also Aramaic.
Turning from language to topic, there are (a) the 'gentile' topics (such
as *Dukus Horant, Ditrikh of Bern, Hildebrand* and others), (b) the 'Jewish
topics' (such as books of laws useful for daily life on kosher slaughtering
and on women's laws), and (c) 'hybrid topics' (most famously, biblical
narrative recast as European epic dramas in the Jewish vernacular). Here
the power factors are more complex and multifaceted: there is the power
within the minority culture and the power of the state (representing the

religious and ethnic majority) over all members of that minority. From the point of view of Yiddish and power, it would be obvious that *any* Yiddish work that can be enjoyed by everyone in the Jewish community (and even those outside it) is an empowerment of the population, with knowledge, information and all the wisdom that comes from the reading of literature. The medieval phenomenon of Yiddish power includes the ability of a woman and her husband to read for themselves the laws pertaining to their private life in their own language as much as it enables enrichment, pleasure and prestige of knowledge, via medieval knightly narratives of external derivation. Whatever one's views on the veracity of the designated readership declarations in the prefaces of many Yiddish printed books in the last seven decades of the sixteenth century, one thing is clear. Women were excluded completely from the serious study of Hebrew and Aramaic texts, and so it is a matter of simple common sense to conclude that Yiddish writings would have, all in all, 'meant more to them' in terms of providing education, knowledge, edification, entertainment and more. If the socioeconomic factor of women 'staying home to look after the home and children' is factored in, then the time available for Yiddish would be all the greater, and their benefit from Yiddish empowerment proportionately higher.

In the scholarly tradition, there are ongoing echoes of the *shpílman* debate between 'the Yiddishists of the 1920s led by Max Erik' and the 'Israeli school of Yiddish literature of the 1970s and 1980s led by Khone Shmeruk'. Some post-debate scholars, including Baumgarten (2005: 142) and Frakes (33), concur with Shmeruk so completely that they cite his 'definitive refutation' of the *shpílman* theory, almost as if the fabled 'fear of Shmeruk' lives on undiminished. Others pass it over in silence as one would a minor skirmish relating to a tertiary point in the history of the literature being studied. But there may be a sociological relationship to the debates between the 'Yiddishists' and the 'Germanists' over the nature of Old Yiddish texts in general ('German or Yiddish?'), and a tendency to side with the 'Jewish side' at least in so far as rejecting the lack of knowledge and respect for Old Yiddish on the part of many Germanists, an issue boldly exposed in Frakes's earlier successful polemic, *The Politics of Interpretation* (Frakes 1989; cf. Katz 1990a).

There are, as ever, ironies. Erik, who was much more 'Yiddishist' than his posthumous critic Shmeruk, was nevertheless taken to task by Shmeruk for having casually taken from German literary studies and refashioned for Old Yiddish a certain term and made it somewhat central to the origins of Yiddish literature. Shmeruk concluded his critique with the wider issue of secularism in older Yiddish literature, accusing the interwar Yiddishist literary scholars of bias in favour of a kind of (for him) anachronistic interbellum secular Yiddishism that most of them believed in 'for the here and now', before the Holocaust that they could not have envisioned, and that Shmeruk knew about all too well from the loss of his family and native milieu of Polish Jewry. For many decades, scholars who came to Yiddish from Germanic studies did not have adequate respect for the integrity of Old Yiddish texts. Frakes led in the corrective to this; but did he and Baumgarten (whose excellent history of Old Yiddish literature Frakes edited and translated into English) perhaps overcompensate? The question then turns back to the medieval period and the broader notion of 'secularism', rather than the narrow notion of a '*shpílman* period' or '*shpílman* literature'.

'Secularism' for older Yiddish literature can have a number of senses. These include derivation from gentile sources, forms of culture not included in the traditional canons or traditions, and ultimately a level of increased overlap with the cultural world of the non-Jewish co-territorial majority population. Being an ideological Yiddishist and active participant in the world of contemporary Yiddish culture, publications and education, the last thing on Erik's mind in the borrowing and remaking for Yiddish of the term *shpílman* was in any way to diminish the 'Jewishness' of Old Yiddish literature. Like any other scholar of Old Yiddish, he delighted in discovering how works taken from German (or Italian) literature were chosen, altered, reworked, de-Christianized, Yiddishized. In addition, like or dislike the term, Erik demonstrated beyond reasonable doubt that, in an era when not many people could own extensive manuscripts of any kind, when surviving literary works are methodically rhymed, they are indicated to have been sung according to this or that melody, include comments intended for an audience, and contain a lot of 'stage-type humour', these works were indeed potentially at times sung or performed in addition to being read. If the proportion of sung or performed to read is lower than Erik thought, perchance, it is not a pivotal issue in his broad conceptualization of the history of Yiddish literature.

There was some transfer of power from those Yiddish slaughtering manuals and women's laws, but it was, at the end of the day, somewhat marginal. The authority of the professional rabbis was never seriously undermined. But the tales of *Dukus Horant, Hildebrand, Ditrikh of Bern* and *King Arthur*, which did not challenge rabbinic authority in the same direct way, brought a whole new realm of literature to potentially everybody, as did the European epic poetic form that had recast biblical works in ways that departed overwhelmingly from the Old Testament texts upon which they were based. Yes, it was cultural material from Europe that enabled Yiddish to empower the typical Ashkenazi with literature, in other words 'secular' culture, which in works like the epics based on 'Samuel' and 'Kings' resulted in east–west syntheses of culture from the ancient orient with contemporary Europe. That synthesis mirrors the very nature of Yiddish itself, and when the twentieth-century layers are scraped off, it turns out that Maks Erik — born Zalmen Merkin — conceptualized it with broad strokes.

6

Power Shifts: West→East, Earlier→Later, Secular→Religious

When it came to unlocking the secrets of Yiddish linguistics in the early twentieth century, the prime unlocker was Ber Borokhov (see Katz 1980, 2007: 274–8). It took more than a sum total of erudition and acumen. It took a veritable genius to kick-start the new field for a stateless language. Borokhov (1881–1917), in his short life, was that person. When it came to coming to grips with the history of Yiddish literature, however, Borokhov stayed more in the box of conventional thought, in applying the schemes for other literatures to this one. His scheme for the history of Old Yiddish literature, based consciously or unconsciously on the sociological needs of the dynamic new Yiddish cultural movement in Eastern Europe, seems to have perceived the need, in terms of the aimed-for societal power of Yiddish in the twentieth century, of a 'classic period' for Old Yiddish literature, that he found in the flowering of Yiddish publishing from the 1530s and 1540s onwards, with its wide variety of genre and orientation, religious and secular alike (see Borokhov 1917: iv).

However, it was not long before Maks Erik in in the 1920s would challenge (the by then deceased) Borokhov on the conceptualization of the history of older Yiddish literature. Erik postulated that the *printing* of Yiddish works was a function of the time when external factors conspired to enable the rise of Yiddish publishing: in fact, the entire period of the first Yiddish age of printing was merely a *transition*, in Erik's view, from an earlier period that he had called the *shpílman* period to a later period, starting at the end of the sixteenth century, that was based on internal Jewish-religious culture, rather than external gentile-secular motifs.

The two masters, Borokhov and Erik, were not 'equal', nor were their biographies remotely identical, though looking back from afar, in time and place, there are striking analogies: their permanent contributions, to Yiddish linguistics and Yiddish studies (Borokhov), and to the history of older Yiddish literature (Erik), came in bursts of energy over the course of some years. Both their lives were tragically prematurely ended, Borokhov's at the age of 36, of pneumonia, when he couldn't resist returning from America to Russia after the Revolution of 1917, and Erik's at 38, by Stalin's Great Terror of 1937. But, if we look back using the understandable post-war critiques such as Shmeruk's, then a few things become apparent. First, Borokhov, best remembered today in wider circles for his founding role in the Labour Zionist (Zionist-Socialist) movement, was able to properly disassociate his politics from his work in Yiddish studies. In the case of Erik, he too constructed remarkable edifices that emphatically did *not* make for the history he would have *liked*, and he inserted his opinions into the narrative in separate value-judgement-laden sentences that are noticeable to the modern reader, but that he apparently felt 'necessary' for the charged secularist Yiddish cultural movement of the 1920s. These anti-religious-culture opinions are perhaps a flaw in his legacy (one that Borokhov meticulously avoided) but they do not interfere with the larger accomplishment. In fact, when prejudices of the day are factored in (or rather, factored out), Erik is the prime post-World War I fulfiller in Old Yiddish literature of Borokhov's dreamed-of new field of Yiddish studies (Borokhov 1913a: 18), just as Solomon A. Birnbaum, Zalmen Reyzen, Max Weinreich and others came to work in the linguistic branches of the new *Yídishe filológye (in Borokhóvishn zin)* — Yiddish philology in the Borokhovian sense — that encompasses all the disciplines of language, literature, folklore and more in a national(istic) spirit that constituted the 'academic wing' of the cultural-social-political Yiddishist movement. Considering the lack of centralized state support, and the myriad politics of the day, the accomplishments of Borokhov's posthumously but rapidly fulfilled dream in interbellum Eastern Europe are all the more astounding.

The flavour of Erik on these issues can be conveyed by a number of passages.

The sixteenth century was the golden epoch of the literatures of many European peoples. Especially in the awakening of literature in the national language, as a result of new turns in the Humanist movement, and even more so in the difficult social struggles in the century of Reformation. [...]

For a long time already Talmud and its commentaries had been dominant in Jewish learning: now, in Poland, Prophets and Hagiographa were not studied at all; *Khúmɔsh* [the Pentateuch/Five Books of Moses] itself was taught minimally; in teaching Talmud, the new *khilúkim* method [the further and further logical subdividing of points, often far from the original meaning or issue at stake] of Rabbi Jacob Pollak, where the Talmudic text is but a springboard for one's own wild and artificially concocted achievements and speculations, and the influence of the Polish Method [in Talmudic studies] carries over quickly into other Jewish areas, especially in Germany.

Literary creativity in Yiddish is in this [i.e. the sixteenth] century tied up with three major occurrences and alterations: with the hegemony of the Polish Jewish community, and as a result, the rise of a *Núsakh Poyln* ['Tradition of Poyln' = Jewish Poland, referring literally to the precise order of the prayerbook and by extension to other traditions that were becoming distinctly different from the Western Ashkenazic rite] *in literature* [emphasis added]; with the start of social differentiation between Jews in the German and, especially, the Polish lands, with which the blossoming of *Múser* [Jewish ethics, morals, traditions] and the first, still very primitive shoots of a societal and polemic literature in Yiddish; and finally, the impact of printing activity in the Yiddish language.

In the second half of the sixteenth century, Krakow [Lithuanian/ standard Yiddish *Krókɔ*, Polish dialect *Krúkɔ*] becomes the prime centre of publishing activity in the Yiddish language.

The Yiddish *shpílman*-type [or, for the sake of argument, read here: 'gentile-genre origin'] epic poetry went under due to an array of reasons. There was impact from those factors that brought about the demise of that genre in German literary life too. [...] It seems moreover that in Poland the Yiddish *shpílman* poetry never even caught on in the first place. It remained a plant that blossomed only on German soil. The gravedigger was the art of printing, which had in an extraordinary way democratized literature itself: massive circles of readers emerged, and it gradually became unnecessary to have a public reader, a reciter, people got used to reading for themselves, and in connection with this, prose won out. Rhymes and rhythmic technique are best appreciated during a recitation. When the recitations died out, people became progressively less interested in following the rhyme patterns. Poetry itself became more wooden from day to day, crude. *Poetry itself became prosaicised* [emphasis in original].

(Excerpts from Erik 1928: 207–8, 210, 220–1
[from the Yiddish])

The 'transitional' (perhaps 'transformational') rabbinic personality Erik cites is Rabbi Jacob Pollak, who would much later in the twentieth century, long after Erik's untimely death, become the symbol for the transition from west to east, from Ashkenaz I to Ashkenaz II for the great historian of the Yiddish *language*, Max Weinreich. On the very first pages of his monumental history of the language, of which an unabridged English translation first appeared in 2008, Weinreich lays out his two symbolic icons for the history of Yiddish:

> Ashkenaz I remained and even expanded in the course of the centuries, but the centre of gravity of Ashkenazic Jewry gradually moved from Central Europe to Eastern Europe. In the seventeenth and eighteenth centuries the centres of Ashkenazic Jewry were no longer Mainz, Worms, Regensburg, nor even Prague, but Cracow, Lublin, Brisk [Brest Litovsk], Vilna, and Mezhbizh [Mezhibozh]. And once again a towering personality as the symbol. Just as the figure of Rabeynu Gershom symbolizes the pioneers of Lóter [nascent Ashkenaz], so there stands by the threshold of Eastern Ashkenaz another great rabbinic scholar, Reb Yankev der Bal-khilúkim [Rabbi Jacob the master of *khilúkim*], and the shift in the centre of gravity expresses itself in the fact that around 1500 — the precise year is not known — Reb Yankev left Prague for Krakow. And there he became the great Rabbi Jacob Pollak.
>
> (Weinreich 1973: I, 5, 1980: 3–4, 2008: I, 3–4)

The German-born Jacob Pollak (±1460–1541) studied in Regensburg in Germany, in Western Ashkenaz. He married a woman from Krakow and moved east, first to Prague and then to Krakow, where he founded (arguably) the first major *yeshiva* in Eastern Ashkenaz. He was a strong personality who had various conflicts with authorities, but in the end was appointed chief rabbi of a large part of Poland by King Alexander in 1503. He went on to develop a now controversial Talmudic method of analysis that became associated with Poland (and against which Jewish Lithuania would later rebel; cf. Katz 2010: 90, 97–8). The 'Polish method' involved a kind of logical gymnastics that critics contend is more apt to be 'charming' or 'entertaining' than 'historically accurate' (or even prone to logic) in text analysis. Nevertheless, the method stimulated the growth of Talmudic study in Poland. As Max Weinreich so eloquently pointed out, Jacob's life symbolized the shift of Ashkenaz from a Germanic to a Slavic epicentre, just as Rabeynu Gershom, a half millennium earlier, symbolized the shift of Jewish legal authority from Babylonia in the Near East to the Germanic-speaking lands of central Europe.

There is moreover another potential analogy. Like Gershom, who formally banned polygamy, Yankev Polak caused a major European Jewish stir on an issue of women's laws, with one tremendous difference. Gershom had (as far as we know) faced little opposition to formalizing monogamy around the year 1000. But Jacob's ruling, on a matter affecting many young women of his time, caused a major conflict, all the more as he was ruling upon a case concerning a member of his own family. His wife's sister, while still a minor, had been contracted to marry an older man, a prominent Hungarian Talmudist who lived in Buda. But before she reached the Talmudic age of majority (12 for a girl [13 for a boy]), she exercised her Talmudic right of refusal. The plot thickened further in so far as she was 'given to the Talmudist' by her widowed mother (Jacob Pollak's mother-in-law), who later supported her refusal to proceed. Rabbi Jacob Pollak accepted the girl's refusal on the basis of ancient Talmudic law, and thus defied what had a half century earlier become Ashkenazic law in Germany, when Menachem of Merseburg abolished the right of a minor to back out of such an agreement. In other words, the upstart Jacob who had married a woman from Eastern Ashkenaz was defying the consensus of the Western Ashkenazic German rabbinate. Jacob considered the girl's erstwhile contract to marry null and void following her refusal, and he allowed her to marry someone else. The rabbis of Germany placed him under a ban (*khéyrəm, herem*), the harshest legal punishment open to rabbinic authority. The lines of the conflict largely followed the division between old (Western) and new (Eastern) Ashkenaz. The endeavour to end forced child marital commitment consolidated a growing east–west differentiation in the realms of culture, tradition, dialect and lifestyle.

Even this ostensibly unrelated 'symbological biography' can on the level of touch-and-feel impressionism illustrate the shift to a culture where *King Arthur*, though 'he' might 'survive for a time', has progressively less to say to the evolving Eastern European Jewry than some new twist on a classic interpretation of a famous passage in the ancient Hebrew or Aramaic literature. Erik found in the history of Yiddish literature the same cultural, temporal and geographic configuration that Weinreich would later find for the history of the Yiddish language and, more broadly, Ashkenazic civilization.

Changes in the east regarding the coterritorial culture

In *both* cases — the 'first half of Yiddish history in the (Germanic) West' and the 'second half of Yiddish history in the (Slavonic) East' — writings in Yiddish were potentially the cultural property of virtually all the Jewish population, most of whom, and all of whose women, were disenfranchised from serious study of the Hebrew and Aramaic texts of Ashkenazic High Culture. In other words, it was a kind of Yiddish power well and truly in both cases, but of a different ilk. In the Western Yiddish area in earlier centuries, it was manuscripts, and perhaps performances, largely of epic poetic renditions, whether of gentile-origin narratives or biblical or other Jewish texts. In the Eastern Yiddish area in later centuries, it was generally printed books increasingly focused on internal Jewish themes. Erik was right that the sixteenth century was a transition period between the two, because of the shift from Western to Eastern Ashkenaz and from gentile-origin literature and entertainment (we need not call it *shpílman* or, for that matter, any other kind of *man*...) to a uniquely Eastern European, East Ashkenazic setting. In this new setting, immersion in Jewish books, learning, law, lore and tradition becomes the be-all and end-all of most popular literature. There is a continuing love of stories, but they are usually modelled or remodelled to have a Jewish moral, in addition to Jewish motifs and characters.

The west to east shift, for which the essentially 'different Maxes' (Weinreich and Erik) of twentieth-century Yiddish scholarship found one and 'the same Jacob' (Reb Yankev Pollak), who moved his yeshiva eastward to Poland, is a shift between two very different kinds of Yiddish power. In Eastern Ashkenaz, as the reprints of the old knightly romances gradually go out of fashion from the late sixteenth century onward, a new Yiddish literature arises whose soul is in the depths of an Ashkenazic society that finds all its sustenance in 'very Jewish books' and has scant interest in the knights and duels of European epic works. The lack of a co-territorial German, linguistically-cognate-with-much-of-Yiddish, body of knightly literature naturally played a major role as well.

In other words, the spiritual trends of mainstream Ashkenazic Jewish culture became even more pronounced in the east, in Ashkenaz II, which became, so to speak, more Ashkenazic than Ashkenaz I ever could be.

There is moreover another point that is awkward for some moderns. While in the west, in the earlier period, whatever one may call it, there were obviously numerous Jewish women and men who looked *up* at least to the entertainment value of *Dukus Horant, King Arthur, Hildebrant, Ditrikh of Bern* and the other Yiddish favourites merrily taken from the outside with various degrees of reworking and de-Christianization. Whether it is called *shpílman* or reading or singing or reciting, it was an activity that Jews willingly adapted from their Christian neighbours, just as they adopted the narratives themselves and enjoyed the same pan-human pleasures of any audience enjoying a good story well presented in whatever genre. In Slavic Eastern Europe, the impact of local literary and narrative culture on the increasingly compact and intensive Jewish life hovered somewhat closer to nil, outside the influences of melodies and of course linguistic impact. There was a crucial difference in receptiveness to the local non-Jewish culture. The 'political incorrectness' here lies, at the end of the day, in coming clean about the differential in *respect*. There was more of it for the surrounding culture in the Germanic west than in the Slavic east, even in times when levels of tolerance were vastly higher in the east. Respect for tolerance (and the lack of religious persecution) is not the same as respect for the supposed superior sophistication of the majority culture of the host country. But the differential in regard for Germanic vs Slavic culture is in each case only one side of the coin. The other is the nature of the Jewish culture per se. When it is open, as it was in the earlier west, to knightly epics and scenes of blood and sensuality, it would have ipso facto been open to well-constructed works making literary use of these elements. When it is inherently relatively closed to non-Jewish narrative, there would ipso facto be more drive to create 'Jewish-Jewish' works in the vernacular. Added to the lack of familiarity with Slavonic literature of any kind, the death knell of secular thematics and form in Eastern Yiddish was for this period a natural consequence.

Shift of Yiddish power to the religious sphere

Erik's second major period in older Yiddish literature was *Di múser tkúfe* ('the Mussar period'). The Yiddish word *múser* is the expected reflex, by the usual sound laws, of classical Hebrew *mūser* (frequently attested in the construct state *mūsár-*). The most frequent modern English and European language transcriptions are *musar* and *mussar*. Its earliest biblical occurrence is in Deuteronomy, where King James and most subsequent translations have 'chastisement' in 'chastisement of the Lord' (Deuteronomy 11: 2). The word has a 'chastisement like' meaning in other passages in the Old Testament (e.g. Isaiah 53: 5). But at some points, it is rendered 'instruction', as in 'receive instruction' (Jeremiah 32: 33). The word established itself for all Jewish prosperity in Proverbs where it occurs about two dozen times, often apparently in the sense of '(moral) instruction' or '(ethical) instruction' or '(ethical) rebuke' or 'lesson-teaching'. These and similar meanings, found in the Hebrew Bible, continued to accrue to the word for millennia, and around a thousand years ago a literature got under way in the Sephardic (Iberian) and Italian centres of Jewish learning that has become known as Musar literature. It is a literature of entire books about ethics in daily life, moral living and living a properly good life, whether in relation to other people or to God. Early classics of the genre include Bahya ibn Paquda's *Obligations of the Hearts* (Muslim Spain, eleventh century), Jechiel ben Jukuthiel Anav's *Virtues of Good Traits* (Rome, later thirteenth century) and Jonah Girondi's *Book of The Fear of God* and *Gates of Repentance* (thirteenth-century Spain). In various times and places, there was a revival of the genre, written in Hebrew. For example, Moshe Chaim Luzzatto, an eighteenth-century Italian kabbalist, penned *Path of the Upright*, which became a classic of Musar literature.

Though itself potentially open to critique (as would be any 'interesting and indigenous-derived' term recycled for the classificatory convenience of moderns), Erik's term *múser* here, for the second major period in Yiddish literary history, *Di múser tkúfe* ('the Mussar period') never ran into *shpílman*-grade troubles. It is frankly easier to name a literary period that takes off *after* the rise of publishing in the language in question. Erik's name for this one could not be disparaged, if only because the word itself started appearing in the *titles* of printed Yiddish books at the very dawn of the age of Yiddish printing in Europe. It was no theoretical construct or functional appelation borrowed from outside the culture.

Some of the earliest printed Yiddish works had the word in their title. *Múser un hanhóge* ('Musar and Behaviour') appeared between 1535 and 1540, and is often thought of as either the second printed Yiddish book (Weinreich 1939a: 203) or the third (Rosenfeld 1988: 121). Printed by the Helitz brothers, like the other Krakow prints of the time, it is a Yiddish rendition of a Hebrew work ascribed to Asher ben Jechiel ('the Rosh'), who lived from around 1250 to 1327. That Hebrew work on ethics of life (including demands for uprightness in dealings with Jews and gentiles alike), was known by various names, usually ones that did not include the word *musar*, and the decision to put the word into the title of the Yiddish print makes it aptly portentous. The title page even notes that the author of the Hebrew original was the father of Jacob ben Asher (±1270–1340), the author of one of the most studied legal codes in Ashkenaz. He is widely known as *der Tur* ('the Tur'), after this work, *Arbe-túrim/Arbóo túrim* ('The Four Sections [or: Columns]'), which became the organizational structure for further codes based upon it, most famously the *Shúlkhon órukh* (Israeli: *Shulkhán arúkh*) of the sixteenth-century Spanish legalist, Joseph Karo.

The title page of *Múser un hanhóge* translates as follows:

> *Múser* and Behaviour. How a person should conduct oneself. It was
> written by the rabbi Rabéynu Ósher [Our Rabbi Asher], the memory
> of a saint be it for blessing, the father of Rabéynu Yánkev [Our Rabbi
> Jacob], who wrote the Four Turim. And whoever cannot under-
> stand everything in the Language of Holiness [or 'Holy Language' =
> Hebrew], has it here explained in *Taytsh* ['translation language' =
> Yiddish], so that everybody would know, what he should do and
> what he should beware of not to do. And also a fine *múser* [work]
> called *Kaaras késef* ['The Silver Bowl'] written by Rabbi Joseph of
> Parpreyne [now Perpignan, France], which he sent to his son, as it is
> written in his preface.
>
> (*Múser un hanhóge* ±1535–1540 [from the Yiddish])

From this title page of this second (or third) known printed Yiddish
book in 1530s Krakow, we see that the word *múser* had, by that time and
place, come to mean in (older) Yiddish 'a book about *musar*' (just as *tfíle*,
usually 'prayer', meant 'prayerbook' in Western Yiddish). Erik's choice
of name for a period of Yiddish literature was on the mark, all the more
so for the roughly half a century before a Yiddish literature *in its spirit*
would define a whole new period of Yiddish writing in Eastern Europe,
not just genre (the classic 'ethical treatise' would cyclically leave and re-
enter East European Jewish literary fashions), but by mood, ambience
and purpose of the work. But the Musar genre per se continued to be
prominent.

Just a few years later, in 1542, when Paul Fagius was the principal figure in Yiddish publishing, came the *Séyfer mídes* ('Book of Good Traits'),
discussed in Chapter 3 in connection with the rise of Yiddish publishing. Yiddish as well as Hebrew manuscripts of this work had been cir-
culating for some time. The book ends with a table of contents of its
27 chapters. They include: Humility, Love, Happiness, Worry, Second
Thoughts, Anger, Envy, Laziness, Meanness, Forgetfulness, Falsehood,
Truth. The final three are Gossip, Repentance, Torah.

Múser power

It was only in the waning years of the sixteenth century that '*múser*
power' really took off in Ashkenaz as a new Yiddish force that was
coming to be more and more publicly addressed to the male population too. Yiddish had by then expanded to include a hefty proportion

of male readers who could be proud to be seen owning and reading a book of sacred Jewish wisdom in the vernacular. The 1590s was a decade of major new publishing activity and one that subtly but noticeably began to usher in a shift from the presumed (but never really) exclusive female readership of certain Yiddish works to a more open and 'official' wish to have male as well as female readers. At first, the gender barrier could be breached only in the 'announced target readership' of a book's title page or introduction, not in most of the actual content. But none of this means that Ashkenazic men and women who were Yiddish readers necessarily started reading 'the same thing' all the time.

It is frankly much easier to establish the target audience of a *múser* work than of an epic or other work of belles lettres. That is because the subject matter has a lot to say about the addressee. One booklet from 1590 is really only for men, and the first great '*múser* encyclopaedia' which was brought out in 1602 was really only for women, despite ritual protestations of the authors to the contrary in both cases. With the advantage of retrospection, it is obvious that both were part of a new process of Yiddish expansion to serve also the literary needs of the majority of males who were not part of the 'Hebrew and Aramaic' elite, in some cases according to interest of each gender. In the realm of *múser*, the differences between men and women in Ashkenazic civilization is vast and unchallengeable. A book that was really only about women would intrinsically not do for a male audience (unlike, say, story books in which anyone can take pleasure). The process under way was toward a lifestyle literature in Yiddish that would cumulatively cater for everybody. That is not to say, by the way, that our sense of 'lifestyle' is remotely a synonym for *múser*. It is not, by far, not least because the current concept is founded in freedom of the individual and the older concept is founded on how the individual can live up to a set of standards in both everyday and religious life that is demanded by his or her God. But the analogy can be useful if the differences are not forgotten. It is a literature about how a person lives out the days of this life.

Earlier Yiddish publications of works on Jewish ethics, such as the *Séyfer mídes* ('Book of Good Traits'), and works on women's laws such as *Hanhóges nóshim* ('Conduct of Women'), had been among the very early Yiddish printed works of the 1540s. They had fulfilled the practical purpose of explaining what the classic sources say, whether about everyday life and ethics, or points of Jewish law which women need to know. There was not necessarily a concomitant attempt at creativity or the providing of literary pleasure in the vernacular, though the aesthetic calibre obviously depended also upon the translator, copyist or editor.

That changed at the end of the sixteenth century. Some claim that this was in part a conscious traditionalist 'response to *Ditrikh of Bern*' in the spirit of 'If you can't beat them, join them'. That no doubt played a role, especially at the level of publishing. Once the Yiddish publishers' genie was released, any and all were in it, as ever, to find new ways to inspire folks to purchase a newly released product.

However, as is often the case, the commercial trends that Erik traced so analytically were part of a wider cultural shift. The Yiddish power of the *King Arthur*s was sinking, though it would be centuries before the good king was forgotten altogether. In the late 1920s, Max Weinreich was able to report that 'Two hundred years ago, still, every Jewish person knew the name and if you wanted to say that someone is living it up, they'd say: Who is this fellow, whose house is like *King Arthur*'s court?' (Weinreich 1928a: 64).

As those collective memories of medieval knights and the literary recombinations of Bible, knightly duels and sensual love were fading, a new wave of creative Yiddish writing in a pious, traditionalist, God-fearing mood was coming into its own. It was inspired by deep feelings of pride and happiness with the traditional Ashkenazic Jewish heritage and all that that implies, a spirit that blossomed in Eastern Ashkenaz. In fact, the notion that one should feel fortunate at being born into this group is a point often brought home in this literature, which strives to help the reader achieve satisfaction with life, and the need to make the best and see the best. This literature progressed over the course of a few years, within the 1590s, from booklets of moral warning to huge 'encyclopaedias', organized by topic, in which the reader could look up the right thing to do in a sizable array of situations.

A 1590 booklet, *Sam kháyim*, obviously intended only for men, was written by Abraham Ashkenazi Ap(e)teker ('the pharmacist'). Apeteker lived in the 'deep' East, in Ludmir (now Vladimir Volynsk, western Ukraine). The booklet was published in the large Jewish 'border city' (of Western and Eastern Ashkenaz), Prague, in a bilingual Hebrew and Yiddish edition, with numerous awkward or forced rhymes which render parts of it less than comprehensible. This is a man who still thinks of rhyme as 'a necessary part of a Yiddish book' — but people who write Yiddish books can't do the old rhyme form anymore; moreover, it is hardly suited to a book of moral critique and observation. Erik, come to think of it, would

Image 6.1 Abraham Apeteker's 1590 *Sam kháyim* ('The Elixir of Life'). From the illustrations chosen for the title page (which would not have amused the rabbis in town) and the male-centric content, it is obvious that this was a book intended specifically for men
Source: Image courtesy of the Bodleian Libraries, University of Oxford.

not have done too badly to call his two periods of Old Yiddish literature Poetry and Prose.

This book's name, *Sam Kháyim*, can translate as 'Medicine that Heals' or simply 'Elixir of Life'. In either case, the author meant to take a pharmaceutical image from his trade and apply it to the moral sphere of daily life. And, like many of the Yiddish authors and publishers of the day, he saw himself as part of a movement of the times that stressed vernacular language and the new liberating force of the printed book. He states the view (here quoted from the Hebrew text) that whoever doesn't *really* understand Hebrew well:

> should look at books printed in Yiddish [*loshn Ashkenaz*, 'language of Ashkenaz'] or in *any* language that he understands, even a non-Jewish language. And it is for that reason that the opportunity is given for things to be printed in every language.
>
> (Apeteker 1590 [from the Hebrew])

For the late sixteenth century, this was a daring pro-Yiddish and pro-everyday-people-power sentiment. The author identifies Yiddish not with women but with people generally and avoids using such stock phrases as 'women and men who cannot learn' and similar formulas that provided Yiddish authors and publishers of the period with an 'excuse' to publish in the vernacular. For him, knowledge of the right thing to do, whether in medical or spiritual spheres, goes hand in hand with what can only be called social protest, terminological anachronism notwithstanding, against community leaders he accused of being more interested in their own wealth than in the people they should be serving. Apeteker explains what is required to be a member of the community leadership: 'to treat the members of the community as they would treat their own children' and not to 'show off power' over others. The book's appeal was limited by the author's clumsy rhymes in a genre that calls for prose, its poor typography and its concentration on the ethics of formal community leadership rather than the broad readership of the wider Yiddish audience. That it is principally a book for men is itself innovative for a Yiddish book of the time. It even discusses a number of male-specific issues such as behaviour of rabbis, of students in a *yeshiva* (traditional Talmudic academy), cautioning, for example, that students of the *yeshiva* should not be in carnival Purim-like mode the whole term, and admonishing them not to 'run after girls all the time'. There is an almost modern ring.

A *Mirror of Fire*

The next rung in the chain was the first major '*múser* encyclopaedia'. It was called the *Bránt shpigl* (*Mirror of Fire*). No one knows exactly when it first appeared because not a single copy has yet been found of the first edition. The earliest surviving print is Basel 1602. The *Bránt shpigl* was written by Moyshe Henoch Yerushalmi Altshuler, a scion of the famous Altshuler family that had spread out from Prague to many parts of Ashkenaz. The book has 76 chapters and around 470 pages. Much of the early parts are meant specifically for women, while most of the later chapters are ostensibly for everybody, though this is not wholly consistent. The title page addresses the book to 'men, women and girls', promising 'eternal life in Paradise, full of joy' as well as a long and good life 'also in this world'. Here is a paraphrased translation of the titles (or, occasionally, the first lines) of a sampling of the chapters. Although there is no subdivision of sections by gender, it is clear that some chapters in this tome are for women, others for everybody.

3. Why the book is written in Yiddish.
6. Why good people are considered wise (and the evil – fools).
7. The good wife and the bad wife.
8. The good that comes from the good wife, and the evil from the bad.
11. When an upright man has an evil wife, and an evil man a pious wife.
12. How women's talk can bring eternal life.
14. How a woman uses wisdom to influence her husband for good.
15. The commandments which women must carry out.
18. How to treat people who work in your house.
21. One should not be a too frequent visitor in a friend's house.
23. One should not hold oneself high to other people.
26. One should not be desirous of wealth.
27. One should say 'It's for the best!' no matter what happens.
28. One should not yell at or complain to God.
30. To give charity and *how* to give it.
31. The wonderful deed of inviting guests.
33. Relationship with one's father and mother.
35. How a woman should act during her period.
37. Lighting candles Friday evening for the Sabbath.
38. How husband and wife must keep a clean bed.
39. A wife should wake up her husband before daybreak [for his prayers].
43. How to conduct oneself at the table.
44. Not to make parties and celebrations on weekdays.
46. Bringing up children to come to good things.
47. All dishes and vessels must be washed and blessed.
50. One should not envy anybody for anything.
54. Do not make fun of anybody.

55. Not to gossip.
56. Not to tell a lie.
58. Not to slur or curse.
59. A woman may not wear men's clothing.
66. To have honest measures and scales.
68. One should not practise magic.
69. How to repent.
74. To visit people who are sick and do good for them.
75. One should accompany a deceased to the grave.
76. Bringing comfort to those who are mourning.

Image 6.2   Bránt shpigl ('Fire Mirror'), Prague, 1602
Source: Image courtesy of the Bodleian Libraries, University of Oxford.

Several points are nevertheless important for the story of Yiddish. The author did his best to be entertaining and make the material pleasurable to read. And whether he succeeded or not, he set out to write a book that would be for men too, even if such devices as (to some extent) 'scattering the woman-specific chapters' do not always succeed in looking natural. Finally, it is important that he wrote and published a large-scale work in Yiddish without directly translating the bulk of it from a pre-existing book in Hebrew. For all its faults, this is a book that became a link in a historically significant chain of events in the development of an Eastern European Yiddish language-fuelled empowerment of a majority of the population.

To understand how the role of Yiddish was being grasped around 1600, it is worth citing some of the content of the *Bránt shpigl*'s chapter 3, which, in everlasting publishing-war tradition, cites by name its prime competitor, the *Séyfer mídes* ('Book of Good Traits'), which had been around in Yiddish printed editions for some 60 years at least. The stock phrase about 'the women and the men who are like women and cannot study' was by then so much a part of the Yiddish preface that it would have been missed had it been absent.

This book was written in Yiddish for the women and the men who are like women and cannot study [the sacred texts] very much. And when Sabbath and holidays come around, they should be able to read and understand what they are reading. Other sacred books are in Hebrew, and write about convoluted Talmudic arguments which they cannot understand. Notwithstanding that there are many fine Books of Good Traits in Yiddish, they do not tell about all the good things in the World to Come, or about the punishments of Hell. Only the great masters of Kabbalah study and write about that. And that is not very easy for everyone to understand. Therefore I have written this book for women and men who cannot really read the sacred books in Hebrew or even the sermons that are preached every Sabbath. I have felt pity and write in Yiddish so that they may thereby know what a person is and why people were created, and how it is better to be among the people of Israel than other nations. And what the reward is for being in awe of God, blessed be He, and serving him with love. And if people will read this book seriously and will keep to what it says, then I will afterwards write about the attributes of the World to Come. As much as I know.

And whoever didn't know anything before will know more than before. Moreover, I have learned from the Torah that God, blessed be

He, said to our teacher Moses: 'Thus shall you say to the House of Jacob, and tell the Children of Israel' [Exodus 19: 3]. Our sages have interpreted in the *Mekhílto* that 'House of Jacob' refers to the women, and 'Children of Israel' to the men. In other words, it was told to the women first and only afterwards to the men. The *Médresh* [homiletic text, referring to the aforementioned work, Israeli *midrásh*] asks further: With what did the women merit that Moses should not convey God's Word to the men first of all? Because it is they who win over children to the study of the Torah, bring them to the teacher and take care of the children and speak God's Word to them and awaken in their hearts the happiness of studying, and of fulfilling the commandments [...]. It says in the Tractate 'The Suspected Woman' [in the Babylonian Talmud] that Rabbi Avohu and Rabbi Chiya bar Abba turned up in a certain city and gave talks. Rabbi Chiya spoke purely about laws. And Rabbi Avohu spoke purely about legends, beautiful stories. And the people listening to Rabbi Chiya went to Rabbi Avohu and listened attentively to his talk. This made Rabbi Chiya feel badly. Rabbi Avohu told him: 'I will tell you a parable. Two people came to a certain town. One of them sold needles. And the other, precious stones. More people came to the one selling needles than the one selling precious stones. And you come and give a talk purely on law, when not everyone can understand it. But in my talk I bring the legends and beautiful stories which everyone can understand, so they come to me' [paraphrased from 40a of the tractate].

(Altshuler 1602, chapter 3 [from the Yiddish])

7
Women (and Men) of Eastern Ashkenaz

The *Good Heart*

Bránt shpigl was popular for a time but it was displaced a generation later by a better book crafted more artfully for a wider readership and 'more proudly in Yiddish'. It was the next step in the progressive story of Yiddish empowerment, specific to the ever more inward-Jewish-looking East (Ashkenaz II, in the Slavonic and Baltic lands of Eastern Europe). That new book was the *Lev tov* (*Good Heart*) that appeared in Prague in 1620 and many times thereafter. In addition to being in many ways more sophisticated (and discernibly less patronizing), it was acclaimed by a number of great rabbis and scholars who would for many years go on to recommend it for women and for men who 'could not study' the sacred texts in the original. It too was not a work of any remarkable originality (at least not in our modern sense, though there is a relativity to originality, not least, as understood by the time, place and people in question rather than by 'us'). It owed much to a Hebrew work on ethics that had first appeared in Constantinople in 1537. The author of the Yiddish *Lev tov*, Isaac ben Elyokum of Posen, did not attempt to hide this, and enjoys beginning chapters with a credit to his source. This is a milieu where the accomplishment of translation into the vernacular and novel compilation and production in themselves constituted an 'original thing' for the time, place and readers in question.

As usual, the title page includes a rhymed commendation for the book, one that is particularly illuminating and helps us better grasp the Ashkenazic mindset of the time, now into the first quarter of the seventeenth century. The words 'all men and women' and 'all who are made by the Creator' reflect a kind of 'creeping universalism' that was becoming incrementally characteristic of evolving East Ashkenaz.

The Book of The Good Heart. All you men and women, and all who are made by the Creator, who want to build This World and The Other World for themselves, come and look at this beautiful book. Anybody who reads it through will not regret it. The reader will find in it all of *Yídishkayt* [traditional Judaism], in its length and its breadth, easily understood and well explained, spread over twenty chapters. Whoever reads through it, not forgetfully but taking it all in, will be wholeheartedly happy, and rejoice with gentility, and will be able to hold one's own in a discussion among scholars. But at the outset, I wish to let you know that knowledge and reading are not the main point. It is a question of keeping these things and performing! The book captivates whatever kind of person may read it. How a person can adhere to all the laws, from birth to old age, and all kinds of behaviour in all their forms. Don't miss the opportunity to buy it cheaply now. And, it is printed with fine paper and ink. That could be seen even by someone who is half blind. Take it for yourself, your wife, and your children. And whoever doesn't pay for it properly would be sinning. With it, you will achieve the World to Come, you and all your daughters and sons, whom you will begat in all the generations. Great honour and wealth will never again run away from you, and you will bid farewell to this place in fine old age. Amen.

(Isaac ben Elyokum of Posen 1620, preface
[from the Yiddish])

Lev tov is a lifestyle book that women and men can enjoy equally. Some of the chapter headings are shortened or paraphrased for brevity in the translation that follows:

1. Everything that God created he created for His honour [Higher purposes of life].
2. Laws of prayer.
3. Laws of repentance.
4. Laws of charity.
5. Laws of good conduct [respect to others].
6. Laws of Sabbath.
7. Laws of humility.
8. Laws of honouring father and mother.
9. Laws of raising children.
10. Laws of marriage to a wife [laws of sex].
11. Laws of studying Torah.

12. Laws of business.
13. Laws of just judgement.
14. Laws of love of friends and charitable deeds.
15. The issues of anger and rage.
16. Laws of gossip and bad language.
17. The topics flattery, mockery and lies.
18. Don't reveal the secrets of your friend.
19. Be happy with what you have.
20. Laws of keeping the commandments.

Image 7.1   Title page of the *Lev tov* ('Good Heart'), Prague, 1620
Source: Image courtesy of the Bodleian Libraries, University of Oxford.

The book's charms include its interweaving of Hebrew and Aramaic bits and pieces to give the flavour of the totality of traditional Ashkenazic civilization. In the table of contents, the names of the chapters are all in down-to-earth Yiddish. In the book itself, they are briefer and more formal, in many cases starting with the word *hílkhəs* ('Laws of' in the old construct state, the Semitic answer to genitive; Ashkenazic *hilkhoys*, Israeli *hilkhót*), a form known to Talmudic students from various codes of law most typically as the start of a section name followed by the name of the topic. The author begins those chapters with a Jewish legal basis with the term, and most of the others with a common word for 'topic'. The book became so popular that it may well have contributed to *hílkhes* entering Yiddish in a wider and humorous sense as 'laws of' juxtaposed with a non-legal issue (as in 'he's really good in the laws of bragging'). And many of the book's chapters conclude with the Aramaic phrase *slíko pírko*, meaning 'end of the chapter'. This is a Yiddish book for men and women that gives the Yiddish reading public, in other words the vast majority of the Ashkenazic population, the feeling that they too can be learned in the major points of law and wisdom of thousands of years of Hebrew and Aramaic texts, the flavour of which is transmitted by these retained short formulas in a work published in Yiddish.

It is important not to anachronize. There was no attempt here to change the roles of men and women, or of Hebrew, Aramaic and Yiddish for that matter, but rather to raise the level of Jewish knowledge of both genders. Where *Bránt shpigl* concentrated in some places on women pleasing their husbands, *Lev tov* is a two-way street, demonstrating how the popularization of Yiddish books, thanks to the spread of printing, was nevertheless affecting attitudes about some gender issues. Now husbands and wives could both read about the respect they owe each other, in their own language, from the same book. The *Lev tov* even touches upon that 'untouchable' family subject: domestic violence. A man who raises his hand as if to hit his wife, even if he does not actually touch her, is considered to be an evil person. He may not be called to say a blessing on Sabbath for the reading of the Torah, and his signature in business documents is null and void until he has properly repented. A husband who forces the sexual act upon his wife when she is not willing, is cursed. Although various ancient platitudes about wives and husbands are repeated, Isaac ben Elyokum of Posen adds that a wife should be as a servant-maid to her husband, *and* a husband as a man-servant to his wife. It does not get more egalitarian than this in the traditional Orthodox environment. This sentence could simply not have occurred in a normative Hebrew or Aramaic text of the time. Anachronism-phobia to one side, this is verily an attested case of literature in the vernacular (Yiddish) coming some modest way closer to the thought of gender equality (by whatever name it is to be called) than would be possible in the two high-prestige languages that were the domain of small circles of highly educated males but whose authority and prestige commanded the respect of virtually all.

This was the Yiddish counter-reformation following the period of knights and duels and secular romances: Yiddish power for empowerment of everyday women and men *within* the largely self-contained world of Eastern Ashkenazic Jewry. The status of 'insularity' results from the group's minority status and its relative separateness from many aspects of the majority's life and culture; of course, from the Jewish Ashkenazic point of view, the majority Christian population would have seemed 'insular'. In the chapter on finding a wife, the *Lev tov* warns against marriage for either beauty or money. The themes of (and for this time and place, inevitable excitement of the novelty of) male–female relations recur, revealing a sprightly 'Yiddish counterspirit' to a male-dominated traditional Near Eastern civilization long ago transplanted to the heart of Europe where it embarked on a new, long and winding European road.

The Yiddish *Women's Bible*

The *Women's Bible* became the Yiddish bestseller of all time. Well over 300 editions have appeared, but nobody knows how many exactly (despite being written in the early 1960s, and concentrating on the period 1786–1850, Shmeruk 1964 remains the best work to date on 'chasing the editions' and is a model of scholarly thoroughness). This *Women's Bible* is a Yiddish elaboration and paraphrase of the 'Ashkenazic canon' parts of the Hebrew Bible — the Five Books of Moses (the *Khúmesh* or Pentateuch); the weekly Prophets readings (haftorahs or Haftaroth, Yiddish *di haftóyres*) and the Five Scrolls. It was compiled by one Jacob ben Isaac Ashkenazi of Yanov. No one is sure which of the many East European towns called Yanov (or Yanova, Jonava, etc.) this is, and the location itself became a source of mystique, an emblematic East European *shtetl*, perhaps for the first time ever in the emerging self-consciousness of *Eastern* Ashkenaz that was in the process of a centuries-long incubation. In modern times, Yiddish humourist Sholem Aleichem's (1859–1916) mythical shtetl *Kasrílevke* has played that role for modern Yiddish culture.

For the book's title, the author followed tradition and found an alluring title in the eternal source for such things, the Bible. He took the Hebrew feminine imperative plural for 'Come out and see!' from a passage in the *Song of Songs*: 'Come out and see King Solomon upon the crown O ye daughters of Zion [...]' (*Song of Songs* 3: 11). In evolved (and in this case remorphologized for use as a single noun book title) Yiddishized pronunciation, these Biblical words, *ṣǝʔέnɔ ūrǝʔέnɔ* (modern Hebrew *tseéna ureéna*) became 'the *Tsèneréne*' ([*cɛnǝrέnǝ*]), a copy of which became the traditional Ashkenazic woman's 'specific' precious possession for centuries to come. And it continues to be reprinted today in contemporary Haredi communities. The first three editions, starting probably in the 1590s, were 'read to pieces' and not a trace remains (notwithstanding some contemporary scholars' refusal to accept that such things happened — at least until the next time a discovery of an unknown edition is made). The oldest surviving edition, from 1622, states explicitly that the first three editions, one printed in Lublin and two in Krakow, were by then totally unavailable.

Instead of 'just translating' those principal parts of the Bible, the author interlaced his narrative with material from midrashic sources and diverse later commentaries. The result was decidedly not a partial (that is, Ashkenazic canon) Bible translation, such as those that had been appearing in print from the 1540s onward, but a new work that told the stories of the Bible in the way they had been interpreted, extrapolated, expanded upon and taught by generations of rabbinic scholars and commentators. In a spirit in which the canon had been taught to so many usually male pupils, it gave many commentaries to women, of the type that learned men revelled in elaborating on and regaling each other with especially at Sabbath and festive meals and services. In a sense, the whole male world of the majority of Ashkenazic males was in one fell swoop opened to the Jewish women of Ashkenaz.

The compiler of the *Tseneréne* dispensed with giving the sources on site, thereby maintaining the 'synchronic' and readily enjoyable continuity of story telling. More learned people could in any case immediately look up any source in one of the original Hebrew editions of scripture with commentaries. The non-academic or even counter-academic format comprised the weaving of a continuous and contiguous narrative without the 'academic disturbance of footnotes in one sense or another'. The millennia of interpretation could now be woven into the narrative seamlessly, and merge into the biblical bare-bones template. The *Tsèneréne* stands on its own, without a cumbersome bibliographic apparatus of cross-references and abbreviations, with which 'male' Jewish literature floweth over.

Image 7.2   Title page of the Basel 1622 edition of the *Tsèneréne*
Source: Rostock University Library, courtesy of Dr Hermann Suess.

Here, to give its flavour, is the first section of Genesis from the *Tsèneréne*. As in the case of the classic commentaries in Hebrew, each section starts with (or includes) 'catchphrases' from the original, highlighted typographically in the original (here *italicized* for contrast), which provide a constant link to the original Hebrew text of the Jewish Bible.

In the beginning God created the heaven and the earth. In the first creation of the heaven and the earth, *the earth was without form and void,* and the throne of honour of God hovered in the air over the water.

And why does the Torah start with the [second] letter of the Jewish alphabet *beyz* [first letter of *Bréyshis*, 'In the beginning']? Because it is the first letter of the word *brókhe* ['blessing']. Therefore the Holy One, blessed be He, started with 'b'. But then [the first letter of the Jewish alphabet] *alef* came flying before God and said: 'No! Start the Torah with me, I am the first letter of the alphabet!' But God answered her and said: 'On Mount Sinai I will give the Ten Commandments, and there I will start with the letter *álef, Onóykhi adoyshém eloyhékho'* ['I am the Lord thy God,' Exodus 20: 2; Deuteronomy 5: 6]. So that is why the Torah starts with the word *bréyshis*, to teach us that the world was created for the sake of the [giving of the] Torah, and it is called 'beginning of His way' [after Proverbs 8: 22, 'God made me as the beginning of His way, the first of his works of old']. Rabbi Isaac says: But why did the Torah write about how God created the world? The Torah is after all the book of commandments, and should have started only with the commandments. But when the Seven Nations [who had earlier lived in the Land of Canaan] would thereafter say to the Children of Israel: 'You are thieves, for you are taking the Land of Israel away from us,' the Children of Israel will answer them: 'God created the world, and gave this land first to you, and now he wants to give it to us.' Our sages said: For three things God created the world: for the sake of the Torah, which is called 'the beginning [*réyshis*] of His way', for the sake of the sacrifices, which were brought in the Sacred Temple [in Jerusalem], which is called *réyshis* because it was created before the world, and for the sake of the tithes for the poor, which are called *réyshis* in the phrase ['the first fruits of your corn', Deuteronomy 18: 4], and because the Torah refers here to the Temple, showing how the Sacred Temple will be destroyed, this by the words *the earth was without form and void* meaning that 'The earth will become without form, when the presence of God will turn away from us, making way for the destruction of the Temple.' And therefore it says *and the spirit of God hovered upon the face of the waters*, showing us that even when we will be in exile the Torah will not be taken away from us, and that is also why it says: 'And God said, Let there be light', showing us that after the Exile will be over, God will bring light to us and send us *Moshíakh* [Messiah, used in Yiddish as a personal name, hence no definite article], for it is written 'Arise and shine, for your light is come' (Isaiah 60: 1). This means: Get up and bring light upon us, for your light has come. *And God said let there be light and there was light.* The Holy One, blessed be He, created two lights, the sun and the moon, to bring light to the world.

And yet another [third] light was created by God for the righteous, when Messiah will come. That light is enormously great. But because the world did not merit such a great light, God kept it especially hidden for good people.

(Jacob ben Isaac of Yanova 1622: Genesis 1 [from the Yiddish])

The text is supra-temporal, ranging through this civilization's clearly fixed and (internally) uncontroversial Beginning of Time to its (internally) uncontroversial messianic End of Days; from quasi-Kabbalistic homiletics about the letters of the Jewish alphabet, and the ancient temple in Jerusalem to the contemporary Jewish situation of exile, and the study of Torah as everlasting consolation. The *Tsèneréne* seamlessly interweaves thousands of years of Jewish texts and ideas in simple everyday Yiddish, without all the cross-references and without the original Hebrew or Aramaic beyond catchwords and lines from the original to provide the anchor and the gravitas. The prestige of the ancient language is as high as ever, even as it is bypassed on the cognitive level by the vernacular. What is hard to fathom for some moderns is that the level of literary excitement here would be, in Eastern Ashkenaz at any rate, greater than in any gentile-origin knightly romance, no matter how gripping the tale. This was a book Jewish women (and some men) loved to read and re-read. To put it differently, the empowerment of simple people via Yiddish shifted from knowledge of knightly epics in the Ashkenazic West to knowledge of the Jewish sources and commentaries on the Torah in the Ashkenazic East.

Moreover, it followed the Jewish weekly cycle of Torah reading with the accompanying set weekly readings from the Prophets, and included the Five Scrolls read in the synagogue during specific Jewish holidays. And that has something to say about why those two complete literal Amsterdam Bible translations, folio editions of the entire Old Testament in Yiddish, by competing publishers in Amsterdam in the late 1670s, were ultimately abject failures (see Katz 2007: 144). Quite a statement, that is, actually: two complete Jewish Bibles in the Yiddish language were the ultimate publishing failures in the Yiddish-speaking civilization of Ashkenaz.

The *Tsèneréne* brought the level of Jewish knowledge up to the status held by many men of middling education: those who had learned to study the Bible and some commentaries as boys in the *khéyder* but didn't go on to the more difficult texts. But to do so in the original meant constantly shifting one's eye from the text to this commentary and to that and back. The *Tsèneréne* is an anthology. It includes what its author chose to include and leaves out what he chose to leave out. The few paragraphs cited derive from the original Pentateuch passages, citations from the rest of the Hebrew Bible, Midrashic and Talmudic literature, and bits and pieces from the commentaries of the Ashkenazic commentator Rashi (1040–1105), the Sephardic Bahya ben Asher of the thirteenth century and others.

The author Jacob ben Joseph of Yanov followed up with a similar compilation on the Prophets and Hagiographa. Again, its name is rich in historic allusion. He called it *Séyfer ha-mágid*, which literally means 'the book that tells' or 'book of the messenger', 'book for the messenger', or by even further extension (all within Ashkenazic thinking and the typical interaction of its Jewish languages in the Ashkenazi mind) 'handbook for a preacher or speaker'. There might be memory of, for example, 'the messenger (the *mágid*, ancient Hebrew *maggîð*) came to David, saying ...' (II Samuel 15: 13). In Ashkenazic society, the *mágid* himself was often a travelling preacher who would deliver a talk in precisely this spirit, interweaving many Jewish sources in a continuous narrative in a style and with a charisma that delighted his audiences. And now, Jacob ben Joseph turned the genre from an oral discourse by a learned man into a second 'Bible tome' for women. Unlike the *Tsèneréne*, it was published together with the original Hebrew and Rashi's commentary and is therefore more of a teacher's handbook than a popular tome. And like many second works by the author of a masterpiece, nothing that author would write could ever compare to the first.

Jacob ben Joseph of Yanov has been called the linguistic Martin Luther of Yiddish, though he didn't have the slightest interest in innovating anything in religious belief. He used the vernacular of his people and the Bible and raised the stature of the vernacular to bring serious knowledge to anyone who could read their native language. Going well beyond Luther's actual Bible translation (albeit only for the books that constituted the Ashkenazic canon), Jacob ben Joseph of Yanov created a synthesis of thousands of years of commentaries and works of the kind that could previously be made in an ad-hoc oral way by teachers and preachers, but was now all there in an easy-to-read printed book, all in the vernacular.

By the end of the sixteenth century, publishing a special work for women, and in Yiddish, and in Eastern Europe, was something that could be trumpeted with pride, rather than with the older apologetics about a book being for those who 'couldn't' (as in couldn't deal with the sacred-language originals).

The *Story Book*

The new 'eastern' style Yiddish empowerment was to get its very own consolidated story book. This was part of a wider series of steps that signalled not only a gradual changeover from external to internal, and from secular to religious, with respect to the nature of the raw material for literature, but also a concomitant genre changeover from predominant rhymed epic (poetry) to predominant narrative (prose) as the centrepiece of popular genre.

Although a number of the stories that were becoming more popular had non-Jewish origins, the overall result of their reworking was nevertheless more works with a profoundly Jewish focus. The three main areas are the past, the very internal life of the Jewish present, and the messianic future, in other words 'vertical'. There is very little that is 'horizontal', in the sense of looking beyond the Jewish world to the wider society around it. The new ambience in this later more Eastern-Ashkenaz-centred period is one of the internal Jewish, not one of trying to enjoy what the larger, external, non-Jewish world was reading. This new ambience emphasized the empowering of women (bearing in mind a baseline that still excluded them from Hebrew and Aramaic literature). It also seems plausible that the Slavic and Baltic milieus provided much less in the way of literary works for 'Jewish reworking' than had been the case in the German language environment earlier on. Much of the non-Jewish cultural impact in the east came by the way of folk tunes and the like, not works of literature.

From the early days of the earlier Western Ashkenaz, stories had circulated about the most beloved personalities of the new Jewish civilization coming into their own in central Europe, both orally and in (largely lost) written traditions. Among them were tales about such early Ashkenazic pioneers as Rabeynu Gershom (±960–1028), Rashi (1040–105) and, above all, the real-yet-semi-mythical personalities at the centre of the 'Pious of Ashkenaz' (Khasidey/Hasidei Ashkenaz) movement. They thereby joined a kind of pantheon starting, no more and no less, with Adam and Eve, about whom stories had long been assembled in the midrashic and later literature from the ancient Near East's Talmudic period in the early centuries of the common era. As ever, there are parallels in Western Ashkenaz with European Christendom. In this case there was a Late Latin analogue to the earlier Yiddish *máyse* (the Yiddish word for 'story', derived from the Jewish Aramaic sense of the prior biblical word *maʕăśé* that originally meant 'work' or 'deed' or 'doing', from the root for 'to do'). That was the Christian *exemplum*, a short tale used by a preacher to illustrate a point, or very frequently to illustrate model behaviour by telling about the life of a saint. *Gesta Romanorum* ('Deeds of the Romans') was one popular compilation that preachers could use to inspire their congregations, and which writers could use as raw material on which to expand (see Meitlis 1958).

By the late sixteenth century, the indigenous Ashkenazic tradition of stories had long been amalgamating into a book in the hands of generations of anonymous compilers. In the age of publishing this was to become part of the traditionalist literary response to the secular books, in other words part of the rise of traditionalist Yiddish literature that is intended to satisfy readers, rather than just to inform them. It was, like the *Tsèneréne*, meant to be pleasurable rather than purely didactic. The oldest known edition dates to 1602, published in Basel under the title *Máyse bukh* (*Story Book*). It was put together by Jacob ben Abraham of Mezritsh, also known as Yankev Polak, or Jacob of Poland, not to be confused with the similarly named Rabbi Jacob Pollak of a century earlier (see Chapter 6).

The 'Story Book' comprises three major threads. The first consists of tales from Jewish antiquity, mostly stories from Talmudic and Midrashic literature that the compiler adopted from *Eyn-Yánkəv* (*Ein Yaakov*), an anthology of legends from the Talmud that was put together by the Sephardic scholar Jacob Ibn Habib (after the expulsions from Spain and Portugal he had settled in Salonika, Greece; he died around 1516). The second part of the Yiddish work is drawn from the legends and stories around the father-and-son team at the centre of the 'Khasidey Ashkenaz' or Pious of Ashkenaz movement, Shmúel ben Kalonymus, the Khósid, of Speyer (twelfth century), and his son Yehúde, son of Shmúel the Khósid, of Regensburg (±1150–1217). The final part comprises a wide variety of tales drawn from far and wide, including adapted non-Jewish sources. Literary scholars have found that a number of beloved tales from the days of rhymed epics about gentile knights somehow made their way into the *Story Book*, but thoroughly Judaicized and transformed into the genre of the short-short story or little tale-with-a-moral, in sharp contrast to the long, rhymed, epic Yiddish versions of *King Arthur* or *Bovo of Antona*, which revelled in length, rhyme, performance and focused mostly on non-Jewish personalities, personalities who could be some kind of entertaining, popular figures from tales in older Western Ashkenaz. That was a glitter mostly outworn in new Eastern Ashkenaz which was focused on the 'Jewish hero' who was the master scholar or saintly personality or both. One thing is for certain: he was not a man of swords, spears and duels over damsels.

Here are three translated and lightly edited samples taken from three different parts of the *Story Book*, chosen for their diversity of origin:

(1) A Conversation Between Two Spirits

[Based on a story in the Babylonian Talmud (Tractate Blessings, 18b). In the Yiddish *Story Book* (No. 102 in the 1602 edition) it is adopted to provide a purposely ambiguous ending.]

This is a story that took place with a pious fellow who once gave a golden coin to a poor person, before the New Year, out of a sense of obligation to fulfil the commandments, in a year in which the prices were very high. His wife therefore got very angry at him, and he was afraid to go home. So he went and spent the night at the cemetery.

At night he heard two spirits of girls speaking to each other: 'Come, let's float around over the worlds and listen in behind that curtain, and find out from God (blessed be He) what kind of year this coming year will be.' The other one answered: 'I can't join you, because I am buried in a shroud made of reeds. You go ahead, and tell me later about everything you hear!' So she went herself and after a while returned to tell her friend: 'I heard that whoever will plant grain *before* the middle of the month Markhéshvon [coinciding with parts of October/November] will have it all spoiled by a hail.' When the religious fellow who went to spend the night at the cemetery heard this, he made a point of planting his seeds after the middle of that month. And then when a hail came and spoiled all the grain that had been planted up to the middle of Markhéshvon, this righteous man's grain that he had planted after the middle of the month survived.

A year later the pious fellow went again to spend a night at the cemetery, hoping again to overhear what the spirits were saying to each other. All of a sudden he heard one of the spirits saying to the other: 'Come on, let's go out and find out what will happen in the world this year!' The other spirit answered her: 'Didn't I tell you already that I can't move from this spot, because I'm tied up in a shroud of reeds? You go yourself, and you'll tell me what you hear.' To make a long story short, she went on her own, and came back after a while and said: 'I heard that whoever plants their grain *after* the middle of Markhéshvon will have it all spoiled by hail.' Once again, the pious fellow went home knowing what he had to do. He planted his field before the middle of the month. Again, hail beat the life out of the grains planted after the middle of the month. But it didn't do the pious fellow any harm, because he had planted his own before the middle of that month.

His wife found it surprising and said: 'How does it happen, my dear one, that the whole world has bad luck with crops and you don't?' He explained to her that it's not all that simple. So, he tells her the whole story, what happened to him, how he listened in on what the two spirits were saying to each other, mentioning that one of the deceased couldn't move from the spot because she was stuck deep in a shroud of reeds.

Not long after that, it so happened that the wife of the pious fellow had an argument with the mother of that girl, the one who had been buried in a shroud of reeds, as sometimes happens with women. And the wife of the pious fellow told the woman off. 'Just look how your daughter was buried in a shroud of reeds!'

The third year, the religious man went to the cemetery once again, to hear what the two spirits were saying to each other. He heard, again, one girl saying to the other: 'Come on, let's go out and hear what will happen this year!'

And the other one answered: 'Forget it! The secret came out. People were listening in to our conversation.'

(2) Torah Secrets and Shortcuts

[This is from the middle to early Ashkenaz-based part of the *Book of Stories* (No. 173 in the 1602 edition). There were many legends about Amram of Mainz, and some comparative literature scholars see a tradition parallel to the Christian figure of St Emmeram of Regensburg, the seventh-century martyr (with impetus from the similarity in the names, too). This tale is about Amram's son Eliezer.]

Now here's a story. In the city of Mainz there was once upon a time a very good person called Reb [rabbi] Amram, and he had a son called Reb Eliezer. Before he died, Reb Amram left a will, in which he forbade his son to ever cross the River Danube.

But Reb Eliezer had heard a lot about Reb Judah the Chosid and his ways, and was simply desperate to see him and to study Torah with him (and by the way, Reb Judah was also a distant relative). To cut a long story short, one fine day Reb Eliezer hit the road to Regensburg to go and find Reb Judah. But he had to cross the Danube, and thereby violated his father's will. When he entered Reb Judah's study, the Chosid said hello and went on to say: 'The truth is that I shouldn't have welcomed you with a *shólem-aléykhem* because you have violated your father's will. If I greet you, it is only out of respect for your late father.' And upon hearing these words, a great fear came upon Reb Eliezer and he went through a lot of anguish.

In the meantime, Reb Eliezer stayed at Reb Judah's for a very long time. His intention was to learn from him the secrets of the Torah, meditations and formulas of Unity with God. But the Chosid always put him off, and taught him nothing.

In the meantime, a whole term had passed, and Reb Eliezer had still not had any guidance from Reb Judah, and suffered serious grief. He had made it there over such a long journey, had remained there for a considerable amount of time and in the end accomplished nothing and learned nothing.

When the eve of Passover came around, Reb Eliezer's sadness became even greater. He became melancholic and his thoughts were full of sorrow. So he thought to himself: 'Here the holiday is coming where every Jewish person makes a *séyder* in his own home, and here I am, cast away and leaning upon a strange table. I had hoped to spend the holiday together with the members of my family, and here I am away from home three terms already. They won't even know what happened to my skeleton!' As he was thinking, he was feeling lower and lower, and this not only because he had been wandering away from home so long, but because on top of that, he hadn't managed to learn one single thing.

Reb Judah saw the sadness of the guest in town and knew very well its cause. He had done it to spite him, because the man had violated the will of his father. But that day, the Chosid said to him in a by-the-way kind of tone: 'It is obvious that you are very sad, and the reason for this is no secret for me. You would probably want to spend the holiday at home, with your wife and children, and make the *séyder* with them, the way it's supposed to be.' Reb Eliezer answered him: 'Yes, of course I would want that, but it would be possible only with God's will. But it isn't possible anymore. Today is the eve of Passover, and it's too late to get home for the holiday.'

Whereupon Reb Eliezer said to him: 'What would you give me if I brought you home today, in time, before the holiday?' And Reb Eliezer became even sadder from these words, and said to the Chosid: 'Ay, *rebbe*, you are just making fun of me!' Reb Judah replied: 'Heaven forbid! I mean it very seriously.' Reb Eliezer said: 'I would give everything I own for that, because I cannot imagine any greater happiness than being at home with my dear wife and child for the holiday.' So the Chosid said: 'It's getting late, we have to go bake the matzahs.

Then I'll see whether you'll be able to get home in time for the holiday.' In his heart, Reb Eliezer was very surprised at the strange words
of the Chosid, but he didn't say a thing.

Soon after that, Reb Judah together with Reb Eliezer went to bake
the matzahs. When they had taken the matzahs out of the oven,
the Chosid said to Reb Eliezer: 'Come here and take a freshly baked
piece of matzah and put it in your chest pocket. I would like you to
bring it home while it is still warm.' When Reb Eliezer heard this, he
laughed to himself, but at the same time prepared himself for the
journey. The Chosid put a piece of still-warm matzah into his vest
pocket and went out with him to an open field. But Reb Eliezer was
still distressed, because he had still learned nothing from Reb Judah,
and here he was being sent away empty-handed. The Chosid noticed
his sadness and said to him: 'I know very well that your intention
was to learn secrets of the Torah from me.' 'Yes,' Reb Eliezer replied,
'That is the reason in essence why I came.' To which the Chosid
replied: 'To be honest about it, I wouldn't be allowed to teach you,
in as much as you have violated the will of your father. But for the
merit of your holy father, who was a relative of mine, and moreover,
a person who was in constant awe of God, I will nevertheless teach
you something.'

During their conversation, Reb Judah took the stick which he happened to be holding in his hand, and used it to write out some sacred
names in the sand. Then he turned to Reb Eliezer and said: 'My dear
Reb Eliezer, read what I have just written out, please.' As soon as he
read the writing in the sand, he experienced a great revelation and
knew just as much as Reb Judah. Then Reb Judah went ahead and
erased the names and covered them over with sand. And suddenly, in
the middle of a sentence, Reb Eliezer forgot everything. The Chosid
repeated this three times one after another, writing the names in the
sand, and then erasing them. Reb Eliezer was full of regret that he
had so quickly forgotten everything he learned.

The fourth time, the Chosid again wrote the sacred names in the
sand and asked Reb Eliezer to lick them off with his tongue. And Reb
Eliezer did what the Chosid told him to do. Barely had he swallowed
the names, in sand, when he again knew all the secrets of the Torah
that Reb Judah knew, and never again forgot anything.

And just as soon as Reb Eliezer had learned all the wisdom from
his teacher, he asked permission to take his leave. The Chosid blessed
him, and Reb Eliezer went out on his journey, revived in spirits and
happy because he had confidence in the words of the Chosid, that

he would yet make it home before the holiday. Before his departure, the Chosid blessed him with the ancient blessing of the priests and uttered a Name, such that Reb Eliezer immediately saw Mainz, where he turned up very quickly.

When the people of the town went to synagogue on the eve of the holiday at dusk, they caught sight of Reb Eliezer and greeted him. They wanted to know one thing only. Where had he been the previous night, because it doesn't befit a Torah scholar to be on the road on the eve of Sabbath or the eve of a holiday. Reb Eliezer told them: 'Strange as it may seem when you look at me, I was in Regensburg today at Reb Judah's and helped him bake matzahs. Here is corroboration in my vest pocket: a still-warm piece of matzah that the Chosid gave me to take to my wife.'

(3) A False Accusation against an Innocent Woman

[This tale, set in a period of Talmudic law in ancient Judea, is from the third section (no. 204 in the 1602 edition). It has analogues both in midrashic literature, where it appears to exemplify the prohibition against slander, and in international sources. The section which echoes the book of Jonah is illustrative for the changes in historical outlook. Not only is the Jonah figure a woman, but the sailors, though gentiles, pray to a single God before throwing anybody into the sea (compare Jonah 1: 5, 14).]

This is a story that happened to somebody who was away from home to do business abroad. He entrusted his wife to his brother and asked him strongly to please keep an eye on her, to make sure that no evil, heaven forfend, came upon her, and also that she should lack nothing, because he knew what a precious, honest woman she was. The brother promised to carry out everything, exactly as befits a brother-in-law.

When the man had left on his travels, his brother took his wife and brought her into his own home, and gave her a separate room in his house. He became a frequent caller to his sister-in-law, and took care that she should not lack anything she needed. On top of all her other attributes, the woman was beautiful and traditionally chaste and modest.

But it came to pass that her brother-in-law was attracted to her. Coming into her room on one occasion, he said to her: 'My dear sister-in-law, be good to me and do as I ask, and I too will do everything that you ask of me.' The honest woman answered him: 'One mustn't even speak about such a thing! A woman who has sex with another man denies God, blessed be He, as well as her own husband. Why should I do such a horrible thing? You know very well that we would both lose our portion of the World to Come! And how can you even ask it of me in this situation, where you know very well that your brother trusted me with you, to keep an eye on me and protect me? How can you even think about such a bad thing? Remember that the Torah forbids this as long as your brother is alive. Our sacred Torah says, doesn't it, that whoever has relations with his fellow's wife is stricken with leprosy and never gets to leave Hell!'

On this occasion, her brother-in-law listened to what she was saying and let her go. But he kept on coming in to her every day to ensure that she was not lacking anything.

And the day came, and the brother-in-law sent his helper out to bring water from the street, and during that time, went into his sister-in-law's room and tried to force her. The honest woman began to scream loudly, but there was nobody at home who could hear her. But she protected herself with all her might, and he couldn't do what he wanted, and so he let her go. Thirsting for revenge, he dashed out onto the street and found two people who would bear witness falsely and testify that they saw this woman committing adultery with a young man, during the period when her husband was away. And the two false witnesses went to the rabbinic court and gave testimony that they saw this woman lying with a young man.

So the court sent for the woman to ask her: 'Could it be? How could she, a married woman, do such a dreadful thing?' All the while, the two false witnesses were standing there, and said it to her face. The woman replied that everything the witnesses said was lies and falsehoods, that it was a completely made-up story, and that the truth would one day come out. During her appearance in the court, she mentioned what had happened with her brother-in-law and how he had tried to force her. The witnesses jumped back at her: 'What does this have to do with your brother-in-law? We have only given testimony about what we have seen ourselves!' The court had no alternative than to sentence the woman to death by stoning. She was led to the stoning ground outside town, and they stoned her. But she remained alive under the mound of stones for three days.

The third day, it so happened that somebody who had come from a far away country and was taking his son to Jerusalem to study Torah passed by the mound of stones and sat down to rest from the journey. Because it was close to sundown and they were afraid that they would not make it to Jerusalem before nightfall, they decided to spend the night at this spot. Obviously they had no idea that somebody was lying under the stones. At night they heard a weak, moaning voice that said: 'Woe is to me, I have been stoned for nothing, all because of slander. I did not deserve such a dreadful death.' When the stranger heard this, he got up from his makeshift bed and began to take off the stones, until he found the woman. She was alive. He asked her: 'What's the story, why were you sentenced to be stoned?' And so she told him what happened to her and how the hired witnesses were able to give her a bad name. Then she asked the man where he was going with his boy. He said that he was taking him to Jerusalem to study Torah. She said to him: 'If you take me home with you, I will teach your son Torah, Prophets and Writings' [in other words, the Hebrew Bible]. The man asked her: 'Are you really able to study and teach? If so, I will take you home with me.' The woman assured him: 'Yes, I know Torah well.'

And so the man, with God's help, went back home and took the woman with him. When he arrived home safely, he built a special house for her, within the distance of the Sabbath boundary from the city, to enable her to live in peace and to make sure nobody would interrupt her studying. He also hired a helper who would bring her food and drink.

And the day came, and it happened that the helper was attracted to the woman and tried to seduce her. But the woman would not hear of it and said to him: 'May God save me from committing such an awful sin. I am a married woman, and with God's help my husband will return to me soon.' The helper got angry, took a sword in his hand, and wanted to kill her. The young lad whom she had been teaching happened to be around, and threw himself on the helper, trying to protect the woman, but he killed the boy immediately with the tip of the blade of his sword. When the helper saw what he had done, he quickly ran away to a wild forest. And a lion, sent from His Dear Name, came and devoured him. That was God (blessed be He) who sent him a punishment for his great sin.

When the righteous woman saw that her pupil was murdered on account of her, she ran away too, though she was completely innocent of any wrongdoing. She just could not bear to look at the sadness of the father and mother over their child. And so the woman journeyed over the roads and the highways until she came to the seashore. At that time, a ship full of robbers was pulling into port.

When they saw the beautiful woman, they captured her and took her with them.

So what does God, blessed be He, do? He sent a storm to the sea that almost broke up the ship. So the sailors screamed loudly, saying that it must be that they are being punished by God. 'Let us therefore cast lots and we will throw into the sea whomever the lot falls upon. After all, we see clearly that the storm is because of us alone, because the other ships are being struck by a light wind and the sun is even shining for them. But we have been destined for bitter weather. Most probably one of us has sinned very badly.'

So they went ahead and cast lots. Then the lot fell upon the good woman. And the sailors asked her: 'Tell us, we beg you, what is your deed that God is so angry about? We are afraid that we will all be drowned at sea because of you!' The woman answered them: 'I am a Jewish woman, and believe in Almighty God who created heaven and earth.' And she went on to tell them everything about her life and experiences, everything that happened to her from beginning to end. The sailors took great pity on her and didn't want to throw her into the sea. They raised their hands in prayer to the One in heaven and did pray, that he should spare them all from evil, and that they should not have to throw this bitterly punished woman into the sea. And God (blessed be He) heard their cry, and the sea turned calm. They sailed back to shore and let the good woman go. In that way she was saved from a calamity and the sailors got on their way once again.

Our good woman always showed her consistent strength and never lost trust in Him who is in heaven (blessed be His name) and that was true now too. At the seashore, she [...]

(*Máyse bukh* 1602 [from the Yiddish])

The story winds on to its eventual happy ending, reunification with her husband, and to the stern moral warning about the propensity for slander to lead to murder. Although the stories had to have a moral, which was sometimes a virtually mechanical tag-on from the literary point of view, the essential criterion was that they had to be enjoyable to read and succeed in the new (increasingly eastern) European marketplace of printed Yiddish books.

This was a new genre: the *Jewish* short-short tale, published in Yiddish, openly for men and women alike, that was a new rung in vernacular stature in society, coming as it did in a printed book readable by all, and being able to hold its own, competitively speaking, in the newly Yiddish synthesis of written literature, vernacular language, internal Jewish thematics and content rivalling the interest level for classical sources, and, now and again, a woman hero. Unlike the Hebrew and Aramaic midrashic literature, with its ancient legends set in the Near East, some of the new heroes were verily heroes of Ashkenaz.

A prayerbook for women

There is no evidence of any standardized canon of prayer for the general populations of Israelites in biblical times, though it is believed there was a canon for priests and nobles of the Jerusalem Temple preserved in some measure in the book of Psalms. The later Jewish prayer canon, its greater part in Hebrew with a smaller but pivotal part in Aramaic, grew over time, particularly after the point when animal sacrifices were discontinued, with the destruction of the Second Temple in Jerusalem in 70 AD. Sacrifices were replaced by the evolving canon of thrice-daily standard prayers, and of the Sabbath and holiday canons. The differences between the Ashkenazic and Sephardic and other European Jewish prayer canons are very important for the communities concerned. But looked at from outside, the traditions are often remarkably similar. The level of standardization and normativism is quite uncanny, bearing in mind there was for most of the post-Temple time no printing press and these were disparate and geographically far-flung communities of a stateless minority. It was the voluntarily granted authority to the rabbinical authorities in many countries and over much time that enabled codification to the remarkable degree attested. Much of the canon is already discussed in great detail in the Talmudic literature of the first half of the first millennium AD.

Alongside this central tradition of canonized community prayer, there was traditionally room for personal prayer, supplementary prayer and prayer for special occasions. Ironically, the biblical tradition on prayer is strongest for precisely such non-canonical prayer. One well-known example is 'Heal her please, O God' (Numbers 12: 13), the five-word supplication of Moses to God, to heal his sister Miriam of the leprosy God inflicted on her as punishment (for speaking against her brother Moses in connection with his choice of a [non-Israelite] wife).

Later post-biblical Judaism revived or recycled biblical terminology to cover various of the categories. The biblical nouns *təfillɔ́* and *təḥinnɔ́* occur next to each other in a famous verse, in which the first is traditionally translated 'prayer' and the second 'supplication'. The original passage reads: 'Whatever prayer and supplication be made by any person [...]' (I Kings 8: 38). The tradition, like so many others, was continued right through the ages, from Hebrew into Aramaic and then Yiddish, where the *tfíles* [tfíləs] (in plural) are the standard Hebrew and Aramaic canon of (mostly) communal prayer, while the *tkhínes* [txínəs] are extra-canonical individual prayers not in the canon, and more likely to be in the unmediated language of the person with the personal prayer.

In the case of women in older Ashkenaz, the prayers that were translated or adapted for women sometimes became quasi-standard women's prayer in Yiddish, used communally (not just individually) by the women in the women's section of the synagogue (most often upstairs, from a balcony or raised platform), while the men for the most part prayed in the original Hebrew and Aramaic (irrespective of whether or not they understood what it was they were reciting). Of course, such a neat division is a historic oversimplification. There were men who prayed in Yiddish, to be sure, and women who prayed in the original. But like many oversimplifications, this generalization encompasses a big chunk of historic truth, and is therefore worth making. By the time of Yiddish publishing, a Yiddish canon for women was developing that was supplementary to the various translations of the Hebrew and Aramaic canon. In its published forms, it came to be known as *Séydər tkhínes* (*The Order of Personal Prayers*), or sometimes more fully as the *Séyder tekhínes u-baKóshes* (*The Order of Personal Prayers and Requests*). These titles were parallel to many editions of original Hebrew prayers called *Séydər tfíles* (*The Order of the* [canonical Hebrew and Aramaic] *Prayers*). In modern literary Yiddish, *baKóshe* (in classical Hebrew *baqqɔ̄šɔ̄*) is just a highbrow, more literary alternative for 'request' but in older times carried the semantic weight of 'a request from the Almighty', which it still carries in traditional communities, especially in the plural *baKóshes*.

Glancing through the *Séydər tkhínes* or *Order of Personal Prayers*, it becomes obvious that these special Yiddish prayers are not Yiddish translations of the Hebrew and Aramaic canon (such as those over which there has been much debate; see D. E. Fishman 1991 for a survey of the intellectual history). That debate was after all over *substitution*, whether people would ditch the canon in favour of 'praying in a language you understand'. For the original Yiddish prayers that were composed and ended up in various editions of the *Order of Personal Prayers*, there is no issue of substitution. Whether the women who use them *also* pray in Hebrew is almost beside the point. The prayers in the *Order* are sometimes supplements to various specific Hebrew prayers. Sometimes they are specific to certain holidays or days of the week. And sometimes they are specific to circumstances in life. There is a prayer for successful childbirth, a prayer for the health of the children, a prayer for a widow and a prayer for a wife whose husband is away on a business trip. It becomes apparent that the *Order of Personal Prayers* is a standardized personal prayerbook in Yiddish for the Ashkenazic woman. Many editions contain specific instructions for specific Yiddish supplications which exemplify a blend of standardization and flexibility that would be unthinkable for the original canon in the classical languages. One famous instruction tells a woman to read this prayer slowly and joyfully, even if it means finishing it only the following day. Another calls, in print, for her to weep when uttering it.

One of the classic editions of the *Order of Personal Prayers* was the Amsterdam 1648 edition. It is titled simply *Tkhínes*. Its title page reads:

These *Tkhínes* are beautifully clear for pious women, wives and girls, for all who have good, clean thoughts to praise God, blessed be He, and to remember the great gift which He gives people every day of their lives, and so these *Tkhínes* are said early in the morning before everything else when they awaken and have dressed, washed their hands clean, and have come to know God, blessed be He, and will thereby come to inherit God's love, and the Holy Land, and Messiah. [Published] here, in the sacred community of Amsterdam.

(*Tkhínes* 1648, title page [from the Yiddish])

The book starts with a personal prayer to be said every day and is followed by specific prayers for each day of the week (emulating the Hebrew *shir shel yom* or 'song of the day' in the men's standard canon). It includes prayers upon baking challah, the Sabbath bread; lighting candles; dressing up in white; immersion in the ritual bath (*míkve*); childbirth; on first rising from the bed after childbirth; for the various holidays; upon visiting a cemetery and specific prayers to be said at the graves of different relatives.

Yet it took quite a few years for the fully developed *Order of Personal Prayers* to emerge. The earlier printed versions contained only a few. For example, a booklet called *Tkhíne zu* ('This Personal Prayer') appeared in Prague around 1590. It is a small bilingual booklet comprising a bilingual Hebrew-Yiddish title page, and two pages of a Hebrew prayer text followed by four in Yiddish. For moderns it can seem strange that finding a way forward other than to enable women to share the same canon as men can be considered empowerment. But such 'modernistic' views are anachronistic and fail the elementary test of looking at a society through its own eyes (the a priori primary test), and the test of common sense. For women to get their *own* prayerbook in the *living, spoken* language of the entire society, in book form, while men keep their ancient one was actually a kind of progress that represented a massive evolution of women's power through Yiddish: one's own prayerbook for talking to God, with specially composed, compiled and published prayers especially for women in a handsome volume that rivalled the canonical Hebrew prayerbook in size, print quality and appearance.

Something else was under way too, something that is hinted at by publications such as the *Tkhíne zu*, which were small booklets of (in effect) single poems authored by a named and female author. Their authors would, retrospectively speaking, be the first Yiddish poets.

Women initiate Old Yiddish poetry

It is a logical progression from the foregoing to the stage where actual named women are authors, something frankly unimaginable in the Hebrew and Aramaic writing tradition of Ashkenaz. But it was perhaps predictable that the chain of events unleashed by the initiation and development of Yiddish publishing primarily for women would sooner or later result in women becoming (named) writers as well as readers and patrons. That came as part of the process of creating specific women's prayers in Yiddish. These poetic creations came not from the earlier, West Ashkenaz centred, secular-literature-dominated period in Yiddish history, but, as it happens, in the transitional and eastern regions, from the late sixteenth century onward, as a striking component in the *múser* period in Yiddish literature, in the Erikean sense.

Twenty-first-century readers who learn that women started publishing the first non-translated Yiddish poetry during the age of earlier Yiddish printing sometimes get excited about what they expect to find in the way of the topics, feelings and purposes of that poetry. If they hope there might be some kind of early 'feminist voice' in any modern western sense, they are at times bitterly disappointed. The poems snugly fit the bill of ancient Jewish law and sensibilities as evolved over the millennia by standard rabbinic Judaism, except in the very fact of the woman's voice speaking up, which is no little thing when it is the first time in the history of a language that it comes to pass. These are deeply pietistic, religious poems, in which the woman talks to God one-on-one, asking, for example, for her male children to be Torah scholars or for her husband to succeed. For the Ashkenazic society in question, it was sensational, and in the history of ideas revolutionary, that a work written by a woman would appear with her name as the author, and be published and sold as such among traditional Ashkenazim, virtually for the first time in the society in question (see Korman 1928: xxvii–lxxxii, 1–38).

This new environment, in which a quasi-standard prayerbook in Yiddish for women was being developed and marketed in the age of printing, inspired women to come out with their own individual signed prayers, *tkhínes*, openly authored by women. This enterprise, as far as is known, began in 1586 in Krakow, by then one of the 'principal cities' of the new Eastern Ashkenazic cultural bloc. A Yiddish edition of the book of Psalms, by one Moyshe Shtendl, was prefaced with an original rhymed poem by an author called Royzl Fishls. In the poem (typeset as continuous prose), she gives a capsule autobiography as it relates to this edition of the Psalms that she is publishing. She is the daughter of the late Rabbi Joseph, and granddaughter of Rabbi Yuda Leyvi who kept a yeshiva going for 50 years in Ludmir (today's Vladimir Volynsk, western Ukraine). She was forced into wandering, and in Hanover found this rhymed translation of Psalms by Rabbi Moyshe that is to be sung according to 'the melody of the Shmuel Book' (see pp. 99–100). This musical instruction statement makes this a potent symbolic transitional icon between one kind of Yiddish commodity from older Western Ashkenaz that was still known, and the new Eastern variety being ushered in. She goes on to say that, seeing how good it would be for men, women and religious girls, she copied out the whole text with her own hand and brought it to press. Actually, the poem becomes a prayer only at its conclusion, where she thanks God and beseeches Him to continue having mercy on her, and to stand by her, just as he stood by David, son of Jesse (traditionally the author of Psalms), and a recurring allusion to eschatological hopes that are gripping throughout traditional Ashkenazic society.

Royzl's poem marks the start of the age of the named woman Yiddish poet, and it does so not entirely in the realm of traditional content. It daringly contravenes the tradition by which a woman's prayer might ask that she be in God's eyes as a worthy successor to Sarah, Rebecca, Rachel and Leah (the biblical Matriarchs). Instead, and significantly for the history of ideas and their published literary expression, she invokes David (ancestor of the Messiah in Jewish, just as in Christian lore; see Finkelstein and Silberman 2006). In a more cosmic sense, Royzl Fishls initiated the tradition of women Yiddish poets that has continued, albeit in different incarnations and social milieus, unbroken. And, given the implications of 'rewriting the manuscript' for the press, it is likely that she did some editing as well, as is the wont of contemporary 'copyists' who prepared works for the press.

Incidentally, the name Royzl Fishls is as classically Yiddish as one can get. *Royzl* is one of the diminutive and name-forming derivatives of the base noun for 'rose'. It is altogether possible that this was an etymologized root spelling and that by the sixteenth century it would have been Eastern Yiddish Reyzl (Polish Yiddish Rayzl). The most venerable way of forming a 'usable Yiddish surname' (as in Fishls = Fishl's) over the generations is by adding a parent's or spouse's or ancestor's name in the possessive. In the Yiddish milieu it would be in daily use when distinguishing two people sharing a forename. Modern Yiddish authors have in an uninterrupted tradition delighted in creating their own literary names by the traditional formula, most famously Isaac Singer who became Isaac Bashevis (= Bashéve's, son of Ba(s)shéve or Bath-Sheba).

Sometime early in the seventeenth century another woman Yiddish poet emerged. As ever it is important to stress that we are all as much as any at the mercy of the currently known sources and peradventure doing unintended violence to the heretofore undiscovered. She was Toybe Pan, wife of Rabbi Jacob Pan and daughter of Rabbi Leyb Pitzker. ('Toybe' in most cases derives from *toyb*, 'dove' or 'pigeon', in modern Yiddish more common in the diminutives *Taybl* and *Táybele*). From the text of the poem it becomes clear that she is both the daughter and wife of high-titled rabbis. Her book is known to scholars as 'Toybe Pan's *tkhíne*' though its printed title is *A* [or: *Eyn*] *sheyn lid nay gemákht*, which can translate as 'A beautiful poem newly made'. It has 54 (or 55) lined stanzas with the refrain 'Father King', and a user's note suggesting it be sung according to the melody for a popular Hebrew prayer.

The three title lines, of which the first two rhyme, are:

> A sheyn lid nay gemákht
> B'lóshn tkhíne iz vor(d)n óysgetrákht
> Benígn Ádir óyem venóyre.

roughly translating as:

> A beautiful poem [or: song] newly made
> In the Language of the Tkhíne thought up
> According to the melody of Ádir óyem venóyre.

The *Ádir óyem vanóyra* (Israeli *Adír ayóm vanorá*) is a mystical poem that is in many traditions sung at the *Meláve málke* ('Escorting the Queen [Sabbath]') on Saturday night, which marks the end of the Sabbath and the start of the new week. It is a poem with acute Kabbalistic yearnings for the messianic age of redemption. Hence this melody is thematically suited to the poem's content. But it is a more immediate kind of salvation that is demanded from the Almighty by this very direct and daring named Ashkenazic woman. The poem concerns a plague or contagious illness that was rapidly spreading. The author begs God to 'call it back'. A most striking element is the argument that Toybe puts forward to God. Yes, a woman, writing in Yiddish, writes a poetic supplication supplementary to canonical prayer (wholly separate from the 'Can you pray in Yiddish?' debate, where the issue was substitution for canonical prayer), constructing an argument with which to confront God. Its opening stanzas characteristically praise God's mercy and ask Him to look at people's prayers rather than their sins. It goes on to explain the loneliness and sense of helplessness caused by this plague, and the specific request that no further victims be 'carried away [that is, dead]'. She takes it upon herself to inform His Holiness that 'five men' are devoting themselves, at great risk, to helping those in need, and God is asked to treat them appropriately. Toybe quickly moves to what women *always* do for sick people (in the original, stanza 9; all five lines rhyme):

> But Goodhearted women all the time,
>
> Do fine things for sick people,
>
> Bringing them company all the time,
>
> At the ready to carry out many good deeds,
>
> May God protect them from all suffering.

After reverting to supplication and prayer mode, and admitting that sins are committed, she asks God, in stanza 21, to accept the repentance for the sin, and to act as He did in the days of King David:

> It happened to King David,
>
> That the Angels of Death ran into him on the street,
>
> But You did have mercy on him
>
> So now too, no more ought die.

The poet dares God to do His work whether or not the repentance carried out suffices. She is making the point that faulty or imperfect repentance should not become an excuse for the plague continuing. She is her people's advocate, interceding with the Almighty:

> We are doing penance, young and old,
>
> But halt the plague!
>
> And if we God forbid were too sinful
>
> Then do it for us as a Gift for naught.

By stanza 26, Toybe is pointing out to God that there is no longer a High Priest or Temple to properly intervene with God, and God is therefore implored to accept this personal prayer:

> We have no Temple, no High Priest
>
> Who will stand for us
>
> And pray on our behalf
>
> So dear God, accept *our* prayer.

By stanzas 29 and 30, God is challenged to 'remember well' His own oath to the Patriarchs, and He is reminded of Abraham's readiness to sacrifice His own son for God:

> O dear God, remember well Abraham, Isaac and Jacob
> of old,
>
> And keep your oath,
>
> That when the people of Israel in great need be
>
> You will help them out of all their misery.

> You promised Abraham
>
> When Isaac lay bound on the altar
>
> That you would keep Your hand over us
>
> For the sake of old Jacob.

The poem takes a kind of 'spiritual ballad challenge to God'. His image is obviously in some local difficulty after the death of the pious rabbi of the community in the plague. The pain and religious decline caused by the death are then 'thrown up' to God (stanza 34), and Toybe intervenes to 'help' God, as it were, by explaining to the people that:

> When God, blessed be He, wants to punish the people of Israel,
>
> He allows the righteous person to escape to Paradise,
>
> Not to be at the scene of plight,
>
> May God take away from us the misery.

Toybe throws up to God the death of tiny children, 'jewels of two three years, and those who can read and pray, too.' She then turns to the people's tears (stanza 41), and appeals to God (stanza 42) to:

> Erase our sins with these tears
>
> You are our father and we your child
>
> We do praise all Your Being
>
> Do not forsake your children, dear father.

With an obvious knowledge of rabbinic terminology, Toybe takes up two of the classic measures of justice, the (harsh) *midəs ha-dín* ('[full] measure of the law') and the (compassionate) *midəs ho-rákhmim* ('measure of mercy'):

> O dear God who sits on the Seventh Heaven,
>
> Pay attention to your poor flock.
>
> Get up from the measure of law,
>
> And sit Yourself down upon mercy's measure.

While some modern critics might find all this naive and simplistic, Toybe was in effect making loud and clear statements of a named woman, in print, in the vernacular, using classic Hebraic concepts from the ancient sources, taking on, not more and not less, God. For Ashkenazic civilization this was a breathtaking 'acquisition of power' for women, for Yiddish, and perhaps for God too.

Around a century later, a not yet 12-year-old girl, Géle (Gella), daughter of a printer-publisher who had converted from Christianity, published her own poem. Her father, who became a rabbi, was Moyshe ben Avrohom (using the usual convert's appellative 'ben Avrohom' ('[symbolic] son of the patriarch Abraham', typical convert's patronymic). He married a rabbi's daughter and published a Yiddish prayerbook at Halle in 1714. The preface, in rhyme, is by his daughter, who typeset the book. It translates as follows:

> This beautiful new prayerbook from start to end, I
>
> Géle daughter of the rabbi Rabbi Moyshe Mádpis [the printer],
>
> I typeset all its letters with my own hands,
>
> And my mother is Freyde daughter of Rabbi Israel Katz of blessed memory,
>
> Who gave birth to me among her ten children,
>
> I am a virgin a little under twelve years,
>
> But don't be surprised that I must work,
>
> The soft and abandoned Daughter of Israel sits long days in the Dispersion,
>
> One year goes by and another comes yet around,
>
> And we have not yet beholden our redemption,
>
> We cry out and beg of God every year,
>
> Would He see that our prayers to God, blessed be He, shall come to pass,
>
> Meanwhile I must remain mum and still,
>
> I and my father's house must not talk much,
>
> As soon as all Israel will come to see it,
>
> So may it happen to us,
>
> As the passage says, all people will rejoice,
>
> Who had bewailed Jerusalem's sack,
>
> And banished great people to exile,
>
> Who will come rejoice at Redemption,
>
>> Amen may it come to pass.
>>
>> Now, my dear people, buy this prayerbook for a pittance,
>>
>> For we have no other living in this world,
>>
>> Because that is how God, blessed be He, wished things to be.

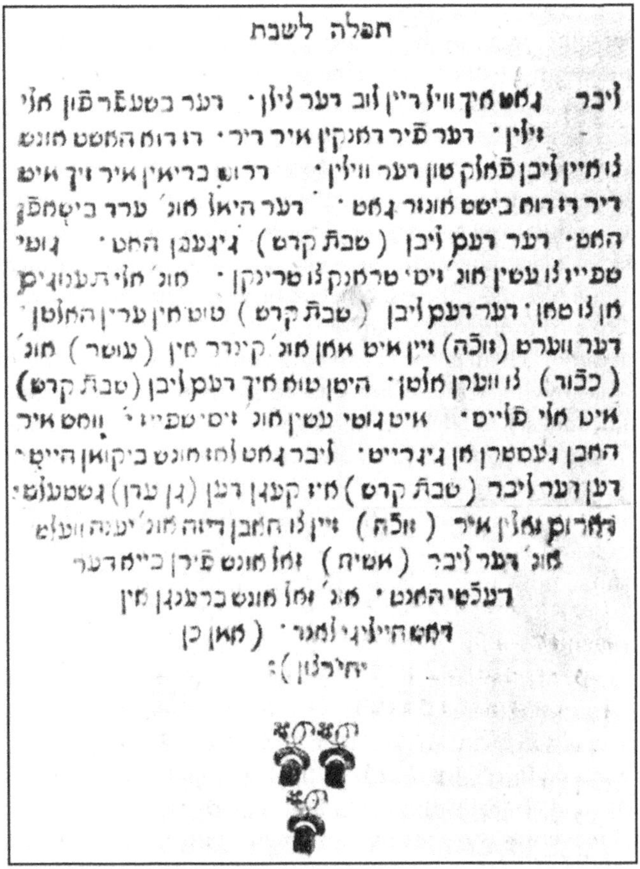

Image 7.3 Khàne (Chana) Katz's seventeenth-century poem to the Sabbath with messianic overtones
Source: Image courtesy of Dr Hermann Suess (Fürstenfeldbruck).

Another female author of *tkhínes* was Khàne (Channa, Hanna) Katz in the seventeenth century. Her Sabbath prayer, to be said at the start of the new month of Elul (a month of repentance before the High Holidays in the autumn), and her 'Sermon for Women' (in fact, a long poem) were published in a single undated booklet in Amsterdam.

The most famous woman writer of devotional Yiddish poetry probably lived in the early eighteenth century. Her name came to assume mythical proportions, and sounds rather like an Ashkenazic literary pseudonym. Its second part was certainly a pen name, but not every pen name is a pseudonym; some can be appellations acquired during the course of a life, more so in societies where surnames were not regularly used and an appellation or nickname often stuck and was adopted by the bearer in the overall spirit of a surname.

She was Sóre [Sórə] bas-Toyvim (Sarah bath Tovim), which at first sight looks like 'Sarah the Daughter of Goodness', but it is probably a more specific Ashkenazic usage. The plural noun *tóyvim* here refers to the set of learned, dignified and prestigious people in a town; it frequently occurred in Ashkenazic documents in the construct state, *tuvey*, especially in the stock phrase *túvey ho-ír* (lit. 'Good Ones of the city/town') which at times referred to a committee or group of respected elders who could be called upon in various circumstances and who convened at fixed intervals.

Sóre bas-Tóyvim, while using this synthesis of her name Sarah and (it would appear) her family heritage as a Yiddish pen name (thoroughly Yiddish in sound, spirit and cultural force, even if etymologically entirely from Hebrew), did not hesitate to identify herself in her works as the daughter of Leah and Mordechai, granddaughter of Isaac of Satanov and great granddaughter of Mordechai of Brisk d'Lite (Brisk of Lithuania; now Brest, Belarus). Her two most famous surviving works both have Hebrew names, as do so many traditionalist Yiddish books. One is called *Shékər ha-khéyn* ('The Deception of Loveliness', a reference to the vanity of emphasizing physical female beauty). The second has a rabbinic-sounding name, *Shlóysho shəórim* ('Three Gates', the image of the gate being frequent in Talmudic and later rabbinic literature). The three components of *Three Gates* are the laws that the woman must keep regarding challah (Sabbath bread), family purity and candle lighting; a personal prayer for the blessing of the new month (in the Jewish lunar-based calendar); and, finally, personal prayers for the High Holidays (New Year, Day of Atonement, Feast of Tabernacles) in the autumn. Sóre Bas Toyvim became the symbol of female pietistic prayer in eighteenth- and nineteenth-century Ashkenazic society.

The Yiddish women's *Tkhínes* have been studied by Freehof (1923), Weissler (1998) and Kay (2004), among others. There remains scope for a monograph on the *Tkhínes* from the viewpoint of the evolving role of women's status in Ashkenazic life. The question of whether men were also readers of the specifically 'women's prayers' has never been properly studied. One research strategy would be to compare texts of those women's prayers that do follow canonical templates with the Yiddish translations for similar prayers in general bilingual Yiddish prayerbooks of the period. Very likely, there would emerge a core corpus of highly similar texts emanating from both.

8
Religious Theories of Yiddish

The eighteenth century gave rise to a new age of arguments over Yiddish in Jewish society in the Ashkenazic lands, arguments whose reformulated incarnations continue to reverberate today.

True, the seventeenth century is 'unfairly' glossed over in many histories of Yiddish (language and literature both). Such is the fate of periods looked back upon as transitional. Novel developments were incipient and would come to some kind of 'enduring visibility' (that is, enduring for 'us') only in the eighteenth century. Looking at the years of birth and formative youth of various personalities who made 'their hit for history' in the eighteenth century, one sees how many were of seventeenth-century vintage. And in some sense, one might think of the 'discussions of the eighteenth century' in this context as a conventional shorthand for culminations of processes that started earlier. This is all in addition to any century-based division of history being a convention of convenience rather than an inherent entity, all the more so in a non-Christian society that didn't even use this calendar, and whose works often refer exclusively to the centuries of the Hebrew lunar-based calendar.

The later seventeenth century was certainly a period of decline of visible products of Yiddish culture of all brands in the west, and of a concurrent and notable rise in the east, notwithstanding some ongoing key western centres of Yiddish publishing, most famously Amsterdam, a cosmopolitan city also in Jewish terms, with a composite Yiddish-speaking community hailing from various parts of Ashkenazic Europe.

The middle decades of the seventeenth century saw some major 'straight history' Jewish-related events that had far-reaching consequences, one externally initiated, and the second (for many historical thinkers a direct reaction to the first) internally generated, and likewise

159

cataclysmic. The Chmielnitski uprisings of 1648–9, though 'officially' of Ukrainian peasants against Polish overlords and landlords, entailed the first mass murder of Jews on East European soil. Many Jews had been involved with Poles as intermediaries, inn managers and in a variety of partnering economic activities. Estimates of victims, once in the hundreds of thousands, now tend towards the tens of thousands (see Stampfer 2003). Whatever the numbers, the utter destruction of entire communities was a seminal event in the history of East European Jewry. Not long after that, a socialized and widespread Jewish hysteria over the false Jewish messiah Sabbethai Zevi (Yiddish: Shábse Tsvi) swept across multiple Jewish communities, with an intensity that led more than a few gullible believers, people with biographies otherwise characterized by caution and common sense, to relieve themselves of their homes and belongings, certain of the imminent messianic transportation to Jerusalem in 1666 (see Scholem 1973). In modern Yiddish literature, the best-known work set in the period is Isaac Bashevis Singer's *Satan in Goray*, available in many languages and editions. These events were of course recorded by works of Yiddish literature too (see, for example, Weinreich 1928a: 192–252). While the Ukrainian massacres of 1648–9 were a catastrophic instance of physical Jewish powerlessness in European history, and the messiah episode was, by contrast, an instance of extreme internal (and foolhardy use of) collective Jewish power, it was not really a time of bold events in the history of *Yiddish* and power.

The theological argument

It is an old story that a certain idea coming from, say, Joe the Plumber, can take on another life when uttered by a learned philosopher (and vice versa). Context and language and the larger assumed identity of the propositioning person are all vital. This is as true of Yiddish and power as anything else. As we saw earlier (see Chapter 4), Yosef bar Yokor, the publisher (/editor/translator) said in his 1544 preface to a translated Yiddish prayerbook that he considers 'the people who pray in Hebrew and don't understand one word to be utter fools. I for one would just like to know what kind of devout intention [*kavónə*] they could possibly have.'

Of course it was the kind of sensational claim that was well noticed by twentieth-century Yiddish-conscious historians of Yiddish literature who collected statements about the use of Yiddish in new realms. Yokor's claim was rediscovered for interwar Yiddish culture by Yisroel Tsinberg (1928: 88). But as anyone not approaching the issue from a twentieth or twenty-first century culturally pro-Yiddish perspective might note, this is a simple case of a business person promoting a new mass-audience product on the market. To paraphrase Yokor's sentence in English: 'New! A prayerbook that speaks your language so you can pray knowing what it is you are saying! Buy it now!' True, it is still important for charting the expansions of Yiddish realms in the new age of printing in the vernacular, but it is more a statement about 'the vernacular' than it is about Yiddish. There is even less direct relevance in the older statements, for example, in the *Book for the Pious* (see p. 44) about the need for prayer in the vernacular [in general] for those who do not understand (cf. D. E. Fishman 1991).

A 'statement from an intellectual' within the culture of Ashkenaz came on the threshold of the eighteenth century from Rabbi Yekhiel-Mikhl (Yechiel Michel) Epshteyn (Epstein; died around 1706). His *Kítsur shney lúkhəs ha-brís* ('Short [Version of] "Two Tablets of the Covenant"'), which first appeared in 1693, was a new summary of a seventeenth-century work, *Yəsód Yóysəf*, that delves deep into certain sins, their cause, and the ways to do penance for them, with a certain emphasis on seminal emissions of the male (on the interest in, or obsession with, the topic during the period, see Hundert 2004: 131–7). The only important 'Yiddish connection' here is that Epshteyn included, in a second edition, a chapter in Yiddish in this otherwise all-in-Hebrew rabbinic work, perhaps a first in Ashkenaz. There is a theological reference about repentance taking place via words in the spoken language (see Noble 1951: 125).

The 'statement' itself was to come in two distinct works of Yekhiel-Mikhl Epshteyn: first, in his Hebrew–Yiddish prayerbook (Epshteyn 1697) and then in his unique *múser* type work of instruction for the Jewish soul (Epshteyn 1703). In both, a rabbi uses Yiddish for a book addressed to men and women, to learned and unlearned alike, in a voice and on topics in which an Ashkenazic rabbi did not usually address his readers in Yiddish. In both he specifically extols the spiritual virtues of prayer in Yiddish. This is part of his message of a rabbinic work, not a title page (or 'book cover') sales pitch for a book in the vernacular by its publisher. It is therefore an inherently new stage in thinking about Yiddish and the status of this thinking within the bounds of traditional Ashkenaz.

The 1697 prayerbook, reprinted numerous times thereafter, has a number of rabbinical approbations (*haskóməs*) for the work submitted by other eminent rabbis. This is usually the format for a *séyfər* (rabbinic book in Hebrew or Aramaic), and was less common for a Yiddish prayerbook which previously had been part of (a) a utilitarian literature to help 'women and simple men' understand the prayers, as so many previous title pages of such Yiddish prayerbooks had indicated, and/or (b) a part of the Yiddish 'counterculture' enabled by the rise of Yiddish printing in the 1530s. But here, in Epshteyn's *Séydər tfílo dérəkh yəshóro* ('Order of Prayers "The Upright Way"'), these approbations were solicited for a bona fide rabbi's book in Yiddish. More than a prayerbook, it offers many explanations about the prayers and how to pray and holds forth on the intricacies of the laws concerning prayer. The 'readership statements' on the title page are stunningly inclusive. The Hebrew-language text near the top of the title page includes the wording:

> for the sake of the knowledge of all the people of the land: old people and youngsters, women and maidens, to know how to pray in the Upright Way in a correct, beautiful and clear way, and upon each part laws and customs that require explanation in the tongue of clear language, and in an easy language, *Loshn Ashkenaz* [...].
>
> (Epshteyn 1697, title page [from the Hebrew])

The Yiddish part of the title page, lower down, includes an invitation to a reader:

> be it a scholar or simple householders and women [...].

There is, in Ashkenazic terms, a tangible theological importance in adding a Yiddish chapter to a Hebrew work on repentance and in producing a learned prayerbook-with-commentary edition in Yiddish for 'all the population'.

However, Epshteyn's prime contribution to Yiddish and power was in fact in a third book: his own *múser* work, *Dérəkh ha-yóshor lə-óyləm hábə*, which first appeared in Frankfurt am Main in 1703. Beyond the novelty of a published *múser* literature work by genre, written by an actual rabbinic scholar himself, in Yiddish, rather than a (watered-down or recombinated) translation of an older Hebrew classic, there is a first in the history of Yiddish: the topic 'Yiddish' is addressed by the rabbi scholar — in Yiddish. This book's title can translate as 'The Upright Path to the World to Come' or just as plausibly as 'A Straight Route to Paradise', in either rendition emphasizing the author's mystical leanings and guidance for fellow Jews to concentrate on the afterlife and a messianic future as their main focus while still here on this earth. Finally, it cannot go unmentioned that Epshteyn, like many innovators who go against the grain, was something of a maverick. In view of his eschatological work in Yiddish, it is perhaps not wholly unexpected that he was among many 'messianic' rabbis suspected of being secret adherents of Sabbateanism, though there is nothing to suggest that other than the indirect impact on the general mystical and messianic mood in Jewish society of the time and place (Katz 2007: 129, 404). Epshteyn's theology of prayer was evident in part from his introduction to his prayerbook. It is a theology that poses a challenge for the 'traditional Jewish orthodoxy' that emphasizes the textual quantification and timing of prayer. For example, his Yiddish mini-treatise on prayer, included in the prayerbook, makes the following point:

> There are many people, men and women, who are religious, and who think that their religiosity lies in praying a lot, but these religious people with all of their praying can actually spoil everything!

The ensuing discussion makes it clear that the profound meditative and transcendental experience that he speaks of is far from the typical legalistic elucidation on the details and laws of 'saying one's prayers as prescribed by law'. There is a special warning for learned people not to recite any more of the canon than prescribed by law, a reaction to 'over-piety in prayer' that was common in some sectors. There is a discussion of how Yiddish prayer is preferable for 'extra-canonical' holy work of the soul, over and above mechanical recitation of 'more' of the original texts than required. It is all rather intrepid for a rabbi's book in Ashkenaz.

It is in that larger context of prayer as a complex subject that language becomes rather more of an issue than the earlier notion of 'understanding the literal meaning of the words'. One theological issue that comes up in Epshteyn's *múser* volume, for example, perhaps unsurprisingly for an age in which popular Kabbalah was in the ascendant, is that of demon-like entities, known as *klípes* ([klípǝs] < *qǝlippóθ* 'husks', 'barks' or 'shells' [remaining from the time of Creation] → 'evil spirits' in various Kabbalistic and popular senses; the singular *klípǝ* came in colloquial Yiddish to mean 'shrew', 'evil woman').When demons force evil thoughts into the mind during prayer, and work cunningly to confuse the mind, then the counter-force prescribed by the good Rabbi Epshteyn is Yiddish prayer as a key part of the arsenal (Epshteyn 1703: chapter 34). An astounding power is ascribed to Yiddish in a culture in which such powers were the realm of rabbinic use of Hebrew and Aramaic.

The commentaries and guidelines provided in Yekhiel-Mikhl Epshteyn's prayerbook were a step in the evolving Yiddish-Kabbalah nexus. His logic, for example, in the preface to his bilingual selections of Psalms to be recited (included in the prayerbook), goes something like this. David's Psalms contain many mystical secrets, because the Holy Spirit of the Almighty rested upon him when he wrote the Psalms. The Psalms include not-so-obvious allusions even to the esoteric names of God. For someone who knows Hebrew well enough to achieve the full layers of meaning from the text, the Hebrew text is fine. For everyone else, those same layers of knowledge can be approached or achieved through *this* special Yiddish version provided. This is very much in a rabbinic-populist spirit of 'giving the same mystical secrets to everyday people', or, to put it differently, a harbinger of the period of Yiddish Kabbalah power for the masses. It must be remembered that Kabbalah is arguably the hardest, most esoteric, highest and most potent sphere of Jewish culture in the society we are considering, and its association with 'power' derives from that circumstance, and additionally, from the supernatural powers often associated with Kabbalah. Both the speculative and practical branches of Kabbalah thereby come into play.

In the *Straight Path to the World to Come*, Epshteyn (1693) went deeper into the question of language, and the understanding of the many gradations of 'knowing Hebrew'. Even among those who could read Hebrew well, very few truly understand every word properly, and he insisted that such people pray in Yiddish instead of Hebrew. He believed Yiddish had acquired a kind of sanctity of its own, and like many kabbalists, believed that prayer should be passionate. The following are translated excerpts from chapter 31, with the caveat, as ever, that many of these things translate awkwardly into twenty-first-century English:

Many women, when told that it is a lot better to pray in the Yiddish that they understand well, reply that they were told that the angels do not understand any language other than Hebrew. But the truth is that they are mistaken, for those same people who told them that, did not study many sacred books, for it is written in the Talmud: 'When one asks [God] for his needs, one should not ask in the Aramaic language [then the vernacular] for the Ministering Angels don't need Aramaic' [Sabbath 12b], which means: Whosoever wants to name his need before God (blessed be He), should not name it in Aramaic for the angels do not link up with this language, Aramaic. But [the medieval commentary on the Talmud] *Tóysfes* [Tosafoth] brings an objection: How could it be that the angels do not understand any language except Hebrew? After all, the angel Gabriel taught Joseph the Righteous all the seventy languages, when he was going to become king in Egypt! *Tóysfes* provides an answer, that the angels know all the languages, but they are repelled by this Aramaic language and don't have much respect for it.

But in the book *Ten Sayings* [by Abraham Brisker/Avrom of Brisk (Brest), who died in 1700] it says [...] that it is obvious that whoever understands Hebrew and does prayer in another language has not fulfilled the obligation of prayer, and the angels do not accept it. But when someone does not understand Hebrew and makes his prayer in whatever language, that he understands with all his heart, with a broken heart, such a prayer is before God (blessed be He) even more pleasant, because it comes more from the heart than a prayer that is said in Hebrew but not understood, for God (blessed be He) 'trieth the heart' [after II Chronicles 29: 17], he tests the hearts of everybody, and no angel is needed for this! For God (blessed be He) accepts the prayer Himself. He also cites for this a passage. It says in Psalms, 102[:1]: 'A prayer of the poor, when he faints, and pours out his complaint before God' which means a prayer of a poor man who turns about with all his heart and pours out his words before God. Concerning this, the author of *The Ten Sayings* comments that the word 'poor' is explained according to its simple meaning, that for a poor man, his prayer is pleasant because he has nothing to rely upon other than upon God.

He further explains the word 'poor' as poor in knowledge, in understanding, he doesn't understand Hebrew and says his prayer in whatever language he understands, and does his praying with all his heart, this person prays to God, and the angels have nothing to be bossy about, for God (blessed be He) Himself accepts it. [...]

Therefore, my good friends, see how our ancestors rendered all our prayers into Yiddish. Everything, whether prayers or Psalms or supplications, everything was rendered into Yiddish. The whole prayerbook is rendered into Yiddish! [...] Were it the case that the angels do not understand Yiddish, our ancestors would not have put such effort and labour into translating it all into Yiddish. [...]

Moreover, women have soft hearts and can start to cry right away. After all, it says in the Talmud that even when all the gates of prayer are locked during the Exile, the gates of tears are never closed off [Tractate *The Middle Gate*, 59a]. It says in the Zohar [Genesis, section 1], that when a person cries in his prayer there is no more that can be said than with weeping. That prayer breaks through all the Heavens, even if the evil angels will be as an iron wall between him and the Holy One (blessed be He), it nevertheless breaks its way through and comes before the Holy One (blessed be He) and the person achieves much with his prayer. Even when a decree has been sealed in Heaven, it can be rescinded.

In the High Holy Days it is much better that the women say all the holiday hymns and penitential prayers in Yiddish, so that they should understand what they say, and even when they don't say many [prayers] it is befitting and in pure awe of the Holy One (blessed be He), and when the women cry on the New Year and the Day of Atonement, they open with their tears all the gates of compassion.

(Epshteyn 1703: §39 [from the Yiddish])

As in the case of Yosef bar Yokor (see Chapter 4), the master historian of Jewish literature Yisroel Tsinberg (Israel Zinberg 1873–1939), brought Yekhiel-Mikhl Epshteyn to the attention of the academic (Borokhovian) branch of the Yiddishist movement in a major paper in the late 1920s series of academic collective volumes that Vilna Yivo published in Yiddish (Tsinberg 1928: 95–7). This was followed up after the war in the circles of the New York Yivo around mid century by Yiddish scholar and Jewish historian Shlomo Noble (1905–86). The rebuttal to Tsinberg and Noble came from the traditionally orthodox scholar Chaim Lieberman, who did not accept any kind of 'proto Yiddishism' in the originals of these works (see Noble 1951; Lieberman 1952; cf. Leiberman 1943; English summary of their debate: *Yivo Annual* 1952). This book sides with Tsinberg and Noble, because however it is sized up theologically and according to religious law, Epshteyn went places where no other Ashkenazic rabbi up to his day had gone, and in context to a point that is somewhat extraordinary. But with one caveat: the daring pro-Yiddish rabbinic argumentation is indeed pro-Yiddish, but Lieberman and those who sided with him were 'also right' in so far as the phenomenon is so essentially different from the later nationalist-inspired rise of secular Yiddishism that there is little empirical justification for seeing a straightforward progression in the history of ideas, or even applying the same word to the two phenomena. It is more a case of replacement of sociolinguistic phenomena where the linear element refers to people and their individual and group progeny, and to different historic stages of the same language. Much might have been solved by some agreed terminological dichotomy, for example, 'pro-Yiddish' vs 'Yiddishist'.

The *Zohar* in Yiddish

Whatsoever Yekhiel-Mikhl Epshteyn would have written about the force of Yiddish prayer, his voice was, for people of the day, that of a contemporary rabbi offering his spiritual analysis and provision of tools to bring to realization for his followers a prayerbook with commentary and a *múser* book. Relative to the usual absence of written works, in Yiddish, by a rabbi, on such matters, both works were in their cultural context a sensation: a rabbi writing in Yiddish for a mixed readership and extolling Yiddish, both in a bilingual prayerbook and in a book of Jewish ethics and lore.

Still, this would be a very modest advance in comparison with the vast library that the *lámdn* (scholar of Talmudic literature) or the *lérner* (lifelong studier of that literature) could access. To be able to truly understand one of the classic texts in Hebrew and Aramaic, in traditional Ashkenaz, entailed an entire childhood, youth and ultimately lifetime of immersion, all in two ancient languages that nobody on this earth spoke as everyday vernacular. The traditional Ashkenazic scholar is, even today in traditionally orthodox communities, an educated male who spent much of his childhood and youth immersed in classical texts in those two ancient Jewish languages, and who does in fact study them for the entirety of his life, whether he is supported to do so or whether he has to hold some job or other that 'wastes' part of his waking hours.

The one-stroke 'slight' empowerment of everyday men and women by Epshteyn's bilingual prayerbook, and his work on morals, would not provide access to the multitude of mainstream, classic works of 'higher mystical thinking'. The rise of classical Kabbalah among the Yiddish-speaking masses of Central and particularly Eastern Europe in the seventeenth century is often traced to two sources. First was the spread of Lurianic Kabbalah from the sixteenth-century mystical centre in the town of Safad, in the hills of the northern Galilee in the Holy Land, and the new widespread spiritual mood its writings and emissaries to Europe inspired. Second was the major pre-twentieth-century Jewish catastrophe in Eastern Europe, the Chmielnitski massacres in the Ukraine in 1648-9 and the Kabbalistic End-of-Days moods they inspired. There was hope for redemption and the messianic End of Days, and there was belief that the world could be witnessing the 'birth pangs of the Messiah', the traditional very bad time that would of necessity precede the redemption. This latter interpretation led to the self-inflicted Jewish disaster of the massacres being used in some people's calculations for the imminence of the Messiah's coming in the service of Sabbethai Zevi ('Jewish millenarianism', as it might be dubbed), but for others it was just an inspiration to start thinking — and living — more mystically, more Kabbalistically.

Not many expected an actual Yiddish edition of the central work of Kabbalah, the *Zohar*. It happened in 1711. But the publication of the Yiddish *Zohar* in Frankfurt that year, by Tsvi-Hirsh Khotsh, came after more than a century of delays with the processing of a manuscript first drafted by Tsvi's great-grandfather Zelig (at least, if the family history recounted in the extensive preface is to be taken as fully accurate). Tsvi-Hirsh Khotsh, of Krakow, was a kabbalist who came from a long line of mystics and rabbis. In his introduction to the 1711 Yiddish Zohar he explains that the published work is based upon a manuscript left by his great-grandfather Zelig, rabbi of Korb (near Lublin) about a hundred years earlier. Hence the book is named *Nákhles Tsvi (Nachalath Zevi)*, the 'Legacy of Tsvi' or 'Inheritance of Tsvi' — a work he inherited from his great-grandfather. He recounts how it came to take more than a century for the Yiddish *Zohar* to reach the press. In a striking application of biblical citation, he uses the words of redemption from the first passage of the book of Ezra, when, 'In the first year of Cyrus king of Persia, God stirred up the spirit of Cyrus king of Persia, that he made...'. We also learn how the publication was held up for many years for various reasons, including the inherent controversial status of the project, and the economic and social disruptions resulting from the Chmielnitski massacres. Here follow some re-collated excerpts, edited for (hopefully some slightly improved) clarity from the large folio tome's lengthy trilingual introductions (actually two introductions, one alternating somewhat inscrutably between Hebrew and Aramaic, the second in Yiddish):

I give thanks to God who performed a miracle for my great-grandfather, the late luminous intellect Zelig, of blessed saintly memory, head of the rabbinic court and the yeshiva of Korb near Lublin, to whom Elijah [the Prophet] appeared in a vision. And, he saw the vision of the Almighty with more wisdom than a prophet or seer. He had four sons, all wise and understanding. Elijah commanded him to call them by famed names from the Zohar. They are my grandfather, the rabbi our teacher Yosi, and his brothers Khiya, Khisda and Abba, all of blessed memory.

In the year [5]361 [=1600/1601], God stirred up my great-grandfather's spirit to translate the Book of the Zohar into Yiddish for He has given vernacular language to His people [a Hebrew sound-play on 'The Lord will give strength to his people' at Psalms 29: 11]. His eye perceived all that is a treasure, the mystical sayings, and ethics and the deeds, so that they would be borne in mind and carried out in order to awaken hearts to the fear of God, that it may be equal to every soul of every person, that they may sanctify and stand in wonderment, by day as at midnight.

And there rose after him his son, my grandfather Yosi of Vienna, and he obtained rabbinic approbations [for publication of his Yiddish Zohar] from all the brilliant scholars whose Torah gave light in those days. And they also answered that to bring such benefit to a fine and pure people is a sacred and a blessed thing.

But he did not manage to publish it. And various mishaps occurred until the time of the evil decrees, in 1648, at the hands of the cursed bandits, may the name of the accursed be blotted out, who butchered and had no mercy and killed every person in that country from the great to the little, until almost no remnant remained. And they did great damage to sacred books, defiling and trampling them, and they became, for all our sins, trampled and dragged all around. Those rabbinic approbations were lost in sorrow and in grief. Nevertheless, by the compassion of God upon us, this remnant has survived, exiled in heaven as on earth.

And from the day that I came to my own senses, I sought and researched, and in accordance with the will of Heaven I clarified all that needed to be clarified. It is my legacy, the inheritance from my fathers that came to my hands, a gift to bring light to the soul that yearns and craves. How wonderful is the writing that is brought to benefit to the masses with its goodness, and for them to be immersed in it. And it will be for me a crown, the *Legacy of Tsvi* [name of this first printing of the Yiddish Zohar in 1711]. There were a number of incarnations and tribulations that kept spinning until it all wound up as my own lot.

And I said: O dear God, Lord of Hosts, show me a sign that it is good to benefit the masses, to purify the hearts that are distanced and depressed, to satisfy the souls of the thirsty, that they might not become unhallowed, but that they be filled by the best of gifts to all seeing eyes.

And if there will be a sign, I would consider it a great miracle. And I lifted my eyes and behold I saw a grand vision: my [great-] grandfather, of blessed memory.

It has been done so that the reader may find pleasure in the words, at their appointed time, each week [according to the weekly portions of the Torah], with nothing missing in the message. It is my inheritance and my destiny, my path and my road, to balm the sins of His people, as it says in the language of the Zohar [Aramaic], through translation from this language of gold and glory to another language [Yiddish].

Was not the language of the Zohar [Aramaic] in those lands a language of the families of the gentiles as a spoken language, as was the Language of Ashkenaz in our land? There too their language was privileged for everybody. And there too, the mystical secrets were for everyone who read them with proper knowledge. Likened unto those, our own wives who read the prayers and the personal prayers, and if their path is paved out for them like an open thoroughfare, the restriction on publishing is removed, and it was for all eyes to see. And moreover, is it not the case that 'there has not risen since a prophet in Israel like unto Moses, whom God knew face to face' [Deuteronomy 34: 10]? And He explained the Torah to him in seventy languages both in what He said and in what was left unsaid. Every word of God, overflowing with knowledge, was divided into seventy languages. Afterward too, it was written on the tablets to be studied by all humankind. And before giving it to Moses, He said: 'Thus shall you say to the Children of Jacob' [Exodus 19: 3]. This refers to the masses of the people and the women, whose inheritance is an easy and pure language.

Our holy Torah has been bequeathed equally to all the communities of Jacob. And from every word there come forth numerous combinations of words and Holy Names that work miracles throughout the world as is known, through their careful and precise application. There depend upon them innumerable spiritual worlds and it can be demonstrated, clear as the morning light, that it is the source of life, even as the early and the late rains [of the seasons in the Land of Israel]. And this is the way of the Torah to be expounded in every language to every desire.

The Talmud and the Aggadoth and the Midrashim are full of mystical secrets, all clothed in simple language, from which they have passed into other works and to other languages.

There are some who say that by studying the Zohar, even without understanding but by just reciting the words with a pure intention and with love in one's heart, one is enlightened and surrounded by the sanctity of the words. That is true, but this book was not made for those intellectuals of great comprehension, who are already some way up the ladder of achievement.

I have instead chosen a path that ignores the complications, and explains things for simple people who otherwise would not reach these depths. Moreover, even for those who understand the Zohar, the book is not always readily available, and those who own a copy find it difficult to discern and focus on those passages that contain the inspiring material, and to set aside the mysteries that would prove too much, or to search for related passages and to know when to omit digressions, like a bird flitting from rooftop to rooftop. If one is able to plumb its depths, it is surely proper and correct to invest all one's strength in its study on Sabbaths and Festivals to atone for both intentional and unintentional sins.

And the living shall take to heart and talk about it, and it then will be as a tree planted on the banks of tranquil waters, one that will give forth fruit at the right time, and all one's works will succeed, and the Light of the Ancient will shine upon this person.

Whoever wishes to attain the depths and to understand attains a level that is accepted, just as [in ancient times] a burnt offering on the altar. The damage of division occurs when the mouth speaks but the heart is far away. That is the reason why [the early first-century AD sage] Rabbon Gamlíel decreed that any student whose inner state does not reflect his outer should not enter the house of study to hear the expositions of the Torah, because otherwise he will not reclaim the birthright of his soul, as evidenced by the fact that 'only one whose inner state resembles his outer appearance may pronounce teachings of the Torah' and this tallies exactly with the [alphanumeric] number of the Holy Name. One who applies himself with due deliberation and wisdom, according to his ability to understand, in whatever language, provided he has faith, God in Heaven will come to his assistance and support in every detail, great and small, even if it be a mystery to those who tread only the path of the revealed teachings, that person will nevertheless be able to ascend the straight path to find respite for his soul in tranquillity and satisfaction and God will rescue and protect him from all evil, and he will be able to extract precious teachings, and even the barren trees will bear fruit. His soul will be reckoned unto those of the righteous in Paradise, crowned and clothed with beautiful garments by God, the creator of the celestial bodies.

And with these indisputable proofs, everyone will rapidly collect around me in rows, and will lift the hems of their garments to run: those who seek to undo the limitations imposed by the earlier sages as well as those who seek to uphold them, both the proud and the humble, the small and the great, all will be united, the rich and poor will meet with holy melody and clear voice, reading the scriptures and delving into the secrets with comprehensive explanations,

because we are strong, together with the illustrious scholars who are
among us today drawing pure water from the depths of the springs,
sitting on resplendent thrones of justice, and together with those
who are no longer among us and whose souls are bound in the bonds
of eternal life, through their [previous] approbations [issued in the
days of Tsvi-Hirsh's great-grandfather who conceived the project and
produced the first draft] to publish for the public good to enlighten
them with these pure words, filtered a number of times, inscribed for
future generations.

And so I girded my loins and, with little backing, I set out on my
way to bring to fruition my idea for the benefit of my dispersed
nation and I reached the holy city, crowned with pure beauty, the
famous Holy City of Frankfurt, and I set my face to the wells of deliv-
erance. In a time of love one cries out, and I raised my eyes to the
high mountains, namely the wealthy, perfect and guileless to come
to my assistance and to enable with their means this book as a way
of being remembered forever, as they are renowned for always being
prepared to come to the aid of those who exert themselves for the
sake of God. They favoured me and loaned me finance to cover the
cost of publication. They are Reb Moushe Shiff and Reb Itzik Hamel
together with the other leaders of the community, may God fully
repay them their deeds, and may they see children and grandchildren studying the Torah. I gave the work to three printers, those with
pure hearts, in order that they complete it as quickly as possible for
the public good.

But our joy was turned to grief over the destruction of the holy
community and its synagogue, as we witnessed the great fire in the
city. I was obliged to omit passages and to abridge the rest as far as
possible, the roots and the branches as well as the fruit. Because of
this necessity, the shortcomings are readily noticeable. I raise my
hands in prayer to God, who gives strength that He should find
me worthy of applying my hand again to publish the entire work
properly as my broken heart had intended, and that He protect me
from His anger and wrath and from every crisis and trouble, so that
I should be able to benefit the Jewish people, who are as beautiful as
the pure sun, and to guide them in the upright path, and that the
crown be restored and we be worthy to see the primeval light of the
seven days of creation of which the sun is only one sixtieth, and to
the rebuilding of the Temple in our days, amen.

So says Tsvi Hirsh ben Reb Yerakhmíel Khotsh of Krakow.

(Khotsh 1711: introduction [from Hebrew, Aramaic and Yiddish])

Image 8.1 Title page of the folio-size Yiddish *Zohar* published by Tsvi-Hirsh
Khotsh at Frankfurt am Main in 1711
Source: Courtesy of Dr Moshe Rosenfeld (Rose Chemicals, London).

Taken with this introduction, the publication of the central work of
the Kabbalah in Yiddish, with these daring thoughts expressed in
the introduction, represents an apogee of Yiddish religious power
within Yiddish-speaking Europe, in one of the last projects to span both
conceptual halves, west and east, of Ashkenaz.

II
Transition in the West

9
Anti-Semitism Targets Yiddish

In 1913, Ber Borokhov established the academic field of Yiddish by the publication of two works, an essay (Borokhov 1913a) and a powerfully annotated bibliography (1913b), that together built out of scattered and unknown components a viable field for modern academia. Much that modern readers learned was startling. For the reader then (and for that matter for some readers now), it comes as something of a shock that section Roman II and subsection Arabic 1) read:

II Sensational writings about Yiddish
1) Trash literature about Yiddish
(Borokhov 1913b: 8 [from the Yiddish])

The word 'trash' in the second heading does not quite do justice to the Yiddish *shund* (cf. German *Schund*, and it is indeed a nineteenth-century borrowing from New High German rather than an old Yiddish word that 'came down the line'). Among Yiddishist intelligentsia, the word took on the notion of sub-standard publications, usually racy stories and novels that were entertaining and titillating, incorporating sex, violence or both. The term was popularized by humorist Sholem Aleichem (Sholem Rabinovitsh 1859–1916) in his one rather non-humorous polemic, *Shómer's mishpet* ('The Trial of Shomer') of 1888, where he blasted Shomer (Nokhem-Meyer Shaykevitsh 1846–1905) out of the new field of serious Yiddish literature (perhaps unfairly; see Grace-Pollak 1998).

With a Borokhovian twist, the founder of Yiddish studies was 'slightly modifying' a by-then popular media (newspaper and magazine) word to fit the new field of Yiddish linguistics, that would itself be highly controversial in the super-charged world of East European Jewish cultural diversity, in which some powerful factions saw merits in developing study of the majority-population languages where Jews lived or of Hebrew, or of both, but not of the Jewish vernacular language. After listing more than 30 entries (Borokhov nos. 32–55, various of them with sub-entries) comes his characterization of this body of literature:

> This so-called 'literature' is disgusting. Still, it must not be dismissed out of hand. First, it is too numerous in quantity of works to be wholly ignored. The greatest part of the older Christian literature about Yiddish consists of ignorant, self-advertising, barking *shund*. A smaller part, however, consists of serious work. Now if you take the German reader, he also comes into the equation: the flood of ignorance does after all demonstrate how much the German public is interested in Jewish 'speech'. Aside from that, Avé-Lallemant is quite right, when he finds at least something interesting in every one of these pieces of trash. For all these booklets, even the scornful mockery of 'Itzig Feitel Stern', were written either by people who knew the coarse language of the lowest strata of Jewish traders rather well, or were simply stolen from other such 'experts'. A person dedicated to academic research must overcome the disgust and still leaf through this referenced *shund* literature. For Jewish folklore (in Germany) this literature has in any case not a smaller worth than for example, Bernstein's collection of impolite Yiddish expressions, *Erotica et Rustica*, which no serious scholar would negate because of its dirty contents. The difference is only that Bernstein himself is a serious and learned researcher, while our *shund*-linguists have no association with any academic seriousness.
>
> (Borokhov 1913b: 12 [from the Yiddish])

The Bernstein referred to is the eminent Yiddish folklorist Ignatz Bernstein (1836–1909), known for his classic compilation of Yiddish proverbs and sayings (Bernstein 1908; Althaus 1969). The section on erotica appeared as a supplementary publication.

The Avé-Lallemant referred to is Friedrich Christian Benedict Avé-Lallemant, a police official in the north German port city of Lübeck who was, improbably, one of the leading Yiddish linguists of the nineteenth century. He had come to the study of Yiddish via criminology and study of the German underworld language Rotwelsch, which had numerous Yiddish (and Hebrew) elements, rendering Rotwelsch studies an important field of historical Yiddish linguistics (see Katz 1996). Avé-Lallemant came to respect Yiddish so deeply that he actually argued for the antiquity and legitimacy of the language against contemporary German-Jewish scholars who had feelings of shame about Yiddish (see Chapter 10). Indeed, criminological works dealing in part or in whole with Yiddish go back centuries, and they too were sometimes (by no means always) part of anti-Semitic discourse. The most famous example is Martin Luther's preface to the 1528 edition of the *Liber vagatorum*. The book, which first appeared around 1510, warned people against fake beggars and ends with a vocabulary of the underworld language. By the time of his preface, Luther had despaired of converting the Jews to his reformed Christianity, and used the obviously Hebraic origin of some of the words of Rotwelsch as 'proof' that the Jews were at the heart of criminal gangs. Intriguing as the subject is, the study of Yiddish for criminological purposes, whether hostile (anti-Semitic), practical (neutral, for example, for helping police) or positive (as in the case of Avé-Lallemant), was sometimes an object of study, not a tool of societal power in the wider sense. We shall therefore return to the eighteenth century.

Incidentally, the German word *Antisemitismus* was coined, virtually in its modern connotation, by German radical nationalist Wilhelm Marr (1819–1904) who founded the *Antisemiten-Liga* ('League of Anti-Semites') in 1879, though a more general sense is attested some decades earlier. Leaving the terminology aside, the phenomenon in earlier times is of course coverable by the modern term, and the study of the phenomenon is today a productive academic field (see, for example, Wistrich 2010; Heni 2013).

In the eighteenth century particularly — though the phenomenon occurred both earlier and later — there was a veritable market saturation, so to speak, of anti-Semitic works focusing on the Yiddish language, though for sure not by that name for the language. These works appeared in German-speaking areas and were intended for readers of German. Many take the form of dictionaries, lexicons and language-learning manuals with sample texts, most often in the Latin (or German) alphabet, thereby revealing more about everyday Yiddish or modern Yiddish linguistics, strange as it may sound, than any Yiddish-in-Yiddish works from the same time and place which tended toward a marketable, common-denominator Jewish alphabet standard with a host of delimiting factors. The inherited writing tradition naturally had its baggage; there was frequent conceptualization of 'German' as more correct, stern avoidance of dialect that could impair international sales, and a typically Jewish, for the time, apathy toward low-brow or potentially compromising vocabulary or content when it came to printed matter. Indeed, Western Yiddish language and literature were in any case in steep decline during the eighteenth century, and the 'photographic capture' of select segments of contemporary linguistic usage remains a permanent treasure of data for linguists and sociolinguists alike.

The anti-Semitic aspects are manifold, including many of the accusations against the Jews from the litany of classic European anti-Semitism of older Christian culture. But if pressed to categorize the major ways in which the study of Yiddish and publication of books about Yiddish could empower a major trend of anti-Semitism in central Europe in the eighteenth century, the answer could be reduced to three key assertions. The first is explicit: that the Jews use their 'secret language' to cheat the Christians. By busting the code, as it were, Christians can acquire self-defence in commerce against Jewish machinations. The second is that Jews despise Jesus Christ and Christianity, and their anti-Christianity is exposed by mere observation of their vernacular lexicon. The third, though often implicit, is nevertheless equally obvious: that from the viewpoint of a German-speaking anti-Semite, the Yiddish language per se is at once barbarically ugly and hilariously comical. The three aspects combined made way for a commercially viable product. The multiple editions of many of these titles serve inter alia to demonstrate their commercial success beyond the realm of scholars and even of businessmen who could learn something 'useful for their business'. Studies of the subject from the viewpoint of Yiddish linguistics include Borokhov (1913b), Max Weinreich (1923b), Katz (1986, 1996b) and Frakes (2007). On Yiddish in German culture see Grossman (2000) and Elyada (2012).

Yiddish-focused anti-Semitism: samples of a genre

The author whom Borokhov rightly crowned 'the father' of the eighteenth-century anti-Semitic literature focused on Yiddish was a baptized Jew who had turned on his erstwhile people, and obviously had native command of the everyday language and even some of its rabbinic registers. His nom de plume was the unexciting 'J.W.'. The book's first known (and undated) editions are generally dated by bibliographers to a time span between ±1702 and ±1714.

J.W.'s book is called *Jüdischer Sprach-Meister* ('Jewish Language-Master') for short and has now been made available in an English edition (Finkin 2010). It is constructed as a book-length dialogue between a Jewish merchant called *Joune* (*Youne*, modern Yiddish *Yóyne* 'Jonah') and a rabbi called *Rebbe Itzick* (Itsik, a Yiddish male forename deriving

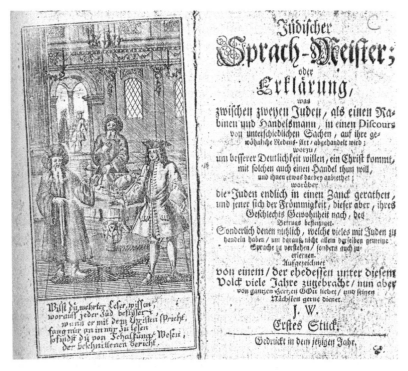

Image 9.1 Frontispiece and title page of the *Juedischer Sprach-Meister* (±1714)
Source: Courtesy of Hermann Suess (Fürsenfeldbruck).

from *Yítskhok*, 'Isaac', hence in effect 'Rabbi Isaac'). Instead of tedious vocabularies and grammar rules, J.W. offers a colourful (and flashingly off-colour) extended series of dialogues between the two, with contemporary Western Yiddish on the left-hand side in Gothic letters, with the exception of words of Semitic (Hebrew or Aramaic) origin which are provided in Latin letters. In either case, this made for the text being readily readable by German readers without having to learn the Jewish alphabet. Facing it, on the right-hand side of each opening, is the German translation, all in the standard Gothic alphabet of the day.

The 'moral of the story' that runs through all the topics covered in the *Sprach-Meister* is that Christians, by unravelling the Jews' 'secret language', have the power to defeat the Jews' alleged purposes: cheating Christians, defaming Christ, behaving unethically, immorally and hypocritically. These prejudices come to the fore via a sometimes hilarious dialogue, containing some of the earthiest items from the lexicon of everyday vernacular Yiddish. Indeed, these are the kinds of items that did not make it into Yiddish writings in Yiddish.

The book aims to undermine perceived Jewish secrets by revealing for Christianity not only the 'secret Jewish language' but supposed 'secret Jewish thoughts' too. On the ultra-sensitive subject of Jewish vs Christian views of the Messiah, Jonah reports to the rabbi the news that Jews are getting impatient with their rabbis' explanations for their Messiah's failure to arrive:

> I asked converts [to Christianity] why they got baptized. So they answered me that the rabbis are liars, and have put on the people of Israel heavy burdens, concerning which nothing is said in all the Torah, and they have stipulated specific dates [for the Coming], according to which Messiah should have come some hundreds of years ago, but is unto this day not come; Therefore Yeishe ['Jesus' in this dialect of Yiddish] is the true Messiah. Hence we have left the Israelite religion.
>
> (J.W. ±1714: 33 [from the transcribed Yiddish])

What is lost in translation is much more than the usual specificities of a language. In the original, this paragraph is peppered with learned Hebraisms embedded in the Yiddish, for example (using modern standard Yiddish transcription), *shóyel zayn* ('ask'), *ol kóved* ('heavy burden'), *ad hayóm (ha) zé* ('to this day'). Others, not naturally occurring in Yiddish, were part of a special style of language meant specifically to defy understanding, for example, *oum't* in his orthography (the modern Yiddish *would* have been *óymed*) 'stands', but in the sense of the Germanic-derived Yiddish *shteyt* ('stands' [physically] in Yiddish). Here it is a playful conscious counter-natural calque of 'stands written', the Germanic construction for 'is written'. The stem replacement would be humorous and secretive both (reminiscent of Rotwelsch, the secret German underworld language; see Katz 1996a). Finally, there are Hebraisms whose sociolinguistic status straddles learning and mockery at once, for example, *shakrónim* ('liars'). These were indeed used by the rabbinically educated and high-prestige language-conscious members of the Western Yiddish speech community.

Elsewhere J.W. veers into sexual matters in an effort to unmask the rabbinate. The rabbi plans to visit a house of ill repute, which initially shocks the naive man, who goes on to warn his rabbinic friend:

> I can't listen to you any longer. Your blasphemies burn me in the heart to the point where I will soon faint. Therefore, quickly, let's go to the police station, and I will revive myself with whisky, and I am

telling you explicitly, that if you will go to the whore house, then I
won't consider it any great sin to rat on you and immediately inform
the judge, and I do so for your own good, for it is better that you
receive punishment in this world than in the world to come.

(J.W. ±1714: 33 [from the transcribed Yiddish])

There is a hilarity of juxtapositions, of such classic Jewish religious
concepts as (modern transcription) *óylem háze* ('this world') vs *óylem
hábe* ('the world to come'), with one of the 'worst' words in the Yiddish
pantheon of curses, *náfke* ('whore') (from the Aramaic root for 'going
out', hence 'one who goes out', 'streetwalker', etc.). There are homely
terms like *nevéyre* for 'sin' (from *an avéyre*, 'a sin', with the indefinite
article 'an' fused into the noun via meta-analysis), and as ever, 'secret
language' concoctions like *Shouters-Baijis* (today that would theoreti-
cally be the non-occurring *shóyter's báyis* 'policeman's house' for 'police
house/station').

The result of the anonymous apostate author having once been a
relatively learned Ashkenazic Jewish fellow leads to numerous intra-
Jewish discussions, which are revealing. The twentieth-century debates
about prayer in Yiddish in earlier Ashkenaz (for example, Noble 1951
vs Lieberman 1952; see now D.E. Fishman 1991) have struck some as
a somewhat anachronistic imposition of modern issues into older and
more westerly Ashkenaz (see Chapters 5 and 8). But the *Sprach-Meister*'s
illustrative dialogues delve into that too in an in-situ eighteenth-
century Western Ashkenaz milieu. When Rabbi Itsik insists that God
only accepts prayer in Hebrew, the simple Jonah challenges him about
how such a prayer can be acceptable, without it being understood and
hence failing to produce the necessary *kavóne* (intent, concentration,
sense of purpose). When the rabbi cedes the point of *kavóne* being
absolutely necessary, Jonah comes right back asking how a blessing can
have the required quality if the person saying it doesn't understand what
he is saying. But the discussion then digresses somewhat to encompass
attitudes toward ejaculation of semen that would, as usual in this book,
lead from the mundane to the shockingly sensational (pp. 52–7).

Some eighteenth-century purveyors of Yiddish as a weapon in the
arsenal of growing anti-Semitism in Germany adopted rather pompous
pseudonyms, including 'Philoglottus' and 'Bibliophilus'. Philoglottus
published his *Kurtze und gründliche Anweisung zur Teutsch-Jüdischen
Sprache* in Freiberg in 1733, noting on the title page that it was intended
for both theological students (generally a euphemism for missionaries) and for *Handels-Leuten* (tradesmen). The missionary literature on

Yiddish is itself a major chapter in the history of Yiddish studies (see Katz 1996b: 237–9).

Following his dedication and preface, Philoglottus proceeds to provide the Yiddish alphabet (using the specific *máshkit* type font of the Jewish alphabet in which actual Yiddish books had by then been printed for around two centuries). He provides rules of spelling, reading exercises and the alphanumeric values for the Hebrew alphabet important for reading business documents. That is followed in turn by the German-to-Yiddish dictionary in the German-Latin alphabet only, invariably providing only Yiddish terms that come from Hebrew or Aramaic that would ipso facto not be comprehensible to a German. At the end, as a sort of epilogue, there is a short text in a stylized Western Yiddish, in the usual German-based transcription, that is then provided in German as a learning tool. It starts with this thought:

> That the Jewish religion today consists of vanity of vanities can be seen from the secrets that the rabbis have invented from the Kabbalah supposedly to guard people from evils and danger.
>
> (Philoglottus 1733: 61–2 [from the transcribed Yiddish])

The section concludes with a pseudo-Hebraic blessing that starts with the usual first word of Jewish blessings, *Borukh* ('blessed be'), and then proceeds to bless God, using four forms of God's name in Hebrew, and also: 'Yeshua Messiah who reigns over the heavens and the earth. Amen and amen'.

By contrast, Bibliophilus, whose own *Jüdischer Sprach-Meister* appeared in 1742, in Frankfurt and Leipzig, offered his readers the inverse of Philoglottus: a Yiddish (more accurately, a mostly Semitic-component-of-Yiddish) lexicon with translations into German. It is followed by five dialogues in the by-then popular format of Yiddish on the left, German on the right. One typographical innovation here is that the Yiddish column appears entirely in Gothic font, including the (many) words of Semitic origin. Sandwiched between the dictionary and the five dialogues is what may be described as the book's introduction, though it is placed between a dictionary and study-aid bilingual dialogues. The seven-page salvo's title translates as: 'Concerning the slander and blasphemy of the Jews against Christ our Saviour, the Holy Mother, and against all Christians' (pp. 72–81). It is a classic 'code-busting' effort, starting out with the argument that in their own internal language, the Jews have uncomplimentary names for Jesus, including (transcription here modified to modern standard Yiddish) *der nótsri* ('the one from

Nazareth'), *der tólui* ('the hanged one' or by extension 'the crucified one') or *der mámzer* ('the bastard'), but, it is lamented, they never deign to call him even by his own Hebrew name *Yeshúa*, which comes from the root for 'salvation'.

Further on he claims that the usual appellations in the Jewish language for Mary include, instead of Maria, *Kharia* (in his spelling *Charja*) which he glosses 'pile of excrement', or *zóyne*, Western Yiddish *zóune* (his: *Zona*) 'whore'. Further on, we are told that Christian women are invariably known by the words *góye* ('Christian woman'), *érltin* (modern Yiddish *órlte*), which translates as 'uncircumcized woman [humorous]', *kláfte* 'bitch', *náfke* 'whore', ending the paragraph with the following flourish: that of Christian women collectively it is said *Hakl náfkes teméyes* 'All of them are unclean whores'. As a contrast to the usual welcoming exclamation *Bórukh habó* (lit. 'Blessed is the comer'), when it is a Christian coming, the Jew is reported to say *Órur habó* ('Cursed is the comer').

Naturally, Bibliophilus was not interested in the neutral or friendly words of Jews for their neighbours. Instead he assembled the most aggressive curse and slang words in the language, in a way that would give his German readers the impression that Jews obsessively spent their days harping on against Christ, Christian holinesses and Christian people at all times and with a developed and multifarious vocabulary. No mention is made of the use of the various terms cited (and many uncited) for using Yiddish to insult other Jews. It is the crystallization of a clear brand of German anti-Semitism that was 'in the air' by the eighteenth century. In the final paragraph of the purported exposé, he explains that he acquired all these terms 'in part from typical Jews, in part also from various rabbis, for I have studied Mishnah and Gemoro [the two comprising the Talmud] [...], I observed and made notes and hereby communicate it to the well-disposed reader.'

Bibliophilus concludes with five bilingual dialogues with the two language columns on each page (as opposed to the facing-page format). The two columns are named *Hebräo-barbarisch* (Hebrao-Barbaric) and *Teutsch* (German), respectively. The first is a dialogue between two Jewish horse dealers, including some terms that were to become part of German horse dealers' slang well into modern times (see Guggenheim-Grünberg 1954). The second is between a poor and a rich Jew on the topic of the fruit trade. The third is between two Jewish traders; the fourth between two Jews, Samuel and Lipman, about the cow trade; and the fifth between a rabbi and his pupil. Bibliophilus's *Jüdischer Sprach-Meister* climaxes with the sixth and final reading exercise: 'Between a Christian and a Jew concerning the Messiah'. The tone switches here from 'code breaking' to persuasion, demonstrating how a Christian can persuade other Jews from their own holy books that passages in the Hebrew Bible (Old Testament) specifically prophecy Jesus Christ, and how generations of rabbis have simply misinterpreted the obvious. It makes clear that mastering the language and holy texts of the Jews is vital to be able to prove to Jews the veracity of Christianity and the falsehood of Judaism. This is a brand of anti-Semitism historically milder (in the sense of less or non-violent) in so far as the evil ones are given conversion as a purportedly honourable way out.

Many of the authors of eighteenth-century anti-Semitic Yiddish grammars, dictionaries and handbooks tended to be focused either on ostensibly theological or ethical categories. While the first group condemns the alleged anti-Christian disposition of Jews, the second is obsessed by alleged Jewish dishonesty in business. Knowledge of Yiddish is offered as a key to surmount the purported obstacle.

A prime late eighteenth-century example of the genre is the anonymous Yiddish-to-German dictionary that appeared in Oettingen in 1790 (apparently a reprint of a work from 1764, see Borokhov 1913b: no. 39). It is a small book titled *Teutch-Hebräisches Wörterbuch*. Here the lexicon provided from (essentially) the Semitic component in Yiddish is referred to as 'Hebrew' (*Hebräisch*) rather than, say, *Juden-deutsch* or *Hebräo-barbarisch*. This author of a Yiddish dictionary is not interested in theology or in characterizing the language as 'Hebrew-Barbarian'; on the contrary, he enhances the brand of the product he is selling by virtue of the word for 'Hebrew'. The author's central idea appears to be that the language of the Jews is their tool for commercial supremacy. The title page includes the text 'in order to be able to act with caution when engaged in doings and dealings with the Jews'. The next page, before the start of the book, carries a three-line warning that translates: 'Whoever wants to understand the Jews, does not have to come from them. Their motto is: bargain!' These two messages at the book's start are reinforced by an unflattering image of a Jew, long nose and all, on the title page (see Image 9.2).

The commercial (rather than theological) focus of the Oettingen *Wörterbuch* of 1790 comes to practical expression in the book's content. It proceeds methodically from an alphabet chart to the Hebraic numbering system, names of coins and banknotes, and the 12 months of the Jewish calendar at the end.

The eighteenth-century corpus of anti-Semitic Yiddish manuals can be analysed into the three primary Yiddish-related German antipathies to Ashkenazic Jews. First, the aesthetic, entailing the notion that Yiddish

Image 9.2 Title page of the *Teutsch-Hebräisches Wörterbuch* (Oettingen 1790)
Source: Courtesy of Dr Hermann Suess (Fürsenfeldbruck).

is a barbaric corruption of German and inherently disturbing. Second, the religious, entailing the claim that the Jews use Yiddish to constantly demean and mock all that is dear to Christians and Christianity, from Christ on down. Third, the economic, entailing the notion that Yiddish is consciously structured (what with Hebrew-derived numbers, names of currency units, months and much more) to facilitate Jewish cheating of Christians in everyday commerce.

These three language-related eighteenth-century pillars of German anti-Semitism were to find new incarnations in subsequent generations, even when and where Yiddish had partly, nearly or completely disappeared, a process under way in that century, and one modified but not eradicated by the German-Jewish Enlightenment (see Chapter 10). In the history of ideas, these anti-Yiddish notions were to be integrated into wider models of the anti-Semitic imagination in Germany and Austria which had their directly descended state of mind in Nazi Germany. An example follows of the language issue in Hitler's *Mein Kampf*:

> A man can change his language without any trouble, that is, he can use another language; but in his new language he will express the old ideas; his inner nature is not changed. This is best shown by the Jew, who can speak a thousand languages and nevertheless remains a Jew. His traits of character have stayed the same, whether two thousand years ago as a grain dealer in Ostia, speaking Latin, or as a flour profiteer today, jabbering German with a Jewish accent. It is always the same Jew. [...]
>
> The motive why the Jew decides suddenly to become a 'German' is obvious. He feels that the power of the princes is slowly tottering and therefore tries at an early time to get a platform beneath his feet. Furthermore, his financial domination of the whole economy has advanced so far that without possession of all 'civil' rights he can no longer support the gigantic edifice, or at any rate, no further increase of his influence is possible. And he desires both of these; for the higher he climbs, the more alluring his old goal that was once promised him rises from the veil of the past, and with feverish avidity his keenest minds see the dream of world domination tangibly approaching. And so his sole effort is directed toward obtaining full possession of 'civil' rights.
>
> (Hitler 1925 [from the German])

The first and rather immediate intellectual impact of the anti-Semitic targeting of Yiddish fed almost seamlessly into the late eighteenth-century launch of the German-Jewish Enlightenment, which rather straightforwardly *agreed* with the anti-Semites' ideas about the Jews' language and set out to stamp out Yiddish, so that Yiddish-speaking Ashkenazic Jewry would be replaced in these lands by a modern German Jewry comprised of culturally and linguistically assimilated 'Germans of the Mosaic faith'.

10
German-Jewish Enlightenment also Targets Yiddish

The 'Berlin Enlightenment' that transformed German Jewry cannot wholly be seen as the result of a movement established by one towering figure, the German-Jewish philosopher and reformer Moses Mendelssohn (or Moses of Dessau, 1729–86). But neither can his overwhelming impact be minimized. His life and times, and the concurrent intellectual and cultural ferment, have been researched extensively (see, for example, Altmann 1973; Low 1979; Bach 1984; Sorkin 1987; Elon 2002; Hertz 2009; Feiner 2011).

From the Yiddish point of view, the antecedent backdrop to the Berlin Enlightenment is vital. In the eighteenth century, Yiddish language and literature were in any case in steep decline in the German-speaking lands, as traditional Ashkenazic civilization was heading downwards by any number of measurements, among them demography, rabbinic authority, creative output (with few exceptions) in Western Yiddish and in Hebrew and Aramaic rabbinic literature. Many Yiddish areas were being Germanized by virtue of attrition to German, the co-territorial language of state, power and prestige, which had cognates with most of the majority Germanic component within Yiddish. Ashkenaz I, to use Max Weinreich's terminology, was in decline, while in the east, the centuries of Jewish settlement in Eastern Europe, in the Slavonic and Baltic lands, had become an Ashkenaz II that was undergoing major growth in demography, rabbinic culture and the independent further development of Yiddish in places where there was no (or no significant volume of) German to be heard among the co-territorial population.

In the west, on German-speaking territory, Western Ashkenaz gave way incrementally to the 'modern Jew' in the sense of someone who may dress like and sound like any non-Jewish German, but who (perhaps privately) adheres to the Judaic rather than the Christian religion.

189

Western Ashkenaz, in its new guise of German Jewry, would also give rise to a (for Jewish history) large number of converts to Christianity, further eroding but never erasing the German Jewish identity prior to the Third Reich.

For moderns, it can be hard to fathom, but before this the Ashkenazic Jew, in east or west, was immediately identifiable by clothing, seemingly constant religious activity and observance and, above all, language. The emerging anthropologically westerner of the Jewish faith was to be a new type in the German-speaking areas of central Europe. Whatever the breakdown in factors leading to the change, it is clear that the 'Berlin Enlightenment' or 'German-Jewish Enlightenment' led by Moses Mendelssohn played a significant role in the transformation (detailed studies of Mendelssohn on language include Grossman 2000 and Schorch 2012).

Mendelssohn's circle believed that Jews could escape their social ghettoization and be empowered on the path to civil equality if their language, clothing, bearing and aura would only be Germanized. On a deeper psychological level, the Mendelssohnians, or *Berliner* as they were often called, more or less internalized the conclusions of the anti-Semitic camp about Yiddish: aesthetically it was just bad German that needed to be stamped out and replaced by standard German. Culturally, the language kept the Jew in a kind of spiritual and social ghetto. Intellectually, it prevented the Jew from pursuing a fulfilling life in German society. Finally, and here the deep psychological link to what the anti-Semites were claiming is evident, Yiddish was bad for Jewish morals. The most famous quotation in the saga was perhaps made in the context of that very rare extant state-recognized Yiddish text: the oath which a Jew would have to swear in a court of law, and which he or she was expected to fully understand. Mendelssohn famously had this to say to those who might think that permitting a person to take an oath in his or her native language is a sign of tolerance and intercultural respect:

> To the contrary I would not in the least wish to see a legal authorization of the Judeo-German dialect, nor a mixture of Hebrew and German as suggested by Fraenkel. I am afraid that this jargon has contributed not a little to the immorality [or: uncivilized bearing] of the common person. By contrast, it seems to me that the recent usage of pure German among my people promises to have a most positive effect on them. It would aggravate me greatly, therefore, if even the law of the land were to promote, so to speak, the abuse of

either language. It would be much better if Mr Fraenkel tried to put the whole oath into pure Hebrew so that it could be read in either pure German or pure Hebrew, or perhaps both, whichever is the best in the circumstances. Anything but this mishmash of language!

(Mendelssohn GS 13: 80; after Gilman 1986: 103; cf. Grossman: 2000: 77–8)

This statement, more than many by Mendelssohn's circle claiming the vernacular to be a corrupt hybrid that impeded assimilation to the majority culture, remains central precisely because it went a step further in relating Yiddish to the alleged immorality of everyday people. Only a retrospective and inherently anachronistic thought experiment could try to say what it is that Mendelssohn might have had in mind. The most likely, although politically incorrect answer, is that the hearty rich Yiddish vocabulary for all levels of a living language, including the lowest echelons of society, and indeed, the registers of the lexicon so heavily 'revealed to the German majority' by the eighteenth-century anti-Semitic literature about Yiddish (see Chapter 9) caused him and his circle grave discomfort.

Mendelssohn's statement in connection with the 'Jewish oath' came in his letter to Assistant Councillor Ernst Ferdinand Klein on the possible reform of the oath's text for use in Prussian courts. What the Assistant Councillor may not have known was that Mendelssohn, with 'pure Hebrew or pure German', was in fact echoing an ancient debate in the Talmud from the early centuries of the common era that concerned the antecedent to Yiddish as Jewry's principal vernacular: Aramaic. One Talmudic sage asked,

'Why Aramaic? Either Hebrew or Greek!' and another said, 'Why Aramaic? Either Hebrew or Persian!'

(Babylonian Talmud, tractate The First Gate 83a; The Suspected Wife 49b [from the Hebrew])

But another sage warned:

Let not the Aramaic language be light in your eyes for the Good Lord has shown it honour in the Bible.

(Midrash on Genesis 74: 34 [from the Hebrew])

The recasting of such ancient preconfigurations of modern issues is not all that rare in a culture so vertically reliant on ancient holy books.

It is not overly difficult to find anti-Yiddish statements by Mendelssohn and by his followers, who went on to build not only the modern academic field now known as Judaic (or Jewish) studies (itself a direct intellectual descendant of the Mendelssohn-circle-origin *Wissenschaft des Judentums*). Such statements have been collected by, among others, Max Weinreich (1973: III, 293–7), Sander Gilman (1986: 98–107) and Jeffrey Grossman (2000: 77–87).

The wider issue of the (at least partial) internalization of the anti-Semitic view of Jewish language as being on the mark about a set of troubles that need to be 'fixed' is a touchy one that is often shirked by modern Jewish scholarship. The most profound exception to date is Gilman's (1986) pioneering *Jewish Self-Hatred: Antisemitism and the Hidden Language of the Jews*, which comes closer than any in recognizing the Mendelssohnian rejection of Yiddish as inherently related to a Jewish self-hate that was itself not unrelated to the image of the Jew in the anti-Semitic imagination in the German-speaking lands.

In recent times, debate has arisen anew about whether Mendelssohn was *really* against Yiddish, or whether the language issue was just a bystanding entity for the debate. David Sorkin, an eminent scholar of the German-Jewish Enlightenment, has injected a note of doubt into the narrative:

> The notion that Mendelssohn was opposed to Yiddish was the invention of a subsequent age. For the possible origins of the idea, see Leopold Zunz, *Die Gottesdienstliche Vorträge der Juden* (Berlin, 1832), 451. Mendelssohn's alleged 'anti-Yiddishism' is an anachronism that has nothing to do with Mendelssohn but everything to do with those who applauded him (advocates of German, Hebrew, or other vernaculars) or attacked him (advocates of Yiddish). For example, the oft-quoted passage, 'This jargon has contributed not a little to the immorality of the common man' [...] has been wrenched out of context.
>
> (Sorkin 1996: chapter 6, note 3)

There is one sense in which Sorkin introduces a corrective into the debate. The present German word *Jiddisch* was nowhere to be found in German of the eighteenth century (and, indeed, in Yiddish itself it was just one of the names of the language, occurring in writing along with the more frequent *Taytsh*, *Loshn Ashkenaz* and other linguonyms). There was no 'Yiddish consciousness' in the present sense, which is in effect the sense of the nineteenth-century nationalism that produced in their precise current sense such analogous concepts as 'Belarusian', 'Ukrainian', etc. For sure, it is an anachronism to accuse Mendelssohn and his followers of being against a movement for the Yiddish language that was not to start for more than half a century after his death, and in Eastern Europe, never in Germany. On the other hand, the Mendelssohnians' hatred for, let's call it, 'the native Jewish language that would in a later period be universally known as *Yiddish*' and their extensive efforts to stamp it out are so well documented in both word and deed that it is not capable of convincing denial on an empirical basis.

The paper trail is solid. Mendelssohn attacks Yiddish Bible translation language as the work of 'stammering lips' (see Altmann 1973: 369). Commenting on one Yiddish Bible translation produced by the eminent Hebrew and Aramaic philologist Elijah Levita, Mendelssohn could only conclude that the luminous Levita could not have really done it (Altmann 1973: 370). In his own philosophical works, he could not resist the opportunity to mention in passing that German Jewish degeneracy, in his view, was inescapably linked to the language of the Jews (cf. Gilman 1986: 103–4; Breuer 1996).

Incidentally, the transition from Western Yiddish (more accurately the majority German-speaking areas within Western Yiddish) was helped along en masse by a very clever mechanism that made it appear to be a natural and incremental development. For many decades, the new language being introduced, modern standard German, was published (especially in the religious realm of Bibles, prayerbooks, traditional ritual and religious texts and translations) not in the German (Gothic) alphabet, but in the same old right-to-left ancient Jewish alphabet. Two additional factors made the transition smoother. First, the same traditional *máshkit* font that had been the typographical bastion of Yiddish from the dawn of Yiddish publishing in the first half of the sixteenth century was now used for German; it looked homely and familiar. Second, the same spelling conventions, alef for *a* and *o* vowels, and ayin for *e* vowels, double yud for diphthongs like *ei* and *ai*, were retained intact. In some instances there were logical, structural improvements, one of which, the addition of the Hebrew diacritics to distinguish alef (that is, *a*) from alef (that is, *o*), entailed simply placing the diacritic under the alef itself, turning the new combination into a conceptually 'separate letter', an overdue break with the strict inherited Semitic writing tradition by which letters were consonantal (and vowel systems were added via systems of diacritics to the preceding consonantal letter). Here, the diacritic was simply moved from the previous consonant (as in Hebrew) to the vowel letter, making for a univalent vowel letter, as in any European language. This simple improvement was later adopted 'back into real Yiddish' in Eastern Europe in one of the curious chapters of Yiddish and Writing, a topic for another book. The transition from Yiddish to German in the west, and its linguistic, orthographic and typographical correlates, merits a new monograph that will be a milestone in the study, inter alia, of normative linguistics in stateless situations.

There was great variation in the speed and the completeness of the transition from Western Yiddish to German speech in everyday life. As ever, some details of accent and pronunciation, perceived Jewish hand movements that accompany speech and similar features were able to outlive the language they had come from. If there was one German derogatory word that dogged the effort from before Mendelssohn and through to Hitler it was *mauscheln*, meaning to speak like a [German] Jew, to not quite be speaking real German but rather German with Jewish features. The etymology is presumed to be 'speak like Maushe' from the Western Yiddish *Moushe*, a popular Jewish male forename ('Moses', modern standard Yiddish *Móyshe*). On the German term *mauscheln*, see now Hans Peter Althaus's (2002) *Mauscheln: Ein Wort als Waffe*.

A few comments about the wider debate are in order. Latter-day Yiddishists who 'accuse' Mendelssohn of being 'against' Yiddish are not accusing him of being an evildoer. He and his circle acted according to their convictions and with the best civic-rights interests of their people at heart, and in context of the time and place. Yiddish was 'on its own' sinking in Germany by the time Mendelssohn came on the scene; he was to become a sophisticated German philosopher who would try to transform his people into a form that he thought would make them acceptable to German society. To comment on the Mendelssohnian circle's antipathy toward Yiddish is therefore to contribute to the variegated intellectual history of the subject, not to 'belittle' Mendelssohn.

Sorkin cites one of Mendelssohn's conceptual followers, the founder of *Wissenschaft des Judentums* in the German-Jewish spirit, Leopold Zunz (1794–1896), as being the key to understanding why Mendelssohn might be misunderstood on Yiddish in modernity. But Zunz and the other enormously accomplished scholars of the Mendelssohnian school can equally be understood to prove just the opposite. So obsessed with anti-Yiddish sentiment were these scholars that even their academic work, which was normally of the highest order in the traditional philological and literary sciences, tended to decline conceptually when it came to anything to do with Yiddish. Zunz, for example, when writing about Yiddish and frankly coming up with some perspicacious conclusions on 'politically neutral' issues like the interrelationship between etymology and semantics of the Yiddish lexicon (Zunz 1832: 439–41), ignored all these findings when it came to any question tied up with German-Jewish 'German nationalism'.

Most famously, in the same section in which he, ever the meticulous scholar, reveals medieval specificities of Jewish language, he finds it necessary to state that the German Jews as recently as 'three hundred years' beforehand, in other words in the sixteenth century, had spoken 'rather correct German' (?), the downfall of which is attributed to (as one might guess) the corrupting influence of 'the Polish Jews' (Zunz 1832: 438). Put differently, the history of Yiddish (and of course Zunz did not see the issue in those terms, because for him Yiddish could only be 'bad German') was in fact the history of the decline of German within the Jewish community.

Of course the German-Jewish Enlightenment's disdain for Yiddish was not a one-person Moses Mendelssohn proposition. The passion for dethroning the already powerless vernacular from any form of societal life or prestige for everyday people (an idea featured on Jewish title pages for centuries), and the idea of thereby improving the lot of European Jewry, was wholeheartedly shared by his fellow enlighteners. One key Mendelssohn ally, Naphtali Herz Wessely (Naftoli Hirts Vizl, 1725–1805), got deeply involved in supporting the reforms of Emperor Joseph II of Austria whose 1781 edict ('Patent of Tolerance') inspired many *maskílim*, as the Berlin Enlightenment proponents became known. Balancing attempts to remain loyal to Orthodoxy with support for the modernization of education became a major and painful theme in his life. He is best remembered for his Hebrew treatise, *Words of Peace and Truth*, where this remark is to be found:

> We ruin our reputation among the nations by being stammerers. It is well known that even a wise man educated in the sciences, who does not have a pure language, and does not know how to place his words into a sentence, is made into a laughing stock. All the more so the simple man when he deals with officials and merchants and speaks a castrated language like us, the Jews of Germany and Poland. He can only attract mockery and scorn in their eyes, and he will be treated as a peasant and one who is despised by people. This is not the case for a man who knows how to speak properly and in good taste. That man will find grace and honour in all who see him.
>
> (Wessely 1782 [from the Hebrew])

This was the age of epistles to German-speaking Jewry. Another major leader of the movement, David Friedlaender (1750–1834), was, unlike Wessely, unconcerned with finding favour among the traditionally religious rabbinate. He wanted to reform Judaism into a modern code of ethics of sorts, and years after Mendelssohn's death proposed a process of 'dry baptism' to make Jews more acceptable to the Christian environment. He wrote in his *Epistle to the German Jews* in 1788:

> This is the first and necessary condition [...]. The Judeo-German that is common among us has no rules, it is vulgar, and it is an incomprehensible language outside of our own circles. It must be eradicated completely, and the Holy Language, and the German mother tongue, must be taught systematically from early youth onward. Only then will it be possible to lay the foundations for a useful and rational education for our youth. Once the child is stuck into the so-called Judeo-German language he cannot have any correct conception of a single thing in this world. How can he be expected to act later on in accordance with any proper principles of behaviour?
>
> (Friedlaender 1788 [from the German in Yiddish script])

Turning from societal views of Yiddish to the scholarly component of the Berlin Enlightenment movement, subsequent German-Jewish scholars over the course of the nineteenth century often sought to 'improve' on Zunz's model from the viewpoint of buttressing Jewish empowerment in the country. They tried to further adjust the history by around a century with the claim that such a precious asset as the true German language could only have been ruined, as they saw it, by the influx of East European refugees from the Chmielnitski massacres in Ukraine in 1648 and 1649 and in ensuing years. J. M. Jost (1850, 1859: 208) posited the westward migration (in schematic Ashkenazic terms: remigration) of 'teachers, cantors, rabbis and community officials'. His theory was energetically developed by M. Güdemann (1887: 105, 1888: 296–7).

From the viewpoint of the history of ideas and scholars' aspirations to civic-rights empowerment for their people, this was analogous to the effort in the Russian Empire later in the nineteenth century of Albert (Avróm Eylióhu) Harkavy (1867) to posit that Jews in the Slavic lands once spoke pure Slavic before this same Yiddish arose on *that* scene. Harkavy, an intellectual combatant for the rights of Jews in the Russian Empire, was trying to bring to the political forum a certain history of their language that would amount to a 'historical argument' on behalf of Jewish rights and standing in czarist Russia.

What emerges as self-evident is that even top scholars can be power-oriented with respect to the anticipated (or feared) social, practical, political and other 'physical' effects of their constructions. These forces, conscious or unconscious, are to outsiders or a later generation often patently obvious in so far as they provide material for readily visible comparisons with the same scholars' conclusions on academic issues that are not conceptually attached to external issues of the day. The same Leopold Zunz whose enormous erudition led him to collect and cite an array of medieval Yiddish specificities in the documents of early Ashkenazic Jewry, and that would long after his death ensure his position as a de facto 'forefather' of modern Yiddish studies, felt the need to somehow calibrate findings to harmonize with contemporary political efforts to improve the lot of his people. At the same time, it is possible for scholars with no particular interest in political ramifications of certain projects to come out with daring and sensational conclusions that set them apart from the mindset of their era. Of course these instances point to a much narrower genre of power, that of personal academic or literary prestige of an author, a prestige that comes with producing original and daring work, but is far removed from current events.

Against that backdrop, the nineteenth century did produce one rather sensational scholarly exchange. A German police chief, who was not overtly pro-Jewish on questions of emancipation and civil rights of German Jewry, was a talented philologist on the side, specializing in Rotwelsch, the secret German underworld language known for centuries for its substantial Yiddish (and Ashkenazic Hebrew) component. His research led him to the profound study of the history of Yiddish and to conclusions on the origin and age of the language that would, as fate would have it, be rather close to those of the pro-Yiddish twentieth-century school of East European Jewish scholars of Yiddish long after his death, and that would set him on a collision course with his contemporary German-Jewish scholars. He also wrote novels on criminological themes, and studied the psychopathology of the criminal mind.

This police chief and criminologist, discussed earlier in other contexts (see Chapter 9), was Friedrich Christian Benedict Avé-Lallemant (1809–92), who spent much of his life in Lübeck, northern Germany. His major philological work is his four-volume opus, *Das deutsche Gaunerthum* (1858–62). Ber Borokhov, the founder of twentieth-century Yiddish studies, had this to say:

> Avé-Lallemant was a police official in Lübeck (Germany), but at the same time a highly trained linguist. As police official he started to

research the lives of German thieves, their history and their language. And — because Jewish thieves brought many elements to the language of their German colleagues — Avé-Lallemant thereby came to the investigation of the Yiddish language. He dedicated nearly the entire third volume of his opus and a large part of the fourth volume. Although now outdated in nearly every sense, Avé-Lallemant nevertheless remains the greatest researcher in the field of older Yiddish philology.

(Borokhov 1913b: no. 103 [from the Yiddish])

That brings us to the most sensational Yiddish scholarly debate of the nineteenth century. Avé-Lallament, whose unbiased research on Yiddish, coming as an adjunct to his study of Rotwelsch, led him to posit an early origin of Yiddish essentially coinciding with the early settlement of Jews (now known retrospectively as the first Ashkenazim) on German-speaking territory. In his research on Yiddish, he replied robustly to the academically 'anti-Yiddish' views of the great German-Jewish scholar Leopold Zunz for whom Yiddish was a relatively recent 'corruption' of the 'correct German' that the Jews in German-speaking lands no doubt spoke earlier. The German police chief was sharp enough to note that Zunz's own observations about the structure of Yiddish demonstrated a primary creative development (see Avé-Lallemant 1858–62: III, 204–7). It was then that another German-Jewish scholar, the greatest Jewish bibliographer Moritz Steinschneider, responded sharply to Avé-Lallemant (Steinschneider 1864: 36–7).

Mendelssohn's Berlin Enlightenment led, in the generations after his death, to some Jews converting to Christianity, and to some assimilating without converting. But it also led to three major streams of modern Judaism, known as Reform (radically changed beliefs and rituals), neo-Orthodox (modern Orthodox) and the compromise Conservative movement. From their origins in Germany and German-speaking areas of neighbouring countries, mostly in the nineteenth century, and with early outposts in Great Britain and the United States, all three movements were for all of that century and much of the twentieth every bit as anti-Yiddish as their ultimate late eighteenth-century founder.

Needless to say, absolutely no 'blame' attaches to anyone for not foreseeing Nazism and the Holocaust. But that caveat cannot enable us to shirk the responsibility to examine with the benefit of hindsight the fate of the explicit claims made repeatedly in Germany by founders and theoreticians of all the German-Jewish trends from Mendelssohn's circle through the scholarly *Wissenshafts des Judenthums*, reform, neo-Orthodoxy, the conservative movement and their outgrowths. All were certain that the shedding of the hated Yiddish speech or its remnants in the ensuing stages of 'Jewish German' would bring an end to anti-Jewish sentiment in German-speaking Europe.

In part through massive Jewish leaders' efforts, the weakened Western Yiddish — the dialects of Yiddish on German language territory (see Map 2) — were wiped out, in most areas nearly completely, with modest pockets of exceptional and highly localized survival on some peripheries, particularly Alsace (see, for example, Zuckerman 1969), a few Swiss villages (Guggenheim-Grünberg 1954) and the Netherlands (Beem 1954, 1975). These exceptions on the linguistic 'borderlands' were all cases of pockets of 'simple people' far from the centres, shakers and events of German-Jewish culture, religious or secular. They stand in sharp contrast to the societal power in the arts, professions and business achieved by the culturally assimilationist majority of German Jewry in a history that spans the late eighteenth century to the years of the Weimar Republic.

What went wrong, as framed by Sander Gilman, one of the few scholars to stare this issue unabashedly in the face, was that:

> The Jews had been seen as the speakers of the true German. Now they were seen as not speaking German at all. It was this thesis more than any other that attacked at the very roots of German Jewry's identity. [...]
>
> The German Student Union in their book burnings [of May 1933] carried out Hitler's dictum that 'a man can change his language without any trouble — that is, he can use another language, but in his new language he will express the old ideas; his inner nature is not changed' [from *Mein Kampf*]. [...]
>
> Hitler's racial linguistics is based on the image of the hidden infiltration, a paranoia echoed elsewhere in *Main Kampf* in his use of the image of the Jews as the cancer hidden within the German body politic. But it is the reality of the language of the Jews that permits them to burrow within. Like the blacks, they will never be able to hide their true nature, and thus like the blacks, they can never become truly German. Their mask has only one purpose: the eventual destruction of the host culture and its language. [...]
>
> The program of action according to which the Jews in Germany would be able to publish in only Hebrew or Yiddish (or present their works as translations) was a natural consequence of Hitler's reasoning. The fact that somewhat less than six per cent of German

Jews even had a rudimentary knowledge of Hebrew did not faze the German Student Union.

(Gilman 1986: 310–11)

Whatever one's conclusions might be, and there is certainly room for multiplicity of interpretations, it is patently — and painfully — clear that the wildly successful German-Jewish effort to replace Yiddish with German, and create generations of German-speaking Jews in Germany who would participate to the full in parts of the majority's life, certainly did not in any way ease or mitigate the rising tide of (ultimately genocidal) anti-Semitism that coalesced so seemingly rapidly in the 1930s. There is every reason to posit that at the deep psychological levels where eliminationist racial hatred survives and develops, the Other that speaks Your language, without being You, is wont to become a greater object of racial loathing than the Other that does not try to speak Your language. The Berlin Enlightenment's project brought social and economic empowerment to generations of Jews before itself becoming part of the target of the most fully enacted genocide in human history. In an altogether symbolic way, the negationist power of Yiddish was unleashed in the time and place where Yiddish was a memory (or an image of the 'barbaric east'), where Yiddish essentially did not exist, and where the descendants of its speakers felt confident that their jettisoning of the stigmatized minority language would pave the path to social integration and acceptance in one of the world's most advanced societies.

III
Rise in the East

11
Religious Power

The exotic history of such exceptional sagas as the Yiddish-related writings of Yechiel-Michel Epshteyn and the appearance of the Yiddish Zohar (see Chapter 8) notwithstanding, the 'encroachment' by Yiddish into the all-powerful daily religious life remained marginal. Usage of Yiddish found various 'openings' in the pervasive and encompassing religious life of Ashkenazim. The exceptions are so noteworthy precisely because they are so exceptional, often involving the intimate need for understanding, and invariably being supplemental to the Hebrew and Aramaic prayers, blessings and recitations. Traditions that became established most famously include songs at the two Passover night *seders* (*sdórim*), women's non-canonical prayer, stock phrases used before the grace after meals or at the conclusion of the end-of-Sabbath *havdóle* ceremony, and in certain kinds of texts, for example, that were recited in connection with searching for crumbs of bread or other forbidden-on-Passover foods during a search for the same before the festival.

But 'power' in society does not come from recital of the very occasional line in the vernacular language, Yiddish, when literal understanding is required by law or practice. Still, it is enticing to consider the 'what ifs' of language and power, not only the 'straight history'. Had Yiddish not been in demographic, literary and societal decline in German-speaking lands, had there not been a potent movement to obliterate it coming both from without (anti-Semitism focused on language) and within (the Berlin Enlighteners and Co.), then those few 'heroes of Yiddish' at the end of the seventeenth and beginning of the eighteenth centuries might have been the harbingers of vernacular power among Western Ashkenazim. But as the Western Ashkenazim were to fade out into a German Jewry, or a German-speaking group of the Jewish faith (or Jewish origins), we will never know.

Still, there was a lone author, whose book came to a 'rather bad end', who had attempted to fuse the religious object of a prayerbook and the desire for modernization into a new kind of Yiddish. One Aaron ben Shmuel of Hergershausen published a novel prayerbook in Yiddish in 1709. To moderns some of the following features might seem minor, but to the still-traditional rabbinic and communal authorities they were both scurrilous and scandalous. The prayerbook was entirely in Yiddish (not bilingual) *and* in the classic 'square Hebrew letters' (*meruba*) reserved in Ashkenaz for the Hebrew and Aramaic classic texts (even the hallowed commentaries had to be in another font, the rabbinic 'Rashi' font). These two culturally rebellious features, taken together, represent a power grab on behalf of the Yiddish-speaking 'Hebraically limited' majority, at the expense of the accepted order. On top of that, the author of this book tinkered with linguistic reform of the actual Yiddish itself, replacing the archaizing Western Yiddish style with a more *au courant* local synthesis of spoken Western Yiddish and standard German. For the traditional eye, one of the greatest symbological outrages comes on the very first page: a blessing for children, but not a 'real Hebrew blessing' that starts with (here in modern Ashkenazic transcription) *Borukh ato adoynóy eloyhéynu mélekh ho-óylom* ('Blessed are you, God, our Lord, king of the world [or: universe]') but with a Western Yiddish parallel (in Western Yiddish!): *Geloubt bistu her unzer got a(n) kinig der velt* (lit.: 'Praised are you, Master, our God, king of the world'). This alone would to this very day send a traditional Jewish religious school teacher into acute shock.

There is a long, winding introduction that starts out quoting from strictly traditional Ashkenazically authoritative sources, principally the medieval *Séyfer Khasídim* ('Book for the Pious') about the imperative of praying in a language one understands, reviving the older debate on that subject (see D.E. Fishman 1991; also Freund 1998). Toward its end, Aaron ben Shmuel veers into educational methodology and argues that Hebrew needs to be taught as 'a language' with grammar rules and incremental structurally organized lessons, instead of by what may now be called the 'Ashkenazic method'. That method, used to this day in the *khadórim* (traditional elementary schools) of Haredi (mostly Hasidic) communities, entails memorizing phrase-by-phrase translations of the Torah and other texts, leading to rather impressive command of classical Hebrew (and for the higher levels, and the academies — *yeshivas* — of Aramaic too). Many a modernizer of Jewish education in more recent times has recommended replacement of the Ashkenazic method with 'language learning' texts. Leaving the merits of the debate to one side, let us turn to a sample of what Aaron ben Shmuel tells early eighteenth-century Jewish parents in Germany on Jewish education and indeed, the educational imperative of instilling religion in children:

> As the Sephardim do it! They teach little children in the mother tongue and then they proceed and only thereafter do they teach Hebrew with roots and grammar for two or three years, thereby enabling them to understand Hebrew books and their prayers, and are expert in the Torah, Prophets and Writings [= the Old Testament]. [...] So we shall hope that God (blessed be He) will help, following this view, to see to it that children understand it in their mother tongue, and so what they learn will truly be fear of God and love; afterwards, Hebrew grammar according to roots and grammar, and then the passage will be fulfilled, as it is written in Isaiah 29 [18–19]: 'And in that day shall the deaf hear the words of the book, and the eyes of the blind shall see out of obscurity, and out of darkness. The meek also shall increase their joy in the Lord, and the poor among men shall rejoice in the Holy One of Israel.
>
> (Aaron ben Shmuel of Hergershausen 1709: [19–20]
> [from the neo-Yiddish of the author])

Incidentally, the author's preference for the Prophets as a source, in the overall absence of Talmudic references, would likely lead to suspicions of influence from 'outside' (the Christian world and the more modern, 'worldly' Sephardic world) as well as to suppositions that in Ashkenazic terms of reference, the author of this book is not particularly learned (which he wasn't).

Be all that as it may, the book was banned by the rabbinate. In 1830, over 120 years after its appearance, most of the press run, torn into pieces, was found in the attic of the old synagogue in Hergershausen. The book could not be burned or thrown out because of the holy names of God therein.

And thus was Aaron ben Shmuel's attempt relegated to the series of unsuccessful Western Yiddish power coups. This one was the most ambitious, perhaps. To be sure, its failure was undoubtedly the most spectacular.

For Yiddish to be associated with any kind of quasi-religious value would have to wait for a place where the language was not co-territorial with German, and for a time when a new revolutionary but masses-based Jewish religious movement would arise in opposition to contemporary rabbinic hegemony over Jewish life. It is a typical irony of history when yesteryear's revolutionaries are today's conservatives, yet that is a rather

Image 11.1   A torn page from one of the many copies of Aaron ben Shmuel's attempt at an innovative Yiddish prayerbook (Hergershausen 1709). Jüdisches Kulturmuseum und Synagoge Veitshoechheim
Source: Courtesy of Dr Hermann Suess (Fürsenfeldbruck).

precise description for Hasidism (Chasidism and other spellings too). But if there is one constant then in Ukraine and Poland and now in far-flung communities concentrated in western countries and Israel, it is the presence of Yiddish, albeit in non-identical ways.

The matter of *place* is important on many levels, of which two are directly relevant to Yiddish and power. As a stateless and internally non-sacred language, Yiddish, for all its demographic force as the universal vernacular for centuries of Western Ashkenazim, was on the linguistic level constantly subject to attrition from the majority and high-culture non-Jewish language, German, to which a majority of its vocabulary is identifiably related. This was true in the west notwithstanding the multitude of minute differences in nuance and cultural evocative qualities researched particularly by twentieth-century Yiddish linguists. The upshot is that even moderate drift in the direction of assimilation and integration by any German-Jewish community would lead to Yiddish forms and nuances being displaced by German ones.

Then there is *time*. There were attempts to incorporate Yiddish into the truly traditionalist canon of classic works of Kabbalah (where Kabbalistic esoterica would suddenly be accessible to a wide audience), to elevate theologically the sanctity of Yiddish prayer, and to introduce a Yiddish-only prayerbook suited to a modernized paradigm for studying Hebrew grammar. But these were attempts at a time, on the cusp of the eighteenth century, when the demographic, cultural and linguistic decline of Western Ashkenaz were well advanced, even before the onset of the Mendelssohnian Jewish Enlightenment movement.

Turning to the positive, there is the question of critical mass. In Eastern Europe, where Yiddish was demographically turning into a language of millions, where there was no great prestige attached to the neighbours' local (Slavic, Baltic and other East Europe) vernacular, and where, further from the contemporary wider western movement toward secularization and modernity, there was, by contrast, a set of circumstances conducive to the opposite: a revival of deep and all-pervasive inwardly self-sufficient religion that would further develop religious Ashkenaz rather than challenge it. Part of that set of circumstances was tied to the great Jewish tragedy of the Chmielnitski massacres of 1648 and 1649, which were the first case of ethno-religiously motivated mass slaughter of the Jewish populations of entire regions, something that had never before happened in Eastern Europe, and that did not before the Holocaust happen in other parts of Eastern Europe.

Hasidism in the East

Israel Baal Shem Tov (±1700–60) is accredited as the primary founder of East European Hasidism in the eighteenth century. It was a deeply pietistic movement, stressing the spirituality of all people, including simple uneducated people, and their call, and inherent ability, to draw closer to God. At the same time, it was a rebellion against the official rabbinate, establishing in many instances opposition to the traditional *rov* ('rabbi with a rabbinic ordination'), their own *rebbe* [rébə]. The word *rebbe* had long been a Yiddish vocative, when addressing in second person a *rov*, and has the additional meaning of 'traditional Jewish religious school teacher'. It was now to acquire the additional and very different meaning of 'dynastic Hasidic grandmaster' or 'grandrabbi' who was (and is) imbued with a somewhat pope-like aura of infallibility, and whose power over his 'court' of Hasidim, usually named after his home town or the town where he or the group set up their Hasidic court, was (and in many cases still is) passed on dynastically. There is a large academic literature on the history of Hasidism (see, for example, Dubnov 1930; Hundert 1991; Idel 1995; Rapoport-Albert 1997).

The naming of Hasidic *rebbes* (of each generation) and their entire followings according to place names entailed the added property of elevating Yiddish place names in Eastern Europe for otherwise often small and 'insignificant' towns to the status of growing Jewish sanctity. For generations now, to people who follow Jewish life around the world, terms like *Gérer* ('of Ger', 'from Ger'), *Lubávitsher* ('of Lubavitch'), *Sátmarer* or *Sátmerer* ('of Satmar') are well known and can serve as different parts of speech.

When someone today talks of a *Gérer khósid* (variously anglicized, for example, Ger Hasid, Hasid of the Ger dynasty and more), they are talking about a Hasidic (ipso facto 'ultra-Orthodox') Jew who is part of the group of Hasidism who belong to Ger, with the traditions, mores and features that affect many parts of life. For this type of modern Jewish discourse, it scarcely matters that Ger is Yiddish for a town that is today in Poland, Góra Kalwaria, southeast of Warsaw, which has, after the Holocaust, no Jewish community. It is frequent that stateless, minority-based geography can outlive political developments of even a long time ago. From the Yiddish culture point of view, 'Satmar' is a major 'Hungarian' Hasidic group, one of the largest and most powerful in the world today, and it matters not that today's Satu Mare is today in Romania. The major Orthodox outreach group to Jews who have become estranged from their religion is today Lubavitch, named for a town, now Lubavichy, in western Russia, not far from the border with northeastern Belarus. But when one speaks of 'Lubavitch' today, not many think of that town, and even less about the town that preceded it as home of its founding *rebbe's* court, Lyadi (today in Belarus, smack on the border with Russia).

As a noun: he/she is a *Sátmarer(in)*. As an adjective: a *Sátmar* er [invariant, uninflected, as is usual for city-derived adjectives] idea, concept, belief, or, alternatively, *Sátmarishe(r)* [as inflecting adjective]. As an adverb: *Sátmar* (referring to a way of thinking, seeing things, doing things). From there it can travel far and wide across the parts of speech, including such interjections as in: *Sátmar!* ('Aha, I recognize that and where it comes from', which could be in praise or in criticism, depending on the all-important Yiddish intonation employed). Both Hasidic and non-Hasidic Yiddish use any number of names of East European towns to signify characteristics of their Jewish culture, adverbially or as interjection. This journey from geography to intimate Eastern Ashkenazic culture would strike current residents of those places as curious. For Hasidim, saying *'Lubávitsh!'* signifies the unique status of this Lithuanian origin (northern) Hasidism from the southern courts and an array of opinions about the group (nowadays most famous for outreach and sending rabbis to actually settle for life in far-flung cities to build Lubavitch-compatible Jewish communities). Among non-Hasidic traditionally religious Litvaks, calling something *'Valózhin!'* (now a backwater town in western Belarus) evokes the rarefied mystique of the high level of rabbinic learning of a certain sort practised there, not unlike the words *Oxford* or *Harvard* in English.

So powerful did such Yiddish place names, and their derivative and culturally loaded vocabulary, become, that these have, in the twenty-first century, sometimes 'outlasted Yiddish' in various circles where Yiddish is no longer spoken but these concepts are part of the contemporary Jewish religious scene.

Such ostensibly minor points are examples of a much larger phenomenon. In Eastern Europe, in the thick of a Yiddish-speaking population undergoing remarkable demographic growth, and in the absence of any of the factors inhibiting Yiddish in the west, the 'incorporation' of Yiddish increasingly into realms that 'feel sacred' was not a statement by this or that rabbi or author who was in some sense or for some intellectual reason 'pro-Yiddish'. It was a natural societal development.

Hasidism, by elevating the spiritual status of simple people and rejecting the administrative authority of the organized rabbinate, was also an economic and cultural rebellion on behalf of the masses. This too fed into elevation of Yiddish in the absence of any kind of modern 'language movement' or philosophy. What often remains outside the calculus in discussion of the eighteenth-century rise of Hasidism in the Podolia region of Ukraine, and its rapid spread, particularly into Poland, is that the lowering of the status of some traditionally learned community leaders who were targeted by the early Hasidim meant ipso facto that Hebrew and Aramaic learning was in some sense downgraded, though not in explicit terms. There was a shift not away from the sanctity of either sacred language, to be sure, but toward a feeling that intellectual acuity in Talmudic and other texts was not everything, and spirituality in the vernacular could blossom, and could now count for a lot.

There were of course many other aspects of Hasidism. These included a Kabbalistic bent, a switch to the 'Sephardic rite' of prayers, a philosophy of 'holiness in everything' that some have associated with pantheism, and a host of developing customs and traditions, including dress (earlocks for men) that would distinguish Hasidim from those in Eastern European Jewry, primarily in the Lithuanian lands, where the opponents of the movement, centred in Vilna (today's Vilnius), became known as *Misnágdim*. The word literally means 'Protestants' though in chronological terms they are perhaps the 'Catholics' of East European Jewry against whom Hasidim raised an innovative societal revolt in the eighteenth century.

When it comes to Hasidic Yiddish and power, there are two inter-locking components. One is the unspoken cumulative force of culture, continuity and society, a de facto view of Judaism as much more than just a demanding religion; it is a view perhaps more of Judaism as an all-encompassing civilization of which language is understood to be a central component. There is a strong case for defining twenty-first-century 'real Hasidim' as by definition speakers of Yiddish as opposed to 'modern Orthodox Jews' who may in some detail or other or 'professed higher philosophy' follow this or that Hasidic court, or may be part of a 'second-tier Hasidim' that is inside the border of (say) American, British or Israeli society, as opposed to those whose separate language makes them an ongoing and distinct linguistic minority.

The second component is more explicit and is best grasped via exam-ples. Léyvi-Yítskhok of Berdichev (±1740–1810) one of the founding Hasidic masters, did much to help spread Hasidism in Poland, particu-larly during the dozen or so years (1772–84) during which he led the Zhelekhov (Żelechów) community. He became known for talking to God in Yiddish and thereby teaching that others, including those who knew only Yiddish, could also use it to talk to God. Conversation with the Almighty did not require the scholarship needed to master tomes in Hebrew, let alone Aramaic. He became known as *der Berdítshever* (or *Bardítshever*), 'the Berdichever', after the town where he served his final stint as *rebbe* and built the long-term court that would outlive him. If *der Berdítshever rebbe* could speak to God in Yiddish, and encouraged the simple people in his flock to do the same, then Yiddish was elevated in its psychical and functional aspects in the societal power scale of Eastern Ashkenazic civilization.

Simple details of language that are mechanical 'grammar' were in the hands of Hasidic masters rapidly 'translated' into aspects of theology. A song by the Berdichever known as *A Dúdele* — [dúdələ] or [dúdalə] — took its name from an older Yiddish verb, *dúdlen*, used for playing a sim-ple folk instrument, a flute or bagpipe associated with shepherds. But it also evoked *du*, the familiar form for 'you' (rendered *di* in the southern dialects of Eastern Yiddish). In this song, the simple line 'Master of the

Universe! I will sing a song to you: You, You, You, You, You!' brings the intimacy of personal passionate love, of necessity in the vernacular, to a for-Ashkenaz novel form of dialogue with God, giving the intimacy of Yiddish a kind of social and psychological power it had never before had.

Yítskhok-Isaac Kálever (or Taub, 1751–1821), a founder of Hasidism in Hungary and *rebbe* at Kalev (now Nagykálló, Hungary), heard a gentile shepherd's love song and recast it in much the same spirit as *A Dúdele*, as a call to God with one key replacement. The word for 'rose' is replaced with Yiddish *shkhíne* (Ashkenazic Hebrew *shkhíno*, Israeli *shekhiná*), which derives from Kabbalistic thought and literature where it is the feminine face of God or the component of Godliness as it is revealed to humans. The word for forest is replaced by *góles* (*golus*, *galút*). Yiddish *góles* has various meanings. As a concept of Jewish history it refers to any of the great Jewish diasporas (after conquest of the ancient kingdoms of Israel in 722 BC, Judah in 586 BC, and following Judea's failed revolt against Rome, from 70 AD which is the 'current/ recent one' resulting in the great two-millennial Jewish Diaspora). As an everyday concept by semantic extension, it can be a quasi-comical reference to, say, being in the doghouse vis-à-vis one's spouse. But here it was acquiring a mystical, Kabbalistic sense of the exile from holiness, spirituality and bonding on a personal level with the Almighty.

Serious mystical thoughts from the ancient and medieval Kabbalah were being disseminated anew in Hungary by a Hasidic *rebbe* who was thereby accomplishing several things. These included the spread of mystical Hasidism and its moods among the masses of everyday Jewish people and as part of that the popularization of Kabbalistic terminology in a Yiddish guise; the spread of the sacred use of Yiddish by everyday people with the overt blessing of their grandrabbi or *rebbe* (in the Hasidic sense); the dramatic enlargement of the circles of 'spiritually elevated people'.

It is important, in achieving some measure of retrograde understanding of an age gone by, to be careful not to anachronize. It is curiously actually helpful that none of these Hasidic founders wrote treatises or even chapters about the concept of 'Yiddish', as did Yechiel-Michel Epshteyn just slightly earlier in Germany (see Chapter 8). They were not purveyors of the 'idea of Yiddish' in the later nineteenth- and twentieth-century sense of 'language of the people', and attempts to see them as such are historically fallacious. Such attempts can arise by modern 'lovers of Yiddish' clutching at presumably 'useful past' morsels that records may provide. But they can also arise, particularly with regard to Eastern Europe, several generations later, in the deep nineteenth century, by a juxtaposition of time, place and large-scale identity of the population under study.

Still, there were occasions when classic foundational Hassidic *rebbes'* mentions of Yiddish transcended the parameters to veer by some degrees toward a differentiation of 'languages as such' on the basis of vernacularity, which of course harks back to much older arguments on behalf of prayer in Yiddish (see pp. 77–8). The most tantalizing case to this day is perhaps that of Reb Nákhmen, or Nachman of Bratslav (or Breslev, Ukraine), whose Hasidim (Hasidic followers) were and still are known as *di Bréslever* (or *di Brátslaver*). Nachman, himself a great-grandson of the Baal Shem Tov, was considered so holy that he was never replaced after his death in 1811, and other Hasidim refer to Bratslaver as *di tóyte khsídim* ('the dead Hasidim', in the sense of 'the Hasidim whose *rebbe* is dead'). The town where he finally settled in Ukraine, Uman, today draws tens of thousands of pious Jewish visitors a year who come to pray at his grave, providing much of the town's economy.

Nachman of Bratslav, or *Reb Nákhmen Bréslever*, put it this way, according to the classic compendium of his words:

> The highest state in which a human being can achieve divine inspiration is in seclusion, where he can pour out his heart and soul to God freely and with intimacy, and in the familiar language, the native tongue, the Yiddish of our lands. Hebrew is barely known to the average person and it is therefore impossible to express oneself fluently in it. The result is that whenever Hebrew is used as a medium of prayer, the ears are not listening to what it is that the mouth is saying.
>
> (Nachman of Bratslav 1806: §2.23a [from the Hebrew])

Reb Náchman represents another tantalizing tilt in the direction of modernity while remaining wholly in the most mystical and 'vertical' traditions of Jewish religious life, where verticality refers to the enormous input into the psyche of the rich past and the yearned-for messianic future with rather less conscious emphasis on the present, and even less than that for the non-Jewish surroundings. That tilt is in the *direction* of the modern Yiddish short story.

Along with the 'primary work' of Yiddish, the compilation of stories known as *Shívkhey haBésht* ('Praises of the Baal Shem Tov'), Nachman's own collection of Yiddish stories, *Sipúrey máyses* ('Telling of Stories') as transcribed by pupils, also appeared at the same time, around 1815 (Bratslaver ±1815). In fact, both foundational works of Hasidism were bilingual, but in a completely different way than in the previous centuries of producing bilingual Hebrew-Yiddish books, generally in the western area. In nearly all of those books, the Hebrew was classic and sacred and beautiful, and the Yiddish was a watered-down, charming-in-its-own-way 'translation language', one that was replete with archaisms (which added an aura of sanctity), but one that was linguistically not seldom a 'lowest common denominator' language in that it opted for 'boring' pan-Yiddish forms, sometimes closer to German, than the vibrant dialect forms of the publisher's area or native language variety. In these two classic works of Hasidism, the Yiddish was fragrant with the immediacy of being rough transcripts of the masters speaking in Yiddish and the pupils transcribing, with no attempt to hide that (though of course many older writing conventions tempered things). The Hebrew was there for appearance's sake, for the sake of sanctity, and was often stilted and not quite suited to the atmosphere of immediacy of here-and-now evoked by the stories in both books. In *Praises of the Baal Shem Tov*, the stories illustrate the master's greatness. In the words of Reb Nákhmen Bréslever, to use his Yiddish name, they were his own romantic, symbolic and mystical stories and allegories. The most famous is *A Story of Seven Beggars*. Almost none are completely clear, but the ambiguities and doubts are themselves part of the aesthetic achievement inherent in the book (see Band 1978; Buber 1999; background: Mantel 1977; Niger 1959: 109–77).

The two classic works of Hasidism, the stories about the movement's founder, the Baal Shem Tov, and the stories by Nachman of Bratslav, in their primary Yiddish versions, cemented Yiddish within Hasidism, not on their own but in the context of the lore of hundreds of other founding personalities of the movement. These were scattered far and wide in the eighteenth and early nineteenth centuries. Yiddish was acquiring a religious and spiritual cachet it did not have before among the masses of everyday religiously observant people in Eastern Ashkenaz.

It might be a step too far to claim that these books and, more widely, the Hasidic *máyse* 'story' also made it a rather shorter jump for modern Yiddish fiction to 'miraculously' emerge onto the arena of Europe just a few dozen years later in the middle of the nineteenth century, but it would not be an inherent case of hyperbole. It is a question requiring monographic investigation using subtle strategies for tracing non-obvious influences of the hagiographical story genre of traditional religion upon modern Yiddish fiction. Various studies have dealt with the ideological progressions (for example, Hasidism to Haskalah/Enlightenment), but the raw linguistic and stylistic analysis remains a desideratum.

For all the de facto incorporation of Yiddish into the power of Jewish religious and mystical spirituality in Hasidism, the Hasidim did not generally make 'Yiddish, the language' into a topic of Jewish law. They didn't need to. They were in the thick of a largely monolingual Yiddish-speaking civilization, they were 'doing sanctity' in Yiddish, and in the course of things, looking back, they did an enormous amount for the language, from Baal Shem Tov's stories told in the eighteenth century down to the hundreds of thousands evolving-into-millions of Hasidic Yiddish speakers right now in the second decade of the twenty-first century.

The ensuing nineteenth-century enshrinement in Jewish law, how-soever marginally, came, as fate would have it, via a *non*-Hasidic nine-teenth-century ultra-Orthodox community that was in profound (and still unstudied) ways impacted by Hasidism. The central personality was, eerily enough, a rabbi who moved from west to east and came to 'feel' the role of Yiddish in full Jewish-as-a-civilization life. He would go on to codify considerable de facto 'language power' to his followers in a way that would impact directly the mostly Hasidic Yiddish-speaking masses of hundreds of years later. Such are the vagaries of history, and, within it, of language and power.

Non-Hasidic 'ultra-Orthodoxy'

It was to transpire in one of the areas of 'transitional Ashkenaz' (see Map 2), in other words an area occupying territories geographically (and culturally) between the large blocks of Western vs Eastern Ashkenaz. The central personality was a German (that is, Western Ashkenazic) Jew who moved eastward to that transitional area. He was Moses Schreiber (Moyshe Shrayber, Shreiber and other spellings), who became known to Jewish history, as was the wont of many famous rabbis through the ages, by the name of a famous book or series of books preceded by the definite article which becomes in this culturally specific case a kind of agentiv-izing morpheme. For Jewish culture he is *der Khsam Sóyfer*. Modern English usage features a wide array of transcriptions, ranging from the Ashkenazic-based *Chasam Sofer* to the Israeli style *Hatam Sofer*. We will use the transcription of the Yiddish *Khsam Sóyfer*, and in the tradition of the culture we are exploring, we will call him that instead of 'Rabbi Schreiber' or some such. In older Yiddish, *shráyber* usually meant 'scribe' rather than '[modern] author' and indeed, a variant of his name was Rabbi Moshe Sofer (or Moyshe Soyfer...). (In the nineteenth century, incidentally, concurrent with the older Yiddish meanings, which in addition to 'scribe' sometimes included 'semi-professional local letter-writer/document-producer', there came the newly imported meaning from modern German, 'modern author' as well. Some dialects preserved distinct pronunciations for the older and new meanings.)

The family name, in the German-based spelling *Schreiber*, actually meant 'scribe', for which the more common word is the Hebrew-derived *sóyfer*, usually a reference to the highly learned specialist who could pen Scrolls of the Torah and other sacred items, such as mezuzahs, using all the prescribed ancient practices and tools and obeying the ancient laws on production and states of mental concentration during production. The phrase *khsam sóyfer* ('seal' or 'signature' of the scribe) occurs in the Babylonian Talmud (in Tractate Divorces, 66b and elsewhere). In the case of the Khsam Sóyfer there was an added Ashkenazic delight: the three Jewish letters that make up the first word are taken as an acronymic for <u>Kh</u>idúshey <u>T</u>óyras <u>M</u>óyshe — 'The [rabbinic] innovations of Torah by Moyshe' meaning Moyshe Shrayber the Khsam Sóyfer.

The Khsam Sóyfer was born in Frankfurt in 1762 and became a disciple there of a stalwart old-fashioned rabbi, Nathan Adler (1741–1800), himself a controversial figure, ultimately because of the East European tradition-alist influences that became part of his world view. The disciple headed east and settled in Pressburg (Pozsony), in the 'Hungarian lands'. Today it is Bratislava, capital of Slovakia. There he built his *yeshiva*, wrote his works on Jewish law and commentaries, and constructed what is known as 'ultra-Orthodoxy' or 'Haredism'. It is, inter alia and in a nutshell, the belief in societal distinctiveness (including language, dress, mores) in con-trast to 'modern Orthodoxy' (or 'neo-Orthodoxy'), itself a German-Jewish philosophy of the nineteenth century that combines observance of the laws with acculturation to western civilization, not only in appearance, language and customs, but also in the degree of cross-cultural contact with 'variously lapsed or modernized' Jews and with non-Jewish society.

The Khsam Sóyfer, in his voice as a rabbinic legal adjudicator (much more than as direct polemicist with the modernizers), provided a legal-istic conception of the origin of the Yiddish language and its standing vis-à-vis German, a point of note in the context of the anti-Yiddish positions taken by the various movements of modernizers in east and west alike (for example, 'Yiddish is a relatively recent Eastern European corruption of German'). As a rabbinic scholar concerned with jurispru-dence, his opportunities for expressing his views arose when a legal question presented an opening. One such question concerned the precise ('correct') spelling (in the Jewish alphabet) of the name of the city Pest (now within Budapest) in a bill of divorce. Such things are no laughing matter in Jewish law. If there is a misspelling in a place name, the whole divorce can be invalidated, and a future marriage of either party to new partners can therefore also be invalid and children from such subsequent unions may one day be judged to be illegitimate (with added woes for their own progeny). Even more emotive were the changes to non-Jewish personal names. To avoid the tragic consequences that could ensue from an invalid divorce document, every care was taken with every detail. For all sides in such cultural debates that centre upon language, 'arcane details' are as vitally important as cultural declarations among moderns (or, by way of another kind of analogy, in the same way perhaps that a 'detail' in a certain word distinguishes that word socially or symbolically as northern German vs Dutch, or Russian vs Belarusian, and so forth).

For the Khsam Sóyfer, the city name has to appear as it always was written previously by rabbinic authorities, in other words, rephrased in modern terms, 'written the Jewish way' both in the sense of alphabet *and* spelling (this all being separate from actual Jewish and non-Jewish, local and non-local phonetic renditions). From the question of the name of the city in Hungary, he takes the opportunity to make a comment about Yiddish per se. For legal precedent, he makes reference to the 'Eighteen Prohibitions' enacted by the students of Shamai (± first century AD) to prevent interaction with gentiles in a time and place of assimilation; these had included prohibitions on gentile wine, oil, bread and language, and inter-community intimate relations. Far from becoming law, they remained in the realm of a set of opinions of the students of Shamai, sometimes rejected by the students of Hillel. Hillel and Shamai, and particularly their schools, were at opposite sides of many debates in Talmudic literature, with Hillel going down in Jewish lore as the champion of leniency and Shamai of strictness. The following reply is from the Khsam Sóyfer's response on a section of the Code of Law:

> And I myself do not understand at all why you need to use the Latin name of the city in the section at the bottom for the signatures, even in a civil contract, or in a certificate of kosherness. This never even occurred to our forefathers, the previous generations of rabbis, preceding your excellencies! In my opinion, those of old could also speak the non-Jewish language well when speaking to non-Jews. But what? The language was intentionally altered because of the [House of Shamai's] Eighteen Prohibitions, as explained in the Jerusalem Talmud, in the first chapter of the Tractate *Sabbath* where it is written; 'and upon their language', and take a look there, and on this

point it is better, bearing in mind our many sins, not to expand on the topic any further.

(Khsam Sóyfer 1859: 6b, §11 [from the Hebrew])

Elsewhere he was asked about a trendy new Jewish-letter spelling of the name of a small town in northeastern Hungary. His answer:

My dear friend! Anything new is forbidden by the Torah. In all cases, there is nothing to renew, leave it the way the earlier masters had it.

(Khsam Sóyfer 1841:12a, §29 [from the Hebrew])

In a reply to a question concerning the qualifications for a congregational rabbi, which had alluded to the pluses and minuses of having someone locally born and bred, the Khsam Sóyfer turned away from the candidate's place of origin to the type of rabbi and person, within the types then in competition for the hearts and minds of Jews in Hungary and far beyond:

May he be from the sages of your own congregation or from elsewhere, but he has to be someone who can be called with the name *rov*, a guide in the ways of God for the people of God, and he should not, God forbid, be one of those who writes polemics, who reads outside books and speaks in a non-Jewish language. From the mouth of such a person it is forbidden to learn Torah, and it would be as if the Asherah-goddess [Old Testament idolatrous deity figure] were placed in the middle of the holy Temple.

(Khsam Sóyfer 1862: 74b, §197 [from the Hebrew])

The Khsam Sóyfer exerted a major influence on the traditionally religious of Eastern Europe, whether Hasidic or non-Hasidic, to maintain their names, language, dress and other characteristics in the face of modernity, irrespective of whether a community lives in a tolerant or intolerant society. He thereby founded ultra-Orthodoxy, or Haredism as it is alternatively termed today, though both words leave something to be desired. 'Ultra-Orthodox', like 'ultra' anything, implies fanaticism and is a view from outside the culture, which on this occasion has no connection to violence toward others or any generically jihadist philosophy that would merit terms such as 'ultra' or 'fanatic'. The average person in this civilization, then, later or indeed now, does not consider him- or herself ultra anything, does not hate anybody else, and is only unreasonably religious in the equally biased eyes of (especially) the modern religious of the same faith group. The term *Haredim* (Yiddish and Ashkenazic Hebrew *kharéydim*, modern Israeli *kharedím*) has biblical vintage, referring to a kind of trembling before God (as in 'Hear the word of God, ye that tremble at his word' — Isaiah 66: 5), backed up by a European Kabbalistic heritage that fed right into Hasidism. A 'recent' pedigree comes from the book *Seyfer ha-Kharéydim* (*Sefer ha-Haredim*), a kind of manual for spiritualism and asceticism, which first appeared in Venice in 1601. It was written by the sixteenth-century Safad Kabbalist Elozor Azkari (or Akzri).

One of the Khsam Sóyfer's top followers was Akiva Joseph Shlezinger (1837–1922). Though only a baby in Pressburg when his master died, his childhood and world outlook were moulded by the Khsam Sóyfer's environment and successors in the Pressburg *yeshiva* and in the town, and by his writings. Because Shlezinger moved to Palestine and believed in working the land, and was one of the first to help build up Petah Tikva, he is even regarded as a founding Zionist. Political history writing certainly makes for strange bedfellows. Shlezinger published the Khsam Sóyfer's ethical will in Yiddish with his own commentary in Ungvar, Hungary (now Uzhgorod, western Ukraine), in 1864. The book, in Hebrew, is called *Lev ivri* ('Heart of the Hebrew'), part 1, the word for 'Hebrew' unusually spelled so as to make an acronym for Shlezinger's traditional name. In the classic rabbinic tradition of a commentary often being many times the length of the text it is written for, the Khsam Sóyfer's will is expounded in a much longer commentary by Shlezinger.

Continuing the age-old tradition of Ashkenazic trilingualism, the wills asks that:

> The daughters should keep themselves busy with traditional books in Yiddish.

It goes on to warn all and sundry:

> Be careful not to change your name, language or clothing to those of the gentile, God forbid.

In his commentary, Shlezinger offers this thought:

> And thus our master [the Khsam Sóyfer] warns us not to do as is done, when someone is given the name Aaron and then calls himself Adolph, or is given the name Moyshe and calls himself Moritz. Among the other nations they also adhere to their names. [...]

Our sacred forefathers altered the national language to become their own language, the language of Judaism as our master has explained. [...]

The Yiddish language of ours has the same law as Hebrew, and thus have I heard it in the name of the sacred Arí, who would not speak any unsacred word on the Sabbath, but would speak in our language, he would speak on Musar and Torah, and he said: 'The language which the Jews have settled on and is unique to them, has sanctity and its law is the law of the sacred language Hebrew.' And therefore, our master of blessed memory commanded us not to change our language in this time, and that is our Yiddish language.

(Akiva Yehosef Shlezinger 1864 [from the Yiddish])

After publishing three learned tomes in Hebrew and Aramaic, Shlezinger turned to Yiddish. In 1869 he published his *Second Call to Jewish People* in Lemberg (Lvov). The text on the title page makes the book's purpose clear:

This book was written in order that Jewish people know how to save themselves and their children from the gentile ways and the hands of the deniers of the faith, to remain steadfastly faithful in the wake of the temptations in our current times before Messiah, our righteous one, will come, may it happen soon in our days, Amen.

(Shlezinger 1869: title page [from the Yiddish])

For any modern who might deign to understand the historical psychology of Haredism ('ultra-Orthodoxy'), there could be no better bulletpoint introduction. Unlike his master's, the Khsam Sóyfer's massive legalistic tomes and his own prior works in Hebrew and Aramaic, this book, in simple Yiddish, is a call to arms to traditional Jews to resist the temptations of the world at large and especially those of modern Jews, sometimes (with variable portions of derision and derisive humour) known collectively to Haredim as *di apikórsim* ('the unbelievers' or 'deniers of the faith'; the word entered Jewish Aramaic from the name of the Greek philosopher Epicurus and has remained popular through to the modern Yiddish period). Shlezinger continues:

Every nation has its own way of life, and doesn't take it to heart if others, even thousands of others, go in different ways. Why is it so hard? Because whoever is greater than his fellow has a greater urge of temptation too. The evil inclination is very strong, and imposes itself on people, and tries to stop them from performing commandments, good deeds, keeping Torah and fasts. This is more difficult than anything. The evil inclination knows very clearly what its purpose is! Therefore, dear Jewish brothers, we have to strengthen ourselves against the evil inclination with the help of God. And to keep ourselves strong in Judaism, with the Yiddish language, with Jewish names, and with all the Jewish customs. And blessed is he who remains in his Jewish clothing even in German regions, and doesn't start living like the gentile.

> (Shlezinger 1869: 65a [from the Yiddish])

As for minimal requirements of governments and societies regarding knowledge of the national language, the way to act is laid out with the same certainty and clarity as everything else in Jewish life:

> When the government insists that children study German or some other language, it is only to the extent necessary for commerce such as writing, reading and arithmetic and so forth, but it is important to take care that these subjects not be taught by a Jew who is also teaching the pupils Jewish subjects. These secular [lit. 'German'] subjects should only be allowed to be taught for some hours in a separate room by a separate teacher, preferably a gentile.

> (Shlezinger 1869: 84a–b [from the Yiddish])

Proceeding to tackle the moderns on their own turf, Shlezinger embraces the concept of *freedom*, but argues that to be oneself and not to assimilate is what constitutes genuine freedom:

> To practise Judaism with a full feeling of freedom, and of our unity, these are the roots of our tree of life. When we strengthen ourselves with these roots, no evil spirits will dare make us weak. The free Jew, who lives in harmony with his creator, will not curl up in fear, notwithstanding what the *apikórsim* and the present-day Sadducees come up with. Let them do what they want, it doesn't bother him. And the more so: if they make fun of him and mock him, the more happily he goes on his own way!
>
> The cold [modern] Jew cannot last for very long. And he will be unable to resist all the temptations that come to bear on people nowadays.

> (Shlezinger 1869: 87a–b [from the Yiddish])

Shlezinger went out of his way to stress that traditional Judaism with all its lifestyle components of language, names and dress must not be confused with the Hasidic movement, with which such God-centred devotion in Yiddish was being identified by the middle of the nineteenth century. Haredism, ultra-Orthodoxy, traditional *Yídishkayt*, whatever one may want to call it, is for Shlezinger a simple matter of the traditionalist interpretation of Jewish law and must not be thought of as ideas exclusive to Hasidism:

> Do not think that all that we have written in this book is Hasidism. In all the books we have written, we have not included one word that is not in the *Shúlkhon órukh* [code of Jewish law, Israeli *Shulkhán arúkh*]. That we have thundered about the issue of gentile lifestyle and replacing the Yiddish language is no more than a case of following what the *Shúlkhon órukh* says (in [its section]*Yóyre-déyo*, section 178), that Jews must be separated, different from the other nations, in clothing and all their ways. 'All their ways' encompasses, as it is written […] and in many other works, the tradition that we have inherited. […] God sees everything, the way Jewish children are being tricked into breaking the covenant with God and into replacing the Yiddish language with the gentile language, but none of this will be forgiven. There is a law and a Judge. The world has a way of keeping watch over itself, and these rabbis who sold their souls will hold sway as long as Menashe the son Hezekiah did with his idol in the temple [see Kings 21: 7].
>
> (Shlezinger 1869: 90b–91a [from the Yiddish])

In the century and a half or so since these words were written, there have been many instances of merger and alliance between East European 'ultra-Orthodox' Hasidim and 'ultra-Orthodox' non-Hasidism. The natural Hasidic fervour for Yiddish practices (like mystical direct communication with God in the vernacular, by the great and small of society alike) was — and in traditional communities still is — in full harmony with the not necessarily Hasidic but deeply legalistic Haredi tradition of the Khsam Sóyfer and his followers, many of whose descendants ultimately, particularly in the post-Holocaust generations in both Israel and diaspora centres, became Hasidic, constituting the Yiddishly loyal backbone of modern Ashkenazic Haredism internationally. One component comprises those originating in the Hungarian lands whose near-term pre-World War II ancestors may have been Hasidic or non-Hasidic.

In nineteenth-century Hungary, two 'extremes' of modern Jewish life, very religious and very assimilated, were in frequently bitter opposition. The anti-Yiddish sentiments and practices of the Hungarianizing (Magyarizing) assimilationists was countered, as it were, by internal Jewish legislation among the traditionalists, setting forth traditions that would one day, far from Hungary, become an Ashkenazic Haredi norm for a then barely imagined twenty-first century.

One of the major events in this process of internal Yiddish legal empowerment (that is, within the institutions of rabbinic Jewish jurisprudence) was a conference of some 25 rabbis convened on 28 November 1865 at Nagymihály (Michalovitch; today Michalovce in eastern Slovakia). Its nine-point document, given the rabbinically powerful name *Psak Din* (the 'Ruling of the Court' or, more literally, 'Decision of Law'), was published in 1866 in Ungvar, Hungary (today Uzhgorod, western Ukraine). The 'Yiddish legislation' in this document must not be viewed *either* through later secular language-empowerment eyes ('rights of the language x') *or* the Hasidic attachment to Yiddish. It was formed plain and simply as a question of Jewish law that was being legislated to prevent Jewish assimilation to the gentile cultural environment. For example, it contains a ruling demanding that a Jew leave a synagogue immediately upon hearing that a sermon is being given in a gentile language.

By the twentieth century, it would usually be Hasidism that assumed the mantle of the non-Hasidic Khsam Sóyfer and Hungarian Orthodox traditionalism of the preceding century. But not only Hasidim. There were returnees to the general fold of East European traditional Orthodoxy. One of the most famous was Nathan Birnbaum, himself a 'reconvertee' to deep religiosity in a remarkable intellectual odyssey that earlier spanned playing a role in the founding of both Zionism and Yiddishism (see Goldsmith 1976/1987: 98–119, 223–30; Fishman 1987; Katz 2007: 267–70, 290–3).

The next step was the 1922 conference of Hasidic *rebbe*s and rabbis at Chop (Tshop, Cop; formerly Csap, Slovakia, now in Ukraine bordering on Hungary). At Chop, the Múnkatsher *rebbe* (*der Mínkatsher* in the local Yiddish), Chaim-Elúzer Shapiro ('the Mínkhes Elúzer', 1872–1937) broke with the 'umbrella traditional Orthodox organization' known as Agudath Israel (*Agúdas Yisróel*), fearing that its leaders were too lenient vis-à-vis Zionism and modernism. The Hungarian Hasidim were now adopting the ethos of the Khsam Sóyfer's Pressburg edicts of the previous century. The Chop conference issued a *khéyrem* (or ban) against the Agudah (as Agúdas Yisróel is known for short). The first signature on the ban was another Hungarian (future) *rebbe* (again 'Hungarian' from the Jewish culture standpoint, irrespective of the shrinkage of Hungary's borders after World War I). He was Yóyel Téytlboym (Joel Teitelbaum, 1888–1979), who would later become the Sátmar *rebbe* (*der Sátmarer rébe*), the spiritual leader of what is today, in no small measure due to his and his court's stubbornness, arguably the largest bloc of Yiddish-speaking Hasidim in the world.

In terms of internal Jewish power among the 'religious far right' (as many modern Jews would call them), Yiddish power was the power of legitimacy and authenticity in the face of incremental cultural compromises by others in the same environment who were *also* (and today, in English, Hebrew and other languages remain) deeply religious and even 'ultra-Orthodox' in the eyes of many beholders. That power streamed forth from two sources. First, from the eighteenth-century rise of Hasidism in Ukraine and its spread through Poland and parts of the eastern Lithuanian lands. Second, from a Hungarian brand of non-Chasidic traditionalist Orthodoxy born in earlier nineteenth-century Pressburg. When the two were joined in the twentieth-century ideology (with a strong political component of anti-Zionism), sometimes via rabbis who were both Hungarian and Hasidic, the nucleus was being created for kinds of Hasidism that were destined, long after the Holocaust, to become the bastions of vernacular Yiddish in the twenty-first century, and if demographic trends prove a reliable harbinger, centuries to come.

12
Secular Power

Stateless secular power can be real when it is there in measurable critical mass. Measures can include the extent in quality and quantity of publications and educational and cultural institutions. More subtly, new forms of prestige need to be studied. Inherent in cultural nationalism is the idea that smaller, weaker nations can also come to the global table with works of literature and the other arts, thus also contributing to the enhancement of global culture. Degrees of success are often evident long afterwards, when translations into larger languages enable evaluations from less biased outsiders not concerned with group loyalty.

In the case of East European Jewry, the story of secular power is inherently more explosive than a tale of break-out of 'the masses' using their vernacular against the educated elites who wrote in one of the long-accepted languages. In many East European societies, the challenge for smaller nations whose languages had not been official state languages was to build language consciousness and standardized varieties for 'high culture' and fine cultural expression in the shadow of the German language powers to the west and Russian to the east. This often entailed a dual challenge of promoting literature among agricultural populations where high-level literacy was generally rare and secondary to promoting the focus on national consciousness and a suitably narrated past in opposition to the narrative of the ruling empire. In the case of Lithuania, for example, the Lithuanian language has an ancient and storied past, studied for centuries by foreign philologists for its ancient Sanskritic heritage; the Lithuanian people also have a glorious past, what with the medieval Grand Duchy of Lithuania and its heritage of multiculturalism. The challenge for budding Lithuanian language nationalism in the late nineteenth century was to inspire young people to activism in the cause of their own language, not the mighty Russian or regionally mighty Polish; to encourage literary and creativity among sometimes-rural masses, and to begin to build modern language institutions including press and literature in the face of the Russian Empire's prohibitions, restrictions and fears (be they political or cultural).

Then take the case of Yiddish empowerment. The differences are stark. Close to 100 per cent of the Jewish population was literate, but quite unable to 'enjoy a good book' in Hebrew, let alone Aramaic, the two classic exclusive-to-the-community *Jewish* languages mastered for prayer, study and, among a precious few, writing of new works. They could not enjoy a new book in one of the classic languages the way some non-Jewish neighbours could enjoy a new work in Russian, German or Polish if they had a middling education. Moreover, the societal power of Hebrew and Aramaic was quite inseparable from the age-old religious structure of the civilization in which the rabbinic scholars were the only elites.

Closely related to modernist Yiddish language stirrings, almost from the start, were feelings parallel to those of neighbouring minority peoples about the wider future in the region. There was the promise and the lure, and with it the danger and the daring. To embark on a competing new enterprise in the vernacular, on the model of the national revival among the co-territorial non-Jewish populations, was to also make an immediate, if implied, statement about non-satisfaction with, and opposition to, the status quo, particularly in the Russian Empire. Added into the mix, increasingly as the nineteenth century wore on, was the mental or more-than-mental tie to politically subversive or outright revolutionary tendencies. That tie was at the same time a big slap in the face to the Jewish authority and organized communities of the day, which naturally shunned revolutionary activity that could bring harm to the entire Jewish community from the powers that be. It was itself revolutionary. Once a spirit disseminating among masses of people turns revolutionary, it can have far and wide effects that are inherently unpredictable at the outset.

Local forms of the word *genre* with reference to a sort of literature may not have been popular, or even known to typical East European Jews in the earlier nineteenth century. Consciousness of the corresponding concept would however come progressively into play, with or without the word. Traditional Hebrew and Aramaic literature, the pride and jewel of the community, took the forms of commentaries, commentaries on commentaries (supra-commentaries), community decrees, responsa or replies to legal and other questions sent, correspondence between the learned and, very rarely, a liturgical poem. Yes, Yiddish literature had its remnant of long-declined versions of medieval romances and of older *múser* literature, and there was even a big East European revival of the latter in the course of the nineteenth century. Yes, Hasidic stories, whether hagiographies or mystical parable, bore some resemblance to short stories (within limits). Yes, there was a thriving Yiddish folklore rich in folksongs, aphorisms, curses and rhymes. Yes, there were plays based on the biblical book of Esther for the holiday of Purim. But for all that, the western concepts of the modern novel, short story, poem, play, article, school book, grammar book or treatise (or even pamphlet) were far, very far, from the traditional psyche. To toy with their rise in the Jewish vernacular was invariably to emphatically and controversially challenge the long-established notions of eliteness, learnedness and suitability for role-modelling and leadership in the Jewish communities of the Russian Empire.

Taking the line of thought a stage further to the internal psychological, social and ideological inclination of the Jewish minds who would be thinking in terms of any kind of rise of a 'secular Yiddish': they would ipso facto be raising the status in their own people's minds of the surrounding gentile culture of 'the nations' (as various polite Hebrew euphemisms refer to gentiles), and in some sense displacing the ancient Jewish culture with a new one largely based on a synthesis of Jewish vernacular and gentile genre and raw material. Who would want to do that?

Those who would 'want to do that' would be those among the first generations of Jewish secularists in Eastern Europe in the nineteenth century who were consciously rebelling against the authority of the rabbis and the hegemony of the ancient culture and at least some of its passed-down beliefs. In the southern, heavily Hasidic regions of Ukraine, Poland and the adjacent countries (see Map 2), these secularists had the added targets of the — to them — particularly unworldly, otherworldly Hassidic *rebbe*s who generally opposed any compromises with modernity.

These 'secularists', especially in the early nineteenth century, were in one sense or another indirect (and, in several famous cases, direct) pupils and followers of Moses Mendelssohn's Berlin Haskalah or 'Enlightenment'. A proponent of the movement was called a *máskil*

(Yiddish *máskl*, Israeli *maskíl*). But in sharp contrast to the ultimate results of mass modernization in the German-speaking west, which were assimilation and baptism (in both cases with the concomitant demise of the Western Ashkenazi as a viable ethno-cultural type beyond some relic pockets), the *máskil* in Eastern Europe became in many cases a forerunner of two distinct modern Jewish cultures within Eastern Europe: modern Yiddish culture, and the rise of a modern Hebrew culture that was transported by migrants to then Palestine and became the nucleus of the Israeli language and culture of today. There are many ins and outs that can fill, and have filled, many volumes (for a brief survey see Katz 2007: 154–256).

The most famous 'early Yiddish story in the progression' concerns a *máskil*, Mendl Lefin (or Sátanover, 1749–1826), an actual one-time pupil of Moses Mendelssohn from Eastern Europe who had gone to study with the master and his circle in Berlin and then settled in Tarnopol, Galicia (in the Austro-Hungarian Empire) to spread the 'German-Jewish Enlightenment'. After many attempts to use German and Hebrew failed, Lefin did something utterly outrageous for the *maskílic* milieu. He translated the biblical book of Proverbs into the rich everyday Ukrainian Yiddish dialect (Southeastern Yiddish to Yiddish dialectologists, see Map 2). Appearing around 1813, it was the first book in history, as far as we know, to be published in fully genuine East European Yiddish (that is, with virtually no compromises with the inherited older Western Yiddish template or with modern German). It was the literary language that would go on to become, in its essentials, the medium of great literary masters for close to another two centuries. It was, from the viewpoint of the development of a new literary medium, a day-and-night contrast with the kinds of Bible translations the German-Jewish *maskílim* and their followers were spinning out, which were ever more German in the adopted-from-older-Western-Yiddish *máshkit* type font. Lefin produced his Proverbs, not only in classic square Hebrew characters but with full vowel pointing, that was usually used for biblical and prayerbook texts. Although structurally superfluous in most cases, this was a statement of the power of typographical aura and its implicit statement, not for the first time in the history of Yiddish (see pp. 58–62). A Yiddish edition of a book of the Bible would be appearing (a) on its own, not in a bilingual edition, (b) in the same font and with the same vocalization as the most sacred classical Hebrew, and (c) in a then shocking and astounding literary codification of the genuine everyday Yiddish of everyday people in Jewish Eastern Europe.

Box 12.1 Two visions of an Ashkenazic language

Bible renditions were used to promote new versions of language and culture, as much among Jews as among Christians. In the early nineteenth century, the traditional Old Yiddish Bible translations in *máshkit* type were supplemented by two new 'linguistic projects'. Versions in German using the Jewish alphabet, intended to 'teach Jews German', emanated from the 'Berliners' of Moses Mendelssohn's circle. On the left, the first page of *Proverbs* by Mendelssohn's disciple I. A. Euchel (1756–1804) which appeared in Desau, Germany in 1804. In 1814, Mendl Lefin Sátanover, originally a Mendelssohn disciple too, defected and published his trail-blazing edition of *Proverbs* in a rich local East European Yiddish (right), igniting a fiery feud.

משלי

א

שפריבע

שלמה'ס זאהנם דור קעניגעם אין ישראל ·

(ב) צור עדקענטעניס דער וייזהייט אונד זיטטנ·
ל'עהרע , צור ערנרינרונג דער ברויכשפריכע
רער פ'רנונפט ; (ג) צור ערלאנגונג פ'רנעף·
טיגר צוכט , בילליגקייט , און רעכטשאפ'ענר
זעכבטשאפ'נהייט · (ד) דיא אונבאנענענען אויף
אייכרלעטונג , רען יונגלינג אויף קעננטנים אונד
פ'אריכט צו פ'יהרן · (ה) אויך דער ווייזע
ווירד דיא העןן אונד אן קעננטנים צו נעהמען ,
דער פ'רשטענדינע אויף דאראטשלענגע נלאנגן ;

משלי א ב

(א) שְׁפְּרוּכוּוֶרְטֶר פֿון שְׁלֹמֹה· דְרַיַהמ זוּן , פֶּלֶך פֿון
יִשְׂרָאֵל : (ב) וַויא אַזו מאַל זַיך פֿארשטיין זאָל חכמה
אין און וואָס מוסר· ווי מאַל זַיך פֿאַר שטיין זאָל וואָס
קלוּגי זַוֹערטער : (ג) מאַל וּיך תָמִיד קענדין
אַשׁקַלְדִיקֶן מוּסר בְּרירוּם נֶעמן , צו עהְלֶעכְקַיים,
נֶעלְכַנטְטֶעקריים:און יֶערעטֶת : · (ד)

[remaining Hebrew text in box]

The *Proverbs* edition was published anonymously. Impassioned conflict broke out in the circles of Mendelssohn-inspired *maskílim* on both the Austro-Hungarian side of the border (Tarnopol) and the Russian Empire side to the east (Berdichev and elsewhere; see Map 3). There were investigations and 'social inquiries'. When the truth came out, they learned that the book of Proverbs, in the East European Jewish vernacular, was a surreptitious, pseudonymous project of their own esteemed colleague Mendl Lefin. This Yiddish Proverbs inspired the first ever explicit work in Hebrew *against* the Yiddish language. That too is a kind of milestone in Yiddish and power! After all, all previous opposition was not to Yiddish the language but because of violation of some non-linguistic sensibility (see Chapter 10); even the Mendelssohnian attacks were grounded in a belief that there is no Yiddish, just a bad German that needed to be jettisoned. But now, Yiddish would be attacked because of its first literary *success*.

The first modern attack on Yiddish, in that sense, was penned in the literary genre of the drama by Hebrew writer Tuvia Feder (1760–1817). Folklore, true or not, had it that he became so heartbroken by this betrayal of the Haskalah that he became ill and died soon after completing his book on the subject in Berdichev around 1814. The book, in Hebrew, is called *Kol Mekhátsesim* after a biblical phrase usually translated along the lines of 'the [loud] voice of dart-throwers' (Judges 5: 11).

Shame, shame on the new translation of Proverbs, which is disgusting and stinks. It should be torn into pieces and burnt, and its name not mentioned again. This *megillah* by Reb Mendl Sátanover is senseless and tasteless, and its purpose is to find favour in the eyes of lovers ['concubines'] and girls.

(Feder ±1814, after Lemberg 1853
[here and below: from the Hebrew])

The usage of *megillah* here has various levels. The dictionary definition of the word is 'scroll'. From there it came to mean 'one of the Five Scrolls' in the Hebrew Bible (Song of Songs, Ruth, Lamentations, Ecclesiastes, Esther). In popular and particularly Ashkenazic culture it became the name for the book of Esther associated with the carnivalesque holiday Purim. And from there, in Yiddish (rendered *megíle*; Israeli *megilá*) it came to have a satiric usage for 'a long complicated drawn-out yarn', often in the exclamation *A lánge megíle* ('A long story!'). So on one level Feder is (subconsciously) using a Yiddishized semantic incarnation in his Hebrew text. But on another there is a more historical, biblical point made. Lefin translated the very serious book of Proverbs (not one of the Five), but it is being called something carnivalesque because it is in Yiddish, which Feder regards as carnivalesque to the point of shamefulness when used for a serious book of the Bible.

A longer introduction accuses Lefin of 'hurling King Solomon's exalted Proverbs into the mud'. Most hilarious, from the literary point of view, is the pamphlet's core content, which is a drama set, no more or less, in Heaven:

How is it possible? How could such a great scholar, a man of so much education and such a wealth of erudition, how can you of all people commit such an act to take the beautiful language [of the Bible] and to mutilate it so badly that it is frightening to look at. [...] You, Sátanover, who were the right hand of the great philosopher Moses Mendelssohn. You lingered in his circles and you absorbed his learning, and suddenly you have made such a fool of yourself, taking off the silk garment and putting on rags instead. How do you come to write things for women and servant girls? But they too will make fun of your degenerate language that is so awful-looking.

Remember now what Mendelssohn did in his time! Those rabbis pursued him and their disciples made things hard for him, but he strengthened his heart like a lion, he ignored them all and carried out his mission. He drove away from anything sacred the ugly, disgusting Jargon and lifted the wonderfully beautiful German language on to the throne. That is the language into which he translated the Bible for the younger generation, in order to make our youth more genteel and refined, and to give them a sense of taste and understanding for all that is fine and pleasing. And when Mendelssohn saw that he would not manage to complete the translation of the entire Bible, he left that worthy task to his faithful pupils. He admonished them to be careful with the magic of the German language in the subsequent books of the Bible. And suddenly here you come, Sátanover, and smash to pieces the whole thing!

You have come and hurled King Solomon's exalted Proverbs into the mud! Would our master Moses Mendelssohn have expected such a thing from you? One must not rest and one must not remain silent, until your book will not be extinguished without a trace, from every Jewish house. Whoever finds it should burn it. Whoever sees it should rip it to pieces. And you, sir, Mr Translator, should wander around the world, collecting together the copies of your book and hide them or burn them. Then you should go to the ritual bath, purify yourself, throw away the old clothes and don new ones. Only then will you be clean.

(Feder 1816 [1853]: 12–15 [from the Hebrew])

The 'literary component' of the pamphlet, entertaining to this day, is a scene set, no more and no less, in Heaven, where the departed, pure Mendelssohn is in an apostle-like setting surrounded by his disciples, the German-Jewish Enlightenment advocates Naphtali Hirz Wessely (1725–1805) and Isaac Abraham Euchel (1756–1804), now with him in the afterlife. They break the shattering news which Mendelssohn cannot believe to be the truth:

Wessely: Why are you so sad here, where there is no anger, no envy and no sadness?

Euchel: Whom have you left to look after those few sheep in the desert? Luzzatto is gone, and Naftali is also gone. And now the ridiculous cripple of a language will raise its head and the beautiful Hebrew language will fall further and further and have no future.

Wessely: But there is left one great man of learning, Mendl Sátanover. He would not allow it!

Euchel: Ha! Mendel Sátanover won't allow it? We have wasted all that energy on him.

Wessely: Why, do you consider his education wanting, his wisdom lacking? He is famous all over the world. Whoever seeks wisdom turns up on the threshold of his door, only his.

Euchel: He has now become a different sort of person, a wild man, he goes around with a new set of values, he cannot stand someone who speaks in elegant language, and he spits at anyone who uses a clear language. He likes the language of the peasants.

Wessely (with anger): Shut up! Keep your mouth closed! Here in Paradise you don't slander a great man. Otherwise, I'll let it drop to Satan and you'll have a bad end.

Itsik Euchel goes out, crying. Wessely returns to Mendelssohn and tells him how Euchel had slandered Mendel Sátanover. Mendelssohn, hearing this, gets even more angry, saying:

Ridiculous! How could someone even invent such nonsense about such a great man as the Sátanover?

In the meantime, Joel Brill and Ben-Ze'ev [two Hebrew grammarians of the period] walk in with a book in their hands. When Ben-Ze'ev hears how Mendelssohn and Wessely are fuming over Euchel, he takes Euchel's part and says that the world has been mightily deceived by Sátanover, and he is not the man he is thought to be.

Seeing that Ben-Ze'ev is holding a book in his hand, Mendelssohn asks him what it is.

Ben-Ze'ev answers: It looks like a German translation of Proverbs. But in truth it is not German but mumbo-jumbo, gibberish, a hodge-podge of all the world's languages. Some little Jew-boy has set out to make fun of us and to come up with such a ridiculous book. [...] This is Mendel Sátanover's piece of work!

Mendelssohn: Read, I beg you, several passages from the Proverbs along with Sátanover's translation, won't you please? *Ben-Ze'ev proceeds to do it.*

A sakh folk iz sheyn far a meylekh; vintsik folk iz a shlimazl af dem poritsl. [Translating Proverbs 14: 28:] 'In the multitude of people is the king's glory; but in the dearth of people is the ruin of a prince.'

A klige ishe boyet a hoyz; a shlimezálnitse spistosshet dos hoyz. [Translating Proverbs 14: 1:] 'Every wise woman buildeth her house; but the foolish plucketh it down with her own hands.'

A kliger koyft zikh sposebes. [Translating Proverbs 1: 5:] 'The man of understanding turns to wise counsels.'

(extracted from Feder 1816 [1853]: 18–23
[from the Hebrew])

As Feder's pamphlet, with its attack on Lefin, and the Mendelssohn-in-paradise scene, was still at the press in Brody, another Galician *maskíl*, Jacob Samuel Bik (1772–1831), intervened to try to halt the polemic conflagration. Bik, a fine Hebrew stylist and satirist, wrote an urgent letter to Feder about his anti-Yiddish, anti-Lefin pamphlet, which became one of the first *pro*-Yiddish statements in history in the modern sense of the term.

To Reb Tuvia Feder: Concerning his [= Mendel Lefin Sátanover's] having translated the Book of Proverbs, it bothers you, you compare it to the twitter of birds and the moos of cows, and screeches of other animals. But remind yourself, won't you, my dear friend! How did our fathers and grandfathers speak for four hundred years? Yiddish was spoken, thought and expounded by the brilliant masters, the *Bakh* [Joel Sirkes, 1561–1640], the *Ramó* [Moses Isserles, ±1525–1572], the *Sma* [Joshua Falk, ±1555–1614], the *Shakh* [Shabsay ha-Kohen, 1622–1663], all of blessed memory, and this is the language in which the Gaon of Vilna [Elijah of Vilna, 1720–1797] of blessed memory spoke. Moreover, the [Christian] scholar Fabro in his book about geography (Halle, 1815, p. 274) counts this language among the daughters of the Germanic language. And if the older German language is so dear to you, why don't you scream and shout about the older Bible translations in the *ha-Mágid* [early seventeenth century Yiddish translation of the Prophets and Writings], the *Tseneréne* [both by Jacob ben Isaac of Yanova], the *Nakhles Tsvi* [Yiddish Zohar of 1711]? These books, useful in their time and for their readerships, though there are many mistakes in them, and one does not find in them all the words necessary in a language, and they lack what is necessary to awaken the feelings and make a strong impression upon a person who has literary [...]

Peasants and simple people work very hard so that scholars may have what to eat and from what to live, so it is only common sense that they should nourish the spirit and the faculties of the people in a language which they can understand. [...]

Moreover, French and English are likewise mixtures of German, Gallic, Latin and Greek, but through the efforts of scholars in each generation for over three hundred years to make something out of them, they were made beautiful, and now, although they are mixed as ever, they are nevertheless used for exalted poetry and the most formal uses. It was only a century ago that German was very poorly considered. Eighty years ago Russian was a language for peasants. Even those very ancient languages, Greek and Latin, when they were born they were also 'common' until their scholars came and developed and purified their words, divided them into rules of grammar until they came to their full development which we so admire. It is the simple people who create the language of every nation and at the beginning, there is no difference between one language and another in terms of the level of inherent fineness.[...]

But philosophers and artists make from raw material a precious utensil and a wonderful picture. In a word, you did not do the right thing, my friend! It won't be to your honour if you publish your insults. Instead write a letter to Mendl Sátanover and apologize for insulting him! This is the advice that is given to you by your friend who always wishes you the best [...].

(Jacob Shmuel Bik, Brody, 19th Teyveys [5]575 [= 1 January 1815]
[from the Hebrew])

There emerged a so-called 'Mendelssohn of Russia', who campaigned long and hard to spread the *maskílic* version of westernization among Eastern European Jewry. He was Isaac Baer Levinsohn (1788–1860), a native of Kremenits, Volhynia in the Ukraine. He had earned the loyalty of Russian authorities for his work on behalf of the Russian army during Napoleon's invasion of 1812. He was hated by traditional Jews, not least because of his active support of government schemes to force Jews into agriculture, plans to limit the number of Jewish printing presses to three in all the Russian Empire, and laws to censor imported Hebrew and Yiddish books. His major work, *Attestation among the Jews* (or *Attestation in Israel*, after Ruth 4: 7), was published in Hebrew in 1828. The Hasidim down south put the book under a ban, but the Russian government awarded him a prize of 1,000 roubles for the book's excellence. It dealt with questions such as the grammatical study of Hebrew, and the Jewish attitude toward foreign languages, sciences and other secular subjects. On the subject of Yiddish:

> The language spoken among us here, in this country, which we took from the Germans and which is known as Judeo-German, is completely corrupt. [...] If we wish to discuss ideas about higher things, Judeo-German will just not do. [...] In this country, why speak Judeo-German? Either German or Russian! Russian is not only the language of the land, it is an exceptionally pure and rich language.
>
> (Isaac Ber Levinsohn, *Teúdo b'Yisróel*, Vilna 1828, pp. 34–5 [from the Hebrew])

As has so often been the case in Jewish intellectual history, what with its vertical inclinations to recycle from the distant past, this too was recycled from the ancient Babylonian Talmud, where the dispute had been over the contemporary Jewish vernacular Aramaic. The 'German or Russian!' cry evolved into 'Hebrew or German' or 'Hebrew or Russian' for those seeking to rekindle profound knowledge of Hebrew. They often invoked a famous Talmudic passage on the subject (see p. 191).

> Rabbi Judah said: 'In the Land of Israel, why Aramaic? Either Hebrew or Greek!' And Rabbi Joseph added: 'In Babylonia, why Aramaic? Either Hebrew or Persian!'
>
> (Babylonian Talmud, Tractate The Suspected Wife, 49b)

The nineteenth-century aftermath: rise of secular Yiddish power

The East European Enlightenment advocates, or secularists as they were increasingly becoming, in fact if not in name, increasingly had to turn to Yiddish. Perhaps a bit of modern Yiddish folklore can explain it better than a sociolinguistic construct: 'Yes, our grandparents told us that some madmen used to turn up in our shtetl with silly shortened jackets and shaved faces. They would stand in the middle of town and give a speech in some hilarious kind of *Dáytshmerish* (Germanish, Germanized Yiddish) telling us all to stop speaking Yiddish and to start talking German! *Meshugóym* (Lunatics)!' (This is not a quote, but an illustrative conflation of folk memories documented in the late twentieth century from aged informants.) To put it differently, the spread of *maskílic* ideas through either German books or Hebrew books failed to make any appreciable impact on masses of readers who did not have the ability to 'properly read either language' even if many words or roots of words were familiar to them.

The upshot was that the *maskílim*, whatever they thought of Yiddish, gave in to writing and publishing their books in Yiddish, thereby spreading knowledge of modern subjects, the ideas of the Enlightenment and the encouragement of engagement with the modern world's literary genres. There were books about Christopher Columbus and about personal hygiene, and the beginnings of translations from world literature. There were polemics and satires targeting Hasidic *rebbes* and the alleged corruption of Jewish religious leaders. Unlike Lefin, *some* influential secularists were developing a literary style of Yiddish impacted by *Dáytshmerish*, as a method of inducing creeping Germanization. Very often the roots being replaced were themselves old Germanic roots. For example, some nineteenth-century *maskílic* writers, particularly in the Yiddish press toward the end of the century, would replace *nékhtn* ('yesterday') with *géstern*, and *ítst(er)* ('now') with *yetst*. At the same time, a whole array of modern words that would remain in Yiddish permanently also entered the written and then the spoken language, for such western concepts as *kultúr, literatúr, román*.

Though it was for years an unintentional by-product, the *maskílic* authors of nineteenth-century Eastern Europe on both the Russian and Austro-Hungarian sides of the border were in the process of building secular Yiddish power as a modest but growing force in society. The spark that was missing was, in a word, love. There was not yet an outpouring of intellectual or ideological love for the language of the people to mirror what was happening in many parts of Europe. That was to come in the 1860s in that newest and most liberal-thinking of Russian Empire cities: Odessa.

Alexander Zederbaum (Aleksander Tsederboym, 1816–93) was a Polish Jew settled in Odessa, where he founded the first modern Hebrew weekly, called *Ha-méylits* ('The Advocate'), in 1860. As lore — and some memoirs — have it, it was a Ukrainian Jew who also relocated to become part of the bustling and daring new Jewish (and non-Jewish) society of Odessa, who convinced the still *maskílic*, anti-Yiddish Zederbaum to multiply his influence (and income...) by adding a supplement in the vernacular. Called *Kol mevéser* ('Voice that brings news', conflated from Isaiah 40: 9), it was an instant hit, providing Yiddish with its first East European newspaper issued in a form of the real spoken language. (There had been a Yiddish newspaper in Amsterdam in the 1680s, see Weinreich 1928b; Pach 2006; 2014; as well as some *maskílic* attempts amounting to German in Jewish letters.)

The man who apparently persuaded the *máskil* Zederbaum to take on the daunting prospect of the first really-in-Yiddish newspaper in Eastern Europe was the Ukrainian-born Shíye-Mórdkhe (Yehoshua Mordechai) Lifschitz (1829–78). He began, in the spirit of wider nineteenth-century language nationalism, to publicly 'fall in love with Yiddish' and, after persuading the Hebrew editor Zederbaum to also become a Yiddish editor, he had a magnificent public tribune that would arrive in the post each week all over the Pale of Settlement in the Russian Empire, and beyond: the new issue of *Kol meváser*.

In one issue, in 1862, Lifschitz published his poem *Yudl un Yehúdis*. Both are everyday Yiddish names, the first masculine, being a diminutive of the word *yid* ('Jew'), and the second the Yiddish realization of 'Judith'. In other words, both names mean 'Jew'. For audiences unaccustomed to even moderate literary subtlety, and this is significant for viewing a modern secular culture in its infancy, he added a single asterisked footnote: 'by this is meant the Jews and their Jewish [in Yiddish: *Yídish*] language', in case someone might fail to figure that out. It is a romanticized dialogue between *Yudl* (representing the Jewish people and its masculine leadership or, more simply, the husband) and *Yehúdis*, or *Judith* (representing their everyday Jewish language or, more simply, the wife). Yiddish is portrayed as totally feminine, the faithful wife in danger of being replaced by an exalted higher-bred woman, Hebrew (on Yiddish and the Feminine see Seidman 1997). It is a hearty poem, in deep authentic Ukrainian Yiddish dialect, rooted in romance and passion for the people's language, a theme that would be taken up by countless Yiddish poets in the twentieth century for whom Yiddish would be the only linguistic lover (see Rozhanski 1967).

The poem is charmingly rhymed in folksong-like cadence. It starts with Judith, as we may call the wife in English, saying to Judah her husband: 'I have something to tell you, so don't interrupt me, okay?' She goes on to complain that he prefers to look at other more elegant women. He admits to that, and explains that they are so beautiful and there is so much prestige in being seen with them, presumably an allusion to Hebrew or Russian or both. That is when Judith starts using language that will entertain the reader as the description is suited for both feminine beauty and the beauty of long-cultivated literary languages: 'Yes, that's an old story, to tell the truth, another woman is more liked, she seems clever, good and beautiful, but they were uglier than now, they once wrote and spoke like a child, but they had good fortunes, they were pampered day and night, so they now play great roles, people dance with them, play with them and laugh with them. Why not try to pamper me, spoil me, and caress me? At first you'll sweat but then you'll have great pleasure.' Judah understands but understands his love for his previous long-term wife (Hebrew) and the great prestige she brought him. Judith explains that it is okay for Judah to still have some relationship with her, but she herself is now the real lover and attempts to recover the previous one will be wasted effort. And so it goes on and on, until the narrator's (poet's) voice takes over, and assures the reader: 'Laugh at me today, laugh at me tomorrow you wise guys, but it's Judith who will one day be famous in the world.' The poem ends on the quasi-comical note of the narrator explaining that he has been the true friend of Judah's, who has shown him the inner and future beauty of his Judith.

'So then, Judah, don't just dream [do it!], and don't forget to thank the peacemaker, Lifschitz of Berdichev', that is, Lifschitz himself, for persuading the editor of the Hebrew *Ha-méylits*, Alexander Zederbaum, to start producing the Yiddish supplement that was the Pale of Settlement's first serious Yiddish newspaper, where of course the poem was being read and enjoyed.

Lifschitz proceeded to publish essays, again, in his friend's *Kol meváser*, advocating the societal rise of Yiddish as the language of East European Jewry. There, in his essayistic mode, his similes are not of other beautiful women but of the great languages of Europe:

> Some people accuse the Yiddish language of not sounding nice for them. So I will have the audacity to say that it sounds very beautiful! I will not even say *more* beautiful, but as beautiful as the nasal French or lisping English, especially for the Yiddish ear. But the joy you can get out of every single thing depends on with which cradle you were cradled.
>
> (Lifschitz 1863 [from the Yiddish])

Lifschitz himself would be one of the founders of modern Yiddish stylistics, principally by authoring splendid Russian–Yiddish (1869) and Yiddish–Russian (1876) dictionaries in which the 'Yiddish half' was neither archaic nor Germanizing, but based on the magnificent wealth, nuance and colour of his native Ukrainian Yiddish. To this day, in any argument over a word being 'real old Yiddish' or not, one of the competent Yiddish teacher's first questions is invariably: 'Is it in Lifschitz?'

Image 12.1   Fragment from Y. M. Lifschitz's 1862 poem *Yudl and Yehúdis* (Judah and Judith)
Source: Courtesy of the Menke Katz Collection.

Lifschitz subsequently persuaded one of the most deeply talented Jewish writers of the nineteenth century, also a settler in Odessa, to try his hand at Yiddish. That was the Hebrew writer Sholem-Yankev (Solomon Jacob) Abramovich (or Broyde). Abramovich, under his eternal nom de plume and personage, Méndele Móykher Sfórim, became the 'grandfather of modern Yiddish literature'. The first instalment of his first novel, *Dos kléyne méntshale* ('The Little Person') appeared on 24 November 1864, a date since heralded by Yiddishists as the birthday of modern Yiddish literature. Méndele was a native of Jewish Lithuania,

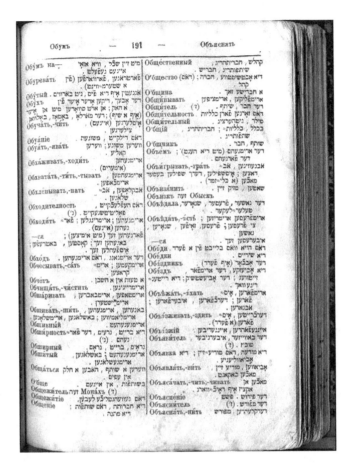

Image 12.2 Sample page from Y. M. Lifschitz's Russian–Yiddish dictionary of 1869. His dictionaries were the first to reflect spoken East European Yiddish, in his native Ukrainian dialect
Source: Courtesy of the Menke Katz Collection.

the shtetl *Kapúle* (today Kopyl, Belarus), who had moved to the depths of Jewish Ukraine, and then on to Odessa. With the gift of a master of literary language, Méndele was able to bring both Lithuanian and Ukrainian Yiddish to the laboratorical synthesis of the new standard literary language. The precise grammatical synthesis he came up with has remained largely intact to this day for those who aspire to modern Yiddish literary usage.

The later nineteenth-century development of Yiddish literature was somewhat startling. It was as if the treasures of Hebrew and Aramaic, and the great European languages with their acknowledged masterpieces of world literature, could all be synthesized in various senses — linguistic, cultural, conceptual, practical — in this new *Yídishe literatúr*, a Yiddish phrase that continues for many admirers of the literature to resonate with a ring that combines the romantic with the sacred. But if the phenomenon of hundreds of major modern Yiddish authors sprouting up all over Eastern Europe in a few short decades in this spirit is considered a miracle, that view is mistaken. The explanation is to be found in the rise of secularism in a fashion that, unlike the Berlin Enlightenment, did *not* entail wholesale rejection of the old ways, life and languages, but recalibration and restructuring on a modern European model of the extant 'linguistic and cultural raw material'. Close to 100 per cent of the great Yiddish authors, and there have been thousands, from the 1860s until roughly the end of the twentieth century, no matter how atheist, socialist, anarchist, communist or otherwise secularist they might have become, were nearly without exception raised in deeply traditional East European Jewish environments. Many were in their youth immersed in the ancient treasures of the Bible, Talmud and Kabbalah. Having acquired subsequent western education, particularly in modern languages, many quickly mastered the art of the novel, or of the story, of the essay, the poem, or the political pamphlet, and were able nearly straight away to produce modern Yiddish literature covering a spectrum of forms and of quality that would be comparable with the emerging nations of Eastern Europe.

Like any new culture, this one too had its developing legends and national traditions. The Lithuanian-Jewish (Litvak) born Méndele, as acknowledged 'grandfather' of modern Yiddish literature, was to be joined by Polish-Jewish short story master Y.L. Peretz (1859–1915), and perhaps the greatest Jewish humorist of modern times, the Ukrainian-Jewish Sholem Aleichem (Sholem Rabinovitch or Rabinowitz, 1859–1916). This triumvirate of modern Yiddish literary classics has survived intact into modern academia (see Frieden 1995).

The major 'power' of secular Yiddish culture was its rise as a source of growing prestige and living use for 'higher' cultural endeavours among an increasing sector of the Jewish population of Eastern Europe. With the mass emigration to the United States, Britain and other countries, primarily from the 1880s onward, in starts, stops and phases, the language and its press, literature, theatre and political organizations would have a diaspora life for at least the lifetimes of the actual immigrants, but only in a tiny minority of their progeny.

It is important not to misconceptualize the notion of 'secular'. In the twenty-first century, it can seem very easy to distinguish, say, an 'ultra-Orthodox Jew' from a 'modern-Orthodox Jew' from a 'secular Jew'. But for the traditional civilization of Ashkenazic Eastern Europe, there were the proverbial '66 varieties' (in fact rather more than that). Many, for example, continued to obey all, most or some of the cardinal religious precepts (like Sabbath and kosherness of food), but could enjoy a modern secular book as well. One pioneering young Hebrew poet in a small Lithuanian Jewish shtetl became known as *der apikóyres* ('the apostate'), because as a protest against rabbinic law, he would pronounce the prayer *shmóyne-ésre* ('The Eighteen Benedictions'), standing, of course, as required, but with his feet apart instead of together as demanded by Jewish law. That was his religious rebellion at that period in his life.

By the early twentieth century, Yiddishism was coming into its own as a viable Jewish secular cultural movement, one of the new 'isms' of Jewish Eastern Europe. Its most famous 'occasion' was the Chernowitz language conference of 1908, held in the town of that name in Bukovina (today Tshernivtsi, western Ukraine). Major Yiddish writers and cultural figures assembled to debate and plan, and after much discussion came up with the resolution that 'Yiddish is *a* national language of the Jewish people', rejecting a more radical resolution with definite article *the* (which would have meant an even more bitter war with Hebraists and others). The conference has been much studied and storied (see, for example, Goldsmith 1976/1987; Fishman 2011; Katz 2007: 264–174). As a by-product it produced material for yet another component of the societal power of Yiddish, the element of academic research and the societal respect it can command.

One of the most daring talks at the Chernowitz conference was given by a 23-year-old scholar, Matisyóhu (German Mattias) Mieses (Yiddish Mízesh or Mízish), whose paper contained the principles for the academic study of Yiddish (alongside a polemic broadside in favour of Yiddish and decrying the Hebraists and their 'cemetery' language that nobody actually spoke at the time). He analysed the structure of Yiddish in the spirit of twentieth-century structuralism, not nineteenth-century etymologism. Though it was a sensation, its effect was limited; it was not published in full until 1931 (as Mieses 1931).

In the early twentieth century, Yiddish scholarship entailing the academic-level study of Yiddish language, literature and folklore came into its own, like the literature before it, in the total absence of state support. It was, as is most often the case for stateless languages and cultures, the work of inspirational individuals and their own inspirees.

Box 12.2   The image of Chernowitz

This image of five Yiddish writers at the Chernowitz Language Conference of 1908 became classic, and was used on a Yiddishist postcard for many years. They are (from left to right): Avrom Reyzen (1876–1953); Y. L. Peretz (1852–1915); Sholem Ash, standing (1880–1957); Yiddishist philosopher Chaim Zhitlovsky (1865–1943); and H. D. Nomberg (1876–1927).

But looking back, the most influential scholarly lecture at Chernowitz was on the structure of Yiddish, presented by young Matisyohu Mieses (1885–1945). His image is superimposed above left. The major political sensation was the proposal by Esther (1880–1943) that Yiddish be declared *the* national Jewish language. Her image is superimposed above right.

That Yiddish scholarship took off was largely due to the influence of one person, who was far from conventional academic life himself, though an extraordinarily talented scholar, whose views on points of older Yiddish have been referred to (pp. 35, 110–11, 177–8). Ber Borokhov (1881–1917) is still best known in Jewish history for being a founder of the Labour Zionist movement which synthesized the ideals of socialism and Zionism in a way whose impact is still felt to some degree in sections of Israeli politics and government. But he was also the founder of the academic component of the modern Yiddishist movement (see Katz 2008).

The Yiddish world was stunned in 1913 when the famed political activist published two daring works in Yiddish and on Yiddish, both of which appeared in the first modern academic anthology in Yiddish, in Vilna (now Vilnius), which for centuries held the symbolic title 'Jerusalem of Lithuania' because of its rabbinic scholarship. It would now become the capital of modern Yiddish scholarship too. One of the two works (Borokhov 1913b) was an annotated and 'narrativized' bibliography spanning 400 years and demonstrating the wealth of previous scholarly interest in Yiddish from myriad groups of researchers, including Christian humanists, missionaries, anti-Semites and more, as noted earlier (Katz 1996b).

Yet Borokhov's achievement vis-à-vis Yiddish and power was to turn scholarship to the purposes of the movement on behalf of Yiddish in society. This he did in his essay *Di úfgabn fun der yídisher filológye* ('The Aims of Yiddish Philology' (1913a)).

Of all the sciences, philology plays the greatest role in the national awakening of the oppressed peoples. Philology is more than linguistics. It is not a mere theory for academic desk-sitters but a practical guide for the nation. It has certain theoretical and historical components, such as the history of the language and literature, the general principles of language development and the like, but its purpose and its educational significance are to be found in the nation's real life.

(Borokhov 1913a: 1 [from the Yiddish])

Lest there be any doubt or confusion regarding such a sensational statement, footnote 1 goes on to say:

I repeat: It is necessary to be clear about the difference between linguistics and philology. Linguistics is a general science, philology a national science. Linguistics can concern itself also with utterly dead and utterly wild languages. Philology, by contrast, works with the assumption that the language it focuses on has cultural and historical value at least for the past. Usually, however, philology goes further and is supportive of the conviction that its language has a national value in the future. Whoever does not believe in the survival of the Yiddish language can maybe still be a Yiddish linguist. But not a Yiddish philologist.

(Borokhov 1913a: 2)

The twentieth-century 'pro-Yiddish' school of scholars (Yiddishist in the double sense of 'specializing in Yiddish' and 'championing the language and its culture') developed an internal-based paradigm of Saussurian structuralist synchrony, first enunciated by Borokhov (in fact a few years before publication of Saussure's *Cours*) in lines that set the future tone for Yiddish studies:

German, Hebrew, and Slavic elements, as soon as they entered the people's language, stopped being German, Hebrew, and Slavic. They lose their former face and take on a new one: they become *Yiddish*.

(Borokhov 1913a: 9)

Borokhov enunciated moreover what effects secularism should have on the new Yiddish culture. Even today, some who come to the field of Yiddish are taken aback by some of his straightforward 'national

Box 12.3   Ber Borokhov establishes Yiddish studies

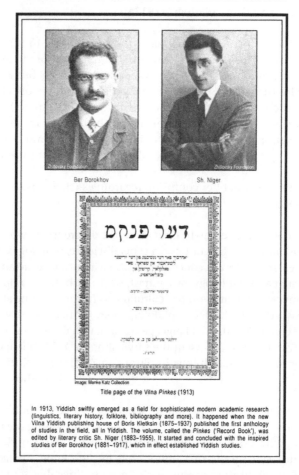

Ber Borokhov   Sh. Niger

דער פנקס

אלגעמיינער פאר דער לעגעומאטע פון דער יידישער
לינגוויסטיק, און ספראך קאר
פאלקלואר, קריטיק און
ביבליאגראפיע.

ערשטער אירגאנג — תרע"ג.

רעדאקטירט פון ש. ניגער.

ווילנער פערלאג פון ב. א. קלעצקין.
תרע"ג.

image: Menke Katz Collection
Title page of the Vilna *Pinkes* (1913)

In 1913, Yiddish swiftly emerged as a field for sophisticated modern academic research
(linguistics, literary history, folklore, bibliography and more). It happened when the new
Vilna Yiddish publishing house of Boris Kletskin (1875–1937) published the first anthology
of studies in the field, all in Yiddish. The volume, called the *Pinkes* ('Record Book'), was
edited by literary critic Sh. Niger (1883–1955). It started and concluded with the inspired
studies of Ber Borokhov (1881–1917), which in effect established Yiddish studies.

self-rebukes'. Here are two of them, from different parts of *The Aims of
Yiddish Philology*:

> [concerning] those uncivil characterizations, that Jews used to
> apply to non-Jews, taking as their point of departure the 'We are
> the Chosen People' point of view [...], this category of disparaging
> vocabulary results from national separatedness, and is found among
> the uneducated classes of all nations. [...]

Implementation of humanism in the language broadly speaking entails turning it into an arsenal for bringing to the Jewish people all the cultural values of modern pan-human development.

(1913a: 11, 17)

13
Party Politics

When discussion turns to any modicum of political power, in the sense of authority emanating from a state or its institutions, Yiddish is the last thing that comes to mind. It is a stateless language par excellence whose surges in society transpired internally by virtue of one kind of private enterprise or another, this or that 'drive for change' within Jewish society; this or that individual, group or movement.

In that paradigm, the incremental and internally diverse tendencies that spurred on these bursts of societal energy can be related to the expanding intellectual realm of women and of the masses of uneducated men, and of the ongoing diversification of Jewish religious trends. Outside the Yiddish-speaking community, anti-Yiddish politics served anti-Semites and assimilationists alike and would in time serve the rise of Hebrew as a vibrant new vernacular in the Land of Israel (see Katz 2007: 310–23; Shur 2000; Tsanin 1999).

However, toward the very end of the nineteenth century, and the start of the twentieth, the modernistic political space of Yiddish was widening dramatically. In contrast to most forms of the Hebraist movement which made a centrepiece of the revival of Hebrew as a spoken language and the degrading of Yiddish — and which believed in migration to the Land of Israel, then part of the Ottoman Empire — the development of Yiddish was becoming more and more attractive to a rainbow of political movements rooted in the 'here and now'. The concept of a 'political rainbow' or spectrum can be deceptive. It can be thought of as necessarily implying a right-to-left spectrum. In the case at hand, it was a rainbow wholly within what we would today call the left (including mostly the far left in so far as revolutionary and Marxist movements are included). Just as religion appears monolithic and homogenous to the non-religious, so leftism can appear monolithic and homogenous to the non-left.

What was common to all the leftist movements that turned to Yiddish was the notion of elevating the vernacular language of the Jewish minority to the status of a modern medium for modern communications for any of the purposes of culture, education, politics and society to which state languages are suited; or, put differently, the notion of the minority rights of languages. In 1908, at the Chernowitz language conference, the 23-year-old scholar Matisyóhu Mieses concluded his daring paper with words that rose above any of the individual movements and parties:

> The nineteenth century gave rise to the rights of people; the twentieth has the high task to give rise to the rights of languages. Whosoever believes in the progress of humanity can join our ranks and with courage and hope strive for our sacred national goal, for providing the means of development for our Yiddish language.
>
> (Mieses 1908, in Mieses 1931: 193 [from the Yiddish])

As a young Yiddishist scholar, Mieses could rise above individual parties and movements and factually centre the Yiddish language in his thinking. His thinking, for all his own rootedness in the ancient Hebrew and Aramaic sources and traditional Yiddish, is thoroughly radical. At first glance, it can seem surprising that such aspirations arose among a national group steeped in traditional Ashkenazic non-militaristic, anti-physical-resistance culture. The answer lies, in part, in the very nature of secularization which comprises 'borrowing' from the wider world not only genres and cultural constructs but, no less importantly, ideas and feelings, and among these were the many stirrings of aspirations for evolutionary or revolutionary changes that would bring about democratic societies that would be multicultural with minority rights enshrined. Moreover, whosoever became a secularist even partially, for example relativizing the sacred religious heritage vis-à-vis modern achievements in Europe, was ipso facto a psychological and usually also a social 'revolutionary'. The person would in most cases fall foul of the elders of his or her community, the rabbis, leaders and elder figures in one's own family. Whoever would latch on to Yiddish as a cause worthy of effort parallel to that being invested in national vernaculars by, say, Belarusians, Latvians, Lithuanians or Ukrainians, in the absence of the constant concomitant of these neighbouring cultures, having a generally defined homeland territory, was ipso facto an extraordinary revolutionary. This is a first given in the discussion, then; those who sacrificed more secure lives and futures for Yiddish, while not as bold as those of their opponents who left it all behind to 'move to the swamplands of Palestine to fight the Turks and the Arabs', had to be in their own way extraordinarily bold even if they remained in their native lands to fight this unlikely and unpromising battle for equal rights for a stateless and not particularly liked minority people, most of whom would in any case remain wed to the ancient religion handed down by their forebears; that is, rejecting the 'brotherly work on their behalf' by the modern campaigners.

Where could such audacity have come from? For many who have written odes to the Yiddish spirit, it is essentially a mystical issue, one that derives from intangible qualities of the Yiddish language and its potentials for the individual, society, literature, the arts and the Jews of Eastern Europe and their progeny worldwide. This opinion can be reformulated away from pure romanticism to one ensuing from potent zeitgeist factors. Determined lovers of their own oppressed minority cultures in Eastern Europe were rising on behalf of their people's languages, taking on board more than a little of the nineteenth-century language romanticism coming from Germany and other European cultures. In many urban and semi-urban locations, the Jews constituted a sizable population (sometimes half or more) of the populations of at least town and city centres. It stands to reason that a new omnibus revolutionary spirit would encompass stateless and dispersed minority cultures alongside those in native countries. Last but not least, a rarely spoken-about factor lay just under the surface. For both the minority concerned and for the majority, it could a priori be *easier* to develop a language and literature and culture that is *not* associated with a potentially violent revolt for independence of an ancient or medieval homeland from the clutches of a great empire. To put it in terms of specific nationalities, the Russian Empire had plenty to fear from a future armed insurrection by Poles, but in a sense zero to fear from even the most thriving Yiddish culture. Nevertheless, the Russian Empire feared Yiddish enough to keep a very tight lid on publishing in the language. That was no doubt related to the evolving revolutionary movements, in which Yiddish-speaking and Yiddish-writing people were surprisingly playing a part (see Fishman 2005: 21–61 cf. Bartal 2006). Moreover, they were playing a part, to the dismay of the rabbinic leadership and the vast majority of Jewish people, who just wanted to get on with their lives.

The earliest images of the Jewish revolutionary, from history books and from modern Jewish literature in Yiddish, Hebrew and also Russian, is of a *yeshíve bòkher* (yeshiva [rabbinical academy] student), seemingly immersed in an arcane passage in the Talmud and wrestling with the Aramaic text and the difficult commentaries that try to explain it while debating it with other pupils. Underneath the large folio tome of the Talmud, in this popular image that became folklore, is the small revolutionary pamphlet printed illegally on cheap paper, in German or Russian, which he can follow only roughly. This scenario crops up both with some of the great traditional *yeshivas* such as the one in Valózhin (province of Vilna, today in Belarus), and it was even more prevalent in the 'modernized rabbinical seminaries' that the Czarist government, colluding with Jewish enlightenment proponents, set up in 1847 in Vilna (now Vilnius, Lithuania) and Zhitómir (now in Ukraine) with an eye to producing modern, Russian-speaking rabbis who would lead their flocks to some cultural assimilation and modernity. They were failures and were closed in 1873.

Looking back, there is also the factor of displacement, perhaps better remembered as *re*placement. Traditional Ashkenazic culture — all the more so its Hasidic incarnation that flourished in so much of the Pale of Settlement and the (eastern) Austro-Hungarian Empire during the nineteenth century — was (and in traditional Haredi communities still is) one of religious fervour and zeal, total and uncompromising devotion to the handed-down beliefs and laws and customs. That is wholly un-western. If only some portion of that fervour were somehow transposed or transferred to the new vernacular-of-the-people movement tied up with some larger movement for a better future, there would be a surfeit of individual and collective energy for the new enterprise.

Finally, in the realm of individual and group psyche, this can in some instances be reduced to romantic daring, that quality of love or sublimated-to-a-language love that can lead to extraordinary risks being taken and achievements being attained. In revolutionary circles in the late nineteenth-century Russian Empire, this led to substantial risk-taking. Involvement in revolutionary circles could and did lead to imprisonment or execution, and these circles attracted people of many traditional backgrounds who were rebelling against staid middle-class type existence by espousing, no more and no less, anti-government activity. That any Jews from the 100 per cent non-violent and politically submissive civilization of Ashkenaz could have joined represented a break with nearly 2,000 years of Jewish history that started in 70 AD, when Jerusalem fell to the Romans, and the long Jewish Diaspora got under way. For many Jews in the Russian Empire, the first shock came with the revelation that one of the conspirators in the successful plot to assassinate Czar Alexander II in 1881 was a young Jewish woman, Gesia Gelfman (1852–82), who had 'just' provided the apartment for the plotters. Her death sentence was postponed, then commuted, but she perished shortly after childbirth, as did her baby daughter, after maltreatment in prison. The story of Hesye Helfman, as she was known in Yiddish, would resound for a number of reasons. She had a traditional upbringing in the depths of Yiddish-speaking Jewry in Belorussia (a town in today's southeastern Belarus), and fled her family to escape an unwanted match made by her parents (a classic theme in Yiddish literature mirroring social trends). She ended up joining the radical revolutionary group Narodnaya Volya. One of the results of the assassination was the unleashing of the first wave of pogroms that shook East European Jewry in the years 1881–4, leading to mass migration. Although another result *might* have been a signal to young Jews to stay away even from peaceful movements that were radical or challenged the powers that be, that was not the case. While the majority remained ensconced within East European traditional Jewish civilization, numerous young people were drifting toward one or another of the radical tendencies, especially those that arose with a Jewish component.

The most famous Jewish socialist organization/party, the Jewish Labour Bund, generally used only peaceful civil disobedience such as demonstrations and illegal publications. It was founded at a secret meeting in an attic of a wooden house in Vilna. Of the 13 founders who assembled, ten had been trained for revolution right there in Vilna (and some had the *yeshiva* background that entailed a clandestine attachment to revolutionary pamphlets). The central personality was Arkady Kremer (1865–1935). He was born in a half-Jewish county-seat town, Svintsyán (today Švenčionys in Lithuania, north of Vilnius), in the thick of a Yiddish-speaking society that was also conversant in Russian, Polish, local Slavic dialects and, in some cases, the Lithuanian spoken to the west. Like others who would become revolutionaries, Kremer was of the small minority of Jews whose parents pushed them toward secular and Russian higher education. He attended technical schools in Vilna and St Petersburg, where in 1884 and 1885 he was inspired by an underground socialist group. After stints in various cities doing both technological and revolutionary work, he returned to Vilna, where in the early 1890s there were heated discussions about whether Jewish revolutionary work should be switched to Yiddish.

By the middle of the 1890s, it was becoming obvious to the Jewish revolutionaries centred in the thick of Yiddish-speaking Jewish populations in the Pale of Settlement area of the western Russian Empire that

Russian would not do the trick. Sophisticated literacy in Russian was low among Jews, though the ability to communicate colloquially with neighbours and countrymen was high. But if one is trying to inculcate the knowledge of the revolution, its methods, short-term ends and final goals, that is not the stuff of market language but of serious reading. That meant Yiddish. In 1895 five issues of a new Yiddish periodical, co-edited by Kremer, appeared in Vilna under the innocuous name *Náyes fun Rúsland* (*News from Russia*). In the 1890s, these circles were far from considering Yiddish much more than the necessary propaganda tool for the politics of their part in the dreamt-of overthrow of the czar they so believed in. It was a kind of intermediate step to the marrying of Jewish socialism at the major organizational level with the educational, cultural, literary and symbological Yiddishist values of the burgeoning Yiddish literary movement. By the turn of the twentieth century, the Jewish Labour Bund, illegal and underground within the Russian Empire, but with productive centres of coordination and writing in western cities, was becoming the first Yiddish-speaking, Yiddish-using and increasingly Yiddish-advocating political party in history (see Haberer 1995; Jacobs 2001; Levin 1977; Tobias 1972).

The full name of the Bund in its Russian Empire years was *Álgemeyner yídisher árbeter Bund in Líte, Poyln un Rúsland* ('The General Jewish Labour Bund in Lithuania, Poland and Russia'; the name 'Lithuania' was added in 1901). It was closely affiliated with Social Democratic movements in Russia, and equally illegal, though also generally far from the violence-supporting branch of the revolutionary movements that would increasingly become known as communism. Still, the Bund's first big sensation was an exception to the policy of non-violence. A young shoemaker, Hirsh Lekert (1880–1902), a native of Hanúsishok (now Onuškis, Lithuania), volunteered for the job of shooting the czarist governor of Vilna, Victor von Wahl (1840–1915), after the governor had ordered the arrest and humiliation of a group of peaceful Polish and Jewish demonstrators on May Day 1902. Lekert's shots lightly grazed von Wahl's hand and foot. When sentenced to death, he refused the officiating rabbi's plea that he express remorse for his acts; instead the shoemaker surprised the witnesses to the hanging with a speech about defending the honour of the Jewish worker. Lekert became the stuff of legend. But the Bund was never again involved in terrorism or acts of offensive violence. It became a powerful political party that was fully legal in interwar Poland and other countries in Eastern Europe.

One of the founders of twentieth-century Yiddishism, Esther Frumkin (1880–1943), in the early years of the twentieth century helped transform the Bund into an ideological bastion of modern Yiddishism. The nexus was neither far-fetched nor complicated. Fighting for the rights of the working class and poor masses meant loving their language. It was also seen to imply that it was vital to develop education in the form of proper schools where the language of instruction and of textbooks would be Yiddish. In fact, the Bund helped pave the way for the most 'radical' brand of Yiddishism in the early years of the twentieth century. At the 1908 Chernowitz it was Esther Frumkin (using her nom de guerre, 'Esther'; she had been born Málke Lifschitz) who put forward the resolution that Yiddish was '*the* national language of the Jewish people', which was rejected in favour of the moderates' 'Yiddish is *a* national language of the Jewish people'. But it was Esther's proposed resolution that went down in popular memory and Yiddish cultural history as the hallmark of that conference, rather than the adopted resolution of a conference with no particular statutory powers.

Esther Frumkin's contributions went beyond being the girl wonder star of the first and most important language conference in the history of Yiddish. She continued to fuse the ideas of Yiddish socialist, secularist nationhood with rapid production of the educational means to educate the Jews of Russia in a twentieth-century western spirit, and in their native language. Her historically significant contributions include the book *Tsu der fráge fun der yídisher fólk-shul* (*On the Question of the Yiddish Elementary School*, Frumkin 1910). Its arguments include the notions that the development of sophisticated education in Yiddish is critical to Jewish life, while recognizing that Yiddish has a long road to travel. The failure of Jewish workers to immerse themselves in education in their own language is a result of their oppression. But, going far beyond the 'language of the workers' arguments of others, she delved into the spirit of language in a deeper sense. For example, in the course of argumentation, she effectively used some lines of a poem by Yiddish poet Dovid Einhorn (1886–1973) to demonstrate that only a Jewish child could fully appreciate them, not least because they contained two very different words for 'to pray': *dáv(e)nen* vs *mispálel zayn* (the first, a warm, everyday word (of disputed origin); the second, more formal and applicable to non-Jewish prayer occasionally, from the Hebrew). And so it came to pass that a modernist approach to the semantic wealth of Yiddish, proudly using its religious-derived arsenal in modern secular literature (rather than negating that arsenal, as was later to happen in the USSR) was fused with the political movement for socialism, social democracy and rights of impoverished, exploited workers. To be sure, the politics were to change dramatically later on in the twentieth century.

Still, the magic of the 'Frumkin formula' is brought into play in so many of the permanent classics of Yiddish literature.

Pioneering Yiddish elementary schools on the modern model started to spring up around the turn of the century. Possibly the first was set up in the famous *yeshiva* town Mir (now in Belarus) in 1898 by Noah Mishkovski (1878–1950). After experimenting with Russian, Mishkovski, a grand-nephew of Yiddish literary master Méndele Móykher Sfórim, found that 'Our language is on a par with other languages and everything can be taught in it' (Mishkovski 1947). Municipal authorities would not charter it, and he went ahead and rebuilt it in 1900, in Nézvizh (Nesvizh, Nieśwież), not far away, attracting more young radical intellectuals to the faculty. One of them, Falk Heilperin (1876–1945), went on to become a prime writer of high-quality Yiddish textbooks used in Vilna and other Yiddish school systems.

The development of modern secular Yiddish schools spread slowly during the early years of the century, and accelerated during the German occupation of World War I, when czarist restrictions were lifted. The period has been studied by various scholars in terms of the Yiddish educational output and the growing 'secular power' of Yiddish education in Jewish society, both in the shtetl (little town) and the larger urban areas (see, for example, Schulman 1971: 1–34; Fishman 2005: 1–79).

The leftist Jewish political scene underpinning the growth of secular Yiddish diverged rapidly and by the early twentieth century, in Eastern Europe and its émigré colonies in the United States, Britain and further afield, it seemed to some that there were almost as many competing varieties as in the variant religious traditions of many centuries' vintage.

Within a leftist rainbow

It is relatively easy to forget that from the viewpoint of twenty-first-century mainstream western perspectives, the later nineteenth- and earlier twentieth-century spectrum of political movements associated with the newly established modernist sectors of Yiddish-speaking Jewry in Eastern Europe would all be classified as 'far left' rather than just 'left'. This was to play a devastating role in places like the United States many years later when the movements modern Yiddish had become associated with would all be taboo for anyone wishing his or her children to be successful in life. Moreover, such an innocuous idea as 'make the best of where you are' would sound devastatingly foolish after the (quite unpredictable) Holocaust. That makes it much more difficult to fathom the late nineteenth-century Jewish secularist mentality, but it is a difficulty akin to many that must be overcome in fathoming the history of ideas in their times rather than from the retrospective stance of our own time, which is burdened with the sheddings of further years down the line of history and the prejudices we all have without realizing them.

In late nineteenth- and early twentieth-century Jewish Eastern Europe, an array of leftist Jewish political groups competed with each other in a market of movements in which some form of socialism was the common denominator. Perhaps if everyday folk joining these movements were then asked what was meant by 'socialism', they would have replied — as indeed they did reply in many memoirs, fictionalized accounts as well as in political propaganda — that it is all about a more beautiful and equal world where simple working people have better lives and share in the joys of their labours, where people of all religions and nationalities (ethnicities) would live in mutual respect and harmony. Sounds good.

However, like other attempts at generalization of internally diverse and divisive subdivisioning, history tends to remember, if not the victors then the largest representative entities. The Bund outshone many of the smaller tendencies, but they too played an important role in bringing Yiddish to modern political activity in Eastern Europe and the emigration centres alike.

The Jewish anarchists were a vibrant group whose famous émigré Yiddish journals included Rudolf Rocker's *Árbeter fraynt* in London and the *Fráye árbeter shtíme* in New York. Many saw the anarchists as the least 'politically toxic' because they were the least prone to be suspected or accused of violent revolutionary activity to overthrow governments (see Fishman 1975; Howe 1989: 104–8; survey by Cohn 2002).

The Jewish territorialists actually had projects to resettle the Jews in a new Jewish homeland, at one point considering parts of Uganda and at others Australia. While destined to political failure, various of their leading personalities played pivotal roles in the development of modern Yiddish culture. One of the most illustrious was Yitskhok Nakhmen Shteynberg (Y. N. Steinberg, 1888–1957), whose most enduring book on the subject was *Gelébt un gekhólemt in Oystrálye* (*Lived and Dreamt in Australia* = Shteynberg 1943).

These and other political groups were part of the growth of Yiddish societal power into a potent (if short-lived) modern secularist Jewish force capable of inspiring tangible and lasting achievements in such modern language realms as literature, education, theatre, press and an array of interlocking political and cultural activities. They represent, with hindsight, a transition (not always chronologically but in a history-of-ideas sense) between the generation of founders of modern Yiddish culture, such as Méndele, Lifschitz and Peretz, and the full-blown modernism launched with the advent of World War I and the concomitant collapse of the two major empires that had between them divided Yiddish (Map 3), the rise of new republics in Eastern Europe, and not least, of the Soviet Union (Map 4).

The political power of Yiddish in the later nineteenth century and the start of the twentieth certainty came from the new revolutionary and secular power of the leftist parties. The practicality entailed simply using what virtually everyone in East European Jewish society spoke and read 'anyway' but now pursued proudly as part of a compatible ideology of 'language of the people', or howsoever that was expressed in each party's and movement's circles. But the point that must not be forgotten is that the language and the growth of its literary, theatrical and public-use products was never the property of any one movement or party, even if the Bund became the central factor later, in the inter-war period, when it had the luxury of being a legal party in non-Soviet Eastern Europe generally compatible with non-Jewish socialist parties that were equally anti-Soviet and therefore no threat to the state. To phrase the notion positively, Yiddish was able to become a modern language because of the confluence of (leftist) parties and movements that chose it for their plans and dreams, and therefore it was able to rise above any one of the parties. It must be kept in mind that as 'similar' as they may all look today, the anarchists, Bundists, communists, Poalei Zion (Zionist socialists), social democrats, territorialists and socialists of many internally differentiated brands looked very different to each other from their time and place, which is where and when culture is measured. The transcendence of Yiddish through them all is particularly evident in the biographies of thousands of influential figures who at different times in their own lives, after abandoning the religion of their youth, flirted with or were active members of one movement before switching to another. Sometimes large groups of writers fell into the status of converts — for example, all those in the United States from 1929 onward who would abandon their American communist circles in protest against Soviet policies to join up with the anti-Soviet 'socialists' (see Katz 2005).

While the return of one Yiddishist theoretician, Nathan Birnbaum, to devoutly orthodox Jewish religion, after being a founder of modern over-the-parties Yiddishism (he was a prime convenor of the Chernowitz Language Conference of 1908) was the greatest one-person sensation, it was those who shifted through the layers within the left who proved the norm rather than the exception. The most famous of those might be Chaim Zhitlovsky (1865–1943) who had been active in an array of movements after moving to Yiddish from Russian, in the first place for revolutionary activity then centring the Yiddish language rather than regarding it as just a party tool. In his later American years, he would champion 'Yiddish is an end, not just a means' in a major debate in Madison Square Garden in New York City with a Jewish communist editor, Moyshe Olgin, who thought the opposite. Zhitlovsky's 'Yiddish comes first' Yiddishism came to expression in an extraordinary number of articles, essays, books and multi-volume collections of writings that achieved enormous popularity both in Eastern Europe and the United States. His late nineteenth-century essay 'Farvós dáfke yídish?' ('Why does it have to be Yiddish?' is a clumsy translation of a very straight Yiddish), was a hit when reprinted in the New York *Fórverts* (*Jewish Daily Forward*) in 1900 (under a pseudonym). It derived from a speech he gave in 1897, after the first Zionist Congress in Basel (which he attended). Zhitlovsky became wary of what he perceived as Zionism's distance from living East European Jewish life, culture and hopes. By the time of his death, he and his voluminous writings, many of which summarized classics of philosophy and other subjects for the Yiddish-reading working public, were available in numerous editions of *Gezámlte shríftn* (*Collected Works*). But it was in earlier years, particularly the *fin-de-siècle* years, when he was one of the singular pioneers of a new 'power of the masses' within Jewish life based on the Yiddish-speaking masses. These were at the time expected to constitute a perpetual population in Eastern Europe from which immigrant communities, particularly in the United States, would forever be receiving new Yiddish blood.

By the eve of World War I, modern Yiddish culture had millions of native speakers of the language interested in one or another aspect of its productivity. This definition, while more nebulous than one that would try (hopelessly) to estimate numbers of 'true followers' of the de facto Yiddish culture movement that was part and parcel of myriad leftist movements during the period, is more useful. When it comes to language and culture, non-statistical measures of critical mass can trump cleverly invented but unprovable statistics. But one statistic that counts is the number of books, editions of periodicals and other culture products. By any count, they number in the many thousands (see, for example, Reyzen 1926–9 and Prager 1982 among the works from which the pre-World War I scope of publications can be broadly extrapolated).

IV
Modernity

14
Interwar Encounters with Official Status

Yiddish power and its limits in the interwar period are topics not just for one future book, but a series of works, looked at from different angles. This short survey of topics and sources is meant as a brief introduction, and hopefully an inspiration, to future scholars. For the purpose of setting the scene, the reader is referred to two masterpieces by Ezra Mendelsohn: *The Jews of Eastern Europe between the World Wars* (1983) and *On Modern Jewish Politics* (1993). These works provide the political background and much of the social context. The political aspects are most important, heuristically speaking, because twenty-first-century readers cannot easily get to grips with a world in which hundreds of thousands, or millions, of native Yiddish speakers are involved in modern manifestations of their culture, in conjunction with an array of political movements ranging from right-wing nationalist to far left, and often with varying degrees of state support. The polaric case is of course full-blown Leninist communism, which was illegal in the free states of interwar Eastern Europe while, quite conversely, being the law of the land in the new Union of Soviet Socialist Republics. Studies of aspects of Yiddishism in the period include Goldsmith (1976/1987), Fishman (1981), Fishman (2005) and Katz (2007). For all the many works on Yiddish literature, periodicals, education and politics, there are still no synthetic works on the broad sweep of Yiddish culture in any of the interwar republics, across a swathe. The reason for that is that the subject has remained too controversial and painful even among allegedly dispassionate scholars who can be loath to tackle an array of ideologies that after the Holocaust remained discredited or tabooed. Sometimes it is because of having to deal psychologically with a culture that failed to anticipate genocide and whose ideologies are regarded as 'losers' precisely on those grounds. Another major hesitation derives from moderns' difficulty in understanding, let alone conveying, the full leftness of many of the secular movements, and the full rightness of the religious traditionalists. Politics looms so large over Yiddish studies to this day that scholars who would wish to represent the full societal force of interwar Yiddish would have to overcome their discomfiture over what is today considered (embarrassingly) communistic far left and (embarrassingly) religious far right. Abilities with relativity are declining in a number of social science disciplines as the different political correctnesses maintain a tight hold over many sectors of academia. All the more so in light of academics' characteristic reluctance to own up to their own limitations and those imposed on them by professional constructs that can impact their career status.

Filling that gap remains a cardinal desideratum. However, there are numerous excellent sources for personalities, places and works, and also for major cultural trends. Two primary encyclopaedic works remain the four-volume *Jewish People Past and Present* (1946–1955) and the *Yivo Encyclopedia of Jews in Eastern Europe* (Hundert 2008). Recent volumes that run counter to the 'reticence' vis-à-vis the leftist background of so much of secular Yiddish culture include Glaser and Weintraub's *Proletpen: America's Rebel Yiddish Poets* (2005), Trachtenberg's *The Revolutionary Roots of Modern Yiddish 1903–1917* (2008), and Pomerantz Freidenreich's *Passionate Pioneers: The Story of Yiddish Secular Education in North America, 1910–1960*. For coverage of the more 'mainstream' trends, the best anthology is still Joshua A. Fishman's *Never Say Die* (1981).

When it comes to Yiddishism of the early twentieth century per se, the central event is the 1908 Chernowitz Conference (mentioned earlier) which proclaimed Yiddish 'a national language of the Jewish people' and brought together literary and political movers along with unknown young talent, inspiring generations of achievement in Yiddish (though, heaven knows, its specific projects mostly failed).

Paris Peace Conference, Polish Republic and more

If any subsequent event came to set the tone for the modern rise of Yiddish in the new states of Eastern Europe, it was the inclusion of the question of Yiddish on the agenda of the Paris Peace Conference. The seminal paper is still Joseph Tenenbaum's (1957–8) memoir; he had himself been a delegate to the 1919 conference representing East Galicia. Concentrating on the educational requirements to be made of the new Polish Republic, and the protection of minority rights, there had been an extensive discussion about the question of Yiddish-speaking schools. Both Great Britain's Prime Minister Lloyd George and the American President Woodrow Wilson took an active part in the discussion. Wilson, lobbied by Jewish groups in the United States, expressed the fear that without explicit protections, there would be a danger of the vernacular language of the Jewish population, numbering millions, being banned at some point. One of the results for Yiddish of the Paris Peace Conference was the enshrinement of educational rights that in great measure came to fruition not only in the Polish Republic, but also in Lithuania, Latvia and other new republics in the heartland of Yiddish-speaking civilization in Eastern Europe. The schools would be producing readers of books and periodicals, and consumers of a wide variety of Yiddish cultural products in Eastern Europe.

Poland's capital, Warsaw, became the international European capital of Yiddish literature. Its environment generated internationally known authors, the most famous of whom, Isaac Bashevis Singer, who migrated to the United States in 1935, would in his advanced years become the only Nobel Prize winner for Yiddish literature (in 1978). The Warsaw Yiddish Writers' Union, at Tlomatska 13, became an international address for Yiddish and the stuff of foundational myths for the new and prodigiously prolific output of Yiddish in the interwar period. Warsaw (Yiddish *Várshe*) became the European queen city of Yiddish *belles lettres*, and home to the prestigious periodical *Literárishe bléter*.

A much smaller city, Vilna, then also part of the Polish republic and known as Wilno (Yiddish *Vílne*), became the international centre of Yiddish scholarship. During and in the immediate aftermath of World War I, young Yiddish scholars converged on Wilno, Poland (now Vilnius, Lithuania). They were all Litvaks, that is, Jews from the Northeastern Yiddish territory — the lands of the traditional Litvaks or northerners among East European Jewry (see Maps 2 and 4). They hailed from cities that after World War I were no longer in the Russian Empire but in Lithuania, Latvia, northeastern Poland and the Belorussian republic of the new Soviet Union. A number of them, led by Max Weinreich (1894–1969), set up in 1925 the *Yídisher vísnshaftlekher institút* (Yiddish Academic Institute or in the contemporary

Box 14.1   A stateless language gets its own academy

In 1923, Max Weinreich, a native of Courland (western Latvia), who had just completed his doctorate on the history of Yiddish studies at Marburg University in Germany, settled in Vilna (then Wilno, Poland; now Vilnius, Lithuania).

Two years later he established the Yivo (an acronym from the Yiddish for *Yiddish Scientific Institute*). The city that had for centuries been known as the 'Jerusalem of Lithuania' for its traditional rabbinic learning had seemingly overnight also become the symbolic capital of modern secular Yiddish learning.

Weinreich married educator Regina Shabad, daughter of the near-legendary Vilna doctor Tsemakh Shabad, who had helped set up a new Yiddish school system in the city during World War I. Shabad arranged the initial financing for the daring new academic venture in Yiddish.

Max Weinreich   Dr. Tsemakh Shabad

Laying the cornerstone for the new Yivo building at Vivulski

Leyzer Ran Collection

The completed building had state of the art facilities for archive preservation. It became an international symbol of 'high culture'

official version, Yiddish Scientific Institute). During its Vilna period, the Yivo published dozens of major works on Yiddish literary history, linguistics and folklore, all *in* Yiddish, thus giving Yiddish a remarkable academic literature — and cachet — in the near-complete absence of universities anywhere seriously including the subject in the interwar period. Following the 1913 'dreams' of Ber Borokhov (see Chapter 12), the Yivo quickly produced an array of academic volumes, including linguistics, folklore research, history and popular education, that verily made it the scholarly academy of the Yiddish-conscious Yiddish-speaking world (see Trunk 1980; Katz 2007: 294–300; Kuznitz 2014). One of the Yivo's co-founders, Zalmen Reyzen, produced a four-volume encyclopaedia of Yiddish writers (Reyzen 1926–9) that established 'as a fact' an international high-level Yiddish literature that could compete in the European arena. The Yivo itself published an impressive array of folio research volumes, most famously the series *Filológishe shriftn* in the late 1920s. All this was *in* Yiddish, as a matter of both practice and principle.

USSR

The one country where Yiddish attained truly official status and varying degrees of de facto state power was in the new Soviet Union. In line with Lenin's nationalities policy and minority rights, Yiddish became a state language in regions where its speakers constituted a considerable portion of the population. In practical terms, that meant principally the Belorussian and Ukrainian republics, but with a national status that also produced Moscow-based institutions of culture and education. There were state-sponsored Yiddish-speaking schools and some higher institutions to train teachers and scholars, as well as a state-sponsored infrastructure that enabled publication and dissemination of prose and poetry and high-end staging of drama. There was also much practical-handbook type publishing for an array of purposes (handbooks on lawyers' and biologists' terminology on Yiddish continue to strike antiquarians today as particularly exciting). In the early and mid 1920s especially, the Soviet sponsorship of Yiddish seemed a kind of paradise for a stateless language, so much so that some famous authors, like Dovid Bergelson and Moyshe Kulbak, actually migrated to the new Soviet Union to be part of what looked like an inspiring new structure for the state sponsorship of Yiddish culture. They were eventually shot during Stalin's purges, Kulbak in 1937 and Bergelson in 1952. But in the early 1920s such dark endings were not foreseen. Events like the Twelfth

Party Congress of 1923, which made way for Yiddish-speaking courts, town councils and cultural organizations, lulled Yiddish personalities to envy the Soviet Yiddishists their good fortune. The Jewish sections of the communist party, set up in 1918 and known in Yiddish as the *Yevséktsye* (from the Russian abbreviated form for 'Jewish section'), were given the power to build a new communist-grade Yiddish culture, and from the start, to fight a war of cultural destruction against non-communist Yiddish culture, and needless to say, against both religious and modern Hebrew Jewish culture. It was not long before the *Yevséktsye* became a beast for destroying its own as intolerance, suspicions of disloyalty to communism and a culture of total intrigue against one's teachers and colleagues set in, in most cases by the late 1920s. By that time, the usefulness of Yiddish for personal career power was setting in with a vengeance for the perceived potential competitors of the person in power, be that a petty official, party hack or actual educator or writer. The *Yevséktsye* was itself closed down in 1930, but the word *yevsék* for one of its members lives on in the sense of 'Soviet Yiddish hack, competent in Yiddish but caring only about his career, and given to permanent intrigue against all colleagues', a sense in which it can still be heard in Yiddish cultural circles today, fairly or unfairly, of those Yiddishly educated in the pre-1991 Soviet Union.

The massive intellectual and financial support for Yiddish in place of building a free modern culture and literature, such as was being successfully created across the border in the non-Soviet East European states, and in the Yiddish satellite emigration centres in North America and elsewhere, resulted in a special kind of Soviet Yiddish. It would be purged by the Soviet Yiddish communist masters of many of its Hebrew and Aramaic lexical items, these being seen as 'clericalistic' and 'reactionary' elements of the language. Many calques from Russian would be accepted in the literary language, giving its syntax a 'Russian cosmopolitan' feel. Most spectacularly for the users of language in such a 'writing-based society' as East European Jewry, the Jewish (Hebrew) alphabet was retained but with mandatory spelling reform that re-spelled Semitic words phonetically, did away with the word-final forms of letters and introduced mandatory diacritics. The look was one of weirdness to the very people for whom the individual alphabetic characters were nearly as 'native' as mother's milk. The net result was the Soviet creation of an artificial, and very temporary, kind of Yiddish. The Stalinist purges of 1937, and then again after the war, from 1948 to 1952 particularly, led to the murder of most of the leading Yiddish writers and cultural personalities. A miniature revival was initiated in the early 1960s with the launch of *Sovétish héymland*, edited by the reliably Stalinist editor Aaron Vergelis until the collapse of the USSR and beyond. One of the ironies, though, is that, by the 1990s, when the Soviet Union had collapsed, his hand-trained younger or early middle-aged Jewish male 'Soviet Yiddish writers' easily took over the weak fields of secular Yiddish culture and publishing in its two centres, the United States and Israel, and for a time at Oxford in the UK (before abandoning it for greener pastures in America), giving much of today's secular Yiddish in the west and in Israel a Soviet timbre that is emotively unattractive to both religious and secular users of Yiddish in the west and in Israel. History is not wanting in ironies.

Then there is the component of modern Yiddish culture built specifically in, for and by the Soviet Union. Those in the lands conquered from the Soviet Union in the aftermath of Operation Barbarossa on 22 June 1941 — the Nazi invasion of the Soviet Union — in present-day Lithuania, Latvia, Estonia, Belarus, western Ukraine and surrounding areas were subjected to the most complete and relenting genocide of the entire Holocaust. In the sense of utter genocide of the entire Jewish minority population in a territory, that is indeed a stage that was launched following this invasion.

We are then left with the uninvaded parts of the Soviet Union, of which only Moscow was a major Yiddish cultural centre. But Stalin's purges of the 1930s, the purges in and around 1937, the 1930s closing-down of Yiddish schools and cultural institutions, had already dealt a blow of the most major proportions to Yiddish in the Soviet Union. Once the temporary wartime alliance with his Anti-Fascist Committee (very useful for winning western financial and political support for the anti-Hitler war effort after Barbarossa) and the surviving famous Yiddish writers were no longer needed, the next major repression got under way in 1948 with the murder, by staged automobile accident, of the actor Solomon Michoels (Shloyme Mikhoels), a process culminating with the 'Night of the Murdered Poets' in Moscow's infamous Lubianka Prison on 12 August 1952 (though poets were a minority of those shot that day). Although its focal years of repression and destruction of Yiddish were shortly before the war (1937–41) and just after it (1948–52), taken in tandem with the Holocaust's having taken out the centres of Yiddish in what was the western Soviet Union at the time of the Nazi invasion of 1941, and bearing in mind the cumulative result, it is fair to say that Soviet Yiddish culture met a grim end in the general period of World War II. Before that, the sheer mass of educated readers and the corpus of literature produced meant that there would be high-quality works of literature created and drama performed, though often tainted by 'red tails' of mandatory communist input to virtually every genre, accompanied by the ubiquitous party atmosphere of unending intrigue to purge colleagues.

The Yiddish experience with 'political power' in the Soviet context, while overwhelmingly disastrous in its outcome, nevertheless produced much of value along the way in the output of education, literature and academic research. There are many studies in English of the topic that might serve the interested reader well, particularly Kochan (1970), Shulman (1971), Gitelman (1972, 2001), Greenbaum (1978), Veidlinger (2000) and, most up to date, Shneer (2004), who uniquely, and from the methodological point of view admirably, aspires to seeing where possible the positive side of things, without ever losing the scholar's sense of judgement. Bemporad's (2013) study of Minsk is perhaps the best to date of an individual Soviet city.

In the permanent canon of lasting Yiddish literature, a number of Soviet Yiddish works might well be included. They might include Kulbak's novel *Zelmenyáner* (*The Family of Zalmen*), from the early 1930s, Der Nister's *Mishpókhe Máshber* (*The Family Mashber*), from the later years of the decade, and Peretz Markish's epic poem *Milkhóme* (*War*) of the mid 1940s. Even an informal canon of works not ruined by communism (in the sense of praise of communism and the regime being the author's theme instead of literary products of his or her free will) is far from being established, and different literary historians have different preferences. When the dust has settled, it will probably become clear that the greatest works of even the giants of Soviet Yiddish literature were in most cases the ones they wrote *before* they were living in the Soviet Union. For the authors cited here, these include Kulbak's mystical *Meshíekh ben Efráyem* (*Messiah, the Son of Ephraim*), published in Berlin in 1924, Bergelson's pre-Soviet novel *Nokh álemen* (*After All*), published in 1913, and Der Nister's *Gedákht* (*Meditation*), which he published while living and working in Berlin in the early 1920s. The best anthology of Soviet Yiddish literature is still Khone Shmeruk's (1964).

In the Soviet Union, secular Yiddishism was, not long after the nation's rise, hijacked to intoxicate millions of Jews (domestically as well as beyond Soviet borders) with the idea that their language and culture were finally achieving official recognition, support and security, the same kind of illusion that the communists were providing to other stateless ('non-territorial') minorities in the Soviet Union. In the bigger scheme of things, Soviet Yiddish culture was no more than an episode: an illusory meteoric rise followed by a brutal and tragic fall.

There have been a number of long-term negative repercussions as far as the story of Yiddish is concerned. One is a huge waste of talent (and life), as fine writers were forced to bend to the party line and were intimidated, imprisoned, tortured and murdered. Another is a huge dent in the prestige of Yiddish during the past generations when there were millions of pre-war East European born speakers of the language. As for those many Jewish collaborators who enthusiastically became the government's mouthpiece for political control and destruction of 'enemies', they have gone down in history in the infamous hall of *mósrim* ('betrayers', 'moles', 'snitches'), who are among the most hated in Jewish history. The post-Soviet issue, as noted earlier, is still felt in the remaining heavily subsidized secular Yiddish circles of America and Israel, though it would be unfair to lump together the results across the board; the ex-Soviets are not to blame for the fact that neither the American nor the Israeli Yiddish establishment had anyone local they cared to invest their remaining endowments in, before passing from life (or years of active work) somewhere in the temporal vicinity of the year 2000.

Standard pronunciation — and spelling

Beyond the usual rough-and-tumble of literary, academic and political environments, there was a certain wider 'stateless power struggle' over which Yiddish would become the international standard. Because the written language had been largely standardized on those points concerning pronunciation (because of the ease with which dialect readers phonetically render the same historic symbols), the most essential debate was between the pronunciation of the Litvaks (the northerners of the historically Lithuanian lands) vs the non-Litvaks (the southerners of Poland, Ukraine and other countries; see Maps 2, 4 and 5). For hundreds of years, the pronunciation of the Litvaks had been considered most prestigious for reasons to do with sacred Hebrew pronunciations, which had been shifting in each dialect area in tandem with Yiddish over the centuries (see Katz 1993a, 1993b, 1994). But the Litvaks were a minority, perhaps a quarter or so of East European Jewry, and it was only natural that the major southern blocks, particularly in the heart of Poland, would attempt to standardize pronunciation on a southern basis. This linguistic 'power struggle' was a kind of subtle reincarnation of older cultural tensions between the Hasidic south and the anti-Hasidic (misnagdic) north (see Schaechter 1977).

In terminology, it is simplest when the discussion is limited to modern East European Yiddish, to speak of the difference between the north and the south. (The approximate boundaries are illustrated on Map 5.) In academic literature one encounters Northeastern Yiddish vs Mideastern + Southeastern (or, for the latter: Central + Southeastern, or simplified to: Southern Eastern Yiddish). In popular folklore, the northerners are invariably known as the *Lítvakes* (Litvaks); the southerners as *Póylishe* or *Ukraínishe*, often subdivided further into *Volíner* (Volhynians), *Podólyer* (Podolians) and *Besaráber* (Bessarabians). Each dialect has 'put-downs' for the others. Southerners may call a northerner a *Lútvak* (with hypercorrect *u*), and northerners may call a southerner a *Páylisher* (with hyper-Polish *ay*), in both cases pressing into service empirically non-occurring forms for lampooning, but using a sound regarded locally as hilarious when it *does* occur in the usual systematic correspondences between the dialects.

Indeed, the most striking difference between the north and the south is in the system of stressed vowels, where the historic 'clock' has moved one notch, leaving a starkly different sounding but generally wholly consistent set of basic correspondences. Among them: northern *o* [ɔ] vs southern *u*: *Nosn* vs *Nusn* 'Nathan'; *zogn* vs *zugn* 'say'; northern *u* vs southern *i*: *shúre* vs *shíre* 'line', 'row; *kúmen* vs *kímen* 'come'; northern *e* [ɛ] vs southern *ey* [ej]: *béged* vs *béyged* 'garment'; *zen* vs *zeyn* '(to) see'; northern *ey* [ej] vs some ['Polish' but not 'Ukrainian'] southern *ay* [aj]: *péysakh* vs *páysakh* 'Passover (holiday)'; *geyn* vs *gayn* 'go'; northern *ay* [aj] vs southern *ā* or *a*: *dáyge* vs *dấge/dáge* 'worry'; *vayn* vs *van/vān* 'wine'.

By the late 1920s it was clear that the northern system had won in Yiddish school systems, including in the emigration lands, though on the native territory of the southern dialects within Eastern Europe this was often a more 'theoretical' victory than a wholesale switch of dialects frequently witnessed, say, in North American secular Yiddish schools. Instead, on the native speech territory in the East European homeland of Yiddish, local adjustments in the direction of the standard were being made. While that was true for educational settings, a modified form of the southern, non-Litvak dialect, based largely on its eastern Ukrainian variant, won out in the realm of Yiddish theatre. By the late 1920s, a southern stalwart, the master Yiddish dialectologist Noyakh Prilutski, was able to proclaim the victory of the south in the standard language of Yiddish theatre, which had emerged as one of the major prestigious products of modern secular Yiddish culture (see Prilutski 1927).

As for orthography, the passionate debates were (and are) not over differences that relate to dialect or geographic origin, but differences on a very different spectrum: from traditionalist and pre-modern, through to anti-traditionalist (the Soviet system, and the 1937 Yivo system that was a compromise with the Soviet model). It so 'happened' that some of the best-known episodes in the debates transpired in the New York 'colony' of Eastern European Yiddish in the decades following the war, and they were largely a process of self-destruction by some of the tiny groups of weak secular Yiddishists themselves.

For traditionalist eyes, various anti-traditional aspects of the Soviet and Yivo systems continued to be unacceptable and to represent, by spelling alone, the anti-traditionalist philosophies of the leftist and far-leftist movements that were developing Yiddish culture in pre-war Eastern Europe. The most famous example is deletion of the silent álef that separates two vovs [v] from one v [u] (or in southern dialects [i]), yielding װוּ instead of the millennium-old װאוּ for the word for 'where'. For much of the second half of the twentieth century, a group of extreme language normativists, purists on vocabulary (trying to take the language 'further from German') and 'Yivoists on spelling', undertook a massive campaign against Yiddish writers, journalists and publications that simply could not stand the Yivo spelling system (or the purists' assault on their lexicon). For some decades, the youth-for-Yiddish group Yugntruf remained focused on these issues, and its one picket action was against the last daily secular Yiddish newspapers rather than against any of the American Jewish institutions that were boycotting Yiddish, particularly Hebrew day schools and modern yeshivas (only one of which had a student movement for including Yiddish; see Bard 1971). At the same time, Yugntruf was the only young secular Yiddishist club for young people that conducted its business in (some kind of) Yiddish. Eventually it developed the highly successful annual *Yídish vokh* ('Yiddish Week') that complements the more academic international summer courses in America, Europe and Israel.

The issues of purism in vocabulary and adoption of an anti-traditionalist spelling variety, however, continued for many years to stymie the progress of the 'Yiddish in Yiddish' camp in the United States and beyond (see Katz 1993a, an openly anti-normativist, pro-descriptivist, pro-traditionalist tract, but with extensive bibliography from all sides of the debate).

Each spelling detail in Yiddish can in fact have a rich cultural history. One famous case concerns the letter *áyin* (classical *'ayin*). For the best part of a thousand years, the Yiddish cognates of unstressed German end of word –*el* or –*en*) were spelled without the áyin that signifies the underlying shewa phoneme. Hence the Yiddish nouns spelled הימל (*himl* 'sky') and לעבן (*lebn* 'life') have 'happily' corresponded with the likes of German spellings *Himmel* and *Leben* for the best part of a millennium. And so it should be: Yiddish writers, scribes, copyists, authors and teachers did not care about 'mirroring' German in their Yiddish cognates and Yiddish developed its own orthographic traditions (not invariable but within a fixed range). In the nineteenth century, Enlightenment proponents and worldly secularist, socialist Yiddishists alike started to 'improve' Yiddish by mirroring modern German spellings by the insertion of the 'silent áyin', yielding הימעל and לעבען, not to be confused with a traditionalist internal East European variation that entailed inserting *yud* before the syllabic consonants (yielding הימיל and לעבין). For decades the German-mirroring innovational spellings, הימעל and לעבען, became the mark of the secularist, leftist Yiddish cultural world. But after 1913, when Ber Borokhov (see Chapter 12) reformed modern Yiddish spelling and threw out the silent letters in a return to older Yiddish tradition, the traditional spellings increasingly, especially in the interwar period, became the spelling of Yiddish academic and educational institutions and publications. The popular press stuck to the Germanized spelling and, increasingly, that spelling became the opposite of what it had been introduced for: it became the mark of traditional orthodoxy that would have nothing to do with the 'reforms' of the secular Yiddishists. And so it remains in some Hasidic circles to this day. A strange old world.

Perspective

On the eve of the Holocaust, modern Yiddish in all its manifestations, centred primarily in its native territory of Eastern Europe, numbered close to eight million speakers. The principal countries (or Soviet republics on the USSR side of the border) and their Jewish populations are estimated as follows (in decreasing order of population and using pre-1939 borders): Poland (3,300,000); Ukrainian SSR (1,530,000); Russian SSR (920,000); Romania (800,000); Hungary (403,000); Belorussian SSR (375,000); Czechoslovakia (315,000); Lithuania (158,000); Latvia (95,000); Estonia (5,000). The actual number of Yiddish speakers is lower because of linguistic assimilation in some countries, but not by much. Knowledge of Yiddish and use of various of its cultural products extended well beyond both the religious and the secular Yiddish bases of the two major branches. Even assimilationists, 'extreme' Zionists and others were usually part of the de facto Yiddish-speaking civilization which seemed eternal on its native turf, where it seemed as natural a part of the human geography as any language or culture in the multi-layered linguistic tapestry of Eastern Europe.

It is that demographic power which in interwar Eastern Europe made way for the more novel kinds of Yiddish power: educational support in the free republics, the investment (until Stalin's purges in the late 1930s) in Soviet Yiddish and, perhaps most remarkably though spoken about less, the role of Yiddishists in the (mainstream) politics of their countries. That often forgotten phenomenon is in its own way the most potent marker of interwar Yiddish power. The greatest Yiddish dialectologist Noyakh Prilutski (1882–1941) was in his time, in Poland, a member of the provisional council of state and a member of the Sejm (parliament). His party, the Folkists (one of the many leftist Yiddishist groupings), won seats in the Polish parliament. For the (fact-based) Yiddish imagination reflecting a certain 'achieved power', the memory that Prilutski had met with US President Warren G. Harding in the course of his political work for humanitarian aid for World War I refugees remained inseparable from Prilutski's role as master of Yiddish dialects (see Reyzen 1926–9: 2, 954–66; Weiser 2011: 202–3).

Yiddish had attained the perceived power of the smaller national languages of Europe by an international fabric of mainline institutions, of education, publication and research, among others, and by being strong in a number of largely free countries in Eastern Europe. For all the many issues and shortcomings arising, the interwar Polish Republic, the Baltics and others, were successful states in which the pre-World War I Yiddishist dream of a Jewish cultural autonomy as part of 'staying where one is' where Yiddish would become the high-culture language as well as the vernacular in its native territory was fulfilled to a spectacular degree, one that can often not be discussed freely today in the wake of the Holocaust.

When the unwritten book on Yiddish in the interwar republics is written, as it inevitably will be, it will reveal that secular Yiddishism of the late nineteenth and early twentieth centuries was one of the most successful power-for-language movements in human history, the more so for coming to pass without direct political power (outside the Soviet Union). A language never standardized by any state or empowered by any government had risen to be the language of education, society, politics, its own Yivo academy and a literature that rivalled, if post-war creations by its surviving writers are included, that of the middle-sized nation-states of Europe.

The internal diversity of Yiddishism ranged from the religious 'far right' to the political 'far left', though it is often neglected that there was a hefty 'silent majority' that synthesized many traditional religious practices with very much of the modern world in the multilingual environment of Eastern Europe. The successfully developed infrastructure of interwar Yiddish, based on both intrastate and cross-border concepts and institutions, was able to fulfil the dreams of the movement. The Jews of Eastern Europe acquired an advanced language of culture rapidly evolved from their own universal vernacular, putting them on one level with their neighbours without coveting local political sovereignty or territory beyond the kind of minority rights formulated at the Paris Peace Conference and various other contemporary conclaves.

The millions of Yiddish-empowered people in the interwar free republics of Eastern Europe, and most conspicuously Poland, not least in view of a Jewish population of more than three million, were all however 'guilty' of one thing: they did not anticipate the most extreme case of genocide in history that was to wipe them off the face of Eastern Europe in a few short years.

Only very recently has some discussion begun to reflect the kind of simple mental acrobatics needed to fathom the interwar framework rather than a post-Holocaust retrospective that is, at the end of the day, an anachronistic imposition. In a 2014 comment on the old Hebrew–Yiddish language debates and disputes, Eli Kavon pointed out in a *Jerusalem Post* opinion piece (Kavon 2014) that earlier in the twentieth century Yiddish was very powerful while Hebrew was very weak, and that he therefore understands the unpleasant means used by the authorities in the pre-state Land of Israel to suppress Yiddish. Kavon does not distinguish these from post-Holocaust manifestations of the same policies (cf. Katz 2007: 310–23; Tsanin 1999). But that is part of another debate. The point for Yiddish and power is that the societal role of interwar Yiddish was projected to the UK, North America, other parts of the west by immigrant communities and even to the sociolinguistically hostile environment of the Land (and then the State) of Israel. The last masters of the language who had grown up in pre-Holocaust Eastern Europe, be they writers, teachers, organizers, performers or just homespun survivalists and educators, managed to keep alive a viable periodic press and literature until somewhere around the year 2000, where the limitations of the human life span took their natural toll.

The leftist-modernist-inspired meteoric rise of a modern Yiddish language, literature and culture, victim of the Holocaust in its homeland, came to its end around half a century after the genocide in the native language territory.

With precious few exceptions — so few that almost each exception was a kind of sensation in the world of Yiddish — the transplanted émigré Yiddishists of America, Argentina, Australia, Britain, Canada, France, Israel and South Africa, among others, utterly failed to convey the full language and their full commitment to the language to their children and grandchildren (see Katz 2007: 352–5).

15

Yiddishless Yiddish Power vs Powerless Yiddish

Looking at the end of the second decade of the twenty-first century, things called 'Yiddish' can be a ticket to various kinds of personal and institutional empowerment to attain prestige or profit, and even some political gain for both left (and far left) and right (and far right). Concurrently, the thinking, speaking, reading and writing in the language per se are particularly powerless enterprises by any measure. The big danger is not remotely the much-trumpeted 'death of Yiddish'. The numbers of native speakers of child-bearing age in compact communities grow each year in ultra-Orthodox/Haredi and particularly certain Hasidic centres, which are safely spread over a number of continents. The big danger for the secular, cultural and literary treasures of Yiddish, and this is the big surprise, is the obfuscation of the very meaning of the word 'Yiddish' as a frequently empty(ish) idol of the market. What *is* in danger of 'death' is continuity of that bona fide secular, literary high-western-culture-model Yiddish language, literature and culture. In its place the PR, marketing and self-aggrandizement *thing* 'Yiddish' can in many instances take over without comment or opposition in light of the disappearance (by death or old age) of secular experts in the language who came to maturity in the pre-Holocaust Eastern European homeland and, when they existed, had some moral authority in speaking out. Even when they (or their supporters) have spoken out, their voice has been small, weak and rapidly disappearing enough to be dismissed as the whines of die-hard killjoys.

How on earth did we get there?

For the history of most languages and cultures, concepts such as 'postwar' became more dated and less usable with each year that passed following the end of World War II. Naturally enough, such notions gradually pass from being cardinal and contrastive with all which came before and since, into being one of numerous epochs of the ever-rich past. It is part of the universal 'time-work' that events that were cataclysmic for a few generations can become sequential links in rather longer chains of demarcative events in collective memory.

On the ground, far from our debates, hundreds of thousands of native Yiddish speakers in Haredi (mostly Hasidic) communities in the world continue to live lives that ipso facto build the demographic foundations for the future millions of native Yiddish speakers (see Katz 2007: 379–97). It is therefore clear that there are innumerable more chapters in the unfinished story of Yiddish that we will not live to see, let alone understand. But we may safely enough posit that 'our sacred notions' will be relegated to much more relative status than we might be able, or care, nowadays to imagine.

For our own times, however, the destruction of East European Jewry in the genocide known as the Holocaust, the most completely executed genocide in human history, meant the loss of the native homeland, of the millions of native speakers in the native territory of the modern language, and the loss of those forms of language viability associated with evolved in-situ language culture. In the framework of this enquiry, that refers especially to the built-up infrastructure of a prestigious culture of native people in their native language: schools, publishing houses, libraries, theatres, research institutions and the intangible quality of 'nativity', 'self-respect' and 'establishment' that are not so easily re-creatable abroad by émigrés, refugees or their progeny.

We are pained by the fate of secular Yiddish culture in the 'relatively safe' countries where neither Hitler nor Stalin ever set foot. Millions of East European Jewish émigrés were out of harm's way well before Hitler's rise to power. The mass migrations to the United States, Britain, South Africa and (the Land of) Israel, among other countries, should have 'on touchdown' led to some transplanted continuity to an 'Ashkenaz III' in the same spirit in which 'Ashkenaz I' centred on German-speaking soil morphed into 'Ashkenaz II' in the Slavic and Baltic lands. In the secular Yiddish world, it did not happen, with no disrespect to the many enthusiasts, supporters, defenders and revivalists who are to be credited with genuine and laudable accomplishments. So small was the micro-percentage of children of Yiddish writers and teachers who became fluent in the language to the point of passing it on further (and an even smaller subset made it into one of their life's prime concerns) that virtually each such case became a sensation, according 'hero' (or 'villain') status to someone who merely continued using their parents' language as a core part of their own career.

Yet the process of disappearance of the last generations of East European born and bred Yiddish speakers (writers, teachers, etc.) was a gradual one over many decades, felt most acutely by personal losses of loved ones by their surviving family members. The sense of loss in the final decades of the twentieth century fed into a new 'love of Yiddish' that replaced the earlier feelings of embarrassment and even shame that American, British and other Jews around the world often felt earlier on concerning the language and its image. That negativism resulted sometimes from assimilationism and the desire to ensure perfect English that would be wholly indistinguishable from non-Jewish native speakers (Labov 2012: 29, 2014).

Often, the negativism vis-à-vis Yiddish among the most Jewishly conscious had resulted from various forms of Hebraism that posited Hebrew as the sole legitimate language of the Jewish future, all the more so after the establishment of the officially-Hebrew-only State of Israel in 1948. It was sometimes compounded by economic and related factors of social psychology; for example, the shame felt by upwardly mobile Americans, competitive in higher education, about forebears who may have been tailors, customer peddlers, small shop owners or factory workers. Hebrew — ancient and modern — equalled prestige and the allure of the romantic past and the faraway revivers of the deserts of the Land of Israel, respectively. Both came to mean 'good' for masses of Jews in America and other western countries, while associations with Yiddish evoked embarrassing images of the immigrant generation of non-native English speakers ('bad').

All of that changed with the gradual disappearance of older loved ones and the recognition that a modern sophisticated literature and culture were being lost, not just the warmth of some homely Coney Island creole. In the second half of the twentieth century, a number of factors fed into the fascinating transformation from shame to love, which is worth a proper study, based on fieldwork interviews with living informants. Sundry factors came into play in the transformation.

First, the acute pain of the loss of a loved one, which can be intensified by the realization that one had failed during his or her life to bother to learn about a unique and very non-American (British/western) heritage, starting with language.

Second, increasing recognition of the scope of the Holocaust and a growing preparedness to talk about it.

Third, the successful translation for the sophisticated English-reading market of a few Yiddish writers into English, demonstrating the world-class status of parts of Yiddish literature.

Fourth, there were western movements to cherish other ethnic and multicultural traditions. In the United States and Britain, the 1960s was the prime decade for that particular transformation, which had a specific and at times noticeable effect also on many Jewish families of East European heritage.

Fifth, there was a potent political factor that few cared (or care) to talk about. The end of the Holocaust was followed in rather rapid succession by the onset of the Cold War, and indeed the McCarthy period, which would de-legitimize any kind of sympathy with communism or the Soviet Union in the first instance — and by extension any kind of socialism too. There are, of course, many individual differences between countries. In the United States, the word 'socialist' joined 'communist' in the list of taboos, in Britain much less so — it would be many more decades before the mainstream Labour Party would, near the end of the twentieth century, finally ditch the 'S word'.

Extrapolating to the mid-century status of Yiddish in America, and elsewhere, that meant that in addition to being associated with the uneducated immigrants from a far away Mars-like place (the East European shtetl), there was even word out on the block, in the 1950s, that an FBI agent could come knocking on the door of this or that Yiddish writer or teacher to ask about connections with communism, or more likely to ask about buddies, mates and others in the world of secular Yiddish culture who might be involved with the Big C. Put differently, there was a rapid obliteration of whatever little legitimacy the various Yiddishist movements in America might have been blessed with in the first place in the eyes of American-borns. This was wholly unpredictable during the war years or beforehand. To be sure, the Yiddishist communists, just like the anarchists, Bundists, (omnibus) socialists, territorialists and all the rest were 100 per cent peaceful citizens of the United States.

By the late 1960s, however, McCarthyism was out and various forms of post-communist liberalism (for example, 'the new left') were coming into vogue, softening the pang of fear felt at the mention of any word associated with notions of the political left. In addition to this change in America, there were the Jewish developments of widening recognition of the Holocaust (Elie Wiesel, the Eichmann trial), a little respect for serious Yiddish (Isaac Bashevis Singer and Sholem Aleichem in translation, particularly via the staging of *Fiddler on the Roof*). The outpouring of pro-Israel feeling in the wake of the 1967 David-and-Goliath Mideast war added to the growing comfort level with certain kinds of out-and-out Jewishness in American Jewish society. By the late 1960s, the anti-Vietnam movement, the stirrings of gay and lesbian equal rights campaigns and a generally anti-authoritarian, anti-conservative culture began, for some limited numbers here and there, to identify with long-forgotten works of Yiddish literature, theatre and press. For Yiddish the major tangible advance was the introduction of Yiddish language courses for credit at American universities, and, from 1968 onward, of intensive summer courses whose heirs continue today to produce more in the way of language knowledge than much else in the sphere of nominally pro-Yiddish activities (see J. A. Fishman 1965, 1991; Hudson-Edwards 1981). But intensive language courses are the 'really Yiddish' part of the secular Yiddish movement. For the rest, something unexpected has often taken hold.

Delinguification of Yiddish

The operative bona fide Yiddish phrase for what happened when Yiddish became popular in late twentieth-century America might well be: *Améritshke gánev*. The literal meaning is 'America [diminutive, possibly with endearment] is a [kind of] thief'. The phrase never referred to stealing or robbery, and is not even necessarily negative, though it is biting. It is instead a humorous Yiddish expression of some vintage that could be 'culturally translated' as 'America is the wonderland of PR' or 'In America you can sell anything!' or 'They can do anything in America!' The following personal memory can clarify that this Yiddish exclamation, probably of late nineteenth-century vintage, is used as often in wonderment as in some kind of moral outrage. In the mid 1990s, I accompanied a very elderly Lithuanian-Jewish gentleman, the late Kalmen Segalovitsh, to the apartment in Brooklyn Heights, New York, where he would be staying during his first foray out of Eastern Europe in his entire life. It was a boiling hot day and I urged him to press the button on the air-conditioner to get cool. He huffed into a long scientific explanation of why you can get warm when it's cold but you can't do anything when it's hot. When, after my continuous begging, he pressed the button, and began to revel in the miracles of cool America, he could the rest of the day say nothing other than *Améritshke gánev!* repeatedly, but never twice with the exact same intonation or accompanying hand and face gestures.

What has been happening for close to half a century now is that the *product* 'Yiddish' has become a major American success story, providing economic, social, academic, educational, political and other forms of empowerment to individuals and institutions without the investment of the time and effort needed to master 'the actual language Yiddish' in the same sense in which one would 'invest in' mastering French, Spanish or German, or for that matter Swahili, Basque or Hindi. What for, when that mastery is rendered socially and commercially superfluous to ambitions to 'save Yiddish', 'rescue Yiddish', 'revive Yiddish' and what not (see Hoffman 1994; Katz 2007: 360–2).

The ongoing process of delinguification by 'the Yiddish industry' was less noticeable in the decades when there were still plenty of East European-born elderly speakers about 'to fill the gap as needed'. But with the demographic collapse of the immigrant generation, and their ongoing gradual disappearance in consequence of the limited human life span (even with the best medicine of *Améritshke gánev*), the fulsome spectre of Yiddishless Yiddish power is coming into its own most dramatically as the current volume goes to the press smack in the middle of the second decade of the twenty-first century.

There has been an audacious (and, in its own American way, remarkably successful) intellectual and PR sleight of hand, moving the goal posts to the present 'postmodernist' stage where the word 'Yiddish' has been redefined to encompass, it sometimes seems, a wide range of activities, with the exception of the one that counts most: creating communities, no matter how modest, that speak and write the language daily while pursuing creative work of one sort or another in the actual language. To be sure, there is a continuum. It includes people as well as websites that sprinkle their English, and particularly their English pitches for donations, with sprightly Yiddish words in the 'Yivo transcription' that gives the usage class and academic cachet, instead of popular Anglo-American spellings that are still the wider norm, for example, *khútspe* instead of *chutzpah*, *dreydl* instead of *dreidel* or *draidel* for the top played with on Chanukah (or Hanukkah), which in its own turn, must become *Kháneke*. Similarly, the delicacy known as a *knaidel* (a kind of dumpling) must be an English-letter *kneydl* for some 'saviours of Yiddish', and this one even resulted in a spelling bee incident that attracted a *New York Times* op-ed in recent years (Horn 2013). Academics, cultural leaders and influential personalities and institutions (American 'winners') have been heavily invested in moving the goal posts to where they are nowadays to be found. In fact, this may become an archetypal chapter of postmodernism as business — with no disrespect to the many serious and productive branches and expressions of postmodernist thought and methodology.

It can be enlightening to work backwards, in the spirit of Saussurean reconstruction, though applied to culture and its societal power rather than the elements of language. What is being solidified today by academic and cultural specialists in Yiddish studies who have been bold enough to take on this irksome topic in the first place is a somewhat macabre redefinition of the word 'Yiddish'. But first, some sociolinguistic background is in order, with America in focus, because it is the country producing most of the relevant Yiddish 'products' under discussion, though similar sets of sequences can on occasion be observed in Britain, South Africa and other countries, and via the internet, globally. It seems to some observers, incidentally, that the idea of Yiddish as a language that must be learned like any other has persevered longer in Yiddishist circles in Melbourne, Paris and Montreal.

'Yiddish' in America was redefined 'downward' as a taste, a feel, a culture, a heritage, an art, a music, a comedy and, simultaneously at the top end of the scale, 'upward' as an academic subject where the language would be treated as a kind of Sanskrit about which learned papers with massive numbers of footnotes and references would be written. The less one would have to master the intricacies of the language, the quicker the route to academic success with 'Yiddish'.

The most famous (and best-endowed) American-born enterprise has been the National Yiddish Book Center in Amherst, Massachusetts, which has many accomplishments, two of which rise far above all the rest. First is its literal saving of millions of Yiddish books that were being thrown out by the close descendants of the immigrants who cherished them, enabling them to be sold and provided to future users, readers, learners and students all over the world. Second, with the help of the Steven Spielberg Foundation, the Book Center has made available free, online, scanned versions of thousands of Yiddish books that are in one fell swoop available to anyone, anywhere, who wishes to study real Yiddish literature. These two accomplishments dwarf, in conceptual terms, the building of a multimillion-dollar impressive and expensive architectural edifice, which in its own way symbolizes the Center's greatest failure: it has not produced one new master of Yiddish who would her- or himself go on to write books *in* Yiddish, teach advanced courses *in* Yiddish, or build any living continuity for 'actual Yiddish'. Over the past forty years, many discussions with staff and supporters alike have elicited the reaction that such goals would be at best 'maximalist' and 'unrealistic' and at worst 'fanatic', 'crazy' or 'whacko'. The very thought of producing a Yiddish master (writer, educator, cultural leader whose work would be carried out *in* Yiddish) would seem so far from the reality within the extant mindset as to be unthinkable even if the benefactions and infrastructure achieved *could have and should have* produced many masters after all these decades, after all those tens of millions of *gríne* ('green ones', a Yiddish term for dollars).

One of the most famous front pages of the Center's glossy magazine, the *Pakntreger* (a genuine Yiddish word for the travelling bookseller of old Eastern Europe), had the ambitious headline 'Charting the Future of Yiddish in America', with a picture of a large staff that communicates 100 per cent in English. They were not by any means deceiving anybody. They were simply redefining Yiddish in the age-old American tradition of redefinition of the entity being promoted to make a success.

Another popular area for the dissemination of 'Yiddishless Yiddish' is English-language book production. Hundreds upon hundreds of publications have appeared. A few are actually masterpieces, like Leo Rosten's *Joys of Yiddish* (1968) and Maurice Samuel's *In Praise of Yiddish* (1971). They are no replacement for a Yiddish course, but they are book-length descriptions of the language and its culture and spirit by true experts who are deeply knowledgeable in the actual language and in the art of conveying its treasures. On the more polemic side of 'Yiddish defences' there have likewise been some memorable writings, including Joseph Landis's 'Who Needs Yiddish? A Study in Language and Ethics' (Landis 1964), which has often been republished in pamphlet form for the arsenal of the pro-Yiddish. Then there is the 'popular end of the market', comprising, just as examples of some of the sub-genres, *Jewish as a Second Language* (M. Katz 1991); Mr P's *The World's Best Yiddish Dirty Jokes* (Mr 'P' 1984), *The Power of Yiddish Thinking* (Marcus 1971) and, in recent times, the highly successful *Yiddish with Dick and Jane* (Weiner and Davilman 2004) and, by the same authors, *Yiddish with George and Laura [Bush]* (2006).

The list and the categories can be expanded significantly. There is the success of *Fiddler on the Roof*, based on Sholem Aleichem's *Tévye der Mílkhiker* (*Tevye the Milkman*), and today in New York the excellent New World Theatre, specializing in productions translated from Yiddish originals of serious Yiddish dramatic works that would otherwise remain unknown. These projects bring usually forgotten treasures of Yiddish literature to English-speaking audiences in America. There are the top comics, such as Woody Allen and Jackie Mason, who have successfully translated Yiddish humour into English (more precisely, certain registers of English that are a notch or two closer to language varieties of segments of the immigrant families of New York and other cities that had become hubs of East European immigrant clustering).

These examples have purposely been taken from the best of Yiddish-in-English enterprises precisely to avoid giving offence. Such offence would occur in the case of *thousands* of cultural products that have nothing at all to do with genuine Yiddish beyond the conjuring of a few emotive words for profit. The Googler may Google 'Yiddish' to find everything from a guide to success in the insurance business to sex toys.

One might expect that 'professors of Yiddish' would be up in arms over such collapse of the very definition. One might a priori expect a professor to say: 'Look, all these activities *concerning* Yiddish, *about* Yiddish, *for* Yiddish, Yiddish singing, Yiddish dancing, Yiddish humour, Yiddish cursing, these are all great, but hey, guys, to learn Yiddish seriously, you have to invest the same amount of time as to learn any language. If you want to be a Yiddish writer, you need to write a real book *in Yiddish*. If you want to be a Yiddish professor, you need to be able to teach in Yiddish. If you want to be a Yiddish thinker, you have to somehow think in Yiddish.'

Not only has that not happened, but a number of eminent and excellent academics have in fact come out with serious works in which delinguification is subtly, or not so subtly, accepted as a kind of fait accompli or even championed. While we sincerely disagree, it does not affect our respect for their work. But there is a real need to launch the Second Opinion into the debate, by reintroducing the notion and trappings of the simple, old-fashioned notion of a 'language like all languages' vis-à-vis Yiddish. Neither a set of insertions into English nor a heavenly feel of klezmer music a language makes. The phenomenon of delinguification has been given a name: post-vernacularity. Its best-known proponent is Jeffrey Shandler in his *Adventures in Yiddishland: Postvernacular Language and Culture* (2006). Among many other examples, he cites (or deigns to cite or reinterpret) as follows from the quotation from the renowned Yiddish musical performer and producer Henry Sapoznik:

[...] in his work, the term *Yiddish* denotes not only the language, but the society and culture served by it. *Yiddish music*, then — be it folksongs, theatre compositions, the singing of cantors, even instrumental music — refers to what has been recognized as music by *yidishe oyern* (Jewish ears), long the arbiters of what gains entry into the soundscape of *Yiddishkayt*.

(Sapoznik, cited in Shandler 2006: 141)

The author, Professor Shandler, comments:

> By focusing on the ears rather than the mouth, Sapoznik shifts the
> agency of defining Yiddish culture from production to reception.
>
> (Shandler 2006: 141)

But Sapoznik is a musician, and musicians inherently think in the
supra-linguistic medium of music. Invoking him here as evidence is
therefore not entirely in order. It soon emerges that, for Shandler himself, a very much more general delinguification is under way. He reports
on an array of American Yiddish phenomena, claiming the existence of:

> [...] a fundamental as well as a transcendent essence that can persist
> despite the absence of actual language. As an idiom or sensibility, Yiddish
> can thrive without lexicon or syntax; indeed, its 'spirit' can inhabit the
> form of another language. The implicit metaphors are both biological —
> language as DNA — and supernatural — language as dybbuk.
>
> (Shandler 2006: 122–3)

There is the ensuing inexorable slide into an aura of teleological
inevitability:

> What has been in decline is not merely the number of speakers or the
> extent of Yiddish discourse, but the unselfconscious, seemingly inevita-
> ble use of Yiddish as a full language (as opposed to isolated Yiddishisms
> embedded in another language) for routine conversation among Jews.
>
> (Shandler 2006: 128–9)

Naturally, there are counter-arguments. First, that to use 'Yiddish' for a
feel, taste, or something else is simply *not* to be studying *Yiddish*, period.
No barrage of academicized or jargonized argumentation can change
that starkly simple empirical conclusion. Second, and here is the rub,
Yiddish is a thriving vernacular in Hasidic communities where children
think in Yiddish, speak in Yiddish to their siblings and classmates,
where hundreds of new books come out every year. Instead of studying the mainstream Yiddish-speaking civilization of *today*, the author
claims, rather counter-factually, that:

> [...] postwar Hasidim are, in their own way, engaging with Yiddish as
> a postvernacular language.
>
> (Shandler 2006: 84)

Shandler's revealing book, incidentally, contains more (and sometimes more illuminating material) on Hasidic Yiddish than many other more linguistics-oriented treatments. For example, in his own book strictly on Yiddish linguistics, focused on the actual language, Neil Jacobs (2005) did justice to the standard secular literary language that has been studied dozens of times, but did not take the opportunity for studying language change under way in Hasidic Yiddish, regarding it all as a kind of corruption of the linguistic norms of secular Yiddish language and literature (cf. Katz 2006). That itself might be an extension of the overly normativist, purist stridency of much post-war American Yiddish-in-Yiddish education (see Katz 1993a) which had championed an ultra-normativist Yiddish that was alien to the then-living Yiddish writers, teachers and cultural leaders in the last decades of the twentieth century. Within the elite, small 'Yiddish-in-Yiddish' circles centred on New York City for decades, a purist spirit of 'power over the language' enabled a tiny handful of expert-in-Yiddish academics and their wholly unexpert students to become campaigners against the Yiddish of the last writers and teachers on the grounds that it was too *dáytshmerish* (infected by modern German words and constructions that had entered Yiddish from the nineteenth century), and did not use the Soviet-inspired but Yivo-compromised 'standard spelling' that is forever unacceptable to Hasidic and Haredi eyes and sensibilities, as well as to secular traditionalists (see Katz 1993a).

So the disconnect becomes even larger when the post-vernacularists in Shandler's spirit, when they do cite Yiddish, cite its 'Yugntruf' incarnations, a reference to an important though very small youth-for-Yiddish group that had genuinely gone against the grain in building a small circle of Yiddish enthusiasts that tried hard to really speak the language and, in a tiny handful of cases, raised secular Yiddish-speaking families in the New York area.

However, the most basic flaw of the current academic trend is to take 'post-vernacularity' from those for whom it is verily post-vernacular (many of the lovers, supporters and donors to 'Yiddish causes' in North America, and a hefty proportion of the teachers and professors too) and to extend it uncritically at a time when spending a month in, for example, the Boro Park section of Brooklyn would afford the opportunity of immersion in a Yiddish-speaking society where 'post-vernacularity of Yiddish' would be equally ridiculous as a word and as a concept. The notion would be laughable to the innumerable thousands for whom it is the one language in the family, on the street, and for life. Go tell it on the mountain of the elevated trainline over New Utrecht

Avenue in Brooklyn, and say unto them from above: 'Thou art verily post-vernacular!'

Shandler is, however, to be credited most sincerely with opening an overdue debate that would invariably attract responses. The main response to date is Tatjana Soldat-Jaffe's more sophisticated and nuanced *Twenty-First Century Yiddishism*. It shows respect both to the East European Yiddish-in-Yiddish secular theorists, like Avrom Golomb (1888–1982), and to present-day Hasidim, of which she writes, correctly:

> Whether the Yiddish Haredim know this as self-conscious pedagogical theory or not, their primers demonstrate that they follow implicit Yiddishism as a cultural-linguistic practice and an ethnic marker. The end, which for secular Yiddishists was only aspirational, Haredi Yiddishists make real.
>
> (Soldat-Jaffe 2012: 67)

It can be argued that in Eastern Europe the secular Yiddishists succeeded splendidly in making it all real, every bit as much as they failed in a sustainable way for American-born generations to make it real in the United States (or the other centres of mass East European Jewish migration in western Europe, South Africa and elsewhere). But that leaves open the question of evaluation of the notion *Yiddishism*, in the current intellectual environment dominated by the 'post-vernacularists'.

Soldat-Jaffe's verdict on Yiddishism (and/or Yiddishness) today:

> If the Yiddish language once created and expressed self-contained group membership and, as such, carried coherently marked societal goals, these were never stable forms of place-identity, and now other values have stepped in. To return to the different faces of Yiddish, Yiddish as a religious and ethnic language still represents a language of resistance to modernity, whereas Yiddish as a secular language has become a language of assimilation to forces of modernity. Yiddishness goes on even when Yiddish cannot.
>
> (Soldat-Jaffe 2012: 127)

Moreover, Soldat-Jaffe well understands that Yiddishless Yiddishism empirically needs to be compared with *whatever it is* that is used to describe the ism-less Haredim who just speak, think, write and perpetuate the language without the language itself being part of a 'movement'.

In all cases, there is a conscious decision to adapt traditional forms of Yiddish culture to diverse ends. Judging by the different forms of adaptation, this process is always in flux. Just as before, Yiddishists today try to invest Yiddish with prestige and status markers, instrumental forms of identity and hybridized claims about authenticity. Authenticity is no longer necessarily singular; it may have become, instead, a second-hand recipe of inherited ingredients, like the books at the [National] Yiddish Book Center [in Amherst, Massachusetts]. Yiddishism's pedagogical imperatives are in sync with this tendency. The reinvention of a non-existing Yiddishland, the acts of repeated re-creation, has left its marks on educational practice. With postmodernism comes a variety of new imagined Yiddishlands. Whereas the Haredim subscribed to a pedagogy of Yiddish language learning without conscious Yiddishism, the New Yiddishists — the new generation of Yivo and the neo-klezmórim alike — in good postmodern fashion advance a pedagogy of Yiddishism without Yiddish.

(Soldat-Jaffe 2012: 107)

Soldat-Jaffe correctly understands the situation. Where one might quibble with her would be on the uncritical acceptance of all and everything that someone claims because something has become part of a satisfying industry in the modern Jewish (and non-Jewish) marketplace (whatever the branding — *Yiddishland, Yiddishness, Yiddish...*). She has certainly correctly identified the abandoning of the Yiddish language by the National Yiddish Book Center, much more painfully by the American Yivo which is meant to be the world centre of intellectual and academic Yiddishism, and less painfully the klezmer music crowd which never pretended to be the intellectual guardian of Yiddish. The next step is for the purported Yiddish, Yiddishism *or* Yiddishness, the collective PR clout of a number of well-oiled organizations that sell and trade in Yiddishless Yiddish/Yiddishism/Yiddishness, to be subjected to critical scrutiny. Otherwise, Yiddish in the secular non-Haredi world is doomed to become a rather perverse joke, where those who know the language well are ipso facto regarded as inherently jurassic and an impediment to a good day's fun and games.

Soldat-Jaffe turns to my own debate with Professor Ruth Wisse of Harvard University:

Yet, like Wisse, Katz's position is defined by a rigid equation between authentic language users and the language itself. One need not be a sociolinguist to recognize that there is more to language than the sum of its lexicon and the tally of its users. [...] [Wisse] may feel that the language is dead, but the culture, the literature, the music, the traditions that still do exist — are they destined for the trash heap of Yiddish history? In an odd way, Katz also defines language futurity too narrowly. A paradigmatically different approach, which I am following here, has been recently proposed by Jeffrey Shandler in *Adventures in Yiddishland*. On the surface, he follows Katz's optimism about Yiddish's prospects, but he departs from both Katz and Wisse in emphasis. Shifting the explanatory weight from language users *per se* to language as a semiotic system, Shandler looks at the transformation of Yiddish since the Holocaust, observing a shift from its role as an ethnic vernacular to a postvernacular laden with symbolic value.

(Soldat-Jaffe 2012: 112)

One point here is both accurate and ironic. Wisse and I have been debating, sometimes sharply, for years (see, for example, Katz 2007: 362–6), being on opposite ends of two debates. First, the 'alive or dead' debate. Wisse believes Yiddish to be a more or less dead language; I claim it is thriving as a vernacular in the Hasidic communities and can continue to thrive small-scale in secular circles that would master it, write in it and teach in it. Second, Wisse claims that the secular Yiddish movement is an enterprise riddled with far-left and liberal causes:

These days, Jewish (and non-Jewish) spokesmen for gays and lesbians, feminists and neo-Trotskyites freely identify their sense of personal injury with the cause of Yiddish. They thereby commit a double fault, occluding the moral assurance and tenacity of Yiddish culture in its own terms and, by attributing value of weakness, retroactively defaming the Jewish will to live and to prosper.

(Wisse 1997: 38)

I certainly do disagree on the identification of all the secular adherents of Yiddish with leftism and 'weakness theory' (one of the 'Three Stigmas' posited in my *Unfinished Story of Yiddish*, Katz 2007: 362–6, the other two being that Yiddish is too *right-wing* because of its Haredi sectors, and 'too *dead*'). I also disagree that believing in human rights and the equality of people and peoples is even remotely a sign of 'weakness' or the 'worship of weakness'; I see in such notions nothing but (far-) right rhetoric. But Soldat-Jaffe has implicitly understood correctly that Wisse and I actually fully *share* a 'narrow' (a better word would be 'literal') definition of Yiddish that is perfectly analogous to the criteria for Portuguese or Swahili, and that leaves no room for the vast swamps of 'postmodernist' claptrap that makes for virtually anything one wishes (right, left or centre....) to be considered 'Yiddish' if an organization develops programmes, say, using the word, and academics then write papers and books about those organizations and programmes giving them a higher degree of supposed existence. Wisse and I agree 100 per cent on what Yiddish is; both of us are old-fashioned empiricists in one of the prime senses of the term. Ironically, the history of ideas of the subject may come to see us on the same side of this (now) larger debate, for all the disagreements on the pro- and anti-Yiddishism spectrum. While agreeing with Wisse that there are (for me: occasional, not dominant of Yiddishism) far-left hijacks of 'Yiddish', I shall maintain that the Yiddishless abuse of the Yiddish heritage is nowadays liable to come from the widest array of causes — including the new far right.

The question of necessity arises: why does a new generation of Yiddish professors in America and elsewhere give succour to the commercial gods of the west, be they of its Jewish branches, be they part of the great can-do-anything American tradition? Surely the work of critics in academia is to call a spade a spade and an evening about Yiddish 'an evening about Yiddish'. It seems strange that a situation could arise when there are *still* hundreds of thousands of elderly East European Jews who speak Real McCoy Yiddish, and well over a million Haredim in the world who speak Haredi Yiddish, many of them of child-bearing age in a society where large families and high percentages of community retention constitutes the actual future of actual Yiddish.

A deeper reason for many secular Yiddishists' proclivity to ignore the Hasidic domain is related to the multi-layered psychological and social divide between modernized Jewry in all its branches (from assimilated all the way to modern Orthodox) on the one hand and Haredism (and its chief Ashkenazic branch, Hasidism), on the other. The Haredim, whose lifestyle is often much closer to the moderns' own ancestors of a century ago in Eastern Europe, cause feelings of discomfort, inadequacy and disdain and unconscious self-questioning in some moderns. Many of the Haredim *are* in modern western terms anti-feminist, anti-Zionist, intolerant, rigid, superiorist about Jews generally, and look down upon other Jews and non-Jews. During a recent research visit to Boro Park, Brooklyn, in connection with this book and a parallel linguistic project on contemporary Hasidic Yiddish, a Hasidic fellow was seen wishing an out-of-town modern Orthodox Jew (that is, a non Boro-Parker identified inter alia by a colourful knitted bobby-pinned *kipá*, instead of the self-balancing larger black *yármulke*), *Khag saméakh!* ('Happy holiday!') using the imitation-of-Israeli American 'Sephardic' pronunciation of Hebrew, and indeed using the Hebrew instead of the Yiddish *Gut yóntef.* The *khósid* turned to our own team (in Yiddish) with a whispered soliloquy as soon as the visitor was out of ear-shot: 'No worries, he wasn't insulted, the *shméndrik* didn't understand that I was *talking down* to him by saying *Khag saméakh*'. Yes, Haredim believe in the absolute truth of their religious society every bit as much as the faithful of other faiths believe in their truths. For Haredim today, the biblical account of creation of the world, the belief in the Messiah to come, in the afterlife, and so much more, are indeed absolutely sacred, as is the belief in Jewish chosenness which so irks modern Jews who are part of western societies that believe uncompromisingly in human equality.

The upshot is that moderns, Jews and non-Jews alike but especially Jews, do not by and large feel comfortable with Haredim, particularly Hasidim, and suffer from as many prejudices and misconceptions about them as any anti-Semite or racist, strange as it is to say. The estrangement between modern Jewish life (including its many academic and educational Jewish studies programmes) and Hasidic communities is so complete that otherwise competent scholars are willing to write books even about the very language only spoken in communities 'by that Other' that ignore, downplay or misrepresent the simple fact that there are multitudes of young Haredim who speak beautiful, rich Yiddish all day, though not the same exact dialect, grammar or spelling used by the academics when they 'play in Yiddish' or write each other Standard Yiddish emails in Latin letters, or culturists who write odes (in English) to the glories of Yiddish or the eternity of Yiddish.

There is in play here a logical route to personal or organizational empowerment that is self-fulfillingly practical. If becoming a powerful success with Yiddishless Yiddish in the modern American scene, personally and institutionally, does not remotely require mastering Yiddish, why on earth invest years to master it, when a fraction of the energy can straight away be invested in fundraising events, kickstarters and promotional videos on YouTube to achieve success?

Yet while Yiddishless Yiddish is thriving as an industry of empowerment, the real future of Yiddish is being crafted elsewhere, though geographically not far away.

The Hasidic future of Yiddish

There are divergent figures about the number of Yiddish-speaking Hasidim. Timothy Gill's *Worldmark Encyclopedia of Culture and Daily Life* estimated 650,000 Hasidim back in 1998. Robert Eisenberg, in his *Boychiks in the Hood. Travels in the Hasidic Underground* (1995), speaking about the United States alone, concluded that:

> Today there are about a quarter million Hasidim in North America. They are growing at a rate of 5% a year, a trajectory which, if anything, is on the upswing, as new generations have ever more children per family. [...] A 5% annual increase translates into a doubling of population every fifteen years. This means that the 250,000 Hasidim of today [in the United States] will number between eight and ten million in the year 2075.
>
> (Eisenberg 1995: 1–2)

Others have worked on estimates for all Haredim ('ultra-Orthodox'), rather than just Hasidim. Professor Menachem Friedman of Bar-Ilan University, one of the leading experts on the sociology of contemporary ultra-Orthodoxy, confirms that exact figures are in dispute but is prepared to offer estimates as guidelines. For 2005, he had reckoned on approximately 1.5 million Haredim in the world, of whom about 700,000 are in Israel. Of the Haredim in the diaspora, the vast majority are Hasidim.

A figure of over a million fully native Yiddish speakers internationally, in 2015, is a conservative, over-cautious low number. It is particularly important to avoid the exaggerations and hyperbolics that have become the staple of 'conferences to save Yiddish' so masterfully lampooned in beautiful real Yiddish by New York's Miriam Hoffman (1994). It is important for the various Jewish population surveys to come to grips with the issue and stop shirking one of the major Jewish demographic questions of our times. It is also important for demographic projects to focus on obtaining more exact figures.

Some years ago the number of Yiddish 'full' speakers in the secular world, who actually use the language as one of the main languages in daily life, dropped to around half a million for the first time, and the figure is now very rapidly collapsing altogether. In other words, the naturally rising figure of Hasidic Yiddish speakers over the last decade 'crossed' the demographically plummeting figure of ageing secular speakers coming to the end of their days.

A recent research trip to Boro Park in Brooklyn found Yiddish to be markedly stronger than several years ago, among certain Hasidic groups that account for the majority. A new Standard Yiddish has emerged, the phonology of which is closely based on the classic southern dialect (Mideastern Yiddish, or Central Yiddish in some schemes, see Maps 2, 4 and 5), which has involved shifts from all other dialects, including the closely related Hungarian dialect. A 'real' Hungarian (or Ukrainian) Yiddish usually can be heard only from older speakers. With few exceptions, the new standard, based on Polish Yiddish, is becoming the Standard Hasidic Yiddish of the imminent future. The application of this phonology to the sacred uses of Hebrew and Aramaic have, of late, become the subject of systematic study within the Hasidic milieu, most notably the recent book by N. Z. Dembitzer (2011). This mode of Haredi study of the subject, taking the incarnation of the dialect's phonology in the sacred Hebrew and Aramaic as the prime object of study (rather than the vernacular as point of departure), is itself a continuation of a venerable tradition from older times spanning both Western and Eastern Ashkenaz (see Katz 1994).

The grammatical system also shows various innovations, most notably from the viewpoint of European Yiddish, the ongoing disappearance of a three-gender system to two and to one, exactly, as it happens, as the founder of modern Yiddish linguistics, Ber Borokhov, predicted over a century ago (Borokhov 1912). Hasidic Yiddish produces hundreds of new books a year, many internet sites, and a lively periodic press (see Box 15.1).

The various Hasidic courts have intra-Jewish power bases that include the businesspeople in the community vying with each other to contribute munificently to buildings, schools, synagogues and *yeshivas*. Because of each *rebbe*'s reliable ability to deliver the bloc vote to politicians, there is a political power base in favour of legislation and largesse that benefit these communities.

However, that is mundane compared to the cultural power within world Judaism of Hasidic Yiddish. That cultural power is founded on the preservation of a veritable civilization including language, dress, mores and laws and customs governing much of the day, a very large birth rate, low percentage of drop-outs from the community and a growing published literature and internet presence that promises to preserve the power of Yiddish *within* world Jewry as a marker of Ashkenazic authenticity and separateness from modern Jews (and in Israel — from ethnographic Israelis or *sabras,* as native-born culturally Israeli people are called).

Box 15.1   New Yiddish magazines for a new century

There can be no 'Hasidic Revival' of Yiddish as a spoken language because traditional Hasidim never stopped speaking it. But during this first decade of the new millennium, there is an unmistakable explosion of Yiddish culture that bears an uncanny resemblance to the rise of classic Yiddish literature in the nineteenth century. Hasidic Yiddish periodicals are rapidly growing in quality, diversity and sophistication. The beginnings of a new prose and poetry are readily discernible.

Courtesy of the Menke Katz Collection.

Turning back to the central theme, Yiddish and power, the question arises: what kind of power will Hasidic Yiddish have over the coming generations. The prophet Amos gave us some sound guidance when he said, 'I am not a prophet nor the son of a prophet.' But eschewing prophecy does not absolve the observer from analysis of the present. A summary of that analysis is graphically represented in Chart 15.1.

The cardinal dichotomy of secular vs Hasidic/Haredi Yiddish does not obviate the need for further analysis of the many different positions

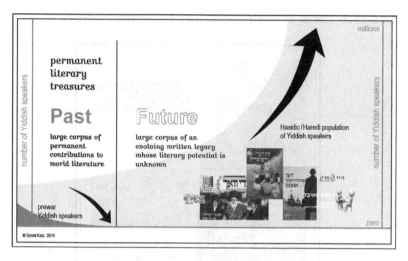

Chart 15.1 Secular and Hasidic Yiddish in the early twenty-first century

within both camps. Generally speaking, in secular circles, the current 'power situation' bears a rather curious inverse relationship to the language per se. In secular circles, those who 'insist' on speaking and writing in Yiddish, on teaching in Yiddish, are often thought of as either weird or strangely 'pro-Hasidic', which secular Jews are 'not supposed to be', given the many topics of substantive disagreement, ranging from the age of the world to women's rights. By contrast, those institutions able to raise millions and carry out many good works in the arena of culture and academic study are often wholly bereft of Yiddish. That situation is illustrated in Chart 15.2, which is an attempt to schematize the current Yiddish situation within the secular camp (which may include participants of a wide range of personal propensities on scales of religiosity or traditionality). Happily, study of literature at many levels remains common to both sub-sectors of today's secular Yiddish scene, though naturally it is discussed and written about in Yiddish among the 'die-hards' but virtually never among those that have amassed societal Jewish and academic power in the Yiddishless Yiddish power environment of the twenty-first century. Within the 'die-hard community', as within any of the others, there are numerous subdivisions. For example, there are some who write each other emails strictly in Yiddish, though with the standard (and excellent) Latin-letter Yivo transcription system; there are those who use the actual Yiddish alphabet for 'important communications' and then those who use *only* the real alphabet for Yiddish, as naturally as Arabic for Arabic, Polish for Polish, Cyrillic for Russian.

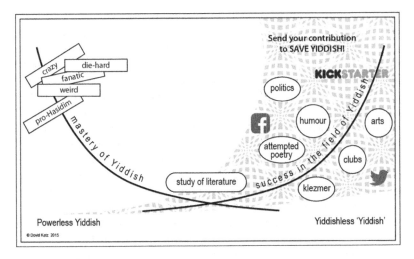

Chart 15.2 Secular Yiddish: the language and the power

Left- and right-wing politics

As noted earlier, in the United States and many other countries, the passion for Yiddish is sometimes tied with liberal values of equal rights for races, genders and sexual persuasions, and anti-war movements; that is, leftist by many definitions. There is an emotional and historic link at work with earlier generations that were socialist or social democrat or otherwise leftist, and there is the (historically justified) aura of classic secular Yiddish culture as pro-minority, pro-underdog, non-violent and at least non-right-wing Zionist alternative in contrast to the 'pro-power nationalist right-wing Jewish camp', or however it might be labelled. The vast majority of supporters of Yiddish in these countries are staunch supporters of Israel, though tending toward the left of politics within the pro-Israel camp. In all events, such proclivities are not politically potent, and are in general terms part of much larger Jewish configurations of 'anti-Likud but pro-Israel' diaspora politics. These features are part of the typical (and stereotypical) profile of the conventional Yiddish enthusiast who is in most cases wholly or partly Jewish by self-identification, and him- or herself of East European Jewish background.

Nevertheless, the propensity of Yiddishless Yiddish — the movement and industry that engage in myriad 'Yiddish' activities but 'not in Yiddish itself' — for extremes of left and right politics continues, remarkably, in the twenty-first century. The simple explanation is that the vast heritage that can be claimed without being studied is an attractive weapon in an arsenal of ideology. In other words, we are leaving the empowerment of self-advancement and organizational grandeur, massive new buildings and enrichment, and we are returning to old-fashioned actual believers in far-left and far-right politics, for whom Yiddishless Yiddish is worth instrumentalizing.

Among some left-wing younger assimilated Jews and perhaps rather more non-Jews, there is a trend to 'take up Yiddish' as a politically and culturally attractive pro-Jewish activity that is consciously or unconsciously intended to counterbalance the worry of being thought of as anti-Semitic in light of extreme anti-Israel politics. While of course Israel is (and should be) criticized as any other state, by citizens, diasporas and outsiders alike, it has often been demonstrated by specialists that the constant, overarching and zealous obsession with Israel-bashing and its rampant demonization, irrespective of the latest news from the Middle East, is a (and in parts of western Europe and the Middle East *the*) major type of contemporary anti-Semitism as unanimously determined by the leading scholars in the field (see Heni 2013: 385–451; Small 2013; Wistrich 2010: 465–542).

In Germany particularly, but also in Austria, Sweden, Switzerland, the Netherlands and Poland, among others, the phenomenon of the politically active left-wing and often anti-Israel student of Yiddish is serially encountered (my colleagues and I have met several thousand over the past three decades in European Yiddish educational settings, especially on summer courses). For them, Yiddish is often much more than a means of proving that one is not anti-Semitic because of a harsh critical stance toward Israel. For many, in the very lands where the Holocaust occurred, there is the identification with the victim rather than the perpetrator or collaborator nation-state. It is at the same time a genuine and profound espousal of a romanticized pre-Holocaust left-liberal Yiddish tradition that is being reclaimed through immersion in the actual learning of a language and its literature. There is the political and emotional feeling that the Holocaust destroyed the ethos of the Bund and other leftist-and-in-Yiddish movements and that this legacy should be reclaimed. For these European, usually multilingual and experienced language-learning students — and here is the paradoxical rub — the investment of time and resources in mastering Yiddish can be vastly greater than among the sentimental Jewish 'adherents of Yiddish' for whom Yiddishless Yiddish, or some or another kind of Yiddish-lite, and love of all that is today Jewish mainstream are the order of the day, without needing to worry too much about vocabulary, syntax, phonology and nuances — or nuisances — like that. Time and again, instructors at intensive international

Yiddish programmes, particularly summer courses, are struck by leftist non-Jewish students who speak and write fine Yiddish, in marked contrast to North American and other western Jewish participants who are proudly Jewish, proudly pro-Israel and proudly pro-Yiddish, though weak on the language-learning side of things. One of the external contributory factors here is the dominant monolingualism of the major English-speaking countries in contrast to the multilingualism that comes naturally to much of continental Europe.

Taken cumulatively over recent decades, the quality of real Yiddish mastered by typically young, mostly non-Jewish, generally European and leftist students has very often vastly outstripped the rudimentary and vaudevillized Yiddish remnants common to many American Jewish 'Yiddish lovers', or the 'purist' Yiddish artificiality of much of the (embarrassingly) tiny Yiddish-in-Yiddish secular youth crowd.

What is even newer, and unique to post-Soviet Eastern Europe, is a tendency of elements of the new far *right* to see in investments in Yiddish a remarkably useful tool for covering for, and deflecting attention from, vast state-sponsored campaigns of Holocaust revisionism and the toleration of neo-Nazi and Nazi-adulating activities. The issue has been most evident in the Baltic states and most burning in Lithuania. The region's nationalist political establishment has invested much national treasure in disseminating the theory of 'Double Genocide' to replace the Holocaust in modern European history (see Katz 2009, 2011). The new model posits absolute equality of Nazi and Soviet crimes. It is rooted in nationalist attempts to deflect attention from massive local collaboration with the Nazis during the Holocaust, which resulted in one of the highest proportions of Jew-killing in Europe (around 95 per cent), largely at the hands of enthusiastic local volunteers. Trying to minimize the historic destruction, the investment in 'Double Genocide' enables the sowing of enough confusion to rewrite the entire history. For example, most local Holocaust perpetrators were also anti-Soviet and many are therefore recycled as 'national heroes' (see Defending History 2014a). In Lithuania, Holocaust survivors were accused of 'war crimes', from 2006 onward, for having survived by joining the anti-Nazi Soviet-sponsored partisans in the forests (see Gloger 2008). From 2011 onward, Holocaust survivors were also accused of 'libelling' national heroes; that is, the Nazi collaborators who were 'also' anti-Soviet activists (see Melman 2011). A number of states in the region have inflated the meaning of the word 'genocide' by parliamentary fiat to encompass most or all Soviet crimes, in order to effect the equalization. The 'constitution' of the revisionist movement is the 2008 'Prague

Declaration', which boasts the word 'same' five times to cover Nazi and Soviet crimes. One of the major engines of the movement has been the Lithuanian state's 'International Commission for the Evaluation of the Crimes of the Nazi and Soviet Occupation Regimes in Lithuania' (see Arad 2012). None of this reflects on the people of the Baltics or of Lithuania, but rather on the nationalist establishments ensconced in politics, academia, media and sometimes the arts. In one of the major shows of force *against* the 'Double Genocide' movement, eight extraordinarily courageous Lithuanian parliamentarians, all social democrats, signed the anti-Prague-Declaration 'Seventy Years Declaration' in 2012 (Seventy Years Declaration 2012). The debate rages on.

What is astonishing for observers of the Yiddish scene is how deeply 'Yiddish' has become involved. In its pre-Holocaust incarnation as Vilna (Polish Wilno, Yiddish Vílne), the Lithuanian capital Vilnius was, as noted earlier, a world-class centre of Yiddish learning and culture. Thanks in part to an imaginative right-wing Jewish politician who took the time and trouble to learn Yiddish, a policy developed of countering the irksome Holocaust issues ('Double Genocide', persecution of Holocaust survivors and glorification of perpetrators, among them) by a lavish array of activities and memorials that give 'honour to Yiddish'. Vilnius might be the world's only city with an appreciable number of city history plaques *in* Yiddish (as well as Lithuanian) on the addresses where famous Yiddish writers and personalities lived. Pre-war Vilna, as already mentioned, was of course home to the Yivo.

Once the incarnation of Yivo in New York moved decisively away from Yiddish per se in recent years, and took to looking for related good causes to justify its existence and fundraising, the Lithuanian government investment got under way. In 2011, there was a major scandal over Yivo's having as guest of honour the then Lithuanian foreign minister, who had been taken to task by the country's small Jewish community for his anti-Semitic pronouncements (see Jewish Community of Lithuania 2010; Berger 2011; cf. Zuroff 2012b). In 2012, the Holocaust survivor community was shocked when the director of Yivo participated in a symposium on the Holocaust in Vilnius allegedly held to camouflage the same week's reburial with full honours of the remains of a major Holocaust collaborator from the United States (see Katz 2012). The same year, Yivo's director became a member of the state's commission on Nazi and Soviet crimes. While Yivo has been the 'biggest catch' for the Lithuanian government's right-wing establishment, it has not been the only one. A number of American Yiddish institutions have participated in state-sponsored events in Vilnius (see Katz 2014b), and it has been part of a larger campaign to include more general Jewish academic, religious and cultural organizations as well, frequently also in London (see Zuroff 2012a).

This far-right 'Yiddish' link has also been evident in a number of books, usually 'roots memoirs' where naive American authors can receive Baltic government support and largesse in return for writing glowing memoirs about their trips to their ancestral home and particularly governments' current 'reconciliation efforts', which are often the PR components in larger history revisionism campaigns that glorify Holocaust perpetrators and support 'Double Genocide' (see Katz 2012b). Then there are the very serious historians who actually believe in a certain levelling of Nazi and Soviet crimes and invoke Yiddish as part of a lost heritage that these countries should be seeking to recover as part of their nationalistic heritage. Now that there are very small numbers of Jews left, the pre-war culture can be reclaimed as part of a political effort to demonstrate the espousal of generous multiculturalism.

One of the more irksome — and surprising — types of political instrumentalization of Yiddish involves anti-Semitism, not in the sense of the eighteenth-century anti-Semitic literature on Yiddish (see Chapter 9), but in a quintessentially twenty-first-century incarnation. The reference here is not to the current left-wing anti-Israel activists who immerse themselves in Yiddish, discussed earlier (p. 296), and who certainly do not think of themselves as remotely anti-Semitic. It is to post-Soviet nationalistic East European states for which events involving Yiddish, from klezmer concerts all the way to 'Yiddish institutes', serve as cover for a policy of simultaneous approval for the anti-Semitic far-right's neo-Nazi marches and events, and programmes and monuments honouring Holocaust perpetrators (see Defending History 2014a, 2014b, 2014c). The politics behind 'promote the antisemitic nationalist establishment and promote Yiddish to show our love for things Jewish' was best described by N. N. Shneidman as an effort to appease simultaneously the west and surviving remnant Jewish communities and also the domestic nationalist camp (Shneidman 1998: 167–8).

One well-meaning Los Angeles-based 'Yiddish' group that specializes in annual historic visits to the Yiddish homeland in Eastern Europe recently found itself curiously used by left and right alike: some of its literature invoked the Yiddish heritage as part of an extreme anti-Israel movement that seeks to cripple the state via 'BDS' (boycott, disinvestment, sanctions), while on-site in Eastern Europe, it fell prey to a far-right 'Yiddish' institution headed by a member of a state commission on Nazi and Soviet crimes rather than a specialist in Yiddish. But the American group and its donors were of course naive rather than in any way sympathetic to either extreme of politics, left or right, that is making hay of 'Yiddish' and that can enlist western visitors in multiple ways. There is, of course, within Eastern Europe a much deeper and much older, formerly Christian-based, anti-Semitism lurking not far in the background. Here too 'Yiddish' makes its weird appearances. Most famously, the historic Bernardinai Catholic church in Vilnius, which continues to feature without curatorial comment an old blood libel plaque commemorating a boy allegedly 'cruelly killed in his seventh year by 170 Jewish blows' fixes things on the PR side with annual Yiddish concerts (see Katz 2013).

While it is natural that our own emphasis in these pages has been the political instrumentalization of Yiddishless Yiddish, whether for current far-left politics in the west or far-right politics in the east, it is important to take note of another side of the story. When resources are thrown at a language, culture, literature, heritage of a people, for whatever primary motive, there are myriad and unexpected results. Whether left or right in motivational origin, the Yiddish-related activities sponsored can take on a life of their own and inspire individuals to become immersed in serious study of the language, and its literature and culture. Critiques of instrumentalization often fail to take into account that courses, conferences, publications and other activities revolving around a language can be of high quality and of educational, research or cultural value, notwithstanding the initial political impetus. To report on the political impetus is to tell today's story of Yiddish and power, not to demean the contributions in many spheres that can be evident.

Concluding thoughts

Looking back over a thousand years, it has been the goal to attempt to see each time and place through its own eyes. At the conclusion of this survey, a certain wholly subjective attempt at some synthesis may be in order.

The constant of Yiddish, from its origin to its unknown future, is its status as the language of traditionally religion-centred Ashkenazic Jewry, with spurts of non-traditional culture or 'secular outbursts' coming on to the scene at various points in time. These energetic episodes include the rise in medieval Europe of a secular gentile-derived knightly romance literature in the earlier centuries of Western Ashkenaz and, many centuries later, the adoption of modern European genres and standards during the rise of modern Yiddishism in nineteenth-century Eastern Ashkenaz. Some of these societally and culturally empowering deviations from the

Ashkenazic 'ultra-Orthodox tree trunk' have left permanent contributions to world literature and to the Jewish heritage more specifically. The twentieth-century flirtations with political power proved short-lived. But would it be presumptuous of the retrospectivist to see therein some teleologically determined fate? Perhaps — or perhaps not. The status of Yiddish in the early 1920s Soviet Union, or throughout the interwar Polish Republic, seemed absolutely secure for generations. The full brutality of Stalinism, which would proceed to decapitate sophisticated Yiddish culture by purging its greatest figures and turning lesser figures into professional betrayers, was not predicted. Infinitely less predictable was genocide; or is it *ever* predictable in times of peaceful multicultural coexistence, when someone who says that all the children, women and men will be killed would be regarded as a hallucinator at best?

The real power of Yiddish has for a millennium rested with its uses and applications within Yiddish-speaking civilization, in a 'vertical', multi-millennial synergy or competition with the other two major languages of Jewish history, Hebrew and Aramaic (with no disrespect to other Jewish languages, the most famous of which is Judzemo, or Ladino, among Sephardic Jewry). Early on, the mobilization of Yiddish for new purposes brought internal Jewish restructuring of power: empowerment to women and to men uneducated in the two inherited classical sacred languages. Much later, it empowered a secular minority to synthesize the native language with the genres of modern European culture. Later still, in its then a priori most promising incarnation, it played a 'normal' political role in a peaceful minority culture for a very short period prior to its destruction in its native homeland.

Looking ahead, the real power of Yiddish within the future of world Jewry has been to confound the standard predictions of either a Hebrew-speaking Jewry or Jewish minorities everywhere assimilated to the host country's national language. In Israel, Hebrew has successfully become the native language of the Israeli people, but the Hebrew movement continues to fail to produce a single Hebrew-speaking family in the diaspora that had not lived in Israel before adopting the language as daily vernacular. In the diaspora, typical Jewish families speak the language of their non-Jewish neighbours with or without injections of Jewish elements for culturally specific phenomena. But both these major trends have for decades obscured the third element. That is, the dramatic demographic rise of a Haredi, mostly Hasidic Jewry, safely spread over many countries, whose birth rate and overall retention of children to the non-western ultra-traditional lifestyle espoused is leading to an international Yiddish-speaking Jewry of millions just a hundred years hence.

That, finally, brings us to a major post-Holocaust surprise. While the Hebrew-speaking population of Israel naturally grows into an ever more distinct Israeli (rather than 'Jewish') linguistic and ethnic identity, and major Jewish communities in the west assimilate culturally, whether or not they observe religion and customs to varying degrees, the Hasidic bloc is growing into what may be the future's one branch of Jewry continuing the decimated thousand-year civilization of Ashkenaz, precisely by maintaining an overall Jewish anthropological profile that refuses to assimilate in dress, mores or language. Just as a sinking Ashkenaz I in central Europe gave way to the rise of Ashkenaz II in Eastern Europe, the destruction of Jewish Eastern Europe by the Holocaust has been followed after a seeming hiatus of half a century or more (that may not be regarded as such by our successors) by the rise of Yiddish-speaking Hasidic societies whose multinational residence in the internet age is giving rise, before our eyes, to Ashkenaz III.

That macro prediction might leave readers with the impression that the micro environments of secular Yiddish are all so deeply flawed as not to be taken seriously. We have been critical, have we not, of both Yiddishless spheres of Yiddish power: the popular culture and the academic Yiddish enterprises; of alleged manipulation by the (far) left and (far) right. That indeed may be the 'Yiddish and power' picture. But cultural value is not necessarily a quantitative issue. The current minuscule presence on the power scale of secular Yiddish projects based on full-blown authentic use of authentic Yiddish should not in any way discount the desirability or potential importance of future achievements. There are today a number of new inspiring projects. During the years in which this book was in preparation, my colleagues and I 'advertised' for submissions about new Yiddish projects that included the goal of mastering the language and provided an early trackable record of achievement. I would like to end this book on the hopeful note of the 'entry' that impressed us the most.

It is the Yiddish Farm recently established at Goshen, upstate New York, 'with the goal of teaching Yiddish and fostering unity and respect between Hasidic and non-Hasidic Jews' (Yiddish Farm 2014). Using the word *yíshev* (which has multiple meanings in Yiddish, including: rural setting in the countryside; new settlement; the settlement of the Land of Israel by the early Zionists), one of its founders, Yisroel Bass, who like the others has mastered Yiddish, explains that the project wants to correct the:

misconception that individuals coming together on occasion to speak Yiddish is somehow saving the language. Yiddish Farm has come to embrace a vision of permanence in order to combat such delusional misgivings. As such it has been the goal of Yiddish Farm's founders to create a Yishev, a settled community, for which Yiddish is the language of daily communication and educational instruction.

(Bass 2014)

Some of the founders of the project are progeny of Yiddishist territorialists in Eastern Europe and New York, of Yugntrufists in New York, and of inspired newcomers. By embracing the notion of a specific 'territory', be it only a farm; by embracing the joining of secular and Hasidic forces; by embracing the notion of 'living in Yiddish'; and by rejecting the normativist purism or spelling obsessions of earlier 'youth-for-Yiddish' groups, the Farm is a veritable conceptual revolution in empirically demonstrable twenty-first-century Yiddishism. It is a far cry from the 1990s, when various secular Yiddish institutions with 'money left over from the old days' could not even find any personnel in America to move forward and had to import newly unemployed Soviet operatives from the just-collapsed Soviet Union to be able to continue at all. Today, Yiddish eyes are on the Farm as a small but authentic 'island' for continuity that would encompass the secular cultural heritage of Yiddish in a way that seeks to join forces with the naturally rising vast modern Hasidic Yiddish-speaking civilization. Whatever its fate, the Farm at Goshen, not far from the upstate Hasidic town Monsey, with which it takes care to be in touch, has made a rapid mark in the history of Yiddish ideas.

That, in turn, in the spirit of exceptions that serve to elucidate the norm, is a statement about where actual Yiddish power of the twenty-first century is heading: toward a Hasidic civilization that is in its own way an Ashkenaz III. After the Holocaust, its linguistic achievement is the rebuilding of a viable international Yiddish speech community. Whether the secularists 'on the Farm', 'off the Farm' or 'in the Academy' can maintain viable secular islands of genuine Yiddish remains the intriguing unknown.

The preface to *Yiddish and Power* ended with a quote from the celebrated mystical poet of London's Whitechapel, A.N. Stencl (p. x). So shall the book. Whenever he received guests from around the world in his favourite, and very poor, café on Fulbourne Street off the Whitechapel Road, Stencl would gently ask to borrow a necklace from one of the ladies in the café. He would ever so gently put it on the floor and even more slowly raise it up high above his head, and say, with the inimitable Yiddish tones of one immersed in both the religious and secular treasures of Yiddish all his life: 'But this necklace is Yiddish. It can fall down, but it is so enchanting that it will not be left on the floor for long. Someone will pick it up.'

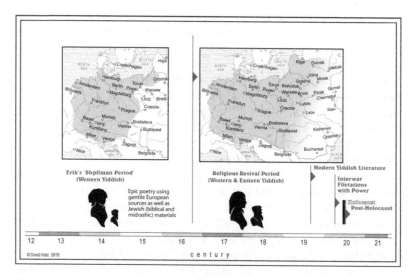

Chart 15.3   Five periods in Yiddish power (twelfth to twenty-first century)

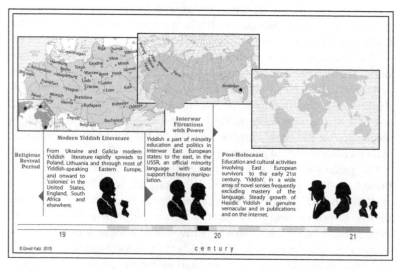

Chart 15.4   Five periods in Yiddish power (nineteenth to twenty-first century)

Bibliography

Aaron ben Shmuel of Hergershausen (1709) *Líblikhe Tfíle óder gréftige artsenáy far guf un neshóme*. Hergerashausen.

Adelkind, Daniel (1552) *Mítsvous ha-nóshim* (Commandments for Women)/ *Frouen bikhlen* (Little Book for Women). Venice.

Althaus, Hans Peter (ed.) (1969) *Ignaz Bernstein, Jüdische Sprichwörter und Redensarten. Im Anhang: Erotica und Rustica. Mit einer Einfürung und Bibliographie*. Hildesheim: Georg Olms.

Althaus, Hans Peter (2002) *Mauscheln. Ein Wort als Waffe*. Berlin and New York: Walter de Gruyter.

Altmann, Alexander (1973) *Moses Mendelssohn. A Biographical Study*. London: Routledge and Kegan Paul.

Altshuler, Moyshe Henoch Yerushalmi (1602) *Bránt shpigl*. Basel: Conrad Waldkirch.

Anonymous (1790) *Teutsch-Hebräisches Wörterbuch* [etc.]. Oettingen.

Apeteker, Abraham [Avrom] (1590) *Sam kháyim*. Moses ben Shabsai (ed.): Prague.

Arad, Yitzhak (2012) 'The Holocaust in Lithuania, and its obfuscation, in Lithuanian sources' in *Defending History*, 1 December 2012. At: http://defending history.com/?p=46252.

Aschheim, Steven E. (1982) *The East European Jew in German and German-Jewish Concsiousness, 1800–1923*. Madison: University of Wisconsin Press.

Assaf, S. (1942–3) 'A rabbinic reply against the composition of law books in Yiddish' [in Hebrew], *Qiryat Sefer* 19: 41–2.

Avé-Lallemant, Friedrich Christian Benedict (1858–62) *Das deutsche Gaunerthum in seiner social-politischen, literarischen und linguistischen Ausbildung zu seinem heutigen Bestande*, 4 vols. Leipzig: F. A. Brockhaus.

Bach, H. I. (1984) *The German Jew. A Synthesis of Judaism and Western Civilization*. Oxford and New York: Oxford University Press and Littman Library.

Band, Arnold J. (1978) *Nachman of Bratslav: The Tales*, translation, introduction, and commentaries by Arnold J. Band. New York: Paulist Press.

Bard, Bernard (1972) 'Yiddish rebels upset yeshiva' in *New York Post*, 14 August, pp. 2, 38.

Bartal, Israel (2006) *The Jews of Eastern Europe, 1772–1881*, translated by Chaya Naor. Philadelphia: University of Pennsylvania Press.

Bass, Yisroel (2014) 'On the new Yiddish farm' (statement submitted for the present volume as personal communication), 12 January 2014.

Baumgarten, Jean (2005) *Introduction to Old Yiddish Literature*. Edited and translated [from French] by Jerold C. Frakes. Oxford: Oxford University Press.

Beem, Hartog (1954) 'Yiddish in Holland: Linguistic and sociolinguistic notes' in U. Weinreich 1954: 122–33.

—— (1975) *Resten van een taal.Woordenboekje van het Nederlandse Jiddisch*, second edition. Assen: Van Gorcum.

Bemporad, Elissa (2013) *Becoming Soviet Jews: The Bolshevik Experiment in Minsk*. Bloomington: Indiana University Press.

305

Berger, Paul (2011) 'Holocaust survivors angry about Yivo's invitation to Lithuanian official' in the *Forward*, 7 September 2011. At: http://forward.com/articles/142398/holocaust-survivors-angry-about-yivos-invitation-t/?.

Bernstein, Ignaz (with assistance of B. W. Segel) (1908) *Yídishe shpríkhverter un rédnsartn* [German title: *Jüdische Sprichwŏrter und Redensarten*]. Warsaw: J. Kauffmann.

Biale, David (1986) *Power and Powerlessness in Jewish History*. New York: Schocken Books.

Biberman, Matthew (2004) *Masculinity, Antisemitism and Early Modern English Literature: From the Satanic to the Effeminate Jew*. Aldershot: Ashgate.

Bibliophilus (1742) *Jüdischer Sprach-Meister, oder Hebräisch-Teutsches Wŏrterbuch* [etc.]. Frankfurt and Leipzig.

Bickel, Shlomo and Lehrer, Leibush (eds) (1958) *Shmúel Níger bukh*. New York: Yivo.

Bik, Yankev-Shmuel (Jacob Samuel) (1815) in Goldenberg 1833: 96–9.

Bin-Nun, Jechiel (1973) *Jiddisch und die deutschen Mundarten. Unter besonderer Berücksichtigung des ostgalizischen Jiddisch*. Tübingen: Max Niemeyer.

Birnbaum, Solomon A. (1929) 'Jiddische Sprache' in *Jüdisches Lexicon* 3: 269–78. Berlin: Jüdischer Verlag.

——— (1939) 'The Age of the Yiddish Language', *Transactions of the Philological Society 1939*, 31–43.

——— (1953) 'Fun daytshmerízm biz der heyl in der Mídber Yehúde', *Yídishe shprakh* 13: 109–20.

——— (1979) *Yiddish. A Survey and a Grammar*. Manchester and Toronto: Manchester University Press and University of Toronto Press.

Bláha, Ondřej, Dittmann, Robert and Uličná, Lenka (eds) (2014) *Knaanic Language: Structure and Historical Background*. Prague: Charles University.

Boeschenstein, Johann (1514) *Elementale introductorium in Hebreas litteras Teutonice & Hebraice legendas*. Augsburg.

Borokhov, Ber (1912) 'Briv tsu Sh. Niger' in Mayzl 1966: 382–423.

——— (1913a) 'Di úfgabn fun der yídisher filológye' [The Aims of Yiddish Philology] in Sh. Niger 1913: 1–22 (also in Mayzl 1966: 53–75).

——— (1913b) 'Di biblyoték funem yídishn filológ' [The Library of the Yiddish Philologist] in Sh. Niger 1913: 1–68 [separate pagination end of volume] (also in Mayzl 1966: 76–136).

——— (1917) 'A por vérter' in [= preface to] M. Basin, *Antologye. Finf húndert yor yídishe poézye. Gezámlt un tsunóyfgeshtelt fun M. Basin. Fórvort un língvistishe ónmerkungen fun B. Borokhov*. New York: Dos yidishe bukh, vol. 1.

Bratslaver, Nachman [Nakhmen of Breslev, Nachman of Bratslav, etc.] (±1815) *Sipúrey máyses*, Ostrog.

Bresh [Brzesc], Leyb [Judah ben Moses Naftali] (1560) *Khamísho khúmshey Tóuro im ktsas péyrush Ráshi vəím ha-haftóurəs ákher kol sédro vəsédro* (The Five Books of the Torah with some of the Rashi Commentary and with the haftorahs following each and every Torah portion). Cremona.

Breuer, Edward (1996) *The Limits of Enlightenment. Jews, Germans, and the Eighteenth Century Study of Scripture*. Cambridge, Massachusetts and London: Harvard University Press.

Brown, Mick (2011) 'Splendid isolation', *Telegraph Magazine*, 26 February: 24–32.

Buber, Martin (1999) *The Tales of Rabbi Nachman*, translated by Maurice Friedman. With a new introduction by Paul Mendes-Flohr and Ze'ev Gries. Amherst and New York: Humanities/Prometheus.

Chazan, Robert (1987) *European Jewry and the First Crusade*. Berkeley, Los Angeles and London: University of California Press.
—— (1996) *In the Year 1096. The First Crusade and the Jews*. Philadelphia and Jerusalem: Jewish Publication Society.
Cohn, Jesse (2002) 'Anarchy in Yiddish: Famous Jewish anarchists from Emma Goldman to Noam Chomsky' in R. A. Forum. At: http://raforum.info/spip. php?article488&lang=en.
Cowley, A. E. (1929) *A Concise Catalogue of the Hebrew Printed Books in the Bodleian Library*. Oxford: Clarendon [photomechanical reprint: London: Oxford University Press, 1971].
Dawidowicz, Lucy S. et al. (eds) (1964) *For Max Weinreich on his Seventieth Birthday. Studies in Jewish Languages, Literature, and Society*. The Hague: Mouton.
Defending History (2012) 'Amherst's NYBC caught up in Lithuanian government's Jew-less Yiddish-less PR library', 23 July 2012. At: http://defendinghistory.com/ amhersts-national-yiddish-book-center-nybc-entangled-in-vilnius-jewish-librarys-turn-to-yiddish/38437.
Defending History (2014a) 'Collaborators glorified'. At: http://defendinghistory. com/category/collaborators-glorified.
—— (2014b) 'Anti-Semitism in Eastern Europe'. At: http://defendinghistory.com/ category/antisemitism-bias.
—— (2014c) 'Double games'. At: http://defendinghistory.com/category/ double-games.
Donsky, Florence Diana (1971) '*Dukus Horant*: Middle High German or Yiddish'. Masters thesis, University of Louisville [University Microfilms, Ann Arbor, Michigan].
Dubnov, Shimon [Dubnow, Simon] (1930) *Toldoys ha-khasidus, al yesod mekoyroys rishoynim, nidposim ve-khisvey yad*, 3 vols. Tel Aviv: Dvir.
Elon, Amos (2002) *The Pity of It All. A History of Jews in Germany 1743–1933*. New York: Metropolitan Books and Henry Holt and Company.
Elyada, Aya (2012) *A Goy Who Speaks Yiddish*. Stanford: Stanford University Press.
Epshteyn, Yekhiel-Mikhl [Epshteyn, Jechiel-Michel] (1693) *Séyfer kítsur shney lúkhəs ha-brís* (The Abbreviated Book of the Two Tablets of the Covenant). Fúrth.
—— (1697) *Séyder tfílo dérekh yeshóro* (Straight Path to the World to Come). Frankfurt am Main.
—— (1703) *Séyfer dérekh ha-yóshor le-óulom habó*. Frankfurt am Main: Jo. Wust.
Erik, Maks (1926) *Vegn ált-yídishn román un novéle. Fértsnter — zékhtsnter yorhúndert*. Warsaw: Farlag Meir Reiz.
—— (1928) *Di geshíkhte fun der yídisher literatúr. Fun di éltste tsaytn biz der haskóletkúfe. Fértsnter-ákhtsnter yorhúndert*. Warsaw: Farlag Kultur-lige.
—— (1979) [photomechanical reprint of Erik 1928 with a new introduction by Elias Schulman (Eyliohu Shulman). New York: Congress for Jewish Culture.
Feder, Tuvia (Tuviohu) (±1816) *Kol mekhátsetsim*. Edition of 1853 with introduction by A. M. Mohr. Lemberg: G. Winiarz.
Feiner, Shmuel (2011) *The Jewish Enlightenment*. Philadelphia: University of Pennsylvania Press.
Finkel, Avraham Yaakov (1997) *Sefer Chasidim. The Book of the Pious*. Northvale, New Jersey and London: Jason Aronson.

Finkin, Jordan D. (2010) *The Eighteenth Century Language Text of Jüdischer Sprach-Meister: A West Yiddish Dialogue Together with an English Translation and Introduction.* Lewiston, NY: Edwin Mellen Press.

Finkelstein, Israel and Silberman, Neil Asher (2006) *David and Solomon. In Search of the Bible's Sacred Kings and the Roots of Western Civilization,* Old Tappan, New Jersey: Free Press.

Fischer, Jechiel (1936) Das Jiddische und sein Verhältnis zu den deutschen Mundarten. [...] Inauguraldissertation zur Erlangung der Doktorwürde einer hohen philosophischen Fakultät der Ruprecht-Karls-Universität Heidelberg. Leipzig: Oswald Schmidt GmbH.

Fishman, David E. (1991) 'Mikóyekh dávnen af yídish: a bintl metodológishe bamérkungen un náye mekóyrim' *Yivo bleter* n.s. 2: 69–92.

—— (2005) *The Rise of Modern Yiddish Culture.* Pittsburgh: University of Pittsburgh Press.

Fishman, Joshua A. (1965) *Yiddish in America.* Bloomington: University of Indiana Press.

—— (ed.) (1981) *Never Say Die! A Thousand Years of Yiddish in Jewish Life and Letters.* The Hague: Mouton.

—— (1987) *Ideology, Society and Language: The Odyssey of Nathan Birnbaum.* Ann Arbor: Karoma.

—— (1991) *Yiddish.Turning to Life.* Amsterdam and Philadelphia: John Benjamins.

—— (ed.) (2011) *The Earliest Stage of Language Planning: 'The First Congress' Phenomenon* [= Contributions to the Sociology of Language 65]. Berlin and New York: Walter de Gruyter.

Fishman, William J. (1975) *East End Jewish Radicals 1875–1914.* London: Duckworth.

Frakes, Jerold C. (1989) *The Politics of Interpretation. Alterity and Ideology in Old Yiddish Studies.* Albany: State University of New York Press.

—— (2004) *Early Yiddish Texts 1100–1750.* Oxford and New York: Oxford University Press.

—— (2007) *The Cultural Study of Yiddish in Early Modern Europe.* New York and Houndmills: Palgrave Macmillan.

Freehof, Solomon B. (1923) 'Devotional literature in the vernacular' (Judeo-German, prior to the Reform Movement) in *Yearbook of the Central Conference of American Rabbis 1923,* pp. 375–424.

Frieden, Ken (1995) *Classic Yiddish Fiction. Abramovitsh, Sholem Aleichem, and Peretz.* Albany, NY: State University of New York Press.

Freidenreich, Fradle Pomerantz (2010) *Passionate Pioneers. The Story of Yiddish Secular Education in North America, 1910–1960.* Teaneck, New Jersey: Holmes and Meier Publishers.

Freund, Richard A. (1998) 'A theology of Yiddish prayer: Yiddish as a creative *lashon haQodesh* (holy language)' in Greenspoon 1998: 265–90.

Friedlaender, David (1788) *Epistle to the German Jews* [German in the Jewish alphabet]. Berlin.

Frumkin, Esther (1910) *Tsu der fráge fun der yídisher fólk-shul.* Vilna: Di velt.

Fuks, L. (1954) 'On the oldest dated work in Yiddish literature' in U. Weinreich 1954: 267–74.

Fuks, L. (1957) *The Oldest Known Literary Documents of Yiddish Literature (c. 1382),* 2 vols. Leiden: E. J. Brill.

—— (ed.) (1965) *Das altjiddische Epos Melokîm-bûk,* Assen, Van Gorcum, 2 vols.

Gilman, Sander (1986) *Jewish Self-Hatred. Anti-Semitism and the Hidden Language of the Jews*. Baltimore: Johns Hopkins University Press.

Gininger, Chaim (1954) 'A note on the Yiddish Horant' in U. Weinreich 1954: 275–7.

Gitelman, Zvi Y. (1972) *Jewish Nationality and Soviet Politics. The Jewish Sections of the CPSU, 1917–1930*. Princeton: Princeton University Press.

—— (2001) *A Century of Ambivalence. The Jews of Russia and the Soviet Union, 1881 to the Present*, second expanded edition. Bloomington and Indianapolis: Indiana University Press.

Glaser, Amelia and Weintraub, David (eds) (2005) *Proletpen: America's Rebel Yiddish Poets*. Madison: University of Wisconsin.

Glinert, Lewis (ed.) (1993) *Hebrew in Ashkenaz. A Language in Exile*. New York and Oxford: Oxford University Press.

Gloger, Dana (2008) 'The Holocaust survivors facing war-crimes trials', *The Jewish Chronicle*, 6 June 2008. At: http://www.holocaustinthebaltics. com/2008June6byDanaGloger.pdf.

Goldenberg, Shmuel Yehude Leyb (Samuel Judah Leib) (ed.) (1833) *Séyfer kérem khémed*. Vienna: Anton Edlen von Schmid.

Goldsmith, Emanuel S. (1976) *Architects of Yiddishism at the Beginning of the Twentieth Century. A Study in Jewish Cultural History*. Rutherford, Madison, Teaneck and London: Fairleigh Dickinson University Press and Associated University Presses.

—— (1987) *Modern Yiddish Culture.The Story of the Yiddish Language Movement*. New York: Shapolsky Publishers & Workmen's Circle Education Department.

Grace-Pollack, Sophie (1998) 'Shómer leór *Shómer's míshpet* le-Shalóm Aleikhem' (*Shomer in the Light of Sholem Aleichem's Shómer's Trial*), *Khulyot: Journal of Yiddish Research*, 5: 109–59.

Greenbaum, Alfred Abraham (1978) *Jewish Scholarship and Scholarly Institutions in Soviet Russia 1918–1953*. Jerusalem: Hebrew University of Jerusalem, Centre for Research and Documentation of East European Jewry.

G[ris], N[oyakh] (1981) 'Shulman, Eyliohu', *Leksikón fun der náyer yídisher literatúr*. New York, Congress for Jewish Culture, 8: 591–3.

Grossman, Jeffrey A. (2000) *The Discourse on Yiddish in Germany: From the Enlightenment to the Second Empire*. Rochester, NY: Camden House.

Guggenheim-Grünberg, Florence (1954) 'The horse dealers' language of the Swiss Jews in Endingen and Lengnau' in U. Weinreich 1954: 48–62.

Gutman, Yisrael, Mendelsohn, Ezra, Reinharz, Jehuda and Shmeruk, Chone (eds) (1989) *The Jews of Poland Between Two World Wars*. Assistant editor Sylvia Fuks Fried. Hanover, NE: University Press of New England.

Haberer, Erich E. (1995) *Jews and Revolution in Nineteenth-century Russia*. Cambridge: Cambridge University Press.

Halevy, Zvi (1976) *Jewish Schools under Czarism and Communism*. New York: Springer Publishing Company.

Harkavy, Albert [Avróm Eylióhu] (1867) *Hayehudim usfas haslavim* [German title page: *Die Juden und die Slawischen Sprachen*]. Vilna: Romm.

Harshav, Benjamin (1990) *The Meaning of Yiddish*. Berkeley, Los Angeles and Oxford: University of California Press.

—— (1993) *Language in Time of Revolution*. Berkeley, Los Angeles and London: University of California Press.

Heni, Clemens (2013) *Antisemitism: A Specific Phenomenon. Holocaust Trivialization —Islamism — Post-colonial and Cosmopolitan Anti-Zionism.* Berlin: Edition Critic.

Hertz, Deborah (2009) *How Jews Became Germans. The History of Conversion and Assimilation in Berlin.* New Haven: Yale University Press.

Herzog, Marvin I., Ravid, Wita and Weinreich, Uriel (eds) (1969) *The Field of Yiddish*, vol. 3. The Hague: Mouton.

Hitler, Adolf (1925) *Main Kampf. Eine Abrechnung.* I. Band, Munich: Franz Eher Nachfolger GmbH.

Hoffman, Miriam (1994) 'An asífe fun yídish-réter' in *Yerusholaymer almanakh*, 24: 302–6.

Horn, Dara (2013) 'Jewish identity, spelled in Yiddish', *New York Times*, 4 June 2013.

Howe, Irving (1989) *World of Our Fathers*. New York: Schocken Books.

Hudson-Edwards, Alan (1981) 'Knowledge, use, and evaluation of Yiddish and Hebrew among American Jewish college students' in J. A. Fishman 1981: 635–52.

Hundert, Gershon David (1991) *Essential Papers on Hasidism. Origins to Present.* New York and London: New York University Press.

—— (2004) *Jews in Poland-Lithuania in the Eighteenth Century. A Genealogy of Modernity.* Berkeley and Los Angeles: University of California Press.

—— (ed.) (2008) *The YIVO Encyclopedia of Jews in Eastern Europe*, 2 vols. New Haven: Yale University Press. At: http://www.yivoencyclopedia.org.

Idel, Moshe (1995) *Hasidism Between Ecstasy and Magic.* Albany: State University of New York Press.

Isaac ben Elyokum of Posen (1620) *Lev tov.* Prague.

Isaacs, Miriam (1998) 'Then and now: creativity in contemporary Hasidic Yiddish' in Greenspoon 1998: 165–88.

Jacob ben Isaac (Yankev ben Yitskhok) of Yanova (1622) *Tsèneréne* [Tse'éno ur'eéno]. Basel.

Jacobs, Jack (ed.) (2001) *Jewish Politics in Eastern Europe: The Bund at 100.* Basingstoke: Palgrave.

Jacobs, Neil G. (2005) *Yiddish. A Linguistic Introduction.* Cambridge: Cambridge University Press.

Jewish Community of Lithuania (2010) 'To the President of the Republic of Lithuania, Dalia Grubauskaitè', *Jerusalem of Lithuania*, 6: 155-6.

J.W. (±1714) *Jüdisicher Sprach-Meister [...]*, Gedruckt in dem jetzigen Jahr.

Joffe, Juda. A. (1954) 'Dating the Origin of Yiddish Dialects'. *Field of Yiddish*, 1: 102–21.

Jost, J. M. (1850) 'Judenteutsch, Jüdisch-Teutsch' in J. S. Ersch and J. G. Gruber (eds), *Allgemeine Encycklopädie der Wissenschaften und Künste.* Leipzig: F. A. Brockhaus, Part 27, section 2, Leipzig: F. A. Brockhaus, pp. 322–4.

—— (1859) *Geschichte des Judentums und seiner Sekten.* Part 3, Books 6–8. Leipzig: Dörffling & Franke.

Kahan-Newman, Zelda (1995) 'The influence of Talmudic chant on Yiddish intonation patterns', *Yiddish*, 10: 25–33.

Katz, Dovid (1980) 'Ber Borokhov, Pioneer of Yiddish Linguistics' [+ partial translation into English of Borokhov 1913a], *Jewish Frontier*, June–July 1980, 47.6 (=506): 10–20.

—— (ed.) (1987a) *Origins of the Yiddish Language* [= *Winter Studies in Yiddish*, 1 = Papers from the First Annual Oxford Winter Symposium in Yiddish Language and Literature, 15–17 December 1985]. Oxford: Pergamon Press.

—— (1987b) 'The Proto Dialectology of Ashkenaz' in Katz 1987a: 47–60. At: http://www.dovidkatz.net/dovid/PDFLinguistics/1987.pdf.

—— (1990a) Review of Frakes 1989 in *Journal of Jewish Studies* 41.1: 140–4. At: http://www.jjs-online.net/toc.php?subaction=fullcontent&id=041_01_140_1& type=bookreview&review=937.

—— (1990b) 'Di éltere yídishe leksikográfye. Mekóyres un metódn', *Oksforder yidish*, 1: 161–232. At: http://www.dovidkatz.net/dovid/PDFLinguistics/1990. pdf.

—— (1991) 'Der semítisher khéylek in yídish: a yerúshe fun kadmóynim' [The Semitic Component in Yiddish: A legacy of ancient times], *Oksforder Yidish*, 2: 17–95. At: http://www.dovidkatz.net/dovid/PDFLinguistics/1991a. pdf.

—— (1993a) *Tíkney-takónes. Fragn fun yídisher stilístik* [Amended Amendments. Issues in Yiddish Stylistics]. Oxford: Oxford Yiddish Press and Oxford Centre for Postgraduate Hebrew Studies. At: http://www.dovidkatz.net/dovid/ PDFStylistics/1993.pdf.

—— (1993b) 'The Phonology of Ashkenazic' in Glinert 1993: 46–87. At: http:// www.dovidkatz.net/dovid/PDFLinguistics/1993b.pdf.

—— (1994) 'Náye gilgúlim fun álte makhlóykesn. Di lítvishe nórme un di sikh- súkhim vos arúm ir', *Yivo bleter*, n.s. 2: 205–57.

—— (1996a) 'Rótvelsh un yídish' in *Yiddish Pen* 27: 23–36. At: http://dovidkatz. net/dovid/PDFLinguistics/1996.pdf.

—— (1996b) 'Tsvelf shítes, zeks húndert yor: di yídishe lingvístik', *Yerusholaymer almanakh*, 25: 225–57.

—— (1998) 'Farvós heysn mir Ashkenázim?' [Why are we called Ashkenazim?], *Yerusholaymer almanakh*, 26: 235–49.

—— (2001) 'Professor Khone Shmeruk (1921–1997) Senior Associate Member 1973–4' in *St Antony's Record 2001*. Oxford, pp. 112–15.

—— (2005) 'The days of Proletpén in American Yiddish poetry' in Amelia Glaser and David Weintraub (eds), *Proletpen: America's Rebel Yiddish Poets*. Madison: University of Wisconsin, pp. 3–25.

—— (2006) Review of Jacobs 2005 in *AJS Review. The Journal of the Association for Jewish Studies*, 30.2: 471–3.

—— (2007) *Words on Fire. The Unfinished Story of Yiddish. Revised and Updated*. New York: Basic Books.

—— (2008) 'Borokhov, Ber' in *The Yivo Encyclopedia of Jews in Eastern Europe*, 1: 218–19.

—— (2009) 'On three definitions: genocide; Holocaust denial; Holocaust obfus- cation' in Leonidas Donskis (ed.), *A Litmus Test Case of Modernity. Examining Modern Sensibilities and the Public Domain in the Baltic States at the Turn of the Century* [= *Interdisciplinary Studies on Central and Eastern Europe* 5]. Bern et al.: Peter Lang, pp. 259–77. At: http://www.holocaustinthebaltics.com/2009SeptD ovidKatz3Definitions.pdf.

—— (2010) *Lithuanian Jewish Culture*. Vilnius: Baltos Lankos [second revised edition].

—— (2011) 'Understanding "Double Genocide": a lethal new threat to Holocaust memory and honesty', *Centre News* [Jewish Holocaust Centre, Melbourne, Australia], September 2011. At: http://defendinghistory.com/wp-content/ uploads/2013/06/Dovid-Katz-on-Double-Genocide-20111.pdf.

—— (2012a) 'An open letter to Yale History Professor Timothy Snyder', *Algemeiner Journal*, 21 May 2012 [in print edition: 25 May, pp. 2, 4, 5]. At: http://www.algemeiner.com/2012/05/21/an-open-letter-to-yale-history-professor-timothy-snyder/.

—— (2012b) 'Respectable memoir, some shrewd manipulation by an East European government – or both?' [review of E. Cassedy, *We are Here. Memories of the Lithuanian Holocaust*], *Algemeiner Journal*, 18 July 2012. At: http://www.algemeiner.com/2012/07/18/respectable-memoir-some-shrewd-manipulation-by-an-east-european-government-%E2%80%95-or-both/.

—— (2013) 'Old blood libel plaque still displayed, without comment, at Bernardinai Church in Vilnius', 17 September 2013. At: http://www.algemeiner.com/2012/07/18/respectable-memoir-some-shrewd-manipulation-by-an-east-european-government-%E2%80%95-or-both/

—— (2014a) '*Knaanic* in the medieval and modern scholarly imagination' in Bláha, Dittmann and Uličná 2014: 156–90. At: http://www.dovidkatz.net/dovid/PDFLinguistics/2014_Knaanic_Medieval_Modern_Scholarly_Imagination.pdf.

—— (2014b) 'The neocons and Holocaust revisionism in Eastern Europe', part 2, *Jewish Currents*, 26 July 2014. At: http://jewishcurrents.org/neocons-holocaust-revisionism-eastern-europe-continued-30677.

Katz, Eli (1963) *Six Germano-Judaic Poems from the Cairo Genizah*. PhD dissertation, University of California, Los Angeles [University Microfilms, Ann Arbor, Michigan].

Katz, Molly (1991) *Jewish as a Second Language. How to Worry. How to Interrupt. How to Say the Opposite of What you Mean*. New York: Workman Publishing.

Kavon, Eli (2014) 'When Zionism feared Yiddish', *The Jerusalem Post*, 11 May 2014. At: http://www.jpost.com/Opinion/Op-Ed-Contributors/When-Zionism-feared-Yiddish-351939.

Kay, Devra (2004) *Seyder Tkhines. The Forgotten Book of Common Prayer for Jewish Women*. Philadelphia: Jewish Publication Society.

Khamisho khumshey Touro im khomeysh megilous vehahaftorous beeyr heteyv beroyv hoiyun milshoyn ivri lilshoyn ahskenazi venidpas poy Konstantsyo habiro shnas dash litsiro (1544) [= the 1544 Constanz Pentateuch]. Constanz: [Paul Fagius].

Khotsh, Tsvi-Hirsh (1711) *Nákhles Tsvi*. Frankfurt am Main: Antona Hensheyd.

Khsam Sóyfer [Chatam Sofer; Moses Schreiber, Moshe Sofer, etc.] (1841) *Seyfer Khsam Soyfer, kheylek Even ho-Ezer* [responsa]. Pressburg: F. Schmidt.

—— (1859) *Seyfer Khsam Soyfer, kheylek Khoyshen Mishpot* [responsa]. Pressburg: F. Schmidt.

—— (1862) *Seyfer Khsam Soyfer, kheylek Khoyshen Mishpot* [responsa]. Vienna.

Kochan, Lionel (ed.) (1970) *The Jews in Soviet Russia since 1917*. London, New York and Ontario: Oxford University Press.

Korman, E. (1928) *Yídishe díkhterins. Antológye*. Chicago, Farlag: L. M. Stern.

Korn, Yitskhok (1982) *Dos gerángl far yidish. Eséyen*. Tel Aviv: Velt-rat far yidish un yidisher kultur.

Kuznitz, Cecile Esther (2014) *YIVO and the Making of Modern Jewish Culture: Scholarship for the Yiddish Nation*. Cambridge: Cambridge University Press.

Labov, William (2012) 'What is to be learned?' [review of *Cognitive Linguistics*, 10, 265–93].

—— (2014) Personal communication, 27 May 2014.

Landis, Joseph C. (1964) 'Who needs Yiddish?', *Judaism*, 13(4): 1–16.
Levin, Nora (1977) *While Messiah Tarried. Jewish Socialist Movements, 1871–1917*. New York: Schocken Books.
Levinsohn, Isaac Ber (1828) *Teúdo b'Yisróel*. Vilna and Grodno.
Levita, Elijah [=Elye Bokher = Elye Leyvi Ashkenazi, etc.] (1541a) *Bovo d'Antouno*. Isny: Paul Fagius.
—— (1541b) *Séyfer ha-Tíshbi le-Eylióhu ha-Tíshbi*. Isny: Paul Fagius.
—— (1542) *Shmous dvórim belóshn ívri uvelóshn róumi gam ashkenázi*. Isny: Paul Fagius.
—— (1545) *Séyfer T(eh)ílim*. Venice: Cornelius Adelkind & Meir bar Jacob.
Lieberman, Chaim [Liberman, Khayim] (1943) 'Tsu der fráge vegn der batsíung fun khsídes tsu yídish', *Yivo bleter*, 22.2: 201–9.
—— (1952) 'Bamérkungen tsu Shlóyme Nobl's artíkl', *Yivo bleter*, 36: 305–13.
Lifschitz, Yehoyshue-Mordechai (Shíye-Mórdkhe) (1862) [under the name: Lifschitz mi-Berditshev, i.e. Lifschitz from Berdichev, Ukraine] 'Yudl un Yehúdis (Dos meynt men di yidn mit zéyer yídish lóshn)', *Kol meváser*, 9 (13/25 December): 135–7.
—— (1863) 'Di fir klasn', *Kol meváser*, 21 (18 June): 323–8; 23 (1 July): 364–6; 24 (8 July): 375–80; 25 (16 July): 392–3.
L[ifschitz], Y[ekhezkl] (1981) 'Shmeruk, Khone', *Leksikón fun der náyer yídisher literatúr*. New York: Congress for Jewish Culture, 8: 731–2.
Low, Alfred D. (1979) *Jews in the Eyes of the Germans*. Philadelphia: Institute for the Study of Human Issues.
Mantel, Martin Irving (1977) *Rabbi Nachman of Bratzlav's Tales. A Critical Translation from the Yiddish with Annotations and Commentary*, vols 1 and 2. Doctoral thesis, Princeton University. Ann Arbor: University Microfilms International.
Marchand, James W. (1959) Review of Fuks 1957 in *Word* 15: 383–94.
—— (1960) 'Three basic problems in the investigation of early Yiddish', *Orbis*, 9.1: 34–41.
—— (1961) 'Einiges zur sogennanten "jiddischen Kudrun"', *Neophilologus*, 45.
Marcus, Martin (1971) *The Power of Yiddish Thinking*. Garden City, New York: Doubleday.
Margaliot, Reuven (1957) *Séfer Khasidím shekhibér Rabénu Yehudá he-Khasíd*. Jerusalem: Mossad Harav Kook.
Margoliouth, G. (1905) *Catalogue of the Hebrew and Samaritan Manuscripts in the British Museum, Part II*. London: British Museum.
—— (1909–15) *Catalogue of the Hebrew and Samaritan Manuscripts in the British Museum, Part III*. London: British Museum.
Mark, Yudl (ed.) (1958) *Yúda A. Yófe bukh*. New York: Yivo.
Marten-Finnis, Susanne and Winkler, Markus (eds) (2006) *Die jüdische Presse im europäischen Kontext 1686–1990*. Bremen: Philo.
Máyse bukh (1602) Basel.
Mayzl [Meisel], Nakhmen (ed.) (1966) *Ber Borokhov, Shprákh-forshung un literatúr geshíkhte*. Tel Aviv: Farlag Y. L. Peretz.
Meitlis, Jacob (1958) *The Ma'aseh in the Yiddish Ethical Literature*. London: Shapiro Vallentine.
Melman, Yossi (2011) 'Expelling the ambassador', *Haaretz*, 7 September 2011. At: http://www.haaretz.com/print-edition/opinion/expelling-the-ambassador-1.382986.

Mendelsohn, Ezra (1983) *The Jews of East Central Europe between the World Wars*. Bloomington: Indiana University Press.

—— (1993) *On Modern Jewish Politics*. Oxford: Oxford University Press.

—— (ed.) (1997) *Essential Papers on Jews and the Left*. New York and London: New York University Press.

Michels, Tony (ed.) (2012) *Jewish Radicals. A Documentary History*. New York and London: New York University Press.

Mirkéves ha-míshne [±1534]. Krakow: Helicz [Halicz, Helits, etc.] Brothers: Shmuel, Osher and Elyokim.

Mieses, Matthias [Matisyohu] (1915) *Die Entstehungsursache der jüdischen Dialekte*. Vienna: R. Löwit Verlag.

—— (1931) 'Matisyóhu Mízeses referát vegn der yídisher shprakh' in Reyzen, Weinreich and Broyde 1931: 141–93.

Mishkovski (Mishkowsky), Noyakh (1947) *Mayn lebn un máyne ráyzes*, vol. 1. Mexico City.

Mr 'P' (1984) *The World's Best Yiddish Dirty Jokes. With drawings by Robbie Stillerman*. Secaucus, New Jersey: Citadel Press.

Nachman of Bratslav [Nákhmen Bréslever] (1806) *Likutey Moharán*. Ostrog.

—— (±1815) *Sipúrey máyses*. Ostrog.

Nextbook (2008) *Jews and Power. New York Festival of Ideas Video and Audio Archive*. At: http://nextbook.org/festivals/ny2008.html.

Niger, Sh (ed.) (1913) *Der pínkes. Yórbukh far der geshíkhte fun der yídisher literatúr un shprakh, far folklór, kritík un biblyográfye. Érshter yórgang — Taráv [=(5)672 = 1911–1912]*.

—— (1959) *Bléter geshíkhte fun der yídisher literatúr*. New York: Congress for Jewish Culture.

Noble, Shlomo (1951) 'Reb Yekhíel-Míkhl Épshteyn — a dertsíyer un kémfer far yídish in zíbetsetn yorhúndert', *Yivo bleter*, 35: 121–38.

—— (1958) 'Yídish in a hebréyishn lvush' [Yiddish in Hebrew Garb] in Bickel and Lehrer 1958: 158–75.

Pach, Hilde (2006) 'Die Amsterdamer *Dinstagishe un Fraitagishe kurantn (1686–1687). Wie jüdisch war die erste Jiddische Zeitung?*' in Marten-Finnis and Winkler 2006: 17–25.

—— (2014) Hilde-Pach Oosterbroek, *Arranging Reality. The Editing Mechanisms of the World's First Yiddish Newspaper, the* Kurant *(Amsterdam 1686–1687)*. Amsterdam: University of Amsterdam.

Peretz, Y. L. (1891) 'Bildung!' [Education!] in Y. L. Peretz (ed.) *Yídishe biblyoték. A Zhurnál far literatúr, gezélshaft un ekonómye*. Warsaw: Brothers Orgelbrand, pp. 5–20.

Philoglottus (1733) *Kurtze und gründliche Anweisung zur Teutsch-Jüdischen Sprache* [etc.]. Freiberg: Christoph Matthäi.

Prager, Leonard (1982) *Yiddish Literary and Linguistic Periodicals and Miscellanies. A Selective Annotated Bibliography. With the help of A. A. Greenbaum*. Darby, Pennsylvania and Haifa: Norwood Editions.

Prilutski, Noyakh (1927) 'Di yídishe bíne-shprakh', *Yídish teáter*, 2: 129–44.

Prilutski, Noyakh and Lehman, Shmuel (eds) (1933) *Arkhív far yídisher shprakh-vísnshaft, literatúr-fòrshung un etnológye*, vol. 1. Warsaw: Nayer farlag.

Rapoport-Albert, Ada (1997) *Hasidism Reappraised*. London and Portland (Oregon): Littman Library of Jewish Civilization.

Ravitzky, Aviezer (1996) *Messianism, Zionism, and Jewish Religious Radicalism.* Translated from Hebrew by Michael Swirsky and Jonathan Chipman. Chicago: University of Chicago Press.

Reiman, B (1962) 'An alter móker far dem yídishn "khóyzek"', *Yídishe shprakh,* 22: 60–1.

Reyzen, Zalmen (1926–29) *Leksikón fun der yídisher literatúr, prése un filológye,* 4 vols. Vilna: B.A. Kletskin.

[Reyzen, Zalmen, Weinreich, Max and Broyde, Chaim] (eds) (1931) *Di érshte yídishe shprákh konferénts. Baríkhtn, dokuméntn un ópklangen fun der Tshérnovitser konferénts 1908.* Vilna: Yivo.

Rivkind, Yitzkhok [Isaac] (1955) 'Fun mayn vérterbikhl (fun der sérye "Vérter mit yíkhes")', *Yídishe shprakh,* 15: 20–30.

Robertson, Ritchie (1999) *The 'Jewish Question' in German Literature 1749–1939.* Oxford and New York: Oxford University Press.

Rosenfeld, Moshe N. (1988) 'The origins of Yiddish printing' in Katz 1987a: 111–26.

Rosten, Leo (1968) *The Joys of Yiddish.* New York: McGraw-Hill.

Rozhanski, Shmuel (ed.) (1967) (*Yídish in lid* [= *Músterverk der der yídisher literatúr* 33]. Buenos Aires: Literatúr gezélshaft bam Yivo in Argentíne.

Rubenstein, Joshua and Naumov, Vladimir (eds) (2001) *Stalin's Secret Pogrom. The Postwar Inquisition of the Jewish Anti-Fascist Committee.* New Haven and London: Yale University Press.

Sampson, Geoffrey (1979) *Liberty and Language.* Oxford: Oxford University Press.

Samuel, Maurice (1971) *In Praise of Yiddish.* New York: Cowles Book Company.

Santos, Fernanda (2007) 'New York rabbi finds friends in Iran and enemies at home', *The New York Times,* 15 January 2007. At: http://www.nytimes.com/2007/01/15/nyregion/15rabbi.html.

Satz, Yitzhak (ed.) (1977) *The Maharíl's Unpublished Responsa* [in Hebrew]. Jerusalem: Machon Yerushalayim.

Schaechter, Mordkhe (1977) 'Four schools of thought in Yiddish language planning', *Michigan Germanic Studies,* 3.2: 34–66.

Scholem, Gershom (1973) *Sabbatai Ṣevi. The Mystical Messiah, 1626–1676.* Princeton: Princeton University Press.

Schorch, Grit (2012) *Moses Mendelssohns Sprachpolitik.* Berlin: Walter de Gruyter.

Seventy Years Declaration, The (2012). At: http://www.seventyyearsdeclaration.org/.

Séyfer Mídes (1542) Isny: author unknown.

Shepkaru, Shmuel (2006) *Jewish Martyrs in the Pagan and Christian Worlds.* Cambridge: Cambridge University Press.

Shiper, Yitskhok (1924) 'Der ónheyb fun "Lóshn Áshkenaz" in der baláykhtung fun onomátishe kveln', *Yídishe filológye,* 1: 101–12, 272–87.

——— (1933) '"Lóshn Áshkenaz" beéysn fértsetn un fúftsetn yorhúndert"' in Prilutski and Lehman 1933: 79–90.

Shlezinger, Akiva Jehoseph [Akíve Yehóysef] (1864) *Séyfer lev ho-Ívri,* vol. 1. Ungvar: M. N. Löwubsihn: Ungvar.

——— (1869) *El ho-adórim ha-shéyni* [Latin-letter transcription provided: *El Huadurem Hascheni*]. Lemberg: M. F. Poremba.

Shlosberg, B. (1938) '"Mirkéves ha-míshne" — der éltster gedrúkter yídisher shprakh dokumént', *Yívo bléter,* 13.3–4: 313–24.

Shmeruk, Khone (1964a) 'Di mízrekh-eyropéyishe nuskhóes fun der Tseneréne (1786–1850)' in Dawidowciz et al. 1964: 336–20 [Yiddish pagination: 195–320].

—— (editor-in-chief) (1964b) *A shpigl af a shteyn*. *Antológye: Poézye un próze fun tsvelf farshnítene yídishe shráyber in rátnfarband*. Tel Aviv: Goldene keyt and I. L. Peretz Publishing House.

Shmeruk, Khone (1964c) 'Di mízrekh-eyropéyishe nuskhóes fun der *Tseneréne* (1786–1850)' in Dawidowciz et al. 1964: 336–20 [Yiddish pagination: 195–320].

—— (1967) 'Di náye edítsye funem alt-yídishn *Mlókhim bukh*' [= review of Small, Cherles Asher (2013) (ed.) *Global Antisemitism: A Crisis of Modernity*, vols 1–5. New York: Institute for the Study of Global Antisemitism and Policy (ISGAP) [Fuks 1965], *Góldene keyt*, 59: 208–15.

—— (1979) 'Tsi ken der kéymbridzher manuskrípt shtitsn di shpílman teórye in der yídisher literatúr?', *Góldene keyt*, 100: 251–71.

—— (1988) *Prókim fun der yídisher literatúr geshíkhte*. Tel Aviv and Jerusalem: Farlag Y. L. Peretz and Hebrew University Yiddish Department.

Shneidman, N. N. (1998) *Jerusalem of Lithuania: The Rise and Fall of Jewish Vilnius*. Oakville, Ontario and Buffalo, NY: Mosaic Press.

Shtif, Nokhem (1928) 'Mikhael Adams dray yídishe bíkher', *Filológishe shrift*, 2: 135–68.

Sh[ulman], E[yliohu] [=Schulman, Elias] (1968) 'Erik, Maks', *Leksikón fun der náyer yídisher literatúr*, New York: Congress for Jewish Culture, 7: 37–41.

—— (1979) 'Aráynfir' in Erik 1979: i–xiii.

Seidman, Naomi (1997) *A Marriage Made in Heaven. The Sexual Politics of Hebrew and Yiddish*. Berkeley and Los Angeles: University of California Press.

Shandler, Jeffrey (2006) *Adentures in Yiddishland. Postvernacular Language and Culture*. Berkeley: University of Caifornia Press.

Shneer, David (2004) *Yiddish and the Creation of Soviet Jewish Culture 1918–1930*. Cambridge: Cambridge University Press.

Shtendl, Moyshe (1586) *Dos Thílim bukh*. Krakow.

Shteynberg, Yitskhok Nakhmen [Steinberg, Y. N.] (1943) *Gelébt un gekhólemt in Oystrálye*. Melbourne.

Shulman, Elias (1971) *A History of Jewish Education in the Soviet Union*. New York: Ktav Publishing House.

Shur, Shimon (2000) *The Battalion of the Defenders of the Language in the Land of Israel 1923–1936* [in Hebrew]. Haifa: University of Haifa.

Singer, Isaac Bashevis [Bashevis, Yitskhok] (1935) *Sotn in Goráy* (Satan in Goray). Warsaw: Yiddish Pen Club.

Small, Charles Asher (2013) (ed.) *Global Antisemitism: A Crisis of Modernity*, vols 1–5. New York: Institute for the Study of Global Antisemitism and Policy (ISGAP).

Soldat-Jaffe, Tatjana (2012) *Twenty-First Century Yiddishism*. Brighton: Sussex Academic Press.

Sorkin, David (1987) *The Transformation of German Jewry*. New York: Oxford University Press.

—— (1996) *Moses Mendelssohn and the Religious Enlightenment*. London: Peter Halban.

Spolsky, Bernard (2014) *The Languages of the Jews: A Sociolinguistic History*. Cambridge: Cambridge University Press.

Stampfer, Shaul (2003) 'What actually happened to the Jews of Ukraine in 1648?', *Jewish History*, 17: 165–78.

St[einschneider], M[oritz] (1863) 'Der Vocalbuchstabe ע', *Hebraeische Bibliographie*. *Blätter für neuere und ältere Literatur des Judenthums*, 6: 35: 119–20.

—— (1864) 'Jüdische Litteratur un Jüdisch-Deutsch. Mit besonderer Rücksicht auf Avé-Lallemant', *Serapeum* (Leipzig), 25: 33–46, 49–62, 65–79, 81–95, 97–104 [part].

Tenenbaum, Joseph [Tenenboym, Yoysef] (1957–8) 'Di yídishe shprakh af der tógòrdenung fun der shólem konferénts in Paríz, 1919', *Yivo bleter*, 41: 217–29. Reprinted in Fishman 1981: 395–408.

Tkhínes (1648) Amsterdam.

Timm, Erika (1987) *Graphische und phonische Struktur des Westjiddischen unterbesonderer Berücksichtigung der Zeit um 1660*. Tübingen: Max Niemeyer Verlag.

Tobias, Henry J. (1972) *The Jewish Bund in Russia from its Origins to 1905*. Stanford: Stanford University Press.

Trachtenberg, Barry (2008) *The Revolutionary Roots of Modern Yiddish 1903–1917*. Syracuse, New York: Syracuse University Press.

Trunk, Isaiah (ed.) (1980) *Yivo bleter* 46: *Lekóved fúftsik yor Yivo, 1925–1975*. New York: Yivo.

Tsanin, Mordkhe [Mordechai] (1999) [typescript memoir in Yiddish on the legislation against Yiddish newspapers in Israel]; excerpt in English translation in Katz 2007: 319–20.

Tsinberg, Yisroel [Zinberg, Israel] (1928) 'Der kamf far yídish in der alt-yídisher literatúr', *Filológishe shriftn*, 2: 69–106 [English version → Tsinberg 1946].

—— (1937) *Di geshíkhte fun der literatúr ba yidn. Zékster band, ákhter teyl. Altyídishe literatur fun di éltste tsáytn biz der haskóle tkúfe*. Vilna: Tomor.

—— (1946) 'A defense of Yiddish in Old Yiddish Literature', *Yivo Annual of Jewish Social Sciences*, 1: 283–93 [translation of Tsinberg 1928].

Weiner, Ellis and Davilma, Barbara (2004) *Yiddish with Dick and Jane*. New York and Boston: Little, Brown and Company.

—— (2006) *Yiddish with George and Laura*. New York and Boston: Little, Brown and Company.

Weinreich, Max (1923a) *Shtáplen. Fir etyúdn tsu der yídisher shprakh-vísnshaft un literatúr-geshíkhte*. Berlin: Wostok.

—— (1923b) *Geschichte und gegenwärtiger Stand der jiddischen Sprachforschung*. Marburg University doctoral dissertation (III vols) [reprint: edited by Jerold C. Frakes, Scholars Press: Atlanta 1993].

—— (1928a) *Bílder fun der yídisher literatúr geshíkhte fun di ónheybn biz Méndele Móykher Sfórim*. Vilna: Farlag Tomor fun Yoysef Kamermakher.

—— (1928b) 'Di bóbe fun der yídisher próse', in *Tsúkunft* 33: 679–83.

—— (1936) 'Form vs. Psychic Function in Yiddish' in Bruno Schindler and A. Marmorstein (eds), *Occident and Orient. [...] In Honour of Haham Dr. M. Gaster's 80th Birthday*. London: Taylor's Foreign Press.

—— (1939a) *Di shvártse píntelekh*. Vilna: Yivo.

—— (1939b) 'A Tentative Scheme for the History of Yiddish' in *Vme Congrès International des Linguistes, Bruxelles, 28 août–2 septembre 1939. Resumes des Communications*. Brussels: Sainte Catherine, pp. 49–51.

—— (1953) '*Yidishkayt* and Yiddish. On the Impact of Religion on Language in Ashkenazic Jewry' in Moshe Davis (ed.), *Mordecai M. Kaplan Jubilee Volume. On the Occasion of his Seventieth Birthday*. New York: Jewish Theological Seminary of America, pp. 481–514.

—— (1954) 'Prehistory and early history of Yiddish: facts and conceptual framework', in U. Weinreich 1954: 73–101.

—— (1959) 'History of the Yiddish language: the problems and their implications' in *Proceedings of the American Philosophical Society*, 103: 563–70.

—— (1960) 'Old Yiddish Poetry in Linguistic-Literary Research', *Word*, 16: 100–18.

—— (1973) *Geshíkhte fun der yídisher shprakh. Bagrífn, faktn, metódn* [History of the Yiddish Language. Concepts, facts, methods], 4 vols. New York: Yivo.

—— (1980) *History of the Yiddish Language*. Translated by Shlomo Noble, with the assistance of Joshua A. Fishman. Chicago and London: University of Chicago Press.

—— (2008) *History of the Yiddish Language*. Edited by Paul Glasser. Translated by Shlomo Noble with the assistance of Joshua A. Fishman, 2 vols. New Haven and London: Yale University Press in cooperation with the Yivo Institute for Jewish Research.

Weinreich, Uriel (ed.) (1954) *The Field of Yiddish. Studies in Yiddish Language, Folklore, and Literature*. Published on the Occasion of the Bicentennial of Columbia University, New York: Linguistic Circle of New York.

Weiser, Kalman (2011) *Jewish People, Yiddish Nation. Noah Prylucki and the Folkists in Poland*. Toronto, Buffalo, London: University of Toronto Press.

Weissler, Chava (1998) *Voices of the Matriarchs. Listening to the Prayers of Early Modern Jewish Women*. Boston: Beacon Press.

Wessely, Naphtali Herz [Vizl, Naftoli Hirts] (1782) *Divrey sholoum v'emes, lik'hal adas Yisroel hagorim b'artsous memsheles ha-keysor hagodoul, ho-ouheyv es bney ho-odom umesameyakh es habriyous, YOZEFUS HA-SHAYNI yr"h* [Words of Peace and Truth to the community of people of Israel who live in the lands of the government of the great king, who loves people and brings to people happiness, Joseph II, may his glory be raised]. Berlin.

Whorf, Benjamin Lee (1964) *Language, Thought, and Reality*. Cambridge, Massachusetts: MIT Press.

Winer, Gershon (2009) *A Memoir: Victory in Defeat*. Israel.

Wisse, Ruth R. (1997) 'Yiddish: past, present, imperfect', *Commentary*, November 1997: 32–9.

—— (2007) *Jews and Power*. New York: Schocken.

Wistrich, Robert S. (2010) *A Lethal Obsession. Anti-Semitism from Antiquity to the Global Jihad*. New York: Random House.

YiddishFarm.org (2014) 'About us'. At: https://yiddishfarm.org/aboutus.html.

Yivo Annual of Jewish Social Research (1952) 'Discussion regarding Rabbi Yehiel Mikhel Epstein', 7: 296–302.

Yosef bar Yokor (1544) preface to *Təfílo* [/*Tfíle*; Prayerbook]. Ichenhausen: Chaim ben Dovid.

Zafren, Herbert C. (1982) 'Variety in the Typography of Yiddish: 1535–1635' in *Hebrew Union College Annual*, 53: 137–63.

—— (1986–1987) 'Early Yiddish Typography' in *Jewish Book Annual*, 44: 106–19.

Zalmen of St Goar (1556) *Maharíl*. Sabionetta.

Ziskind (1953) 'Batrákhtungen vegn der geshíkhte fun yídish', *Yídishe shprakh*, 13: 97–108 [= Mark 1958: 146–57].

Zuckerman, Richard (1969) 'Alsace. An outpost of Western Yiddish' in Herzog, Ravid and Weinreich 1969: 36–57.

Zunz, Leopold (1832) *Die gottesdienstlichen Vorträge der Juden, historisch entwickelt*. Berlin: A. Asher.

Zuroff, Efraim (2012a) 'A shameful Shoah whitewash', *The Jewish Chronicle*, 4 February 2012. At: http://www.thejc.com/the-holocaust/44728/a-shameful-shoah-whitewash.

——— (2012b) 'Pardoning Nazism, in the name of Lithuanian-Jewish relations. The once-venerable Yivo Institute in New York is giving credence to the canard of equivalency between Nazi and communist crimes', *Times of Israel*, 14 October 2012. At: http://www.timesofisrael.com/pardoning-nazism-in-the-name-of-lithuanian-jewish-relations.

Index

Index of Yiddish Words

CPSIA information can be obtained at www.ICGtesting.com
Printed in the USA
LVOW01*1014291214

420748LV00006B/14/P